MW00831920

The Servant and the Ladder

The Servant and the Ladder:

Cooperation with Evil
in the Twenty-First Century

Andrew McLean Cummings

GRACEWING

First published in England in 2014
by
Gracewing
2 Southern Avenue
Leominster
Herefordshire HR6 0QF
United Kingdom
www.gracewing.co.uk

No part of this publication may be reproduced, stored in a
retrieval system, or transmitted in any form or by any means,
electronic, mechanical, photocopying, recording or otherwise,
without the written permission of the publisher.

The right of Andrew McLean Cummings to be identified as the
author of this work has been asserted in accordance with the
Copyright, Designs and Patents Act 1988.

© 2014 Andrew McLean Cummings

ISBN 978 085244 854 0

Typeset by Gracewing

Cover design by Bernardita Peña Hurtado

Cover illustration by Miriam Lademan

ILLI REVELATIONIS VIRGINI

CUI TOTA SUA VIRTUS DEBITA EST

HOC OPUSCULUM

AB ILLO

CUI TOTA SUA VITIA DEBITA SUNT

SUMMISSE GRATEQUE

DEDICATUM EST

CONTENTS

PART III: A NEW PERSPECTIVE

Abbreviations

DS   H. Denzinger and A. Schönmetzer, *Enchiridion Symbolorum, Definitionum et Declarationum de rebus fidei et morum*. Barcelona: Herder, 1973.

ERD   National Conference of Catholic Bishops. *Ethical and Religious Directives for Catholic Health Care Services*. Washington DC: United States Catholic Conference, 1995.

ST   Aquinas, T. *Summa Theologiae*. See Corpus Thomisticum Project of the University of Navarre at www. corpusthomisticum.org.

INTRODUCTION

... filii Dei
sine reprehensione
in medio nationis pravae et perversae
inter quos lucetis sicut luminaria in mundo ...

Philippians 2:15[1]

CHRISTIANS ARE NOT like the rest of men. Set apart by the will of God, transformed by grace, instructed by a new commandment, they have been from the earliest days conspicuous. The ultimate proof of authenticity of the message they bear and the holiness it brings is their refusal to do evil. The readiness to die rather than sin is not the exclusive patrimony of Christians, but it is characteristic of them. No less essential, however, is the motif of leaven in the dough, the soul enlivening the body of mankind,[2] the ever-increasing kingdom in the midst of the world. Christians cannot, as a rule, separate themselves from the milieu in which God places them, for they are enjoined not only to save themselves but others, too. Christians must not only eat with sinners, as their Master did, but share a great variety of activities with them.

The experience of an inevitable tension resulting from the presence of the Christian in the world, a tension between purity and practicality, the ideal and the possible, has only increased over the centuries. Social structures—economies, politics, healthcare systems, communications and so forth—have become more complex. Meanwhile, the effects of evil have grown exponentially more devastating. Could a first century Christian ever have imagined such scenarios as working at a nuclear missile factory or investing in a cable company that supports pornographic programming? The scale and gravity of cooperation today, especially in the context of what John Paul II has labeled "the culture of death", demands a review of Catholic moral theology's understanding of the matter to ensure that it is adequate to the task.

Two problems with the present state of analysis have prompted this study. The first is that even trained moral theologians disagree about what sorts of cooperation are to be considered formal and what material. This fact and its importance can be seen in a recent observation by a member of the Pontifical Academy of Life:

> In this paper I have offered an interpretation of the notion of formal cooperation which suggests that what some would identify as material cooperation (and even defensible material cooperation) should be classified as formal cooperation, and choices that others would regard as formal cooperation in wrongdoing should not be thought to embody an intention which can be so characterised. It is clearly important to have a true understanding of formal cooperation because of what is at issue in choices that count as formal cooperation in grave wrongs against human life: one's acting on reasons which should *never* characterise one's choices, and which, if they do, will seriously corrupt one's character.[3]

Secondly, even if there is some disagreement regarding the application of this distinction, the lack of disagreement is still more worrisome. Even if many theologians retain the category of implicit formal cooperation in theory, it is rarely employed except in discussing immediate cooperation. Most cooperation is considered material and therefore allowable for a sufficient reason. Theological experts, who realize how serious illicit cooperation is for individuals and society, may emphasize that cooperation is often too proximate or scandalous, especially if the harm involves the good of life. Still, these are prudential decisions, as is to be expected in the realm of material cooperation. But if the formal category has been effectively set on one side, virtually all cooperation cases become questions of prudence. Those with responsibility for guiding souls are left with only guidelines to offer. By distinguishing formal and material cooperation more precisely, we hope to make categorical statements about the impermissibility of some forms of cooperation more possible.

Various kinds of involvement with evil have recently been distinguished, which will not concern our study. Following the nomenclature of Christopher Kutz,[4] one can speak, on the one hand, of *unstructured harms*. Here individual agents seek some personal benefit, and evil comes about as a by-product of the collectivity itself; environmental damage provides a prime example. Since the evils in this category result from collective action without coordination, the notions of cooperation and intention only apply in a loose or even analogous way. *Structured harms*, on the other hand, are evil effects brought about by the coordinated action of governments, companies, or smaller groups. Presumably these collective agents act for some good end, such as the end of a war, cure of a disease, or making of profit. Members of such organizations who desire these goods but contribute nothing to the evil are still somehow involved, a question Kutz terms "symbolic responsibility".[5] This sort of cooperation seems akin to that kind of involvement with evil that Cathleen Kaveny has named *appropriation of evil*.[6] Here one contributes nothing to the bringing about of the evil, because in the clearest case, it has already been caused. The agent in these cases is improperly named a "cooperator"; he benefits from evil done by another but does not promote it in any demonstrable way. These important aspects of the question do not concern our study, although the nature of the subject is such as to resist containment within firm boundaries. Our theme concerns what Kutz calls *facilitation*. Here a participant in a structured harm plays a real role in bringing about the evil, even if he makes only a marginal contribution. He may have no interest in the success of the project initiated by the principal actors or approved by the majority of participants. He may play his role for his own private purposes, perhaps with reluctance, often because he finds himself under some kind of duress. This situation will be recognized as the classic arena of debate on cooperation within the Catholic tradition.

Serious reflection on the problem that came to be known as "cooperation with evil" began in earnest in late renaissance Europe with the challenges presented by the discovery of the new world, the fallout from the Reformation, and other developments. At this time Catholic moral theology in general was emerging as an independent discipline. As our review of the question will indicate, the first two centuries of reflection by Catholic thinkers, culminating with St Alphonsus Liguori, produced an enduring analytical advance: the formal/material distinction. However this term pairing is defined, the central idea concerns the intention of the cooperator. Sin and innocence depend upon the will of an agent, expressed by his intention, which is the free, rational ordering of acts towards an end: *intentio proprie est actus voluntatis*.[7] Since the intention of the end gives the moral act its form, formal cooperation denotes any cooperation in which the cooperator shares the evil intention of the principal agent. Material cooperation is defined in reference to formal. It refers to any contribution that is *praeter intentionem* and has the nature of a side-effect. As the facilitation of evil is outside the intention of the cooperator, his will need not share in the bad willing of the principal agents.

From the foregoing it follows that the distinction between formal and material cooperation will be just as clear as is the concept of intention. Usually, the concepts of willing and intending go together: one does willingly what one intends to do and intends to do what one wills to do. A *willing* cooperator can be described as "approving" the evil of the principal agent, even if he cooperates for some other reason than that motivating the principal agent. In such a case, cooperation is formal, willed as a means to an end. Often enough, however, a cooperator acts "on purpose", intentionally, yet *unwillingly*, and here the trouble begins. It can happen that duress brings about such a lack of freedom that there is no cooperation of ethical significance at all.[8] However, assuming that we are dealing with a moral act, even if reluctantly posited, we must seek to assess its objective moral value; to what extent fear will diminish eventual culpability is another question. When cooperation takes place under various kinds of threat or pressure which do not completely deprive the agent of responsibility, it can appear that there is at least no intention to bring about the evil of the principal agent. It can then seem that formal cooperation is excluded, since the cooperator does not "approve" of the evil. This, however, would be an unwarranted conclusion. Duress cannot imply, *ipso facto*, material cooperation; this would be to equate intention with desire. Thus, despite the problems for moral analysis created thereby, it is certainly possible to share in the evil intention of another, and in his bad will, by giving assistance reluctantly or unwillingly.

The term "implicitly formal cooperation" refers to this problematic category of acts. These are actions that, by contributing to the commission of an evil primarily engineered by other agents, involve their author (the cooperator) in the evil intention of the other agents, even though the cooperator himself is indifferent or even opposed to the evil goal they seek.[9] Some authors ignore the existence of such a class of acts. One example is the Manualist, Henry Davis, who defines the formal/material distinction in the following terms: "(1) Co-operation is formal when A helps B in an external sinful act, and intends the sinfulness of it, as in deliberate adultery. (2) Co-operation is material when A helps B to accomplish an external act by an act that is not sinful, and without approving of what B does."[10] By identifying formal cooperation with approving (and bad willing with willing the bad act *qua* sinful), he ends up qualifying all theologically challenging cooperation as material. Not surprisingly, it is in reference to *material* cooperation that he observes "there is no more difficult question than this in the whole range of Moral Theology."[11] Notwithstanding such authors, the greater part of moral theologians of the Manualist period recognized a much wider range of formal cooperation. The use of the term "implicit" to describe it is found here and there, in such authors as Tanquerey, Noldin and Zalba.

For our part, implicit formal cooperation will refer to acts which, in virtue of the aspect of cooperation itself, have a disordered *finis operis*, that is, a proximate or built-in intention such that the cooperator cannot choose them without willing some evil. Clearly, identifying such acts of cooperation will require a sophisticated understanding of human action. Livio Melina calls for a renewal of the discussion of the classic divisions of cooperation made by the Manualists in the light of a theory of action which is better equipped to identify the moral object of the cooperator's action. "It is decisive to establish the objective identity of the act of collaboration, that is, the intrinsic intentionality that connotes it."[12] We agree wholeheartedly with this summons. Yet, little indication of where to start is offered in Melina's article except the tantalizing suggestion that prudence will be required. "It belongs to the virtue of prudence to grasp the context in which one acts and thus to recognize the intrinsic intentional traits of the action which objectively determine its identity."[13] It is the goal of this study to provide further guidance for determining what sorts of cooperative actions must be considered formal, by reason of their "intrinsic intentionality" or moral object.

We would do well to state at the outset what makes describing the contours of formal cooperation so difficult. How is it possible that some respectable theologians could fail to recognize the greater part of this class of action? We must recall that the task of defining any action morally—identifying its moral object—is problematic, if one wishes to be absolutely precise. Murder, for instance, is not simply killing, but killing the innocent. Moreover, we must add that it is killing the innocent *directly*. And still, it will be difficult to show how the direct killing of a lunatic on a rampage does not violate this definition. Certain elements of a situation combine to specify the object; others are circumstantial. Genuine circumstances may be morally relevant, but they cannot make a bad moral object choice-worthy. With cooperation, a special problem lies in the fact that cooperators by definition do something *other* than the principal agent. They take part, provide assistance, omit interference and so forth, but from a phenomenological viewpoint their action is distinct. The question arises: is the cooperator's moral object also distinct from that of the principal agent? If so, when? When would the foreseeable facilitation of evil be a *mere* circumstance—albeit a morally relevant one—of the good or neutral action of the cooperator? When, on the other hand, would the foreseeable facilitation be no longer a circumstance, properly speaking, but a defining element of the moral object of the cooperator's act?

Debate about this issue crystallized at the end of the 17th century around one case, illustrative of the problem: the case of the Servant and the Ladder. If a servant holds a ladder by which his master will ascend through a window to commit a crime, what is the object of the servant's act? Is he "holding a ladder" or is he "committing the crime"? Is the harm caused—in the case in question, the violation of a young woman—accidental to his essentially good action, or is the fact that he was holding a ladder (not forcing a door) accidental to his essentially bad action of visiting harm on an innocent? Antiquated, perhaps, in its details, this case is more relevant than ever in its basic problematic. It serves us well both for presenting the historical development of thinking about formal and material cooperation, and for providing a test for the conclusions we hope to draw.

The case of the Servant and the Ladder gained fame as "Proposition 51" when one version was condemned in 1679 along with a list of laxist propositions by Pope Innocent XI. Chapter 1 will present the background of this condemnation in hopes of providing some keys to its interpretation. We will follow the debate that it ignited in Chapters 2 and 3 until the point when St Alphonsus Liguori defined the terms formal and material in a way that appeared to settle the matter.

The beginnings of moral theology as a specific discipline coincided with the arising of extra-ecclesial forays into moral philosophy. In Chapter 4 we will look at some conclusions of secular ethical thought that provide a counterpoint to the technical reflection within the Church known as casuistry or the Manualist tradition. In particular the tendency towards consequentialism in secular circles called theologians to defend their notion of intrinsic evil and the related principle of double effect. Elizabeth Anscombe is a critic of consequentialism with excellent secular credentials. Her effort to deepen our understanding of intention spurred much thought both within and without the Church which is relevant to our theme.

Chapter 5 picks up the discussion of cooperation proper where we left it at the end of Chapter 3. We follow the development not only of St Alphonsus's definitions of formal and material cooperation, but also of the underlying theological notions, which are discussed in Chapter 6. As previously mentioned, the solidification of moral teaching in the manuals was challenged by secular voices, but it also had to contend with the emergence of new moral issues. Trends emerged within the Catholic world (viz. proportionalism) which seemed ever so akin to the consequentialism usually found in the halls of non-ecclesial academia (cf. Chapter 7). At this point, Providence intervened in the form of the Second Vatican Council which pointedly included moral theology in its call for renewal.

Beginning in Chapter 8 we examine the first steps towards a renewed look at key notions of fundamental moral theology, frequently referred to as "action theory". This effort, we recall, is what Livio Melina suggested could bring new clarity to the traditional teaching on cooperation. Often, one senses a vagueness that has resulted from a failure to analyze exactly in what the cooperative action consists, a lack of analysis that greater precision in "action theory" could overcome. Here, the topics are all interconnected: intentionality, the moral object, intrinsic evil, absolute moral norms. In the following chapters we consider three leading thinkers on the contemporary stage who accept *Veritatis Splendor* enthusiastically but who do not entirely concur in their interpretations of it. We will survey their positions with an eye, always, to what light their views of intention and action might shed upon the question of cooperation in evil.

Finally, in Chapter 11, we can begin to draw conclusions. In particular, we hope to provide a satisfactory analysis of the Servant and the Ladder case. More generally, we will see that despite everything the category of implicitly formal cooperation has emerged, survived and even solidified over time. Our effort is aided and its results confirmed by an authoritative definition[14] of formal cooperation issued by John Paul II in 1995. It must be admitted that a clarified and expanded place for the category of implicitly formal cooperation holds potentially dramatic consequences. This is because formal cooperation is something that should never be given under any circumstances. Consequently, our study closes with a consideration of the practical effects, including the valuable advantages, which can be expected from putting more emphasis on this largely ignored, but very important, category of moral acts.

Notes

[1]   "... children of God, without blemish in the midst of a crooked and perverse generation, among whom you shine as lights in the world..."

[2]   "To speak in general terms, we may say that the Christian is to the world what the soul is to the body. As the soul is present in every part of the body, while remaining distinct from it, so Christians are

found in all the cities of the world, but cannot be identified with the world. As the visible body contains the invisible soul, so Christians are seen living in the world, but their religious life remains unseen. The body hates the soul and wars against it, not because of any injury the soul has done it, but because of the restriction the soul places on its pleasures. Similarly, the world hates the Christians, not because they have done it any wrong, but because they are opposed to its enjoyments... Such is the Christian's lofty and divinely appointed function, from which he is not permitted to excuse himself." Anonymous, "Letter to Diognetus," Chapter VI, in *The Apostolic Fathers*. The Fathers of the Church, ed. L. Schopp, vol. 1 (New York: Christian Heritage, 1947), p. 362.

[3] L. Gormally, "Personal and social responsibility in the context of the defence of human life: the question of cooperation in evil," in *Christian Conscience in Support of the Right to Life: Proceedings of the Thirteenth Assembly of the Pontifical Academy for Life, Vatican City, 23–25 February 2007*, eds. E. Sgreccia and J. Laffitte, pp. 92–111 (Vatican City State: Libreria Editrice Vaticana, 2008), at pp. 110–111.

[4] Professor of Law, University of California at Berkeley, and author of *Complicity: Ethics and Law for a Collective Age* (Cambridge: Cambridge University Press, 2000).

[5] Kutz, *Complicity*, p. 190; this means "being a faultless member of an organization systematically at fault in causing harm", p. 203.

[6] M. C. Kaveny, "Appropriation of Evil: Cooperation's Mirror Image," *Theological Studies* 61 (2000), pp. 280–313.

[7] Cf. *ST* I-II, q. 12, a. 1. Latin quotations from St Thomas Aquinas are taken from the Corpus Thomistcum Project of the University of Navarre found at www.corpusthomistcum.org.

[8] Russell Smith writes that "duress implies threat and force to such a degree that the victim of this duress has a reasonable loss of will in light of the situation... [causing an eventual act's removal] from the realm of the purely voluntary *in an ethically significant sense*, and therefore, from the realm of *the principles of cooperation as they were conceived in the tradition*." R. Smith, "Duress and Cooperation," *Ethics and Medics* 21 (1996), pp. 1–2, at p. 2. This comment is difficult to comprehend. Historically, as we shall see, the principles developed out of the debate over Proposition 51, which certainly involves duress. The principles of cooperation have their primary application where an agent has legitimate goals that can only be attained by fostering the evil in question. The

prospective frustration of these legitimate goals—career advancement, financial security, physical safety, etc.—will be experienced as "having to" contribute to a harm that the agent otherwise would not contribute to. There are certainly many gradations of pressure and corresponding gradations of loss of voluntariness, but removal from the ethical realm would be an extreme case.

9 Our phrasing is awkward, for even the principal agents do not really "seek an evil goal," but some good by a disordered means. This fact—that human agents inevitably act for a good end, the evil being somehow *praeter intentionem*—underlines the reality of implicitly formal cooperation: it would be simply another way of intending evil while pursuing a good.

10 H. Davis, *Moral and Pastoral Theology* (London: Sheed and Ward, 1958), I, p. 341.

11 *Ibid.*, p. 342.

12 "Decisivo è invece stabilire l'identità oggettiva dell'atto di collaborazione, cioè l'intenzionalità intrinseca che lo connota." L. Melina, *"La cooperazione con azione moralmente cattive contro la vita umana,"* in *Commento interdisciplinare alla 'Evangelium Vitae',* ed. E. Sgreccia and R. Lucas Lucas, pp. 467–490 (Vatican City: Libreria Editrice Vaticana, 1997), p. 478. Note that all translations are mine unless otherwise noted. The reminder ("translation mine") will be given, when the text in the original language is not also provided.

13 "Appartiene alla virtù della prudenza cogliere il contesto in cui si agisce e quindi riconoscere i tratti intenzionali intrinseci dell'azione, che ne determinano oggettivamente l'identità." *Ibid.*, pp. 477–478.

14 Here and in Chapters Eight and Eleven, the term "definition" should not be taken to mean a dogmatic, even infallible, statement, but simply a clarification of terms carrying the weight signified by the form of teaching used.

PART I

A PROBLEM RAISED

CHAPTER 1

THE CASE OF THE SERVANT AND THE LADDER

1. An Overview

I N 1679, POPE Innocent XI issued a list of condemned propositions. One of the propositions described the case of cooperation with evil with which we are particularly concerned: the case of the Servant and the Ladder.

> A servant, who knowingly helps his master climb through a window to violate a virgin by offering him his shoulders and many times assists him by holding a ladder, opening a door, or cooperating in like manner, does not sin mortally, if he does this out of fear of a notable harm, such as that his master will treat him badly, look at him angrily, or expel him from the house.[1]

Along with the other propositions, this affirmation was "condemned and prohibited ... as at least scandalous and in practice pernicious."[2] Such is the delicate nature of cooperation with evil that this attempt to clarify authentic Catholic teaching spawned great controversy instead. The aim of our study is to examine this legacy and contribute yet another installment to the debate. We will begin with a brief overview of the question.

The times in which this condemnation was issued were particularly significant for a study of cooperation with evil. One hundred years after the Council of Trent had demanded more stringent formation of clergy, the teaching of moral theology, led by the Jesuits, had become a science in its own right. Cooperation with evil was just emerging as a theme for analysis. It involved a number of difficult concepts which can be seen in the proposition chosen for condemnation: the importance of the levels of knowledge and freedom possessed by an agent for assessing moral responsibility, the difference between mortal and venial sin, the existence and nature of intrinsic evil, and the nature of responsibility for unintended consequences of one's actions. Clearly, a condemnation of a single proposition, issued without commentary, could not hope to settle such questions but only to stimulate and orient discussion.

Initially, as the proposition occurs among those condemned as laxist, it was natural for commentators to want to interpret it strictly. Pope Innocent himself, while not a Jansenist, was considered by some to lean in the direction of rigor.[3] Not surprisingly, therefore, three years after the condemnation, Ramón Lumbier published a work interpreting the cooperation of the servant as intrinsically evil, and thus, to be forbidden for any cause.[4] A number of scholars followed suit while expressing varying degrees of perplexity. Cardenas,[5] Viva,[6] and Sbogar[7] all wrote commentaries on the condemned propositions in which they show some hesitation regarding the authentic meaning of the decree. One reason for doubt is the inclusion of relatively light motives for the servant's cooperation (such as fear of an angry look from the master). This could be taken to indicate that the reason for the condemnation lay in insufficient grounds for cooperation in so serious a matter, and that such cooperation would be permitted by the Pontiff, if a very serious detriment such as death was to be feared.

Nonetheless, the bulk of authors adopted the stricter interpretation. For seventy years attempts were made to explain cooperation with evil in such a way as to prohibit actions such as those of the servant absolutely. St Alphonsus Liguori also followed the strict reading, prohibiting such cooperation under any circumstances, in his first published work, a commentary on the popular book of Herman Busenbaum. Nonetheless, when his own *Theologia moralis* appeared in 1753, the saint had taken a different point of view on the matter.[8] He now supported the idea that the intent of the condemnation was to highlight the insufficiency of the motives suggested.

Not surprisingly, the authority of St Alphonsus, backed up by his beatification, canonization and declaration as Doctor of the Church in rapid succession, tended to cement this interpretation of Proposition 51. This is especially understandable in the climate of probabilism, in which the authority of a given opinion was of primary concern. Thus, the idea that the servant's cooperation was material and condemned by Pope Innocent XI only for lacking a sufficient justification became the dominant view found in the Manualist era. For example, in the entry "Laxisme" in the *Dictionnaire de Théologie Catholique* of 1926, we read the following commentary on Proposition 51:

> There are cases where purely material cooperation in the fault of another is licit. The precise conditions are enumerated in Volume III. In the censured proposition, [these conditions] are not realized; in particular, there is not the *grave inconvenience*, which in certain cases can excuse the completely material assistance made to the sin of a neighbor.[9]

The fact that the servant's cooperation had been thought formal by some, and was indeed solemnly condemned as such in Paris two centuries earlier,[10] is not even mentioned.

Nevertheless, the debate concerning this particular problem appears only to have been quieted by the authority of Saint Alphonsus—not resolved. In our day, while the

Saint's intervention has been lauded as a decisive step forward in a doctoral dissertation by Roger Roy, Cssr,[11] other voices seem less sure. Only a few years earlier, Alphonsus's analysis of this case was called into question by another one of his sons in religion, Bernard Häring, Cssr. In his *Law of Christ*, Häring writes: "It might be more to the point to reason as follows: the action [of the servant] in this case because of the circumstances of place and time, and above all because of the total absence of any morally good motivation, is so unequivocally determined as contributing to the sin of another that it can be conceived only as formal cooperation."[12] Likewise, at about the same time, the author of an article in the *New Catholic Encyclopedia* gives the fetching and setting up of a ladder in response to a burglar's request as an example of formal cooperation that is not formal by explicit intention but "by making an unambiguous contribution to the performance of the act".[13] The great contemporary Catholic philosopher, Elizabeth Anscombe, referred to this case as a notorious example of "directing your intention".[14] Thus, despite two centuries of relative quiet, the controversy of the Servant and the Ladder calls again for attention.

2. The context of probabilism

Development of probabilism from Cajetan to Caramuel

Proposition 51 and the condemnations that accompanied it must, of course, be interpreted within the context in which they were made. We must consider the person of Pope Innocent XI (Benedetto Odescalchi) and his perspective on the moral controversies of his day. While the connection between moral laxism and the moral system known as "probabilism" has been denied by many,[15] the historical coincidence of laxism and probabilism is beyond question. After three-quarters of a century of dominance, probabilist writers began to venture opinions that were considered laxist and condemned as such. The condemnations made by Innocent XI find their place in line with those that came just before and after him. Alexander VII issued two series of condemnations of laxism (24 September 1665 and 18 March 1666), while Alexander VIII continued Innocent's work by condemning two more propositions on 24 August 1690. Taken together, these papal acts formed one sustained effort by the Holy See to stem the trend towards laxism that had already contributed to the appearance of a rigorist reaction, known as Jansenism. There was a sense that an unhealthy tendency was developing that urgently needed to be curtailed.[16]

While the declarations of these Popes do not constitute a condemnation of probabilism as such, some of the propositions speak rather directly of the system itself.[17] Moreover, Innocent XI issued a public statement that, despite debate concerning both its authentic wording and meaning, clearly favors what is known as "probabiliorism".[18] Likewise his support of Gonzalez de Santalla, an opponent of probabilism, indicates that Innocent XI perceived a connection between the probabilist mentality and the laxist trend that he was seeking to uproot. Consequently, in order to elucidate the meaning of his condemnations, we must strive to understand the probabilist thinking that led to the offensive propositions. In addition to a brief review of the history, we will entrust ourselves for analysis to Gonzalez de Santalla, who, more than any other figure, can be presumed to reflect the mind of Innocent XI upon these matters.

The history of probabilism is so long, complex and contested, both in questions of fact and doctrine, that we must make every effort to restrict to the minimum our entry into so thick a wood of controversy. Fortunately, this requisite discussion of probabilism is more possible today than it was as recently as the middle of last century. Servais Pinckaers's book, *Les sources de la morale chrétienne*,[19] masterfully shows that by the mid-1980's it was possible to place the question probabilism in its context between the decline of the Scholastic age and the Manualist era and to survey it with sufficient perspective to gain insight for present efforts to renew moral theology. In any event, the violent passions that characterized the polemics from the mid 17th to the beginning of the 20th century have thankfully subsided.

At first it is perplexing to consider how the central tenet of probabilism—that one acts safely in following a moral opinion provided it is probable—should lead to such a wide variety of opinions that were judged erroneous, including the opinion that, to protect his interests, a servant could help his master without mortal sin to carry out such a vile plan as that suggested in Proposition 51. To understand the connection, we must recall that the decline of Scholasticism, including the nominalism of William of Ockham and the splitting of disciplines into specializations, had led moral theology to be increasingly divided from spiritual theology and identified with law. In time, this trend would continue, so that the very titles of works in this field would no longer lay claim to being *"theologia moralis"* but mere *"casus conscientiae"* (handbooks treating morally problematic situtations). The emphasis on law brought to the fore questions such as a subject's ability to fulfill the law, the conditions for its promulgation, the capacity of a law to cover particular concrete cases, and so on. The efforts of all minds were turned to avoiding scrupulosity and torment for individual consciences while maintaining the validity of commandments and precepts.[20]

In this context Thomas de Vio Cajetan also lived and worked. Cardinal Cajetan was a legend in his own day and is still considered one of the first and greatest commentators on St Thomas Aquinas. Great as he was, he appears to have laid a key foundation stone for probabilist thinking; on this stone Francisco Suarez would later build, bringing probabilism into full bloom. The point concerns the relation between speculative and practical reason.

> It is necessary to distinguish the mode, whether such hesitation or vacillation be in the speculative or practical mode: that is, whether one doubts about the liceity or illiceity [of the act] in itself, or according to the meaning of the act here and now. For, if someone should doubt, whether to play an instrument on Friday is licit or illicit, and however does not doubt that it is for him at this moment licit to play it, he would not sin by playing (...). And, on the other hand, if someone were certain that the act of playing in itself, is something permitted on Friday, and, however, wavers about the playing being done now by him, such that the rationale for setting himself to play is applied with ambiguity, he would play illicitly: the speculative intellect, indeed, says nothing about action.[21]

The role of translating the law (speculative knowledge) known by conscience into a practical dictamen binding in actual circumstances should be the work of prudence. In this passage, Cajetan drives a wedge between the two orders of knowledge. He does not speak of practical certainty as a motive for revising and making more precise the speculative understanding that is expressed in law, nor, on the other hand, does he speak of speculative certainty as a cause for the agent to question his practical estimation of the situation. Rather, Cajetan opens up the possibility of genuine, persistent inconsistency between speculative and practical knowledge. His concern is not so much, how to resolve a conflict in the interest of truth, but which authority to consider binding. His answer favors practical certainty, since "intellectus speculativus nihil dicit de operando."[22]

One must not hold Cajetan responsible for developments of his thinking that he neither could have anticipated nor would have condoned. Nonetheless, nudged by the influential doctor, the idea began to gain momentum that speculative investigation could not provide definitive answers to an agent confronted with the infinitely variable circumstances of daily life. Concepts such as prudence and *epikeia* which had complemented the role of speculative reason now fell into the background. Rather, cases would have to be treated individually; jurisprudence would speedily need to be developed. The agent would then have as his guide not abstract reasoning but concrete opinions of learned men who had confronted similar cases before. As the legalist mentality progressed, the importance of discovering intrinsic reasons for determining the morality of an act decreased; it was superseded by the judgment of extrinsic authorities. An opinion was a sound as the number and reputation of authors approving of it.

While probabilism has root causes stretching far back before Cajetan to the decline of the Scholastic period, its budding as a visible moral system can be assigned a date.[23] In 1577, Bartolomew Medina raised the question that lies at the heart of the probabilist controversy: in a moral quandary, can one licitly follow an opinion that one has reason to consider probably correct, even if other opinions are more probably correct? He answered affirmatively: "it seems to me that if an opinion is probable, it is licit to follow it, even if the opposite opinion is more probable."[24]

Francisco Suarez soon followed, carrying Cajetan's division of speculative and practical orders still further.

He argued that "a man can rationally persuade himself that he can here and now licitly not operate according to such a speculative judgment."[25] This did not mean that practical reason encountered factors that would have to be incorporated into a more precise speculative understanding. Rather, a certain speculative judgment could reasonably be ignored on the basis of the priority of liberty to act in doubt (regarding the here and now). Moreover, Suarez presumed that a law that is perceived as less than certain can be considered insufficiently promulgated and, therefore, inapplicable. These two lines of argument could effectively bolster small practical doubts until they were capable of overcoming any speculative certitude. The status in moral theology of probable opinions in concrete cases was raised above that of universal moral norms, which were considered but speculative and abstract. Full blown probabilism had arrived.

Paul Laymann, who was considered one of the greatest Jesuit moral theologians of his day, assumed the perspective of Cajetan regarding the roles of the speculative and practical orders. He expressed the import of this position, and so the essence of probabilism, with astonishing frankness. After noting that all agree that one can only act rightly if one has a morally certain practical judgment,[26] he asks what suffices to give the practical intellect this certitude. He not only answers that probable opinions will suffice, but that this is so because certitude comes *not* from intrinsic principles but from extrinsic ones:

> You ask, by what reason can he be certain in operating who follows an uncertain and dubious opinion; when from the uncertain it is not possible to obtain certainty? I respond that it is apparent from what was said above. Certainty of conscience, which the agent must have is not speculative, acquired from

> the intrinsic principles of a thing, but it is practical,
> drawn from practical and extrinsic principles of a
> thing; for instance, the opinions of Doctors teaching
> that something is probably licit to do...[27]

Thus, Laymann explicitly affirms the turning away from
the intrinsic truth of human action as an essential part of
the probabilist project. Deman comments that, after this
contribution of Laymann, "it is impossible to say with
more force that the objective truth is no longer the
measure of action."[28]

The most extreme statements of the probabilist position are found in authors who are also responsible for
many of the condemned propositions. Once the source of
practical certitude has been placed in extrinsic sources, it
is logical to take this final step: to reduce to a minimum
the ability of these sources to limit liberty of action. So
Thomas Tamburini, the most likely font of Proposition
51, remarked: "The least probability, be it of authority or
of reason, suffices to act well."[29] Johannes Caramuel
Lobkowitz asked: "What is required that an opinion be
probable to the reason? That it not be evidently false."[30]

In sum, as the idea of probabilism evolved, moral
theologians found it increasingly difficult to avoid coming
to ever laxer moral conclusions, which often were dubbed
"benign". It is only fair to observe that we have attempted
to highlight the dangerous aspect of probabilism, and this,
with the benefit of hindsight of several centuries. One
should not criticize too harshly writers who were, in the
main, brilliant, industrious, well-intentioned and even
holy men. It is likely that even the doctors employed by
the Holy See in condemning erroneous opinions operated
to a large degree on intuition and were unable to explain
exactly what was wrong with the ideas they rejected. One
author, however, whose analysis of the ethical system was

both contemporary and penetrating was Thyrsus Gonzalez de Santalla.

The criticism of Thrysus Gonzalez

As mentioned, the mind of Innocent XI on probabilism is revealed by his extraordinary support for Thyrsus Gonzalez de Santalla, s.j. Thyrsus Gonzalez was one of the few Jesuit professors at the close of the 17th century to argue against the growing tide of probabilism. In 1674, he wrote a book arguing strongly in favor of a stricter approach to moral decision-making, but due to the unpopularity of his approach, particularly among his confreres, its publication was prevented. Pope Odelscalchi came to know of Gonzalez's work, however, and intervened to force his promotion to Superior General of the order in 1687. Amazingly, the opposition to Gonzalez's anti-probabilist position was still so strong that his book would not see the light of day until the next pope, Innocent XII, intervened again. Thus, it was finally published in Rome in 1694 under the title, *Fundamenta theologiae moralis: de recto usu opinionum probabilium.*[31]

The brief outline of the trajectory of probablist thinking given above—from Cajetan to Caramuel—indicates that a progressive displacement of the focus of moral theology from reality to legislation, from an intrinsic morality to an extrinsic one, is the characteristic feature of the age. The existence of moral truth and the most fundamental duty of the moral agent to follow it became obscured. In his *Fundamenta*, Gonzalez sets himself the task of restoring this perspective. "Our goal, therefore, in which we find fulfillment, and the North Star, to which we must look, is truth. And so in questions needing to be decided, it is not necessary to attend to which opinion is rigid and which benign, but to which is true."[32] He eloquently distinguishes this position

from rigorism, indicating the goal as "non quaerere sever-
itatem sed veritatem"[33] (not to seek severity but truth).

Gonzalez argues that the fundamental error of the probabilists who followed Medina was to lose the idea of probability as "vere probabilis" (truly probable) and as "veresimilior
quem opposita"[34] (more likely true than the opposite) in the
estimation of the agent. Repeatedly, he insists that the agent
can only follow a probable opinion when he himself is
convinced that it is the most probably true, even if this path
were generally thought less probable. Thus he comes forcefully to the defense not only of truth, but of the individual's
capacity and responsibility to discern it.

Thus, Gonzalez vindicates the irreplaceable role of
personal conscience. A probable opinion, he says at the
end of his work, is a "relative rule" which only serves as a
"correct rule for those who prudently approve it as true."[35]

Still, Gonzalez clearly avoids the danger of permitting
the subjective conscience to marginalize the truth of moral
action. He quotes St Thomas in this regard:

> That which is done against the law (namely a law
> which someone can and should know—Gonz.), is
> always evil, and is not excused by the fact that it is
> according to conscience; and likewise what is
> against conscience is evil, although it may not be
> contrary to law. What is neither against conscience,
> nor against the law, however, cannot be sinful.[36]

It is critical for the purpose of interpreting Proposition 51,
and for assessing the possibility of implicit formal cooperation on the part of the servant, to attend to Gonzalez's
criticism of probabilism for compromising the notion of
implicit intention in various ways. For instance, continuing his argument that subjective tranquility of conscience
does not absolve an agent, Gonzalez affirms that someone
who knows a law but considers himself *hic et nunc* exempt

may well still sin in acting: "for in order that the act of the will be evil, it is not necessary that its evil be known reflexively, but it suffices that the agent know the object to be evil and prohibited by divine law, and nevertheless, choose it voluntarily and freely."[37]

The tendency to see concrete circumstances (such as, perhaps, the potential hazards to the servant of not cooperating) as capable of overruling a general law is central to the probabilist outlook. Gonzalez does not deny that circumstances can at times justify or excuse behaviors, but he rejects the idea, originated as we have seen by Cajetan, that practical reason can be set in opposition to speculative reason. "Let it be confirmed that … from a speculative or universal doubt there necessarily will result a practical doubt regarding a particular action here and now to be performed, with which doubt it is certain that no one can licitly act."[38] Using the example of usury, he describes the reasoning process that he opposes. Suppose that one prudently doubts whether an act is *secundum se* usury. If there is speculative doubt that the proposed action is intrinsically evil, then it can be doubted that it is *hic et nunc* prohibited to me. This practical doubt, the argument goes, makes it certain that for me, here and now, acting would not be a sin.[39] Gonzalez rejects as specious such a passage from speculative doubt to practical certainty. This question of the relation of intrinsic evil to circumstances (*hic et nunc*) will have a prominent role in the debate following the condemnations of Innocent XI.

In conclusion, Gonzalez does not consider the laxism of his day to be an aberrant fruit on a healthy tree, but rather he seeks to identify the diseased roots feeding the thought of many of his contemporaries.[40] Gonzalez wrote his critique of probabilism before the condemnations of Innocent XI were issued; thus, it cannot be suspected of being a forced reaction to them. As the *Fundamenta* was only published five years later, thanks to papal intervention, it is able to make explicit reference to Proposition 3 on a number of occasions.[41] In essence, Gonzalez makes two crucial points against probabilism. The first and most fundamental problem he identifies is a practical agnosticism regarding moral truth. A truth exists concerning right human action, he insists, no matter how difficult it may be to discover in certain cases. The second foundational assertion that he makes is that an agent who can or does know this truth, or who remains in doubt regarding it, cannot act in opposition to it with a security founded solely upon the opinion of experts. The good alone, as it truly is, or at least as the agent in good faith genuinely perceives it to be, is what primarily determines the goodness of the will that chooses to act. The agent may genuinely wish to avoid sin, but there will be an implicitly evil intention if he freely chooses to act in disregard to the truth of objective reality.

Analysis of the condemnations by the Holy See (1665–1690)

As we have seen, Medina's announcement of the tenet that gave probabilism its name was followed by seventy-five years of development. A theoretical system and a mentality developed far beyond his imagining. We examined Gonzalez's analysis of this phenomenon which had definitely gained the day despite the unease of the Magisterium, manifested most clearly by Blessed Innocent XI. We have argued that the probabilist mentality led to the practical conclusions, which finally spurred a vigorous reaction on the part of the Holy See. We now propose to examine the papal condemnations themselves in light of this theoretical background. Although only Proposition 51 deals with cooperation with evil directly, it is a product of the same spirit that produced the other condemned opinions. By seeking to see how the principles behind laxism were translated into concrete practical judgments, we can gain insight into what lay behind the formulation of Proposition 51 and perhaps what the Holy See found objectionable. Only an analysis of the full context of the case that concerns us, the Servant and the Ladder, will prepare us to consider it anew in light of contemporary thought.

We have noted that the salient characteristic of the moral thinking of the time was legalism. Not only the probabilists but all theologians labored under a conception of law that was opposed to the "liberty"[42] of the agent. When this legalism became exaggerated, some thinkers, zealous to protect agents from the demands of the law, drew a number of conclusions that were condemned as laxist. They proposed a variety of ingenious arguments to reduce the applicability of the law. This tendency might appear to be the whole cause of laxism, but this is not the case. Other elements of the theoretical background that we have sketched underlie many of the condemned propositions, including Proposition 51.

Let us begin however with the legalist aspect. Certainly propositions are not lacking that are the result of identifying morality with duty to fulfill the law and identifying the reduction of that duty with the mission of a benign theologian.

The legalist optic attenuated the link between moral norms and the intrinsic truth of man and his nature, so that even behavior contrary to the natural law came to be considered as wrong only because prohibited. Here the legacy of Ockham is particularly evident. Three of Innocent's propositions combat the idea that sins of lust are wrong only because God prohibits them,[43] and even, in the case of adultery, only because the husband prohibits it.[44] Thus, a legalist, extrinsic perspective caused some to doubt the foundations of absolute moral norms.

The zeal to protect an agent's liberty from the burden of the law, also led to the claim that positive precepts did not have to be fulfilled consistently. The obligation to believe in the essential dogma of the faith could be fulfilled by making an act of faith but once in a person's life.[45] Three propositions sought to reduce the obligation of loving God, from every five years, to once in a lifetime, if at all.[46] Some authors arrived at the point where the commandment to love God was pared down to simply not hating him.[47]

Several condemnations of Alexander VII counter attempts to claim liberty of action when a law is for some reason considered not yet expressly promulgated or evident.[48] Innocent XI closes other loopholes designed to limit the extent of the law. For instance, he denies that uncertainty concerning the fact of ensoulment should translate into freedom to procure an abortion.[49] He also rejects the idea that reciting the remaining hours of the Office will make up for omitting Matins and Lauds.[50]

Most significantly, for our analysis of Proposition 51, one notes a tendency among the laxists to suggest circumstances that might excuse or justify an otherwise immoral action. The degree of *incommoditas* that the fulfillment of a commandment required had become, especially with Suarez, a full criterion of moral evaluation.[51] Some of the condemnations clearly sought to circumscribe the tendency to exaggerate the significance for moral evaluation of such inconveniences for the agent. In a few propositions, an attempt is made to reduce the obligation of *positive* precepts for the sake of the agent. For example, one proposition claims that scarcely ever (*vix*) is one required to give alms as one only rarely has goods that should be considered superfluous.[52] Likewise, the duty for priests to confess as soon as possible (*quamprimum*) a mortal sin they may have committed is interpreted as a counsel to be fulfilled in the priest's good time.[53]

By contrast, other propositions reduce the force of *negative* precepts. In the interest of the agent's *commoditas*, rights were exaggerated with the effect of justifying what otherwise would be considered intrinsically evil. Thus, in the case of theft, the attempt to extend the right to take another's goods in extreme necessity to grave necessity was rejected[54] as was the putative right of a servant to make up for unjust wages by pilfering.[55] Furthermore, Pope Innocent insisted that the right to defend one's property with lethal force was not maintained no matter how small the amount in question, let alone a single gold coin.[56] In the same vein, several of the condemnations seek to prevent the right to self-defense from being expanded to the preservation of one's good name. A girl could not justify abortion to protect her reputation.[57] Nor could one avert calumny and like offenses by killing the offender.[58]

Some of the pressures suggested as significant enough to alter the moral judgment in a case were absurd. Thus, for instance, Alexander VII had to condemn the idea that one could retain a concubine, if sending her away would cause life to be too burdensome or dull.[59] On the other hand, when the threat to an agent's *commoditas* is very great, the serious question arises of fear and duress. Innocent indicated clearly that some actions cannot be justified even to escape very great ills. Thus, the simulation of the sacraments "urgens metus gravis" (prompted by great fear) is still to be refused.[60] Amman, in his commentary made in 1926, remarks that "the sacraments are too holy for it to be permitted, for whatever reason, to turn them into derision."[61] Clearly these propositions bear upon the question of how to interpret Proposition 51: are the actions of the servant such that no feared consequences could justify them (such as dueling, abortion, keeping a concubine, or committing sacrilege)? Or does the servant have a legitimate right to act in protection of his interests, provided the interest in jeopardy is sufficiently great?

In the examples above, the underlying principles justifying the condemned positions regard the limits of law to bind agents and the role of circumstances to excuse them. Clearly laws cannot be written to apply in all circumstances, and legitimate excuses exist. Nonetheless, one can already see how the legalist perspective tended to lose sight of the connection between the agent's good will and the good that the law sought to protect. As we continue our examination of the condemned propositions, it will become clearer that the displacement of the locus of morality from the interior of the agent to external considerations lay at the heart of the distorted moral vision that the Holy See opposed.

In this sense, Innocent XI rejected the idea that a person could receive the sacraments without interior faith. It was even necessary to affirm that those lacking faith through their own fault could not receive the sacraments;[62] nor would a provisory faith based upon fear or other motives suffice.[63] The will has an essential role to play in the act of faith.[64] Still less could a purely formal but voluntarily nullified confession[65] or a sacrilegious communion[66] satisfy the precepts of the Church. Similarly, Alexander VII rejected the idea that internal conviction "no matter how evident" was not sufficient to obligate a person to denounce a heretic.[67]

If the law concerned only external acts, the interior attitude of the agent, or his intention, became easily separable from and ultimately irrelevant to the morality of his behavior. Innocent XI condemned two propositions that claimed it was possible to fulfill the commandment to love one's neighbor by purely external acts.[68] Alexander VII had to reject the idea that fidelity to one's neighbor was not harmed by accepting stipends for more than one mass while saying only one, "even having promised by signed oath."[69]

As long as there was no connection between a subject's interior state and his exterior actions, he was free to desire evils, even the death of his father, provided this desire was not efficacious. Innocent XI condemned three propositions of this sort. It was not, for instance, to be considered licit for a son to rejoice in the parricide that he committed when drunk, even if his joy was due only to the thought of the inheritance that was due to him.[70] The imaginativeness of such hypotheses is itself indicative of the separation of moral reasoning from reality. Some authors indulged in a veritable competition of devising bizarre and perplexing problems, substituting morbid conundrums for the noble science of moral theology. Nonetheless, artificial as such a case may be, it also serves as a paradigm from which analogous cases would be solved. It is a serious matter whether one can permit oneself "to desire the death of one's father not as an evil for the father, but as a good for the beneficiary."[71] This purported ability to direct one's desires echoes the "directing of intention" for which casuistry is notorious. It will have to be carefully distinguished from a legitimate concept of "indirect voluntary".

Other manifestations of this dangerous tendency can be found among the condemned propositions. Failing to observe a religious feast would only be wrong if done out of contempt.[72] For a just cause, it was supposed to be licit to speak under oath "without meaning it" (*sine animo*)[73] or misrepresent the truth without lying.[74] Simony was not simony, allegedly, if the money exchanged was not demanded as payment but accepted as a voluntary gift.[75] Usury was not usury, if the interest were paid as a debt of gratitude.[76] Likewise, Innocent rejected the right of a penitent to absolution simply if he claimed sorrow, while grave reasons to suspect the contrary existed.[77]

Various attempts were made to reconfigure or dissect the execution of an act in such a way that it might admit of a good or at least not mortally sinful intention. Among the attempts rejected: one would not break a fast if one ate as much as one wanted but in small quantities[78]; nor would one commit theft if one took small amounts over time[79]; nor would one be guilty of usury if various artificial transactions were made that had the same results.[80] Also significant is the condemnation of three claims that one can enjoy carnal pleasure purely for its own sake (*ob solam voluptatem*) without sin.[81] Here, also, we perceive facile attempts to sever behavior and intention, attempts which the Holy See rejects. The agent cannot with a good will ignore the end for which the behaviors of eating and engaging in sexual intercourse are intrinsically attractive to a rational being; it does not suffice simply not to hinder those ends.

Alexander VIII ended the laxist condemnations with two of his own. These also indicate a rejection on the part of the Magisterium of tendencies toward extrinsicism, which divided a subject's interior acts from his external actions. In the first case, it was established that a materially good act, separated from the agent's will to please God, is not sufficient actually to do so. Thus, it does not suffice to conform an act formally to the moral law that it be oriented to the final end (God) implicitly (*interpretive*); such a claim, as the proposition itself admits, has the effect that "a man is not held to love either at the beginning or during the course of his life."[82] In an only apparently contrasting statement, the Pope held that a bad act will offend God even if this is not the specific goal of the agent. The notion was rejected that one could not offend God simply by doing what was offensive to right reason, and thus divine law, but that one must do such offensive deeds *so as* to offend him in order to commit a sin meriting eternal punishment.[83] While some maintain that the possibility of this so-called "philosophical sin" was misunderstood by Alexander VIII,[84] nonetheless, as a product of the mentality separating internal and external acts, it justly merited the epithets it earned: scandalous, temerarious, offensive and erroneous. The claim also reminds us of Pascal's accusation that the probabilists he opposed so strenuously only forbade "sinning for the sake of sinning".[85]

Before considering the proposition that dealt explicitly with the question of cooperation with evil, it would be opportune to summarize the foregoing analysis. The propositions condemned by Innocent XI and the two Alexanders can appear to be a heterogeneous mix of far-fetched opinions. Sometimes they are presented not only as having no relation to probabilism but no relation to the thought of any actual writers.[86] This approach explains neither the origin of these ideas at that time nor why the Holy See considered the opinions so dangerous. Having reviewed the fundamental ideas at work in probabilism, both from the perspective of nearly four hundred years' distance and from the insightful analysis of Gonzalez that was endorsed by Innocent himself, we sought to link them to the practical conclusions that came to be condemned. While some of the condemned notions were simply attempts to minimize or circumvent the force of law, the majority reflected the moral aberration that both Gonzalez and Deman denounced: extrinsicist morality that ignores the truth of human action and so severs the connection between the agent's search for this truth and the goodness of his will. This tendency showed itself in two ways, both of which were targets of the papal interventions. On one hand, an agent cannot choose a bad exterior action with impunity, under the pretense of intending some praiseworthy action. Revenge, lying, simony and so forth remain such no matter what the agent claims to be doing. On the other hand, the Pontiffs did not allow an agent to produce disordered interior acts (desiring harm, nullifying confession, seeking carnal pleasure alone) even if the exterior act complied with the law. The intrinsic truth of human acts and the rapport between this truth and the agent choosing to act must remain the focus of authentic moral evaluation. We will have to keep rooted in this insight, as we consider the attempts to grapple with the problem of cooperation described in Innocent's Proposition 51.

Notes

[1] "Famulus, qui submissis humeris scienter adiuvat herum suum ascendere per fenestras ad stuprandam virginem, et multoties eidem subservit deferendo scalam, aperiendo ianuam, aut quid simile cooperando, non peccat mortaliter, si id faciat metu notabilis detrimenti, puta ne a domino male tractetur, ne torvis oculis aspiciatur, ne domo expellatur." DS 2151.

[2] "Omnes propositiones damnatae et prohibitae, sicut iacent, ut minimum tamquam scandalosae et in praxi perniciosae." DS 2166.

[3] It should be noted in this connection that Pope Innocent XI encouraged frequent and even daily communion. Moreover, he has now been declared "Blessed" by decree of Pius XII.

[4] R. Lumbier, *Observationes theologicae morales* (Barcelona: typ. Mathevat, 1682), nn. 460–461.

[5] J. de Cardenas, *Crisis theologica* (Venice: Pezzana, 1700), diss. XXXI, nn. 4–5.

[6] D. Viva, *Damnatae theses ab Alexandro VII, Innocentio XI, & Alexandro VIII*, 9th ed. (Padua: apud Joannem Manfre, 1720), Prop. LI, n. III.

[7] J. Sbogar, *Theologia radicalis*, 3ʳᵈ ed. (Prague: Typ. Caroli Jannis Hraba, 1725), Tract. 79, cap 1, n. 6.

[8] A. de Liguori, *Theologia moralis*, 9ᵗʰ ed. (Gaudé) (Rome: Vatican, 1905), lib. II, tr.3, cap.2, dub. 5. "De scandalo," art. 3, n. 66, quaer. 4.

[9] E. Amman, "Laxisme," in *Dictionnaire de théologie catholique, ed.* A.Vacant and E. Mangenot (Paris: Librairie Letouzey et Ané, 1938), IX i, col. 82.

[10] While the comment, prepared by Bossuet, and solemnly approved by the assembly of French clergy is brief, it would be hard to interpret as supporting the view that the cooperation described in Proposition 51 is only wrong for lack of sufficient reason. It reads: "This proposition is scandalous, pernicious, openly contrary to the words of the Lord and the apostles, and heretical. 'Or what shall a man give in return for his life?' (Mt 16:26) and 'Though they know God's decree that those who do such things deserve to die, they not only do them but approve those who practice them' (Rm 1:26)." The possibility of subtle or implicit "consent" is more perceptible in the Vulgate version that was used: Digni sunt morte, non solum qui ea faciunt, sed etiam qui consentiunt facientibus. Cf. Jacques-Benigne Bossuet, *Oeuvres complètes de Bossuet*, ed. F. Lachat (Paris: Louis Vives, 1885), XXII, p. 757.

[11] Cf. R. Roy, *Notion de la coopération selon Saint Alphonse et ses sources* (Rome: Pontifical University of Saint Thomas Aquinas in the City, 1969); and the article which is drawn from it: "La Coopération selon Saint Alphonse de Liguori," *Studia Moralia* 6 (1968), pp. 377–435.

[12] B. Häring, *Law of Christ*, tr. E. G. Kaiser (Westminister, MD: Newman Press, 1961), II, p. 498.

[13] F. E. Klueg, "Sin, Cooperation in," *New Catholic Encyclopedia* (New York: McGraw Hill, 1967), XIII, p. 246.

[14] G. E. M. Anscombe, "War and Murder," in *The Doctrine of Double Effect: Philosophers Debate a Controversial Moral Principle*, ed. P. A. Woodward, pp. 247–260 (Notre Dame, IN: University of Notre Dame Press, 2001), at p. 257.

[15] In his article, "Laxisme," E. Amman criticizes Bossuet, alleging that "he wanted always to see [in probabilism] the source of all lax morality" (p. 59). One author who openly blames laxism on probabilism is Ludovicus Masius, who entitles the very first section of his book: "Probabilismi cognatio, nexusque cum Laxismo" (cf. *Incommoda probabilismi*, 2ⁿᵈ ed. [Valencia: apud Josephum Thomam Lucas, 1767]). Successive article headings describe the

actions taken by the Holy See as a war against probabilism which, beginning under Alexander VII, "inflicted wounds," continued under Innocent XI "leaving [probabilism] half dead," so that, at the time of the reigning Clement XIII, it "lies lifeless."

[16] In 1658, Julius Mercorus describes this snowballing towards laxism. "Tunc ulterius observo, spatio quadraginta, aut quinquaginta ab hinc annis plusquam centum opiniones laxas antea singulares, factas esse communes, & illas oppositas rigidas, quae prius erant communes, ut antiquatas, nunc communiter reici." J. Mercorus, *Basis totius moralis teologiae, hoc est praxis opinionum limitata: Adversus nimis emollientes, aut plus aequo exasperantes iugum Christi* (Mantua: apud Osanas, 1658), Pars III, art. v.

[17] Cf. especially the first four propositions of Innocent XI, DS 2101–2104.

[18] Decree of the Holy Office, June 26, 1680, DS 2175–2177.

[19] S. Pinckaers, *The Sources of Christian Ethics* (Edinburgh: T&T Clark, 1995). Following Pinckaers, we consider trustworthy the detailed and penetrating analysis of the question provided by T. Deman in his renowned article, "Probabilisme," in *Dictionnaire de théologie catholique*, ed. A.Vacant and E. Mangenot (Paris: Librairie Letouzey et Ané, 1938), XIII–i, pp. 417–619.

[20] This is the time when Martin Luther, imbued with the spirit of Ockham, would escape from his powerful scruples by devising a radically new understanding of the relation of law and grace. Cardinal Cajetan would be sent by Pope Leo X to reason with him.

[21] "...distinguere oportet de modo, an huiusmodo haesitatio seu vacillatio sit modo speculativo, vel modo practico: hoc est, an dubitat de licito vel illicito secundum se, vel ut est ratio operis sui hic & nunc. Nam si quis dubitaret, an pulsare in die sesto sit licitum vel illicitum, & tamen non dubitaret sibi tunc esse licitum pulsare, iste non peccaret pulsando (...). Et per oppositum si quis esset certissimus de actu pulsandi secundum se, quod est licitus in die sesto, & tamen fluctuaret de exercenda nunc a se pulsatione, ita quod ratio applicandi se ad pulsandum cum ambiguitate applicat, illicite quis pulsaret: intellectus siquidem speculativus nihil dicit de operando." T. de Vio Cajetan, *Summula de peccatis* (Leiden: G. a Portonarijs, 1565), t.1, tr. xxxl, rsp. xiii, dub. 7.

[22] The dangers to which the separation of the practical and speculative realms can lead is manifested in David Hume, of whom Philippa Foot writes: "For, as [Hume] says, no such factual proposition could ever have a necessary connexion with the will

of the man who accepted it, while it is an essential fact about a moral judgement that it does have this practical force... thus conclusions of reason have a merely contingent connexion with action, whereas the propositions of morality are necessarily practical..." P. Foot, "Hume on Moral Judgement," in *Virtues and Vices and Other Essays in Moral Philosophy*, pp. 74–80 (Oxford: Clarendon Press, 2002), p. 78.

[23] Even this point concerning the origins of probabilism is controversial. Vasquez can be cited affirming that the opinion of Medina was already common, while Antonius de Cordova can be cited to the contrary. Cf. T. Gonzalez de Santalla, *Fundamentum theologiae moralis: id est, Tractatus theologicus de recto usu opinionum probabilium* (Rome: J. J. Komarek, 1694), col. 1430.

[24] "mihi videtur quod si est opinio probabilis licitum est eam sequi, licet opposita probabilior est." B. Medina, *Expositio in primam secundae...d. Thomae Aquinatis* (Venice: apud Bernardum Basam, 1590), q. XIX, art. 6.

[25] "Homo sibi rationabiliter persuadet hic et nunc licite posse non operari iuxta tale iudicium speculativum." F. Suarez, *De bon. et mal. hum. act.*, disp. XII, sect. iv, t. iv, p. 447, cited by T. Deman, "Probabilisme," p. 473.

[26] "...ad recte operandum requiritur judicium practicum moraliter certum ... omnes doctores consentiunt." P. Laymann, *Theologia moralis quinque libros complectens* (Lyon: Aubin, 1681), lib. I, tract. I, cap. V, sec. I, nr. 4.

[27] "Quaeres, Qua ratione in operando certus esse possit, qui incertam & dubiam sententiam sequitur; cum ex incerto non possit colligi certum? Respondeo patet ex supra dictis; Certitudinem conscientiae, quam operans habere debet, non esse speculativam ex principiis intrinsecis rei petitam, sed esse practicam, ex practicis & rei extrinsecis principiis desumptam; verbi gratia sententia Doctorum probabiliter docentium aliquid esse licitum agere...." *Ibid.*, lib. I, tract. I, cap. V, sec. II, nr. 8.

[28] "Il est impossible de dire avec plus de force que la vérité objective n'est plus la mesure de l'action." Deman, "Probabilisme," pp. 484–485.

[29] "qui aliquid operatur motus ex opinione probabili, bene operatur, & sine peccato (...) dum probabilitate sive intrinseca, sive extrinseca quantumvis tenui... modo a probabilitatis finibus non exeatur..." T. Tamburini, *Explicatio decalogi duabus distincta partibus* (Lyons: Ioan. Ant. Huguatan, 1659), Pars I, bk. I, cap. III, sec. 3, nr. 3.

[30] "Quid requiritur ut sententia sit probabilis a ratione? Ut non sit evidenter falsa." This quotation is attributed to him by E. Amman, "Laxisme," col. 54. A similar comment taken directly from Caramuel: "...afferit paritatem fore probabiliter veram, quamdiu non demonstretur & evidenter probetur esse falsam." J. Caramuel Lobkowitz, *Theologia moralis fundamentalis* (Lyons: Laurentii Anisson, 1657), Lib. II, cap. vi, fund. 58, nr. 1716.

[31] For this history see the series of articles by P. F. Mandonnet in *Revue Thomiste* (Sept. 1901 - Jan. 1903) especially "Le Décret d'Innocent XI contre le Probabilisme," *Revue Thomiste* 9 (1901), pp. 460–481, at p. 472. Despite the following indication that Gonzalez commented on some of the condemned propositions, no direct commentary on Proposition 51 can be found in his extant works or letters. "Le nonce apostolique de Madrid, le futur cardinal Mellini, eut connaissance qu'un jésuite, Gonzalez, professeur à Salamanque, avait déjà, depuis plusiers années, combattu le probabilisme et quelques-unes des propositions que le pape venait de censurer" (p. 472).

[32] "Noster itaque scopus, in quem collimare, et stella polaris, quam inspicere debemus, est veritas. Nec in quaestionibus decidendis attendi debet, quae opinio sit rigida, et quae benigna; sed quae vera." Gonzalez, *Fundamenta*, col. 1426.

[33] *Ibid.*, col. 1402.

[34] *Ibid.*, col. 1429–1430.

[35] "regula respectiva ... recta regula pro his qui illam prudenter approbant ut veram ..." *Ibid.*, col. 1476.

[36] "Illud autem quod agitur contra legem (scilicet quam quis potest et debet scire—Gonz.), semper est malum, nec excusatur per hoc quod est secundum conscientiam; et similiter quod est contra conscientiam est malum, quamvis non sit contra legem. Quod autem neque contra conscientiam, neque contra legem est, non potest esse peccatum." T. Aquinas, *Quod. lib.*, 8., art. 13, cited by Gonzalez, *Fundamenta*, col. 1450.

[37] "nam ut actus voluntatis sit malus, non opus est ut reflexe cognoscatur eius malitia, sed satis est quod operans cognoscat objectum esse malum et lege divina prohibitum, et nihilominus illud voluntarie et libere eligat." Gonzalez, *Fundamenta*, col. 1455.

[38] "Confirmatur quia... ex dubio quasi speculativo seu universali necessario resultat dubium practicum circa actionem particularem hic et nunc exercendam, cum quo dubio certum est neminem posse licite operari." *Ibid.*, col. 1460.

[39] Cf. *Ibid.*, col. 1461.

[40] At one point, acknowledging the dominance of probabilists, Gonzalez makes his own the lament of St Jerome concerning Arianism: "ingemiscens orbis terrarum se Arianum esse miratus est." *Ibid.*, col. 1447.

[41] This condemned proposition refers to the formulation of Tamburini cited earlier. "Generatim, dum probabilitate sive intrinseca sive extrinseca quantumvis tenui, modo a probabilitatis finibus non exeatur, confisi aliquid agimus, semper prudenter agimus." DS 2103.

[42] Pinckaers convincingly argues that the bane of moral theology from the decline of Scholasticism to contemporary times has been a skewed understanding of liberty as opposed to law, a "freedom of indifference" in place of a "freedom for excellence." Cf. Pinckaers, *Sources*, pp. 242–243 and Part III.

[43] "Tam clarum videtur, fornicationem secundum se nullam involvere malitiam, et solum esse malam, quia interdicta, ut contrarium omnino rationi dissonum videatur." DS 2148. "Mollities iure naturae prohibita non est. Unde, si Deus eam non interdixisset, saepe esset bona et aliquando obligatoria sub mortali." DS 2149.

[44] Innocent XI, Prop. 50: "Copula cum coniugata, consentiente marito, non est adulterium; adeoque sufficit in confessione dicere, se esse fornicatum." DS 2150.

[45] Innocent XI, Prop. 17: "Satis est actum fidei semel in vita elicere." DS 2117. Cf. also Innocent XI, Prop. 65 DS 2165, and Alexander VII, Prop. 1, DS 2021.

[46] Cf. Prop. 6, 5, 7, respectively, of Innocent XI, DS 2105–2107.

[47] Cf. Deman, "Probabilisme," col. 494.

[48] Cf. Prop. 20, 32, 36, 45 of Alexander VII, DS 2420, 2052, 2056, 2065.

[49] Prop. 35, DS 2135.

[50] Innocent XI, Prop. 54: "Qui non potest recitare Matutinum et Laudes, potest autem reliquas Horas, ad nihil tenetur; quia maior pars trahit ad se minorem." DS 2154.

[51] Cf. Deman, "Probabilisme," col. 474.

[52] Cf. Prop. 12 of Innocent XI, DS 2112.

[53] Cf. Prop. 38 and 39 of Alexander VII, DS 2058, 2059, respectively.

[54] Innocent XI, Prop. 36: "Permissum est furari, non solum in extrema necessitate, sed etiam in gravi." DS 2136.

[55] Cf. Prop. 37 of Innocent XI, DS 2137.

[56] Innocent XI, Prop. 31: "Regulariter occidit possum furem pro conservatione unius aurei." DS 2131.

[57] Cf. Prop. 34 of Innocent XI, DS 2134.

[58] Cf. Alexander VII's propositions 2, 17–19, DS 2022, 2037–2039, respectively, and Innocent XI's Prop. 30, DS 2130.

[59] Alexander VII, Prop. 41: "Non est obligandus concubinarius ad eiciendam concubinam, si haec nimis utilis esset ad oblectamentum concubinarii, vulgo 'regalo', dum, deficiente illa nimis aegre ageret vitam, et aliae epulae taedio magno concubinarium afficerent, et alia famula nimis difficile inveniretur." DS 2061.

[60] Innocent XI, Prop. 29: "Urgens metus gravis est causa iusta sacramentorum administrationem simulandi." DS 2129.

[61] "Les sacraments sont choses trop saintes pour qu'il soit ainsi permis, pour quelque raison que ce soit, de les tourner en dérision." Amman, "Laxisme," col. 78.

[62] Cf. Prop. 64 of Innocent XI, DS 2164.

[63] Cf. Prop. 21–23 of Innocent XI, DS 2121–2123, respectively.

[64] Innocent XI, Prop. 19: "Voluntas non potest efficere, ut assensus fidei in se ipso sit magis firmus, quam mereatur pondus rationum ad assensum impellentium." DS 2119.

[65] Cf. Prop. 14 of Alexander VII, DS 2034.

[66] Cf. Prop. 55 of Innocent XI, DS 2155.

[67] Cf. Prop. 5 of Alexander VII, DS 2025.

[68] Innocent XI, Prop. 10: "Non tenemur proximum diligere actu interno et formali." DS 2110. Innocent XI, Prop. 11: "Praecepto proximum diligendi satisfacere possumus per solos actus externos." DS 2111.

[69] Alexander VII, Prop. 10: "Non est contra iustitiam, pro pluribus sacrificiis stipendium accipere, et sacrificium unum offerre. Neque etiam est contra fidelitatem etiamsi promittam promissione, etiam iuramento firmata, danti stipendium, quod pro nullo alio offeram." DS 2030.

[70] Innocent XI, Prop. 15: "Licitum est filio gaudere de parricidio parentis a se in ebrietate perpetrato, propter ingentes divitias inde ex hereditate consecutas." DS 2115.

[71] Innocent XI, Prop. 14: "Licitum est, absoluto desiderio cupere mortem patris, non quidem ut malum patris, sed ut bonum cupientis; quia nimirum ei obventura est pinguis hereditas." DS 2114.

[72] Innocent XI, Prop. 52: "Praeceptum servandi festa non obligat sub mortali, seposito scandalo, si absit contemptu." DS 2152.

[73] Cf. Prop. 25 of Innocent XI, DS 2125.

[74] Cf. Prop. 26–28 of Innocent XI, DS 2126–2128, respectively.

[75] Cf. Prop. 22 of Alexander VII, DS 2042, and Prop. 45 of Innocent XI, DS 2145.

[76] Cf. Prop. 42 of Innocent XI, DS 2142.

[77] Innocent XI, Prop. 60: "Paenitenti habenti consuetudinem peccandi contra legem Dei, naturae aut Ecclesiae, etsi emendationis spes nulla appareat, nec est neganda nec differenda absolutio, dummodo ore proferat, se dolere et proponere emendationem." DS 2160.

[78] Cf. Prop. 29 of Alexander VI, DS 2049.

[79] Cf. Prop. 38 of Innocent XI, DS 2138.

[80] Cf. Prop. 42 of Alexander VII, DS 2062, and Prop. 40 and 41 of Innocent XI, DS 2140 and 2141, respectively.

[81] Cf. Prop. 40 of Alexander VII, DS 2060, and Prop. 8 and 9 of Innocent XI, DS 2108 and 2109, respectively.

[82] Alexander VIII, Prop. 1: "Bonitas obiectiva consistit in convenientia obiecti cum natura rationali: formalis vero in conformitate actus cum regula morum. Ad hoc sufficit, ut actus moralis tendat in finem ultimum interpretative. Hunc homo non tenetur amare neque in principio neque in decursu vitae suae moralis." DS 2290. Note that Pope John Paul II cites St Alphonsus Liguori in support of the contrary idea: "[an] act then attains its ultimate and decisive perfection when the will *actually does order* it to God through charity" (*Veritatis splendor,* 78).

[83] Alexander VIII, Prop. 2: "Peccatum philosophicum seu morale est actus humanus disconveniens naturae rationali et rectae rationi; theologicum vero et mortale est transgressio libera divinae legis. Philosophicum, quantumvis grave, in illo, qui Deum vel ignorat vel de Deo actu non cogitat, est grave peccatum, sed non est offensa Dei, neque peccatum mortale dissolvens amicitiam Dei, neque aeterna poena dignum." DS 2291. The error has resurfaced in our day in the form of misguided suggestions of a third class of sin between venial and mortal (cf. Pope John Paul II, *Reconciliatio et Paenitentia,* 17).

[84] In defense of those targeted by this condemnation, one Jesuit author writes: "We will make precise the meaning of philosophical sin by distinguishing the *error* and the *hypothesis.* The *error* would

consist in teaching that it is common and ordinary for men to violate the moral law without offending God. In the *hypothesis*, one holds this type of sin to be metaphysically possible but unrealizable in fact—except perhaps in some abnormal cases. This fundamental distinction is indispensable if one wishes to understand the debate and explain the position which many authors of the Society of Jesus have long held in this matter." (translation mine) H. Beylard, "Le Péché philosophique," *Nouvelle revue théologique* 62 (1935), pp. 591–616, at p. 593.

[85]   B. Pascal, *Pensées et les Provinciales* (Paris: Booking International, 1995), VII, p. 425.

[86]   R. Roy cites Gilles Estrix, an author of the time, as claiming that the propositions were "fabricated of whole cloth by the theologians [of Louvain] who, seizing at random on a phrase in a work, took it from its context, amplified it and so deformed it." Roy, "La coopération," p. 413.

CHAPTER 2

THE HISTORY OF COOPERATION BEFORE PROPOSITION 51

HAVING EXAMINED THE general tendencies that began to produce laxist opinions—the slighting of both the intrinsic truth of human action and the subject's responsibility to choose in accordance with it—we now turn to issues directly related to Proposition 51. Whence did the condemned proposition come? What was the state of the question on this sort of problem before the papal intervention? Surprisingly, problems of cooperation were not widely discussed before the 17th century. Indeed, all sides surely will agree that the condemnation of Proposition 51 led to giving greater attention to this type of moral problem. Most of the opinions that we will review are from authors cited by Roger Roy, whose study is thorough but not, as we shall see, entirely convincing.

Saint Antoninus Florentiae (1389–1459)

We begin with an author who substantially predated the development of probabilism: Saint Antoninus of Florence. His main work is an enormous four volume commentary on St Thomas's moral theology which only reached print posthumously in 1477. Writing approximately one century before Cajetan, Antoninus comes well before the advent of the intricate and imaginative case studies that characterize casuistry. Thus, he makes no assertions that can be considered direct antecedents of Proposition 51.

Still, he does touch upon the theme of cooperation in other terms, when he treats, as did St Thomas, the question of restitution. Commenting upon a line in Psalm 49, "si videbas furem, currebas cum eo" (if you saw a thief, you ran with him), he speaks of participation in theft. After noting that what he says about theft holds all the more for adultery, he comments: "He runs therefore with the thief, who participates with him in a theft, which, as Cardinal Hugo notes concerning the above-mentioned verse of the psalm, happens in nine ways contained in these verses: command, counsel, consent, flattery, sheltering, participating, keeping silence, not impeding, not manifesting."[1] This categorization of modes of cooperation had been a touchstone from Hugo's day (early 13th century) and would remain so into the 20th century.

Regarding cooperation by a servant, the saint acknowledges that a servant is generally obliged to obey his master, but he immediately observes: "In illicit matters he should in no way obey, not even if forced by threats or beating, as Jerome notes (11. question 3) saying: If a master orders those things, which are not contrary to the sacred scriptures, let the servant obey his lord. If, however, he should order something contrary, he would better obey the Lord of the spirit than of the body."[2] In this period before casuist ingenuity gained momentum, cooperation is presumed to be always wrong. The reason lies, evidently, in the *prima facie* difficulty of conceiving of an agent voluntarily facilitating sin without consenting thereto. In this connection we provide one more text of Antoninus, which speaks of those who mediate the sin of luxury.

> Mediators in these evils, who lead the practitioners of such deeds, be they men, be they women, or who persuade them, or who carry letters knowing that they are for the contracting of evil friendships, though they may contain honest things, too; without doubt, all such sin mortally. Worthy,

> indeed of death (eternal, that is—Anton.) are not only those who do such things, but also those who approve those doing them, Rom. 1. One mode of consent is by cooperation, as here, and much more by sending the letters themselves, knowingly receiving them, and reading them.[3]

Worthy of note is the fact that St Antoninus considers the action of carrying amorous letters to imply consent to the author's immoral intentions. Many subsequent authors will try to distinguish the carrying from writing, allowing the one for grave reason but not the other.

Thomas Sanchez (1550–1610)

Thomas Sanchez is a key figure in the development of reflection upon our theme. He was a Jesuit author of holy reputation who exercised particular influence on the moralists who followed him. His *De praeceptis decalogi* appeared just after his death in 1610. While his books did not escape censure, it is possible that he was to some degree ahead of his time and to some degree not careful enough in his exposition.[4]

In Sanchez, the question of cooperation is not yet treated in the terms of formal and material, but the way is prepared under the notions of direct and indirect.[5] Thus he affirms that "no one is considered the direct moral cause of that which he neither orders, nor counsels, nor intends, nor in fact effects."[6] A person would cooperate indirectly, by contrast, if he merely provides the material for the action of the principal agent "by which [action] the matter itself offered to him is abused."[7] Sanchez notes that all agree that it would be bad to cooperate with the same evil intention as the principal agent or "even without such an intention" to provide services "which by their very nature are ordered to evil, and touch upon it, or are part of it."[8] Since one could hardly be faulted for providing indifferent services that one had no suspicion would be abused, "the entire difficulty" resides in evaluating the provision of a service or material that could be used well or badly but that the cooperator foresees in all likelihood to be abused.[9] Sanchez observes that this "difficulty" can be solved in three ways: by permitting the provision of any sort of aid that is foreseen to be abused, by prohibiting the provision of all such aid, or by attempting to distinguish between aid which is of its nature neutral and that which "of itself is destined to evil use."[10] Roy notes that this sort of distinction was also made by Saint Thomas in a text which Sanchez appears to have in mind.[11] In his discussion of the morality of fabricating adornments for women, Thomas observes that some products cannot be used without sin (such as idols) while some can be well or badly used (such as swords and arrows).[12] In addition, he notes that some are frequently misused while not being illicit by nature (de se non sint illicitae). St Thomas says that the production of these items should be banned by the state. From this text it is not at all clear if the production of things likely to be abused would be considered intrinsically evil by Thomas; still less clear is the moral quality of such a production, in a given case in which a product was sure to be abused. Nonetheless, Sanchez's position capitalizes on this ambiguity, considering the act of production as indifferent.

Notwithstanding this conclusion, Sanchez admits that such an action is so proximately ordered to sin that it can be deemed intrinsically evil. In this way, he analyses the question of a servant's cooperation in terms that directly resemble those of the condemned proposition. He likens actions such as holding a ladder to producing an item not illicit in itself, but that is likely to be abused. That such aid is ordinarily to be condemned is vigorously expressed (*nemo excusaret*), as it should be considered intrinsically evil. Yet, a significant proviso is added that strikes the modern reader as an apparent contradiction.

> If an indifferent thing is so proximately ordered to sin, that it should rightly be considered evil *per se*, although in some case it might be licit, as was said in num. 7, the helper is not excused from blame, even though he should know for certain that the other is ready to sin and would find another who would supply him the matter. That no one would excuse someone who should move a ladder, or lift with his shoulders, when someone wants to steal, or kill a man, or fornicate (...) And the reason is that such acts are so proximately connected to sin, and are ordered to it so that they are worthy to be called evil *ex se*, unless they are excused for some urgent reason.[13]

In other words, having introduced a notion of *quasi* intrinsic evil, Sanchez claims only that it must *almost* never be done. In the passage alluded to (num. 7) Sanchez speaks of actions in war, such as setting fire to innocent people's houses, which are to be considered intrinsically evil due to the proximity of the evil effect, but which can be excused in cases of extreme necessity. It seems that Sanchez is struggling to make sense of intrinsic evil without the benefit of concepts to be developed later, such as the indirect voluntary and the doctrine of double effect. Roy also notes the ambiguity in Sanchez's terminology: either an act is intrinsically evil and never worthy of being the object of choice, or it is not.[14]

In sum, Sanchez claims both that the servant's act of cooperation is worthy of being treated as if it were intrinsically evil and that "extreme excusing necessity" prevents the agent's intention from being evil.[15]

Paul Laymann (1574–1626)

Another landmark on the landscape of the emerging analysis of cooperation with evil is Paul Laymann, s.j. His *Theologia moralis* stood out amongst the competition, needing to be reprinted repeatedly for almost a century after its appearance in 1625. In fact, Laymann's treatment is remarkably close to the doctrine on cooperation that St Alphonsus will make his own and pass on to the Manualist tradition.

We have just seen how the concepts that we know as the formal/material distinction are identifiable in Sanchez under other terms (as they were in Gregory of Valencia, see note 6 of this chapter). In Laymann, the modern terminology is used clearly for the first time. "For this reason, rightly is it said by some: it is illicit to cooperate in the sin of another formally, as it is sin; it is licit, however, to cooperate materially in a work which is a sin."[16]

Laymann confidently likens material cooperation to the sort of cooperation that God provides,[17] an argument that will return even in contemporary discussions of the principle of double effect. In addition, the three conditions that Laymann provides in order for material cooperation to be permitted can be matched quite neatly with three of the four conditions of the double-effect principle.[18] Significantly, as we will have occasion to note later, he provides no condition corresponding to the third condition of this principle.

> To concur or operate only materially with sin by providing an object or ministering the matter and faculty of sinning, is not always wrong nor prohibited; but rather it is licit, if three conditions are present: 1. That the cooperation be morally good or at least indifferent in itself. 2. That it be done with good intention or from a motive of some virtue; and in no way by the intention of moving

> the other to sin (...) 3. That you be unable to
> prevent the sin of your neighbor or at least that you
> be not bound to prevent it; but for some reason
> you can permit it...[19]

Some other points remain unclear in Laymann's treatment. Firstly, he has not yet distinguished cooperation from scandal; cooperation is examined in the section on "Charity" under the heading "Scandal". Nonetheless, the essential difference, namely, that in cooperation proper the principal agent is presumed to be already determined to sin, emerges when he notes, that in cases of formal cooperation "although you be not the cause of the internal evil proposal, which is the beginning of sin; you are, however, the cause of sin according to its execution or continuation."[20] Nonetheless, the issue of inducing the other to sin seems to remain the criterion of formal, never to be permitted cooperation. Such assistance is equated with assistance that cannot be put to any good moral use by one's neighbor. He gives the examples of asking a witch for a curse, a usurer to lend money at interest, an infidel to call upon his gods, a priest without jurisdiction for sacraments, a person to drink to drunkenness. Laymann is seeking to draw a thin line, however, as he permits requests which are *most likely* to be fulfilled by means of sin, to wit: "if necessity or utility urges one can ask an excommunicated priest for sacraments, ask a usurer for a loan; an infidel to swear."[21] (The idea is that the usurer need not charge interest, the infidel need not call on his false gods, etc., but it is foreseen that they will.) In the same vein, Laymann provides some examples that are more proper to the cooperation of servants. A servant can aid his master in designs that he knows to be evil if his part is "satis remota". He could, for instance, open a window for a mistress, but not lead her to the house. Actions which appear to be of a nature to induce to sin are forbidden.

With this notion of proximity, another lack of precision arises in the terminology employed in the attempt to distinguish acceptable and non-acceptable assistance. The proximate/remote binomial is not distinguished from that of *per se / accidentaliter*. "Finally, a graver reason, other things being equal, is required, as the material cooperation in sin is more *per se*, or nearer: a lesser cause is required, if the cooperation is only *per accidens* or remote."[22] Yet, the very idea of "magis per se" seems inconsistent.

It should also be noted that Laymann explicitly permits the providing of material help even when omitting such help would impede the performance of the sin. He notes that in this case a "more grave and urgent cause or necessity is required."[23] Still, surely cooperation in these circumstances is a sort of "cause according to the execution or continuation", which had been considered formal cooperation.

Laymann, finally, is loathe to speak of the cooperator's act as intrinsically evil. He does not use this term and indicates that the cooperator's act will only be formal if it constitutes an invitation to sin: e.g. the offer to borrow money at interest, the inviting a woman to visit a lascivious master. In this connection, he also speaks of certain materials, such as poison, which cannot be sold since they cannot be put to good use. Fernando Castro Palao, however, will emphasize that virtually any matter can be put to good use. (Indeed, poison could be used to poison something other than a man). This leads quickly to the position that an act of cooperation is only intrinsically evil when the intention with which it is proffered is bad. A case in point is the writing or carrying of evil letters to a concubine, an activity which Sanchez, Laymann, and most

others will consider off limits, but that is permitted by
Castro Palao:

> Because to write or deliver these [vile] things does
> not seem to be intrinsically evil if there is absent
> from you an evil end; vile words indeed can be
> written, as doctors [of Moral theology] write them
> for the sake of pondering the evil of those who offer
> them for an evil purpose, and can be written or said
> not on one's own part but for another. Or again,
> not seriously but in jest. Therefore, to write these
> vile things is not intrinsically evil in itself, because
> they are only vile and evil insofar as they proceed
> from a perverse mind and to a perverse end are
> directed. Therefore, apart from such a mind and
> such a perverse end, they do not appear to be evil
> and *a fortiori* nor will it be intrinsically evil to carry
> such writings to a concubine, for indeed he could
> take them to her not so that she be moved to sexual
> union, but so that she laugh at them and burn
> them. Therefore, the very act of delivering, insofar
> as it proceeds from you, can serve a good use. [24]

It should be born in mind that Castro Palao enjoyed a
superb reputation for both holiness and learning during
his life and after.[25] The fact that the concept of intrinsic
evil was still in formation, leading to some dubious conclusions, must not lead us to impugn many holy and
learned men as mere laxists or sophists.

Matteus de Moya (1610–1684)

In 1657, another Jesuit, Matteus de Moya, published a
book under the fictitious name, Amadeus Guimenius.
Such a precaution indicates the anticipated reception of
the author's theses; indeed, the book includes over a dozen
of the opinions that were condemned as laxist by Alexander VII and Innocent XI. It was put on the Index in 1666

and condemned again by Innocent XI in 1680.[26] Certainly, this does not indicate that every opinion held by Moya is suspect. Nonetheless, he clearly operated from principles which led to erroneous, laxist conclusions. Both popes just mentioned sought to steer theologians away from his approach. One would want to adopt his position on cooperation, and more specifically on what servants can or cannot do, with appropriate caution.

In fact, he treats of cooperation in the very last case of his condemned book. Here he entertains the question of whether a cleric who sells arms to a man that is certainly going to use them for an unjust killing should be considered irregular. Significantly, he sides with Thomas Hurtado, an author whose book had been put under interdict seven years previously "donec corrigatur"[27] (until corrected).

> When one selling or offering hands over indifferent things (such as weapons) to one about to abuse them, even if it could be avoided without detriment to oneself, one does not sin mortally, if the other is determined to sin, and has sinned by an internal act... And Cajetan writes (2.2 quaest. 10. art. 4.) saying: By selling such common things with knowledge, & without intention of the future bad use, one does not directly give an occasion for sinning. And later [he continues]: the evil use which follows, is not so voluntary with respect to the seller, such that it should be imputed to him, and for this reason it is not a sin. I say that these doctors agree with Hurtado, because if the one giving the weapon is excused from guilt, he cannot not be free from punishment and thus from irregularity.[28]

The ease by which the vendor is exculpated, even if it would not cause him any detriment to refuse, is all the more surprising since the example was not new. St Thomas raises the question in regard to the notion of *epikeia.* Thomas notes not only that one is not obliged to return a sword to a person likely to use it improperly, but that it would be wrong to do so.[29]

Thomas Tamburini (1591–1675)

Writing contemporaneously with Moya was a Jesuit with a great reputation for virtue and learning, Thomas Tamburini. He would contribute significantly to the post-Tridentine systematization of moral theology and the emergence of the Manualist tradition by *Institutiones morales.* Despite the fact that he frequently reasoned well to a correct conclusion, in the estimation of St Alphonsus,[30] several of the weaknesses inherent to the moral reasoning of the time find in him their logical development and clearest expression. We have mentioned his defense of *any* probable opinion "quamvis tenui" (however small). In addition, the difficulty of conceptualizing what essentially constitutes intrinsic evil persists, leading to artificial distinctions that appear as so much quibbling, or to essentially holding only those actions to be wrong which are done for an evil end—again, what Pascal dubbed "sinning for the sake of sinning".[31] Note especially, in the passage to be cited, the unconvincing claim that a servant can invite an enemy of his master to come at dawn to an out of the way spot, as long as he does not openly say that his master wants to duel with him.

This position leads to another characteristic of laxism, namely the reluctance ever to call something wrong absolutely. Thus, painting something very lewd, which will surely lead many to sin, cannot be called intrinsically evil in Tamburini's estimation, but a painter might be allowed once or twice to do so in dire necessity.[32] Representing such things by acting, which is held to be closer yet to performing an intrinsic evil, is still not ruled out altogether. Nonetheless, what is called today "immediate" cooperation is categorically rejected by Tamburini.

Such are the principles and reasoning that produced the formulation of the Servant and Ladder case that appears nearest to that condemned in Proposition 51:

> Moreover, a servant, not only by reason of his role as servant, but from fear of notable harm (such as might be, if he feared that, reporting this to his Master, he would be forced to seek another to his annoyance and detriment; or that he would be maltreated by his Master, looked at harshly, or expelled from the house to his harm) the servant, I say, will be excused if he should inform an adulteress or an enemy to come at such and such an hour to the house of the Master or an agreed upon place (but he must not say that the other should come to sin, or to fight in a duel; these indeed are intrinsically evil); if by order of the master he should follow a girl, to see or discover where she lives, and nothing more; if by order of the same he should not only open the door, but inform her where his master is; if he should help his Master to climb through a window, by which he would enter a place where he will sin. These things indeed, and similar ones, are somewhat closer to the sin of the abuser, and require a somewhat graver reason than the duty of a servant; and what has been said is considered more than sufficient enough.[33]

Several of the phrases used are identical with those in Proposition 51. The most significant difference is the implication of adultery in place of rape. The point here is not only that the latter is graver, but the it further removes the case from the ambit of scandal. The proposition's formulation highlights the harm that the servant's cooperation causes apart from facilitating the sin of those who are already disposed (*iam iam paratus*) to sin.

Casting a glance back over the early references to the problem of cooperation, one perceives a growing doggedness in distinguishing and analyzing this issue. Certainly political and economic changes increased the demand for accurate judgments on what behavior a Christian could undertake in an increasingly complex world. Most of the pertinent issues have been raised: the concept of intrinsic evil, the question of proximity, the relevance of duress. Notably absent is specific talk of the intention of the cooperator and what exactly determines it. This is to be expected in the climate described earlier as legalist and extrinsicist. The general result contains substantial ambiguity and contradiction. The Holy See seized upon a particular example of these imperfect efforts, the future Proposition 51, to help redirect the work of theologians. Now we turn to the reaction to this intervention, examining those thinkers who spoke directly to the issue of the Servant and the Ladder in the aftermath of the condemnations.

Notes

1. "Currit ergo cum fure, qui participat cum eo in furto, quod ut notat Hugo cardinalis super versu supradicti psalmi, fit novem modis contentis in his versibus: iussio, consilium, consensus, palpo, recursus, participans, mutus, non obstans, non manifestans." Antoninus Florentinus, *Summa theologica: ad vetustiores libros exacta et correcta...* (Verona: apud Carattonium, 1740), tom. II, pars II, tit. i, cap. xiv, col 228–229.

2. "Sed in rebus illicitis nullo modo obedire debet, nec etiam minis vel verberibus coactus, quod notat Hieronymus 11. quaest. 3. dicens: Si dominus ea jubet, quae non sunt adversa sanctis scripturis, subjiciatur domino servus. Si vero contrari praecipit, magis obediat spiritus quam corporis domino." *Ibid.*, pars III, tit. iii, cap. vi, col. 200. Pope John Paul II reminds us that Christian doctrine has not changed on this issue: if an order is determined conclusively to be incompatible

with the law of God, opposition must not stop before martyrdom: "It is an honor characteristic of Christians to obey God rather than men (cf. Ac 4:19; 5:29) and accept even martyrdom as a consequence, like the holy men and women of the Old and New Testaments, who are considered such because they gave their lives rather than perform this or that particular act contrary to faith or virtue." (*Veritatis Splendor*, 78).

3   "Mediatores autem in hujusmodi turpibus, qui portant ambassiatas de talibus materiis, sive viri, sive mulieres, vel qui persuadent, vel qui deferunt litteras scienter in istis etiam honesta continentes, sed ad contrahendam malam amicitiam; nulli dubium, quin peccent mortaliter. *Digni* enim *sunt morte*, æterna videlicet, *non solum qui faciunt hujusmodi, sed etiam qui consentiunt facientibus*, Roman. i. Unus autem modus consensus est per cooperationem, ut hic, & multo magis mittentes ipsas litteras, & scienter recipientes, & legentes." Antoninus, *Summa Theologica*, pars III, tit. v., cap.i, col. 646.

4   This might account, for instance, for his teaching on mental reservations becoming the subject of Innocent XI's Prop. 26. Cf. T. Sanchez, *Operis moralis in praecepta Decalogi tomus* (Lyons: Laurentii Anisson, 1661), III, vi, n. 15.

5   L. Ugorji, *The Principle of Double Effect. A Critical Appraisal of its Traditional Understanding and its Modern Reinterpretation* (Frankfurt: Peter Lang, 1985), p. 65, n. 15.

6   "Quod nemo causa moralis directa censeatur eius, quod nec praecipit, nec consulit, nec intendit, nec re ipsa efficit." Sanchez, *De Prec. Decalogi*, I, i, cap. 7, n. 8. This phrase appears verbatim in the work of Gregory of Valencia, whose volume concerning moral issues was first published 1595. Cf. Gregory of Valencia, *Commentariorum Theologicorum tomi 4* (Ingolstadt: Sartorius, 1603), t. III, disp. 1, q. X, pt. iv, col 1517c.

7   "... in actione, qua ipse materia sibi exhibita abutitur." Sanchez, *De Prec. Decalogi*, I, i, cap. 7, n. 8.

8   "... etiam absque praedicta intentione ... quae suapte natura ad flagitium ordinantur, illudque attingunt, vel pars illius sunt." *Ibid.*, I, i, cap. 7, n. 2.

9   "...tota autem difficultas est." *Ibid.*, Lib. I, i, cap. 7, n. 3.

10 "...res ex se ad pravum usum destinata." *Ibid.*, Lib. I, i, cap. 7, n. 3. What might distinguish these services from those mentioned in footnote 8, which are ordered to evil by their nature, is not made clear.

11 *ST* II-II, q. 169, a. 2, ad 4, mentioned by Roy, "La coopération," p. 396, n. 36.

12 Gregory of Valencia comments that anything could be put to good use, even an idol "ad comburendum nimirum, vel ad memoriam, etc." (*Comm. Theol.*, t. III, disp. 1, q. X, pt. v, col. 498b). What St Thomas says about effects which usually follow an act would seem to argue against the value of Gregory's point. "Si autem eventus sequens non sit praecogitatus, tunc distinguendum est. Quia si per se sequitur ex tali actu, et ut in pluribus, secundum hoc eventus sequens addit ad bonitatem vel malitiam actus, manifestum est enim meliorem actum esse ex suo genere, ex quo possunt plura bona sequi; et peiorem, ex quo nata sunt plura mala sequi. Si vero per accidens, et ut in paucioribus, tunc eventus sequens non addit ad bonitatem vel ad malitiam actus, non enim datur iudicium de re aliqua secundum illud quod est per accidens, sed solum secundum illud quod est per se." *ST* I-II, q. 20, a. 5, cor.

13 "Si res indifferens sit ita proxime ad peccatum ordinata, ut per se mala sit merito censenda, quamvis in aliquo casu possit esse licita, juxta dicta num. 7, suppeditans non excusatur a culpa, quamvis certo sciat alium paratum ad peccatum et inventurum alium, qui materiam suppeditet. Ut nemo excusaret admoventem scalam, vel humeris sustentantem, quando quis vult furari, aut hominem interficere, aut fornicari (...) Et ratio est, quia tales actiones ita proxime peccato accedunt, ad illudque ordinantur ut ex se malae dici merito quaeant, nisi causa aliqua urgenti excusentur." Sanchez, *De Prae. decal.*, Lib. I, i, cap. vii, n. 16.

14 Roy, *Notion*, p. 94. Also, compare this point with what Viva will say in the next chapter, p. 59.

15 "...per se mala nuncupamus, quamvis in casu raro licita sint, gravissima excusante necessitate, et ita ut intentio ad illa non fertur." Sanchez, *De Prae. decal.*, Lib. I, i, cap. vii, n.7.

16 "Quare recte a quibusdam dicitur; nefas esse cooperari alterius peccato formaliter, ut peccatum est; fas tamen esse interdum materialiter cooperari operi quod peccatum est." Laymann, *Theologia moralis*, Lib. II, tract. III, cap. xiii, nr. 4.

17 "...in genere causae efficientis, non praeveniendo sed concomitando." *Ibid.*, nr. 4. However, in the following number, he asserts that our cooperation cannot extend as far as that of God, who is "the absolute and universal Lord of things."

18 To see the similarity with double effect reasoning, assume the more standard enumeration of the conditions by which (1) the act

itself must be good; (2) the bad effect cannot be intended for itself; (3) nor as a means, leading to the good effect [to this Laymann provides no counterpart]; and (4) there must be a proportionate reason [which can be seen reflected in Laymann's third condition requiring a sufficient "reason" to permit the evil effect].

[19]   "Ad peccatum concurrere seu cooperari materialiter tantum exhibendo objectum, vel ministrando materiam ac facultatem peccandi, non semper malum, ac prohibitum; sed interdum licitum est, si tres conditiones adsint: I. Ut cooperatio secundum se moraliter bona vel saltem indifferens sit. II. Ut bona intentione, sive ex motivo aliqujus virtutis fiat; & nequaquam intentione movendi alterum ad peccatum. (...) III. Ut proximi peccatum impedire nequeas, vel saltem impedire non debeas; sed ob aliquam causam permittere possis...." Laymann, *Theologia moralis*, Lib II, trac III, cap xiii, nr. 4.

[20]   "quia licet non sis interni mali propositi, quod est peccati principium; causa tamen es peccati secundum executionem vel continuationem...." *Ibid.*, nr. 3.

[21]   Cf. *Ibid.*, Lib. II, tract. III, cap. xiii, nr. 8.

[22]   "Denique tanto gravior causa, caeteris paribus, requiritur, quanto cooperatio materialis ad peccatum magis per se, sive propinquior est: minor autem causa requiritur, si cooperatio sit tantum per accidens, sive remota." *Ibid.*, nr. 5.

[23]   "...gravior et urgentior causa sive necessitas requiritur." *Ibid.*, nr. 4.

[24]   "Quia haec [turpia] scribere vel deferre non videntur intrinsece mala si absit a te malus finis; turpia enim verba scribi possunt, sicuti scribunt doctores, ad ponderandam malitiam illorum qui ea ex malo fine proferunt, possuntque scribi et dici non tanquam ex proprio parte sed ex alieno. Item non serio, sed irrisorie. Ergo scribere haec verba turpia de se non est intrinsece malum, quia solum sunt turpia et mala quatenus a pravo animo procedunt et in pravam finem diriguntur. Ergo, secluso hoc animo et hoc pravo fine mala non esse videntur et a fortiori neque erit intrinsece malum scripta illa deferre ad concubinam, poterat enim illa deferre non ut moveatur ad coitum, sed ut illam irrideat et comburat. Ergo illa actio deferendi, quatenus a te procedit bono usui deservire potest." F. Castro Palao, *Operis moralis: de virtutibus et vitiis contrariis* (Venice: Pezzana, 1690), Punct. XI, n. 7.

[25]   "St Alphonsus numbers [Castro Palao] among the principal authorities on moral theology" *New Advent Catholic Encyclopedia*,

"Fernando   Castro   Palao"   [accessed: 25.01.2008],
www.newadvent.org/cathen/ 03415b.htm.

[26]   Cf. DS 2022*.

[27]   Cf. DS 2026* concerning Hurtado's *Tractatus varii resolutionum moralium.*

[28]   "*Qui Petro arma petenti concedit, certo cognoscens, aut timens ad iniustam Ioannis occisionem illa petere, non manet irregularis, nisi ex intentione occisionis praestet. Gaspar Hurtado Iesuita disp. 2. de irregul. diff. 9. nu. 32.* Author citatus expresse fatetur esse peccatum laethale contra iustitiam indirecte; quo ad irregularitatem vero nil determinat, sed proposita ratione dubitatndi, inquit difficilem sibi videri contrariam sententiam... Dum tradit vendentem seu ministrantem indifferentia, (qualia sunt arma) illis abusuro, etiam si absque sui detrimento vitare possit, non peccare laethaliter, si alius sit ad peccandum paratus, & actu interno peccaverit....Et tradit Caietanus 2.2. quaest. 10. art.4. dicens. [Vendendo ista communia cum scientia, & sine intentione usus mali futurui, non dat directe occasionem peccandi.] Et infra, [Malus usus qui sequetur, non est respectu sic vendentis volunta-rius, ita ut sibi imputetur, ac per hoc non est peccatum.] Dico hos doctores sentire cum Hurtado, quia si praestans arma a culpa excusatur, non poterit non, & a poena liber esse, & consequenter ab irregularitate...." M. Moya, *Adversus quorundam expostulatio-nes contra nonnullas Iesuitarum opiniones morales* (Bamburg: Nicolaum Bua, 1657), pp. 196–197.

[29]   "Sicut lex instituit quod deposita reddantur, quia hoc ut in pluribus iustum est, contingit tamen aliquando esse nocivum, puta si furiosus deposuit gladium et eum reposcat dum est in furia, vel si aliquis reposcat depositum ad patriae impugnationem. In his ergo et similibus casibus malum esset sequi legem positam, bonum autem est, praetermissis verbis legis, sequi id quod poscit iustitiae ratio et communis utilitas." *ST* II-II q. 120, a. 1.

[30]   Cf. *New Advent Catholic Encyclopedia*, "Thomas Tamburini" [accessed: 25.01.2008], www.newadvent.org/cathen/14441a. htm.

[31]   Pascal specifically criticized the tendency of theologians at the time to permit servants to fulfil almost any request of their master (*Pensées*, VI, p. 419). His criticism portended the intervention of Innocent XI.

[32]   "For the same [i.e. that it is not licit to paint regularly] I think is to be held of painting very lewd things, or even concerning actors representing the same, on account of which it is morally known that

many will sin. I have said [regularly] if indeed the necessity of the Painter or Actor be so great that he lacks money for food or something similar, I would not deny that one time only, or a second time it could be permitted..." (Nam idem [i.e. non licet regulariter pingere] puto sentiendum de pingentibus valde turpia, imo de Histrionibus eadem representantibus, ex quibus moraliter scitur multos peccaturos. Dixi [regulariter] si enim tanta esset Pictoris vel Histrionis necessitas ut eo lucro indigeret ad victum vel quid simile, non recusarem semel, aut iterum licere...) Tamburini, *Explicatio decalogi*, Pars II, lib. V, cap. 1, n. 28.

33 "Praeterea, subditus non ex sola famulatus ratione, sed metu notabilis detrimenti (quale esset, si quis timeret ne Dominum hunc deferens, cogatur alium cum sua molstia, & damno quaerere; ne a Domino male tractetur, ne torvis oculis aspiciatur, ne ex domo cum suo detrimento expellatur) subditus, inquam, excusabitur, si referat adulterae, vel inimico, ut tali hora ad Domum heri, vel ad condictum locu accedat. (Sed ne dicat, ut accedat ad peccandum, vel ad pugnandum in duello; haec enim sunt intrinsece mala) si iussu heri insequatur puellam, visurus vel requistiturus ubi ea habitet, & nihil aliud; si iussu eiusdem non aperiat modo ianuam, sed doceat ubi herus sit; si Dominum adiuvet ad ascendendum per fenestram, quo ingrediatur in locum ubi peccaturus fit. Haec enim, & similia cum sint aliquanto propinquiora peccato abutentis, indigent causa aliquanto graviore, quam sit ratio famulatus; & ea, quae dicta est, sufficiens satis superque censetur." *Ibid.*, n. 19.

CHAPTER 3

HISTORY OF COOPERATION AFTER THE CONDEMNATION OF PROPOSITION 51

1. The initial reaction

ESTABLISHING THE PRECISE chronological ordering of the many manuals of moral theology is not easily achieved. Some took years to publish, and some only reached a wider audience in translation with later editions. Some of the earliest commentaries upon the condemnations of Innocent XI surely have been lost. Thus, beginning our examination of the aftermath of the condemnations with François Genet is not without some element of arbitrariness, justified, however, by the balance it will provide, as the period closes with St Alphonsus, the most illustrious student of Genet's famous "morale de Grenoble".

François Genet (1640–1703)

François Genet published his popular text first in French between 1676 and 1684. It appeared in Latin in 1702.[1] He mentions Proposition 51 twice. On one occasion he draws such a wide conclusion on the issue that precision will certainly be needed.

> Because, if such masters should want their servants to be participants of their crimes, by exciting or impelling them to do evil, in such an occasion, the servants cannot obey their masters without grave sin: since we are held to obey the commandments

> of God rather than the orders of men, it is God
> rather than men we should obey; and they should
> not be induced by any temporal advantage, to
> cooperate with the sins of their masters.[2]

He explains his position more clearly in the chapter dedicated to the study of intention in the first tome. Here he asks "whether it is licit for a servant to serve his master in amorous matters, while intending only to earn as much money as he needs for his food?" The answer he gives is that such an act is "so illicit, that no circumstances can make it licit" which judgment is confirmed by the full quotation of the condemned proposition.[3] The motivations for this judgment, given in the previous questions, reveal once again the difficulty had by theologians in describing intrinsic evil. The previous question, dealing with women's clothes, spoke of vain outfits as "ex se malus" in the absence of circumstances which made them honest, such as the order of a husband.[4] He does not deny that it would be evil to wear truly scandalous clothing under any circumstances, but he confirms the opinion set forth still one question earlier that some actions would be wrong unless circumstances removed the evil. In this question, which explicitly treats the directing of intention, he affirms that some actions are evil "ex natura sua" and others are evil unless circumstances, remove the evil, thus making them good.[5] Thus, for Genet, the servant's actions in the condemned proposition are intrinsically evil *ex natura sua*.

One further point can be made from Genet's analysis. The circumstance which might have justified the servant's cooperation is, of course, fear of great injury. Genet asks "Whether grave fear excuses from sin, although it does not take away all freedom?"[6] In other words, although sin is not imputed to one completely deprived of freedom by fear, can one say that under the circumstance of grave threat, something ordinarily sinful could become choice-worthy should the person remain free enough to make a deliberate choice? His answer distinguishes between negative precepts of natural and divine law from which fear can never excuse and positive precepts (he speaks only of those instituted by the Church) which are not *per se* necessary for salvation and not intended to bind under grave inconvenience. While he clearly considers the action of the servant, along with a woman wearing scandalous attire, to be violations of a negative precept, other authors, both before and after Genet, saw forbearing to cooperate as a positive act of charity towards one's neighbor which, for that reason, did not bind under grave *incommoditas*. Thus, without explicitly stating it, Genet is the first author to intuit that more is at stake in cooperation than scandal. The main sin is not against the master, whom one confirms in sin, but against the girl, the victim of his design.

Patritius Sporer (c. 1610–1683)

Patritius Sporer was a Franciscan minor from Bavaria, whom St Alphonsus much appreciated and cited.[7] Sporer's explanation of Proposition 51 is nearly as opaque as the formulation itself. He notes that material aid can be given if it is not necessary for the crime, or can be easily obtained elsewhere, and that it must on occasion be given out of justice, for instance by servants, even if it is foreseen that the other will sin.[8] Thus a servant can take money to a usurer for his master or serve him meat on fast days. In contrast, however, referring to the condemned thesis, Sporer notes that *proximate* aid, even if it is indifferent by nature, cannot be justified "ex sola ratione famulatus".[9] Thus the door is left open that a more urgent reason than fear of notable harm could justify such actions by the servant. Yet, he immediately adds that to lead a concubine, or knowingly deliver evil letters, or those provoking to a duel, "can never be licit: since these things appear intrinsically evil, & and a sort of pandering." This extremely awkward result—that one could in dire necessity help one's master commit a rape and yet must accept death rather than deliver (or at least, rather than write) letters to his mistress—will remain as a call for reexamination of this issue through St Alphonsus and into the twentieth century.

Nonetheless, Sporer may have called the servant's holding of a ladder "indifferent" simply in function of clumsy terminology. He certainly wants to proscribe formal cooperation, which he equates with proximate and immediate cooperation. Indignantly, he asserts: "It is most certain and unworthy of questioning: you cannot cooperate with your neighbor proximately and formally in the very sin, or in the sinful action itself of your neighbor." This he contrasts with cooperating "remotely and materially".[10] Thus we can legitimately read him as anticipating the question: what is the correct moral description of the servant's act? Is it "indifferent" or truly part of the crime itself?

Next, Sporer repeats what Sanchez taught in regard to Christian captives assisting the Turks. "Forced by threat of death", they can harm the external goods of their countrymen provided they do not constitute a grave threat to the Christian cause. Still they cannot be excused from killing, mutilating, or setting fire to boats, even under threat of death, as these are "intrinsece mala".[11] This implies another thorny question: what goods or values are absolutely inviolable? On what grounds can one destroy one's own or another's physical goods? Non-essential body parts? Is the violation of the virgin in Proposition 51 more like destroying external goods or like killing and maiming? The explanation that Sporer gives regarding theft cannot illumine the servant's choice in Proposition 51: Holding ladders for would-be thieves and otherwise assisting them "certainly is excused by certain fear of death or other very grave evil proportioned by the judgment of a prudent person with the harm inflicted on neighbors, who, likewise, will not reasonably be unwilling [to suffer the harm under such circumstances]; hardly, however, will they be excused who assist thieves in murder &c."[12] Since grave bodily harm is presumably included in this "&c", should not "stupra virginis" be as well?

Salmaticenses

A few years later,[13] another significant voice is heard asserting that the condemnation of Innocent XI indicates that the actions of the servant are to be considered intrinsically evil. Sebastien de S. Joachim treats of it in the fifth tome of a six-part work put out by the Discalced Carmelites of Salamanca. He writes:

> But now examining this matter *ex professo* we assert: all these things are illicit even under the urgent danger of mutilation or death. And the reason is that what is intrinsically evil in no way (...) can be made honest even if the danger of death is present; but to help the master, by offering his shoulders, or by bringing a ladder so as to violate a virgin or fornicate with a concubine, here and now is intrinsically evil and in no wise indifferent.[14]

Sebastien defends his position by attempting to distinguish between an action that could be used well or badly and one which, in the given circumstances, can only be used for evil.

> For cooperation with any evil action is then not intrinsically evil but indifferent and on account of grave fear licit, when the principal agent of that act can then execute the act well or badly and of his own

malice it happens that the act turns out evil: for which reason we may ask for a loan from one inclined to usury (...) but the master here and now is not able to ascend, or open the door for the violating of the virgin or fornicating, without sinning in his actions. Therefore, neither may the servant cooperate in them, or help either immediately by offering his shoulders, or by placing the ladder, even on account of fear of death: the conclusion is clear, for otherwise he would be cooperating in an intrinsically evil action, which the master is not able to licitly execute here and now.[15]

Roy calls Sebastien's argument "original" not only in the sense of never before encountered, but with the implication of eccentricity.[16] It may be, however, that in hastening to discount this perspective, Roy concludes erroneously that the act of the servant is not being evaluated "in itself, in its objective morality".[17] Certainly, the claim that the master could not but use the ladder to sin is awkwardly put; nonetheless, the new emphasis on the context of the cooperation as constitutive of the object of the servant's act is an innovation not to be disdained.

Claude Lacroix (1652–1714)

Another text worthy of note is that of Jesuit, Claude Lacroix.[18] His basic position parallels that of the Salamaticenses: the circumstances are such as to make the action contemplated by the servant *per se* and proximately ordered to sin, and therefore illicit.[19] A new contribution is made by his emphasis on the servant's knowledge of the master's plan: "when crimes are not presumed, then for a good reason one can cooperate materially."[20]

But it is in nowise easy to see how Lacroix's judgment fits with what he says about returning a borrowed sword:

> He sins who returns to an irate owner his sword,
> with which it is foreseen he is about to kill another,
> unless the fear of grave inconvenience excuses. The
> reason is that, although the return is something
> indifferent in itself, however, in these circum-
> stances it is proximately related to the killing,
> therefore you are held not to return it if you can
> without grave inconvenience.[21]

Roy observes,[22] with reason, that this is essentially a reprise of Sanchez, who spoke of quasi-intrinsic evils, actions which are considered such, except in extremely urgent cases.

Juan Cardenas (1613–1684) and Johann Kugler

A similar view of the matter, in some respects, is provided by another Jesuit, Johann Kugler. He wrote an addendum to the manual of Juan Cardenas with the idea of updating it in light of the condemnations of Innocent XI. It was printed separately as a small book in 1714. Like Lacroix, he points out that the servant's certainty of the master's plan is a key factor[23] (a point included in the condemned proposition with the term *scienter*). He calls the actions referred to by the proposition as well as other actions (e.g. writing amorous letters, investigating a prospective con-cubine for a master) as "cooperation in the lust of the master" which is prohibited. He contrasts these actions with others which "are indifferent, and not here and now cooperative in the lust of the master."[24] Nonetheless, he asks whether it is "entirely and intrinsically illicit" in the face of very great potential harm including death. Kugler points out that Cardenas thought cooperation was justi-fied under such duress, but he adds that this is a question which the Holy See needs to clarify. He formulates the argument for cooperation under such circumstances in surprisingly contemporary form: "a decision, however, needs to be sought from the Roman See, whether such actions could sometimes be made honest, so that someone could be said to intend *per se* the avoidance of the very great evil, & *per accidens* aim at the sin of the master."[25]

In summary, then, for Kugler as for Lacroix, the context of the servant's action removes it from the realm of "indifferent" actions, yet the label "intrinsically evil" with the consequence of needing to face death, is one that is hard to embrace.

Dominicus Viva (1648–1726)

The condemnations gave rise to a small genre of writings giving interpretations of them. Like Kugler, Dominicus Viva provides a prime example. His analysis is a cautious one in line with the opinions that we have seen. He begins by noting that the motives given are certainly insufficient. Then he points clearly to the key issue: intrinsic evil. For, indeed, all theologians agree that cooperation is prohibited, if it is intrinsically evil. The condemnation persuades him that it is "more probable" that the servant's actions would indeed be intrinsically evil because here and now proximately ordered to sin.[26] An example of intrinsic evil given by Viva could lead to confusion concerning his meaning of "proximate" ordering to sin:

> If indeed [the action] be intrinsically evil, v.g. to help the master climb through a window for the violation of a virgin, as it is intrinsically evil to set fire by military catapults when it is foreseen that death will follow for innocents, certainly not even fear of death can excuse a servant from such cooperation.[27]

It could appear that Viva intends to say that setting fire might be justified, but not when the certain collateral damage is foreseen.[28] Calling such an action intrinsically evil under the condition of certain collateral harm to innocents appears to ignore the issue of indirect intention—the very point raised by Kugler. However, Viva has made clear earlier in the article that he is speaking in the context of Christian prisoners working artillery for Turks warring against Christendom. The foreseen deaths are direct killings for Viva, described by him as "actiones de se connexas cum morte innocentis" and "actio de se occisiva".[29]

Still, a difficulty in identifying intrinsically evil acts remains in his use of the inadequate category of "proximity" to the sin. He notes that "those actions are indifferent, which are remotely related to sin, such as the selling of a lamb to an infidel, whom I know wants to sacrifice it to an idol."[30] But this leads back to the problem that anything, no matter how proximate to a sin, can seem to be usable for the good, at least in theory. The infidel could have changed his mind and eaten the lamb; the Turks could use the rowing of Christian slaves for good as well. He quotes Castro Palao as saying that an action will be indifferent as long as it is "not immediately preparative for such a crime".[31] But, Viva wonders, could not even the holding of the ladder in the case in question have been used for helping the virgin? Thus, Viva concludes in some doubt: whether or not Proposition 51 proscribes such cooperation even in the case of fear of death depends upon whether the actions in question are intrinsically evil or indifferent—a difficult question indeed.[32]

Constantino Roncaglia (1677–1737)

Roncaglia cites both the Salmaticenses and Viva and follows their lead. The context of an action, here and now, can indeed specify the act as intrinsically evil. "If actions which otherwise might be indifferent are sufficiently proximate to the sin of the other such that they cooperate proximately, they cannot be excused even by reason of imminent grave evil."[33] While the idea of "proximity" is not new, Roncaglia puts an accent upon the *causality* of the servant's role: "He is always proved to act badly, who is the proximate cause of an intrinsically evil action ... It will be intrinsically evil to cooperate proximately in such an [intrinsically evil] action; for indeed, to the proximate cause is always imputed the effect which follows."[34] Roncaglia essentially questions the grounds upon which the servant's action can be presumed morally different from the master's. Just as you cannot make a request that cannot be fulfilled without sin, you cannot offer a service that cannot be made use of without sin.[35]

It is worthy of note that Roncaglia reminds his audience that active scandal can be caused without the spiritual ruin of the other being a goal or motive of the scandalous act.

> Not a few think that scandal is then only a special sin opposed to charity and fraternal correction when, by a less than upright word or deed the spiritual ruin of one's neighbor is expressly intended ... However, much more probable, it seems to me, is the contrary opinion which states that the special sin of scandal arises even if the spiritual ruin of one's neighbor is not expressly intended, if one does or says something from which it seems probable that his spiritual ruin will follow.[36]

As we shall see (p. 133 below), this aspect of St Thomas's teaching on scandal was a cause of significant controversy in years to come. In this regard, Roncaglia retains and highlights the idea that a person must be said to intend certain consequences of his actions implicitly, even if those particular consequences are of no interest to him.

On the less perceptive side, Roncaglia's treatment of scandal is confused with his treatment of cooperation. The very title of the section in which he discusses cooperation is "When actions, otherwise indifferent, must be omitted because from them follow scandal for a neighbor."[37] As a result, a determining factor of whether or not cooperation is proximate is, for Roncaglia, the degree to which it increases the likelihood of the sin coming about. In other words, for him cooperation becomes intrinsically evil when it is necessary, in which case it constitutes an inducement to the principal agent. Regarding accompanying a mistress to the master, Roncaglia writes: "...for if she were to come because the servant would accompany her, but otherwise would not have come, the service rendered would not be indifferent, but would proximately influence the sin of the master; he, indeed, would be providing him an occasion for sinning."[38]

Benjamin Elbel (1690–1756)

Benjamin Elbel authored a treatise on moral theology, *Theologia moralis decalogalis*, which first appeared in 1731. In the position he takes we can see the emergence of at least two points regarding cooperation that will soon become firmly established. Firstly, he explicitly distinguishes cooperation from scandal, stating that the cooperator does not lead another into sin, but only helps in the order of carrying out the sin. For this reason, the servant would be guilty of a sin against chastity and not of scandal.[39]

Secondly, Elbel divides cooperation into two parts but in such a way as to confuse the concepts which are now designated by the "material/formal" and "remote/immediate" binomials. He writes: "Cooperation in the sin of another can happen in two ways, namely (1) offering material for sinning, e.g. excessive drink, or meat on a day of abstinence, etc., or (2) concurring with the other in the same sinful action, e.g. theft, murder."[40] Indeed in Elbel, various ambiguities hitherto noted seem to be combined. He equates remote cooperation with *per accidens* cooperation.[41] While such an action would be *per se* indifferent, he speaks of it as becoming "intrinsically" wrong if done with bad intent.[42] Cooperation that is proximate is necessarily done with bad intent: "Besides it is evil to knowingly cooperate in the sin of another by an action proximately influencing in the sin itself ... Whoever indeed concurs proximately in a sinful act is considered to want the sin."[43]

Honoré Tournely and Pierre Collet (1693–1770)

At about this time the Venice edition of *Praelectiones Theologicarum* by P. Honoré Tournely began to appear. Pierre Collet is considered responsible for the moral section. Collet provides yet another clear example of the trend that has been growing for sixty years of considering an otherwise indifferent action which is *hic et nunc* part and parcel of a crime to be intrinsically evil.

> Therefore Sylvius maintains that it is not licit to offer a ladder to a thief or help him to climb up it, because such actions, although they are in themselves undetermined or indifferent, here and now, however are intrinsically evil, insofar as here and now they cooperate in the evil taking of the good of another: but equally whoever carries off booty, here and now cooperates in theft...[44]

In like manner, Collet says that Christians must rather die than row the galleys of Turks into battle. "Never is it licit to bring help to those who are striving to kill others unjustly: but the ships of the Turks are bent on this purpose, to bring unjust death to Christians; therefore, Christians may not help them in this case, but rather should undergo death."[45]

Nonetheless, also in Collet ambiguity remains. As in Elbel, the issue of duress remains an open question as another case indicates, in which cooperation apparently becomes merely material in face of a threat. Without explanation, Collet considers giving wine to drunken soldiers for fear of injury to self as only permitting drunkenness for an urgent reason ("solum illud permittere ex urgenti causa") whereas ordinarily giving wine to those who would abuse it would be considered cooperating in their sin ("eorum peccato cooperari").[46]

Pio Tommaso Milante (?-1749)

The position of Dominican, Pio Milante, whose *Exercitationes dogmatico-morales*, appearing in 1739, treated Innocent XI's Proposition 51, can be seen as a sort of summary of the reflection that the condemnation engendered. Tired out by the effort, theologians seemed unable to make any more significant contributions to this problem until the arrival of St Alphonsus Liguori. (There is a minor exception, the Jesuit, Mazzotta, a sort of precursor of Alphonsus on this issue, who will be treated next.)

For Milante, cooperation was still confused with scandal. Seemingly oblivious to the possibility that the master is set of his own accord on sinning, the servant's actions are deemed wrong because they "bear *per se* on the sin of the master" (per se influit in peccatum heri) and "lead to the offense" (conducit ad culpam).[47] The servant's role is considered intrinsically evil, because of the concrete *hic et nunc* circumstances. Awkwardly, proximate cooperation is equated with *per se*, while remote with *per accidens*.[48] Material and formal are still terms without a clearly established meaning; they are used by Milante to refer to the causal structure of the act and not to the intention of the cooperator. Not surprisingly, this unsettled theory leads to inconsistent applications. An example is the claim that opening the door to the master's mistress would be

intrinsically evil, but accompanying him to a brothel or
duel indifferent.[49]

Nicoló Mazzotta (1669–1746)

Although Daniel Concina will do a better job than his
confrere, Milante, at articulating the importance of the
circumstances of the servant's actions, a certain limit had
been reached after six decades of attempting to explain
why the holding of the ladder should be considered
intrinsically evil. In his *Theologia moralis*, published
posthumously in 1748, Father Mazzotta essentially abandoned this line of reasoning and so anticipated the reversal
that Alphonsus was to make decisively.

Mazzotta demonstrates a somewhat visionary tendency
by more clearly separating cooperation from scandal than
any of his predecessors with the possible exception of
Elbel. More striking still, he defines formal and material
cooperation in terms that sound distinctly modern.

> [One is said to cooperate] formally, when directly or
> indirectly one intends the sin of one's neighbor
> conjoined with one's operation ... Materially ... when
> one offers only material indifferent in itself, which
> the other out of his malice abuses for sin, which abuse
> one either does not foresee, or, if one does foresee it,
> in no manner is held to intend it.[50]

For Mazzotta, the notion of formally cooperating "indirectly" refers not to the agent's relation to an intrinsically
evil act, but to a lack of proportionate reason for positing
an otherwise indifferent act. This terminology will be
eliminated by Alphonsus. Unjustified material cooperation
is not for Mazzotta simply wrong, but it becomes formal
cooperation. Roy observes that this manner of speaking is
not helpful: "The text of Fr Mazzotta leads thus to this
rather strange conclusion that an illicit material coopera-

tion constitutes formal cooperation."[51] Nonetheless, it may be seen as portending the opinion of those who hold that, in applying the principle of double effect, a want of proportion in the 4th condition, can be taken as an indication of a willingness to cause the evil directly. In any case, the result is that Mazzotta can consider the servant's act wrong because of a lack of sufficient cause, and yet classify this wrongness as "formal". This seems the reverse of calling it wrong *in se*, intrinsically evil, but allowable in urgent necessity (like Sanchez). Both authors would seem to seek to have their cake and eat it, too. Not surprisingly, Mazzotta recalls the doctrine of Sanchez explicitly and comments that Innocent XI does not contradict it.[52]

Thus Mazzotta has essentially retreated from the position held by Milante and others, that the circumstance of proximate cooperation is decisive in indicating intrinsic evil. An action must be considered in the abstract, he counters. For example, he will defend rowing for the Turks, saying "rowing is in itself indifferent to good or evil use of it."[53]

2. The position of Saint Alphonsus Liguori (1696–1787)

The period of reflection following the condemnations of 1679, which we have rapidly traversed, certainly lacks unanimity, confidence, and perfect coherence.[54] Roger Roy interprets this as the effect of fear inculcated by the papal condemnations. He concludes that they distorted the free progress of theology, forcing theologians to justify positions they would not have come to on their own and in which they did not really believe. From this, Roy argues, a courageous St Alphonsus liberated us. One might view the period, however, in a more positive light. Did not the condemnation of Proposition 51 spur a period of reflection that can be judged fruitful even if chaotic? Surely it is a positive result to have stimulated the development of a new perspective not only on cooperation but on intrinsically evil acts as well. Saint Alphonsus acknowledged this new direction as plausible and predominant in his first published writing, a commentary on Busenbaum printed in 1748. Still, the identification of "proximate" cooperation with "intrinsic evil" was clearly an unstable and unsatisfying solution. Ever on guard against the harm that rigorism could do to souls, St Alphonsus saw a danger in failing to clearly delineate the limits of intrinsic evil. He claimed to have employed "great effort"[55] in search of a solution which appeared in his *Theologia moralis* of 1753.

St Alphonsus's central contention is that the act of the cooperator and that of the principal agent must be kept separate. The servant's act (holding the ladder) must be considered in itself, isolated from the evil intentions of the master. The master's evil intentions, Alphonsus argues, cannot cause the servant's action to change from indifferent to intrinsically evil.[56] He characterizes this cooperation more as the principal agent abusing the cooperator's innocent act than as the cooperator participating in the principal agent's sin. "For, truly, your action is not *per se* joined with his evil will, but he joins his evil will with your action."[57] This desire to isolate the cooperator's act leads St Alphonsus[58] to the clear and simple definition of formal and material cooperation that has become classic: "That [cooperation] is formal, which concurs in the evil will of the other and cannot be without sin; material [cooperation is] that which concurs only in the evil action of the other, beyond the intention of the cooperator."[59] From this perspective, in which formal cooperation is identified with an explicit sharing of the principal agent's goal, Proposition 51 appears to be concerned only with material cooperation. This is why St Alphonsus thinks the words "de similis cooperando" in Proposition 51 imply that the kind of cooperation under discussion is material.[60] In other words, he argues that the very wording of the proposition proves that the servant's actions are indifferent—an argument that the theologians who preceded him would surely find unconvincing. Roy allows this claim to pass without comment.[61]

Roy enthusiastically applauds St Alphonsus's "return to the ancients",[62] by which he means Sanchez.[63] He interprets St Alphonsus's isolation of the cooperator's act as the definitive and long-awaited overcoming of the confusion between scandal and cooperation. In moral theology, scandal was presumed to be always wrong, an "actus minus rectus", even when "indirect", that is, done not for the purpose of leading the other into sin, but merely foreseeing the scandalous effect. The association of cooperation with scandal, Roy argues, caused all cooperation to be considered to be, like scandal, "less than correct". He contends that theologians, motivated by fear engendered by the condemnation, first judged the cooperator guilty by association with the principal agent,[64] and then proceeded to explain this guilt as caused by the circumstance of the principal agent's known intentions which renders the helping action intrinsically evil.[65] Roy saw the failure to develop the formal/material distinction earlier as evidence that theologians were not considering cooperation apart from scandal.

In fact, however, Roy fails to note a much more serious consequence of cooperation's origins in the discussion of scandal which persists even in the thought of St Alphonsus. Alphonsus presumes, as is right if one wants to analyze cooperation and not scandal, that the principal agent is already determined to sin. Yet, from this he concludes that the cooperator's act is merely material, arguing that his assistance does not render the principal agent's will evil and so does not cause the sin.[66] This amounts to reintroducing scandal in another guise: in effect, because the cooperator is not committing scandal, his action is to be deemed indifferent. This, however, is a *non sequitur*.[67] The question proper to cooperation is not: is the servant inducing the master to sin, but *is the master inducing the servant* to sin? We cannot leap from the cooperator's lack of influence on the will of the other to the conclusion that he does not share the principal agent's evil intent. That is to reject the possibility of implicitly formal cooperation out of hand.

Some other aspects of St Alphonsus's solution appear troubling. Here follows a significant portion of his reasoning:

> The reason is because when you offer an indifferent action without evil intention, if the other should want to abuse it to accomplish his sin, you are not held to impede that except out of charity. And because charity does not oblige under grave inconvenience, therefore, positing your cooperation with just cause, you do not sin: Then indeed his sin does not come from your cooperation, but from his own evil which abuses your action. Nor does it hold to say that your action, although indifferent, nevertheless having been conjoined with the circumstance of the evil intention of the other, turns out evil; for, truly, your action is not *per se* joined with his evil will, but he joins his evil will with your action; whence your action will not then be a cause *per se* influencing the sin, but only an occasion, which the other abuses in order to sin.[68]

The attempt to separate the action of the cooperator so clearly and definitively from that of the principal agent leads to the incongruity of saying that the master, in our case, is "abusing" the servant's action. There can be no doubt that he is abusing the servant by constraining him to do things contrary to his will and station, but the master is hardly abusing the holding of the ladder; he is not making any use of this action other than the one both master and servant agree it is supposed to serve.[69] Furthermore, Alphonsus is forced to describe the servant's action as failing to impede a harm about be done to a third party, so as to claim that the demand of charity does not bind him to act in case of grave inconvenience to himself. However, as Gustave Waffelaert observed on the opening page of his treatise on cooperation, this description would apply only to a case of "negative cooperation".[70] The concern ignored by the holy doctor is that a servant, by helping his master commit this crime, risks violating not a positive commandment to "help thy neighbor" but the negative commandment, "do not rape."[71]

These awkward aspects of the saint's solution serve as signs that there is a more fundamental problem. It is a subtle problem, not introduced by Alphonsus, but inherent to the question of cooperation, and it remains problematic in our day. Consider Alphonsus's statement: "But the latter [material cooperation] is licit when the action is good or indifferent in itself, and when one has a reason for doing it that is both just and proportionate..."[72] Now, do we know that the servant's action is material because it is indifferent, or do we know that it is indifferent because it is material? The role of intention is only considered in this passage as it concerns the formal/material distinction. But if the judgment on the action's good or indifferent nature does not depend upon the agent's intention, upon what does it depend? Barring a situation in which two distinct sins are involved (for instance, the servant might be asked not to hold a ladder but to strangle the night watchman so as to facilitate his master's crime) the help of the cooperator will always appear indifferent. Precisely because he is cooperating, and not doing the evil itself, what he is "doing" appears indifferent. The physicalist perspective from which all thinkers approached the problem in that day obscured the possibility that the cooperator's action could fail to be indifferent solely in virtue of its relationship to the master's crime. For Alphonsus, this possibility is ruled out by definition: the kind of cooperative action with which we are concerned is not formal because that has been defined as intending (explicitly) the principal agent's goal, and it is not illicit material cooperation as it is not evil "in itself" (apart from the master's crime). Conceptually, there is no room for implicitly formal cooperation.

For St Alphonsus, the concurrence of the cooperator with the principal agent's evil will proper to formal cooperation is only verified if the helping action augments that evil will. "Wherefore I only call those actions intrinsically evil which augment the evil will of the thief."[73] Actions which are "ex se determinata ad peccatum", such as seeking a concubine for a master, making idols and the like, must in some way be luring the principal agent further into his evil choice.[74] In the case of writing letters to a mistress, this is also deemed intrinsically evil, because it induces another person, even if not the master, to sin. Apart from this connection with scandal, the cooperator does not appear capable of positing an intrinsically evil act of cooperation no matter how close his relation to the rape itself. St Alphonsus only observes that the cooperator cannot actually do the crime. In this light one understands the rather curious example he suggests to illustrate the two modes by which one can participate in the sin of another: "Cooperation is formal when one cooperates actually in the sin, as happens in fornication, or when one cooperates in the evil will of someone..."[75] Short of such an extreme case of "immediate cooperation", implicitly formal cooperation has been defined out of existence.

Again, it must be recalled that all parties to these debates, including St Alphonsus, were writing in the climate of legalism and extrinsicism earlier described. It seemed natural to divide human action neatly into exterior and interior parts, the physical and the intentional. Formal cooperation would be contributing to both; material cooperation to the physical action only. The cooperator could consider his action as only "physical" matter which would be abused. Only an appreciation of the intimate relation between external and internal act reveals the "chicken and egg" problem underlying the Saint's definition of licit material cooperation as an indifferent action posited for just reason. The difficulty of specifying precisely what the cooperator is doing, what constitutes the object of his act, was a problem that St Alphonsus not only did not solve but could not even see. Such deeper questions about action theory have only emerged over the last two hundred years.

None of this criticism, based upon two centuries of hindsight, should take from St Alphonsus the credit due for his contribution to this question. The patron of moralists achieved a result in this area similar to that which he achieved in regard to probabilism. Faced with competing opinions, the dangers of rigorism and laxism, and the need to provide without delay clear, practical guidance to confessors, he indicated a trustworthy path. For this he has been justly commended by the Church for all time. Nonetheless, presuppositions underlay the debates of his day that no one, including St Alphonsus, was able to discern fully.[76] The resolution of the problem of cooperation with evil presupposes a clear understanding of what constitutes intrinsically evil actions. Real progress on this issue was not possible in the legalist climate of probabilism. As we shall see, this debate continued throughout the Manualist era to our own day.[77] In his analysis, Roy takes for granted that the circumstance of the master's plan does not render the servant's action intrinsically evil. He writes: "The gravest confusion of Fr Milante comes from the fact that, whatever he may say, he has not considered the morality of the act [of the servant] taken in itself, but has judged it already engaged in the cooperation and as informed by that."[78] Roy offers no explanation of how to limit the descriptions of an act taken "in itself". As we shall see in a subsequent section, Elizabeth Anscombe will ask why I cannot describe my action of stabbing you in itself, as "swinging a knife through the air", taking your physical proximity as a mere circumstance.[79]

In conclusion then, we can only see St Alphonsus's intervention as a sort of stalemate, which could silence critics for a time but not convince them entirely. It provided practical guidance, a rule of thumb for confessors, but only put off an elucidation of the problem for future generations. The question of St Alphonsus's sparring partner, Daniele Concina, in which he saw "the hinge of the difficulty" remains open: "when by reason of circumstances do operations or cooperations contract evil?"[80] It is a question that requires, as Concina indicated,[81] a deeper understanding of the relationship between the physical and the moral orders, and of the authentic nature of practical reason. It called for a confronting of the alleged "naturalistic fallacy", which, unbeknownst to Concina and Liguori, David Hume was contemporaneously elaborating. It is a question that involves some of the great debates, moral and otherwise, of modern philosophy and theology. To this question we now must turn.

Notes

1.   Cf. R. Gerardi, *Storia della morale: interpretazioni teologiche dell'esperienza cristiana* (Bologna: Edizioni Dehoniane, 2003), p. 388.

2.   "quia si tales Domini vellent servos suos esse suorum scelerum participes, eos ad male agendum excitando, aut impellendo; in tali occasione servi Dominis obedire non possunt sine gravi peccato: cumque Dei mandata potius, quam hominum iussa servare teneamur, Deo potius quam homini debent obedire; neque aliquo commodo temporali induci debent, ut peccatis Dominorum suorum cooperentur." F. Genet, *Theologia moralis, juxta sacrae scripturae, canonum, & SS. Patrum mentem*, 2nd ed. Lat. (Venice: apud Paulum Balleonium, 1705), t. 6 tr. v, cap III, qu. 5, p. 298.

3.   "Licet-ne famulo in negotiis amatoriis domino inservire, dum intendit tantum lucrari ea, quae sibi sunt ad victum necessaria? Resp. Cum haec actio ita illicita sit, ut in nulla circumstantia fieri licita possit, nulla intentio illam excusare valet, ut patet ex doctrina Sancti Augustini & Sancti Thomae superius relata. Unde sancta Sedes sequentem propositionem damnavit 51 Propositio damnata." *Ibid.*, t. I, tr. I, cap. XVI, qu. 8, p. 232.

4.   "Hic actus est ex se malus, dum non adsunt illae circumstantiae, quae possent illum cohonestare." *Ibid.*, qu. 7, p. 231.

5.   "Actus malus, potest-ne per aliquam intentionis directionem fieri bonus?" He answers that "Certum primo est, illud quod ex natura sua malum est, numquam posse fieri bonum per quamvis intentionis rectitudinem" citing "bonum ex integra causa." But, he continues, "Sed illi actus qui ita mali sunt, ut tamen in aliquibus circumstantiis possint esse liciti, fiunt boni, dum adsunt illae circumstantiae quae pravitatem talium actuum tollant, modo cum recta intentione fiant." *Ibid.*, qu. 6, pp. 129–30.

6.   "Quando-nam metus gravis excusat a peccato, licet non tollat omnino libertatem?" *Ibid.*, t. 1, tract. 1, cap. XIII, qu. 2.

7.   Gerardi, *Storia della morale*, p. 367.

8.   "Quando aliquid alicui ex justitia debetur, praestandum est, etsi per illud alter peccaturus sit: si tu peccatum aliunde impedire non debeas, vel commode non possis." P. Sporer, *Theologiae moralis super decalogum* (Venice: apud Nicolaum Pezzana, 1726) t. II, pars V, cap. 1, sec. iii, n. 95, p. 83.

9.   "Contra vero in iis, quae propinque, vel proxime se ad peccatum habent, juvant, vel ordinantur, etsi de se indifferentia, non possunt

famuli, & ancillae obsequi dominis ex sola ratione famulatus, vel servitii. Immo modo post propositiones damnatas, non amplius excusat metus cujusvis notabilis detrimenti... (...) nunquam potest esse licitum: cum haec videantur intrinsece mala, & species lenocinii." *Ibid.*, t. II, pars V, cap. 1, sec. iii, n. 100.

[10] "Certissimum et quaestione indignum est; non posse te proximo cooperari ad ipsum peccatum proxime et formaliter, seu in ipsa actione peccaminosa proximi." *Ibid.*, n. 70.

[11] "metu mortis coacti." *Ibid.*, n. 103–104.

[12] "nimirum excusari certo metu mortis, vel alterius gravissimi mali prudentis judicio proportionati cum damno proximis inferendo, qui similiter non debebunt esse rationabiliter inviti; minime tamen excusantur juvantes latrones ad homicidia &c." *Ibid.*, n. 103.

[13] On the authority of Roy (cf. *Notion*, p. 141, n. 1) the date of publication cannot be fixed, but the author died in 1714. According to R. Gerardi, *Storia della morale*, p. 370, Sebastien died five years later.

[14] "Sed nunc ex professo rem examinantes asserimus: haec omnia illicita esse etiam urgente periculo mutilationis aut mortis. Et ratio est, quia quod est intrinsece malum nullo modo (...) honestari potest etiamsi adsit periculum mortis; sed adjuvare dominum, humeros supponendo, vel deferendo scalam ad virginem stuprandam aut fornicandum cum concubina, hic et nunc est intrinsece malum et nullo modo indifferens." Salmaticenses, *Cursus theologiae moralis* (Madrid: apud haeredes D. Michaelis Francisci Rodriguez, 1751), t. V, tr. XXI, cap. VIII, punct. V, n. 75.

[15] "Quia tunc cooperatio ad aliquam actionem malam non est intrinsece mala sed indifferens et ob metum gravem licita, quando principalis causa illius actionis potest tunc bene aut male eam exequi et ex sua malitia provenit quod male fiat: quapropter possumus petere mutuum ab usurario parato (...) sed herus hic et nunc nequit ascendere, aut aperire portam ad stuprandam virginem vel fornicandum quin in his actionibus peccet. Ergo nec famulus ad eas cooperari, aut immediate subjiciendo humeros, aut scalam apponendo etiam ob metum mortis, adjuvare: patet consequentia, alias coopereretur ad actionem intrinsece malam, seu quam hic et nunc licite exequi herus non potest." *Ibid.*, t. V, tr. XXI, cap. VIII, punct. V, n. 75.

[16] "ne manque pas d'originalité" and is "une conception de l'action intrinsèquement mauvaise que nous n'avions pas rencontrée jusqu'ici." Roy, *Notion*, pp. 145 and 147.

[17] "L'acte du serviteur n'est plus jugé en lui-même, dans sa moralité objective." *Ibid.*, p. 147.

[18] C. Lacroix, *Theologia moralis antehac ex probatis auctoribus* (breviter concinnata a R.P. Herm. Busembaum) (Koln: apud Servatium Noethen, 1710–1720).

[19] "the action undertaken in those circumstances seems to per se and proximately tend to sin, and therefore to be intrinsically evil and cannot be made honest by any reason." ("… operatio posita in illis circumstantiis videtur per se et proxime tendere ad peccatum, ideoque esse intrinsece mala nec posse ex ulla causa cohonestari.") *Ibid.*, Lib. II, tr. III, cap. II, dub. V, n. 254.

[20] "cum delicta non praesumantur, tumque ex justa causa posset materialiter cooperari." *Ibid.*, n. 253.

[21] "Peccat qui alteri irato reddit suum gladium quo praevidetur occisurus alterum, nisi excuset metus gravis incommodi. Ratio est quia licet illa redditio sit res de se indifferens, tamen in his circumstantiis proxime se habet ad occisionem, ergo teneris non reddere si possis sine gravi incommodo." *Ibid.*, n. 265.

[22] Roy, *Notion*, pp. 156–157.

[23] "It is not prohibited, however, if the servant does any of the afore-mentioned acts not knowing that his master intends evil, although he may suspect it." ("Non prohibetur tamen, si famulus aliquam ex supra dictis actionibus exerceat non sciens, quod herus malum intendat, licet de hoc suspicetur"). J. Kugler, *Brevissima atque acuratissima explicatio LXV Propositionum ab Innoc. XI damnatarum* (Pavia: apud Petrum Antonium Magrium, 1714), pp. 192–193.

[24] "Aliae actiones indifferentes, & non cooperativae hic & nunc in luxuriam heri, licet concubinae exhibeantur, non sunt prohibitae." *Ibid.*, p. 193.

[25] "decisionem tamen dicit petendam a Sede Romana, an tales actiones possint aliquando honestari, ita ut quis dicatur per se intendere evasionem gravissimi mali, & per accidens sequi peccatum heri." *Ibid.*, p. 193.

[26] "Actiones illae in thesi expositae sunt intrinsece malae, eo quod, hic, & nunc sint proxime ad peccatum ordinatae." Viva, *Damnatae Theses*, p. 299.

[27] "Si enim sit intrinsece malum, v.g. adjuvare herum ascendentem per fenestras ad stuprandam virginem, sicut est intrinsece malum admover ignem tormentis bellicis quando inde praevidetur secutura mors innocentis, certe ne metus quidem mortis potest

famulum excusare ab ea cooperatione." *Ibid.*, p. 299.

[28] compare with Sanchez's mention of this example (p. 37).

[29] *Ibid.*, p. 298 and p. 299, respectively.

[30] "Esse vero actiones indifferentes, quae remote se habent ad peccatum, ut vendere agnum infideli, quem scio velle ut immolet idolo...." *Ibid.*, p. 300.

[31] "... non sit actio immediate parativa talis sceleris." The action could be used for good also: "herus ea cooperatio famuli uti ad subveniendum virgini ille, & ad bene operandum." *Ibid.*, p. 299.

[32] "Utrum autem proscibatur implicite, & virtualiter, dependet ab ea quaestione, num actione, de quibus thesis loquitur, sint intrinsece malae, an vero de se sint indifferentes?" *Ibid.*, p. 299.

[33] "Si actiones, quae alias possent esse indifferentes, satis sint proximae alterius peccato, ita ut proxime ipsi cooperentur, non possunt excusari etiam ratione gravis mali imminentis." C. Roncaglia, *Universa moralis theologia* (Venice: typ. Francisci Pitteri, 1740), t. 1, tr. VI, cap. VI, r. III, pp. 183–184.

[34] "semper enim convincitur male agere, qui est causa proxima actionis intrinsece malae ... erit intrinsece malum cooperari proxime hiusmodi [intrinsece malae] actioni; causae enim proximae semper imputatur effectus, qui sequitur." *Ibid.*, pp. 183–184.

[35] "Primo igitur non licet petere actionem a qua hic et nunc non possit separari malitia." *Ibid.*, p. 184.

[36] "Non pauci sentiunt, tunc solummodo scandalum esse speciale peccatum opppositum Charitati, & fraternae correctioni, quando dicto, vel facto minus recto expresse intenditur ruina spiritualis proximi... At, meo videri, valde probabilior est contraria sententia, quae asserit consurgere speciale peccatum scandali, etiamsi non expresse intendatur Proximi spiritualis ruina, si quis faciat, vel dicat aliquid, ex quo probabiliter videat sequuturam illius spiritualem ruinam." *Ibid.*, p. 183.

[37] "Quando actiones, alias indifferentes, omittendae sint, quia ex illis sequitur scandalum in proximo." *Ibid.*, p. 183.

[38] "... nam si iret quia famulum comitem haberet, alias non itura, non esset indifferens famulatus, sed influeret proxime in peccatum heri, ipse enim ad eum deferret occasionem peccandi." *Ibid.*, p. 185.

[39] "Hac de causa R.D. Augustinus Michel ... recte concludit quod famulus hero jam de se determinato ad fornicandum succollet, ut

possit ascendere per fenestram ... peccet quidem eodem gravi peccato quo dominus contra virtutem castitatis, non tamen peccato scandali; quia dominum non induxit ad peccandum, sed tantum adjuvit in ordine ad exequendum peccatum." B. Elbel, *Theologia moralis decalogis*, (Augsburg: sumptibus Mathias Wolff, 1733–1741), II, n. 374. Roy observes that Elbel does not stick to this insight (cf. Roy, *Notion*, p. 168, n. 89).

40 "...cooperationem ad peccatum alterius dupliciter fieri posse, scilicet vel 1. praebendo materiam ad peccandum, v.g. potum excessivum, vel carnes die prohibite, etc., vel etiam 2. concurrendo cum eodem ad eandem actionem peccaminosam, v.g. furti, homicidii." *Ibid.*, n. 361.

41 "...advertunt hujusmodi cooperationem subinde fieri posse per actionem de se prorsus indifferentem et ita quidem ut haec vel remote dumtaxat et per accidens, vel etiam propinque aut proxime omnino deserviat ad peccatum." *Ibid.*, n. 361. Again, in giving the first condition under which one could cooperate he says: "...cooperatio de se sit honesta aut saltem indifferens & ad peccatum proximi merum remote ac per accidens se habeat, ita scilicet, ut nec phyisce, neque moraliter in illud influat..." *Ibid.*, n. 363.

42 "Si fiant ad finem malum, ut si famulus succollet hero, sternat lectum, vocet puellam, etc., eo quod idem dominus velit cum ea habere rem, hujusmodi actiones evadunt male et quidem ... intrinsece." *Ibid.*, n. 361.

43 "Insuper nefas est scienter cooperari peccato alterius per actionem proxime influentem in ipsius peccatum ... Qui enim proxime concurrit ad actum peccaminosum, convincitur velle peccatum." *Ibid.*, n. 362. Contrary to many authors, Elbel includes serving meat on a day of abstinence as an example of unacceptably "proximate" cooperation.

44 "Ideo enim existimat Sylvius non esse licitum scalam praebere furi eumve cum ascendit juvare, quia hujusmodi actiones, licet de se sint adiaphorae seu indifferentes, hic et nunc tamen intrinsece malae sunt, quatenus hic et nunc iniquae boni alterius acceptioni cooperantur: at qui pariter praedas vehere, hic et nunc est cooperari furto...." H. de Tournely—P. Collet, *Universa moralis theologia, sive Praelectionum theologicum* (Venice: Pezzana, 1736–1758), tom. 1, tract. de iustitia et iure, pars III, cap. II, art. v, sec. iv, pp. 279–280.

45 "Numquam enim licet iis opem ferre qui alios injuste occidere nituntur: atqui eo tendunt Turcarum navigia, ut injustam Chris-

tianis mortem inferant; ergo non possunt Christiani hoc in casu
iisdem opem ferre, sed potius mortem pati debent...." *Ibid.*, p. 280.

[46] *Ibid.*, tom. 3, tract. de Praec. decal., cap. I, art. iii, sec. vii, punct 1,
p. 335.

[47] "Famulus enim qui submissis humeris herum adjuvat ut per
fenestram ascendat domum virginis stuprandae, etc., per se influit
in peccatum heri, illiusque crimini formaliter cooperatur: quia
praestet ei medium quo ad executionem criminis perveniat.
Medium autem istud tunc per se influit in culpam quum per se est
ordinatum ad peccatum, vel ex peculiari quadam circumstantia
habet talem influxum: qua propter quum proxime per se, vel
ratione adjuncti, conducit ad culpam, est medium per se influens
in culpam. Secus vero quum solum remote et per accidens quia
tunc solum materialiter ad alterius peccatum concurrit, nec per
se influit in culpam." P. T. Milante, *Exercitationes dogmatico-
morales in propositiones proscriptas* (Naples: ex typographia
Januarii, 1738–1740), vol. II, p. 302.

[48] He says, for instance, that a servant preparing a horse that will be
used for some evil purpose, such as visiting a mistress, "nimis
remote ad domini crimen concurrit, non dicitur formaliter cooperari eius delicto." *Ibid.*, p. 303.

[49] "dicendum est peccare lethaliter et alterius peccato proxime
cooperari (...) servos et ancillas aperientes ostium amasio vel
scorto ad turpem finem accedentibus..." yet "sicut etiam remote
concurrunt famuli obsequii causa comitantes heros etiam ad
lupanar vel ad duellum euntes...." *Ibid.*, p. 303.

[50] "Formaliter, quando directe aut indirecte intendit peccatum
proximi cum sua operatione conjugendum.... Materialiter dicitur
quis cooperari, quando praebet dumtaxat materiam de se
indifferentem, qua alius ex sua malitia abutitur ad peccandum,
quod ille vel non praevidet, vel si praevidet, nullo tamen pacto
censetur intendere." N. Mazzotta, *Theologia moralis in quinque
tomos distributa* (Venice: typ. Remondiniana, 1760), t. I, tract. II,
disp II, qu. I, cap. III, sec. IV. Note that Roy's translation of this
last sentence—"que le coopérateur prévoit ou non, mais qu'il
n'approuve en aucune façon" (*Notion*, p. 178)—seems to betray a
blindness to the possibility of implicit intention; he identifies
intention with approval.

[51] Roy, *Notion*, p. 178.

[52] Mazzotta, *Theologia Moralis*, t. I, tract. II, disp. II, qu. I, cap. III,
sec. IV, quaeres secundo.

53 *Ibid.*, quaeres primo.

54 Yet another example of this halting consensus is the forward written for the 1740 edition of St Antontinus of Florence's commentary on St Thomas. While refraining from calling the servant's actions intrinsically evil, the author concludes that knowingly to "accommodate such a deed" as the master undertakes is to "consent at least indirectly" to his plan, which "no fear of evil" can justify. "Licet scalam deferre, aperire januam, & alia ejusmodi per se indifferentia sint opera, quibus dominus in rem non malam uti posset; quum tamen in dato casu iisdem utatur, ut adjuvetur ad malum; servus qui id noscit, a cooperatione & scandalo activo excusari non postest. (...) At sicut non sunt facienda mala, ut eveniant bona, quod Paulus Apostolus docuit; ita nullius mali metu consentiendum est malo, cui sane saltem indirecte consentit, qui eidem opem & operam accommodat." Antoninus, *Summa theologica*, Praelectio V, de Scandalo, col. cxiii.

55 "Quest'è un punto di molta importanza che mi è costato molto fatica a decifrarlo." A. de Liguori, *Practica del confessore per ben esercitare il suo ministero* (Modena: Tip. Immacolata Concezione, 1948), n. 23.

56 "...malitia alterius nequit mutare naturam actionis, ita ut de indifferenti evadat intrinsece mala." Liguori, *Theologia moralis*, lib. II, tr. 3, cap. 2, dub. 5. "De scandalo," art. 3, n. 66, quaer. 4.

57 "...nam revera actio tua non est per se conjuncta cum mala voluntate illius, sed ille conjungit suam malam voluntatem cum actione tua...." *Ibid.*, n. 63.

58 Roy also admits that the formulation of formal and material, while placed first in his exposition, is "the fruit of the work of reconstruction on the problem of cooperation." Cf. Roy, "La coopération," pp. 424–425.

59 "Illam esse formalem, quae concurrit ad malam voluntatem alterius et nequit esse sine peccato; materialem illam, quae concurrit tantum ad malam actionem alterius, praeter intentionem cooperantis." Liguori, *Theologia moralis*, lib. II, tr. 3, cap. 2, dub. 5. "De scandalo," art. 3, n. 63.

60 "Nec valet dicere quo praefatae actiones sunt per se malae quia cooperantur ad peccatum stupri; idque probari ex ipsa propositione damnata, ubi dicitur: 'aut quid simile cooperando'. Nam respondetur quod 'cooperando' non intelligitur de cooperatione formali sed de materiali, cum de ea solum locuti sint auctores propositionis; et in tali sensu, certe fuit propositio proscripta."

Ibid., n. 66., quaer. 4.

[61] Cf. Roy, "La coopération," p. 420.

[62] *Ibid.*, p. 420.

[63] *Ibid.*, p. 424.

[64] Cf. Roy, *Notion*, p. 170.

[65] Note that this theory ignores the fact that all of these thinkers, e.g. the Salmaticenses, did identify certain actions as remaining indifferent even in the likelihood that they would be the occasion of sin for another, such as asking for a oath from someone likely to perjure themselves.

[66] Cf. passage about to be quoted in note 73.

[67] It can be hard to believe that theologians could have been so preoccupied with the possibility of causing the evil effect of the master's sin as to ignore the causing of the evil effect of the rape itself. Yet, cooperation was treated along with scandal under "sins against charity" (meaning against the charity owed to the principal agent) right through the twentieth century. Even in 1985, one finds this extraordinary description of the Servant and the Ladder case: "Thus, [the servant], by cooperating, cannot be said to be the cause of [the master's] sin that is already existing [in the master's evil will] before his [the servant's] intervention. His refraining from helping in the circumstances would not have impeded [the master's] sin. At best it could have prevented the resulting harm done to the virgin." (Ugorje, *Principle of Double Effect*, p. 51). The main issue in cooperation should be the moral quality of the contribution made to harming the virgin, and this is tendentiously described as failing to 'prevent … harm'.

[68] "Ratio, quia cum tu praestas actionem indifferentem sine prava intentione, si alter illa abuti voluerit ad suum peccatum exsequendum, non teneris nisi ex caritate illud impedire. Et quia caritas non obligat cum gravi incommodo, ideo ponens tuam cooperationem cum justa causa, non peccas: Tunc enim peccatum illius non provenit ex cooperatione tua, sed ex malitia ipsius qui tua actione abutitur. Nec valet dicere quod tua actio, etsi indifferens, conjuncta tamen cum circumstantia pravae intentionis alterius, evadit mala; nam revera actio tua non est per se conjuncta cum mala voluntate illius, sed ille conjungit suam malam voluntatem cum actione tua; unde tua actio non erit tunc causa per se influens in peccatum, sed tantum occasio, qua ille abutitur ad peccandum." Liguori, *Theologiae moralis*, lib. II, tr. 3, cap. 2, dub. 5. "De scandalo," art. 3, n. 63.

⁶⁹ The master is abusing the ladder, just as using a gun to shoot an innocent is an abuse of this instrument, but the action of holding the ladder in that place and time, like giving a gun to a vengeful man, are not convincingly described as "abused."

⁷⁰ G. J. Waffelaert, *Ètude sur la coopération et sur l'espèce morale du scandale* (Bruges: Vandenberghe-Denaux, 1883), p. 5. (See the discussion of Waffelaert on p. 132). On the great moral significance of this distinction note, for instance, the following from *Veritatis Splendor*: "Finally, it is always possible that man, as the result of coercion or other circumstances, can be hindered from doing certain good actions; but he can never be hindered from not doing certain actions, especially if he is prepared to die rather than to do evil" (n. 52).

⁷¹ Even Roy shows discomfort at St Alphonsus's lingering use of the scandal category. Roy notes: "But there is, however, a fundamental distinction, for he who permits pharisaic scandal situates himself uniquely in the occasional order, without participating in the act of his neighbor; the cooperator, on the contrary, gives occasion to the fault of his neighbor in causing it with him by an active participation." Roy, "La coopération," p. 410.

⁷² Liguori, *Theologiae moralis*, lib. II, tr. 3, cap. 2, dub. 5, art. 3, n. 63.

⁷³ "Onde quelle azioni solamente dico intrinsicamente male, quelle che aumentano la mala volontà del ladro." A. de Liguori, *Instruzione e practica per i Confessori* (Milan: Volpato, 1855), t.1, cap. x, n. 57.

⁷⁴ "semper autem est intrinsece mala illa actio, quae ex se determinata est ad peccatum: uti esset, quaerere domino concubinam, idola fabricare, et quid simile...." Liguori, *Theol. mor.*, lib. II, tr. 3, cap. 2, dub. 5. "De scandalo," art. 3, n. 63.

⁷⁵ Liguori, *Practica del confessore*, n. 23.

⁷⁶ In the context of natural law and epieikeia, Martin Rhonheimer makes a comment that is relevant here: "Alphonsus' spirit is absolutely correct, but his methodology is of course misleading (he tries to argue within a legalistic framework)." M. Rhonheimer "Intentional Actions and the Meaning of Object: a reply to Richard McCormick," *Thomist* 59 (1995), pp. 279–311, at p. 304.

⁷⁷ Cf. J. Murtagh, *Intrinsic evil: an examination of this concept and its place in current discussions on absolute moral norms* (Rome: Pontifical Gregorian University, 1973).

⁷⁸ "La confusion la plus grave du P. Milante provient de ce qu'il n'a pas, quoi qu'il en dise, considéré la moralité de l'acte pris en

lui-même, mais de l'avoir jugé déjà engagé dans la coopération et comme informé par elle." Roy, *Notion*, p. 175.

[79] G. E. M. Anscombe, "Medalist's Address: Action, Intention, and 'Double Effect'," in Woodward, *Doctrine of Double Effect*, pp. 50–66, at p. 63.

[80] "In hoc porro difficultatis cardo solvitur, quandonam ratione circumstantiarum operationes seu cooperationes malitiam contrahant." D. Concina, *Theologia christiana dogmatico-moralis* (Rome: apud Simonem Occhi, 1749–1751), tom. II, diss. ix, cap vii, n. iii.

[81] "Utique si physice, vel metaphysice spectentur indifferentes sunt. Sed theologus eas considerat ut practicas et ut reipsa omnibus circumstantiis subjacent. Porro moralis natura, ut sic loquar, istarum actionum (propositionis damnatae) mala est et vitiosa." *Ibid.*, tom. II, diss. ix, cap. xii, n. iv.

PART II

SOME TERMS CLARIFIED

CHAPTER 4

THE CONTRIBUTION OF
BRITISH MORAL PHILOSOPHY

WE MUST BEGIN this chapter with an explanation for what may appear an unwarranted interruption of the history of Roman Catholic thinking on the problem of cooperation by an excursus into modern British philosophy. Still, were we to introduce a discussion of this tradition after completing our review of pre-*Veritatis Splendor* Catholic thought, it would be no less inconvenient.

The difficulty in finding a place to address the contribution of British moral philosophy derives from the fact that it developed parallel to Catholic thought. The end of scholasticism, which gave rise to such dramatic changes in Catholic moral theology, issued in a new intellectual landscape outside the Church as well. Renaissance figures from Lorenzo Valla to Machiavelli began a new direction in moral thinking by finding inspiration directly in classical sources. The separation of faith and reason, philosophy and theology, led eventually to an intellectual tradition with little or no contact with explicitly Catholic thinkers. While empiricist, rationalist, and idealist philosophers also treated moral issues, the concerns raised and the positions taken were at great variance from those of Catholic moral theologians. Only recently has it become increasingly apparent to Catholic thinkers that there are fruits of secular moral thinking which can be of service in making a more profound analysis of human action.[1]

A word must be said about why, of all secular moral philosophy, recent Anglo-Saxon analytical philosophy is of particular interest. Indeed, it is perhaps not coincidental that the writers within the Church who stand out in the development of action theory today, and who will be studied in Chapters 8 through 10, either come from an Anglo-Saxon background or are comfortable in dialogue with English language writers.

As noted at the end of the last chapter, even as St Alphonsus was bringing Catholic moral thinking to a certain high point, David Hume was delivering a formidable challenge to the whole project with his radically empiricist notions. In particular, morality could not, Hume argued, be derived from observation of the world around us. Catholicism, by contrast, with its emphasis on natural law, was generally held to be inseparable from "naturalism".[2] Hume's influential arguments would lead secular thinkers in a variety of directions. Some who wished to retain the truth value of moral statements would, like the rationalists, seek absolute moral norms in formally derived *a priori* duties. Others, while accepting Hume's basic position, insisted that there was an objective moral value attainable by intuition or some other philosophical method. For a great many, exemplified by the positivist line, morality became purely an expression of emotion and sentiment. Nonetheless, since men have to live together, moral problems turned into a question of social contracts, evolutionary development, and pragmatic considerations. Legal theory and moral theory became very much intertwined.

The positivist penchant for scientific precision, along with the development of logical analysis, led, especially in Britain, to the close examination of ordinary language. Towards the middle of the twentieth century these "analytic philosophers" turned their attention to the language used to describe human action. This method, as it turns out, has much to recommend itself to Catholic thinkers.[3] As we will argue in Chapters 5 and 6, Catholic thought was at this time very much in need of deeper understanding of human action, so as to explain its moral convictions more convincingly, especially as new problems arose. Ordinary language analysis could lead to genuinely new insights in the realm of action theory. Moreover, it could keep a moral theory from departing far from reality, as ordinary language functions as a sort of check on the adequacy of a theory.

With this justification in mind, we now turn to an examination of the recent debates among Anglo-Saxon secular thinkers[4] in a search for ideas which appear to be of some promise in our effort to understand the problem of cooperation in evil. We will begin by looking at the strong support for some notion of intentionality that appears as a *tertium quid* between fully intended action and fully unintentional action. We will then consider the attempt to define precisely the notion of a means to an end. Finally, we will examine the question of whether a single moral description of an act is an attainable goal.

1. Intention

An enduring point of reference in this field is the study entitled *Intention*, made by the young Elizabeth Anscombe in 1957. Early on she offers the now familiar example of "Lying on a bed":

> For example, someone comes into a room, sees me lying on a bed and asks "What are you doing?" The answer, "Lying on a bed", would be received with just irritation; an answer like "Resting" or "Doing Yoga", which would be a description of what I am doing in lying on my bed, would be an expression of intention.[5]

In this simple way, Anscombe indicates that a purely physical, external description of an act will not express the intentionality present, nor, as a consequence, count as a moral description. When we ask "What are you doing?" we are usually seeking the reason why the agent is doing what we can observe for ourselves he is physically doing. What description, we want to know, makes this a reasonable, choice-worthy activity? While this may be distinct from what is ordinarily called a motive (e.g. I am preparing for a long drive to London—by resting), we still seek a kind of motive (e.g. I am resting—by lying still on my bed). Since morality has to do with this self-orientation of the agent, it can appear, as one extreme, that the agent's intention, and the corresponding morality of his action, is a purely private affair. Says Anscombe: "Now it can easily seem that in general the question what a man's intentions are is only authoritatively settled by him."[6]

The other extreme is represented by thinkers whose moral philosophy and legal theory are closely allied. Jeremy Bentham stands out as insisting that the exterior results, not the interior intention, are decisive in describing an action. For Bentham, and the law in general, one is responsible for all of the foreseen consequences of an action, not just for those that one claims to intend. H. L. A. Hart comments: "This almost exclusively cognitive approach is one distinctive way in which the law diverges from the ordinary idea of intentionally doing something, for in ordinary thought not all the foreseen consequences of conduct are regarded as intended."[7] Anscombe coined the term "consequentialism" in her concern to rebut this notion in its most extreme form.[8] Nonetheless, there is obviously some limit that must be set to an agent's assessment of what he is doing when he causes various consequences. As Anthony Kenny remarks: "It has long been a maxim that 'a man must be taken to intend the natural consequences of his acts'."[9]

Early on in her study, Anscombe shows that ordinary language has difficulty making distinctions here. One wishes to call merely foreseen consequences voluntary but not intentional. Thus she says: "Something is voluntary though not intentional if it is the antecedently known concomitant result of one's intentional action, so that one could have prevented it if one would have given up the action; but it is not intentional..."[10] Yet she then adds that these actions might be considered involuntary if the agent feels "compelled" or "regrets 'having' to do them." She admits, however, that ordinarily we will call them "reluctant" not "involuntary".[11] Surely, the relevance of this discussion to any judgment on Proposition 51 is obvious. The notion of formal cooperation drawn from St Alphonsus—concurring in the intention of the principal agent—will remain as unclear as our understanding of the concept of intention itself.

Oblique intention

Bentham introduced a term, "oblique intention", to describe the agent's relation to consequences that are foreseen and for which the agent should be held responsible though he deny having intended their production. Legal theorists see a need for highlighting the existence of such a category of action. As one writer commented in reference to a clinician who provided an underage girl with contraceptives: "[she may] not want the offence to be committed: but intention need not involve desire; and her knowledge that her action will facilitate unlawful sexual intercourse constitutes an intention to assist the commission of that offense."[12] R. A. Duff suggests that we distinguish between what is "intentional" and what is "intended". Thus, a man might *"intentionally* 'travel on a plane piloted by a woman': but he does not *intend* 'to be piloted by a woman', since that would imply that he boards the plane partly because its pilot is female."[13] On one hand, he recognizes that "ascriptions of intentional agency are, as a matter of meaning, ascriptions of responsibility," and therefore intentional actions are not to be immediately identified with actions that are "not unintentional".[14] On the other hand, there are consequences for which the agent is fully responsible even though he has not intended them in the sense that he caused them "partly because" he foresaw they would follow. Philippa Foot compares imaginary merchants, who knowingly sell poisonous cooking oil just to turn a profit, with gravediggers, who do the same so as to get clients for their graveyard. Although the former are not interested in the foreseen deaths of their customers, Foot comments that "in morality, as in law, the merchants, like the gravediggers would be considered as murderers."[15]

Some Catholic thinkers might take exception to Foot's claim, in their effort to keep the "intention/foresight" distinction from getting blurred. As Anscombe has observed,[16] the insistence on intrinsically evil actions typical of Catholic thought requires that some means be found to distinguish clearly between cases of inevitable or accidental infringement of goods protected by negative norms, on one hand, and the deliberate violation of those norms on the other. There is, as a result, a tendency in some quarters to reserve the notion of "intention" only to the effects that are sought as an end or as a means to it, and to regard the use of the term "oblique intention" as suspect.[17] Yet, the doctrine of double effect clearly indicates that the agent is still responsible for all the foreseen effects even if they are not intended explicitly or, perhaps in contrast to obliquely, directly.[18] Surely effects for which we are morally responsible (in an extreme case, the victims of Mrs Foot's oil merchants) are *in some way* intended effects. Steven Brock forcefully argues that "such results [even the marathoner's wearing down of his sneakers] must in some way fall within his intention."[19] Referring to the case raised by St Thomas Aquinas of a man who gets his feet wet when he goes to a muddy place, Brock observes: "what Aquinas means is that, although he does not intend simply to get his feet wet, this still falls under his intention."[20]

Eric D'Arcy is another Catholic author who attests to the utility of a "term such as Bentham's 'obliquely intended'," since "if a person does X knowing that Q will be produced by it, one can hardly describe Q simply as 'unintended'."[21] The term used in the Catholic tradition, *praeter intentionem*, simply covers too much. To make his point, he contrasts two cases in which an action is taken which is foreseen to be lethal to one man and lifesaving for several: in the first case a group of people throw a bomb soon to explode out of a window, beneath which stands an unsuspecting passerby, while the second case concerns the now famous party of pot-holers, equipped with dynamite, who are stuck in a cave behind their stout leader. The death in the first case is considered "obliquely intentional" and licit, while the second would be "directly intentional" and illicit.[22]

Not a few additional arguments that support the idea of "oblique intention" have been devised by contemporary moral philosophers. Roderick Chisholm, of Brown University, proposes a "principle of the diffusiveness of intention" whereby "if a rational man acts with the intention of bringing about a certain state of affairs p and if he believes that by bringing about p he will bring about the conjunctive state of affairs *p* and *q*, then he *does* act with the intention of bringing about the conjunctive state of affairs, *p* and *q*."[23] This does not mean, however, that the agent acts with the intention to bring about *q* alone.[24]

Jack Meiland, of the University of Michigan, proposes the terms "purposive" and "non-purposive" intention.[25] The latter would describe the wear on a crankshaft that someone foresees to result from an intentional drive in a car. He makes a second distinction in intention, between "conditional" and "non-conditional" intentions which gets at the same issue.[26] Here Meiland shows that our intentions often (or perhaps always) include conditions. These he describes as either "exclusive" (I intend to do X only if Y obtains; e.g. to play golf provided it doesn't rain) or "inclusive" (I intend to do X even if Y obtains; e.g. to return a borrowed sword, even if the owner is seeking revenge).[27] He notes that "the condition is in some way *part of what is intended or part of what the intention is about.*"[28]

Finally, John Searle, of the University of California, Berkeley, speaks of "unintentional action". While this terminology seems problematic, he is concerned with the same issue. The term refers to "an intentional action, whether successful or not, which has aspects which were not intended in it, i.e. were not presented as conditions of satisfaction of the intention in action."[29] Since every action has such aspects, we need a way of describing them: aspects which the agent does not aim at, but which are part of his action *qua* human act and for which he will be responsible.[30] In this context he asks the question that is of paramount interest, putting his finger on the *punctum dolens*: "How do we distinguish between those aspects of the complex event under which it is an unintentional action and those aspects which are so far from the intention that under them it is not an action?"[31] We will clarify his meaning by the example he provides: Oedipus intended [a] to marry Jocasta, but did not intend [b] to marry his mother or [c] "to move a lot of molecules, cause some neurophysiological changes in his brain and alter his spatial relationship to the North Pole."[32] An apparent distinction between [b] and [c] is at issue, a distinction unconnected with Oedipus's knowledge of facts. The point is that all would agree to call [c] effects "side-effects", even if they are foreseen, but we are not so ready to call [b] a mere side-effect if it is foreseen. Searle frankly admits, however: "I do not know of a clear criterion for distinguishing between those aspects of intentional actions under which they are unintentional actions and those aspects of intentional actions under which the event is not an action at all."[33] In the terms with which we are familiar, he is acknowledging his inability to distinguish clearly between obliquely intended and completely unintended effects.

Even the most ardent Benthamite admits that there is a difference between what we do on purpose and what we foresee as a byproduct of an action. Law has always recognized gradations in murder from "premeditated" to "manslaughter". Yet, the analytical tradition seems to warn against a distinction between the two that is as pat as that offered by Thomas Cavanaugh: "Foresight is an awareness of causal relations" (the [c] effects in Searle's example), while "intention is an agent's volitional commitment to effecting a good as planned"[34] ([a] marrying Jocasta). There seem to be too many sorts of "causal relations" and even other sorts of relations[35] to warrant being lumped together as "*praeter intentionem*". The matter is extremely delicate, of course. It seems that Elizabeth Anscombe evolved considerably on the point in the quarter century between writing *Intention* and her "Medalist's address" to the American Catholic Philosophic Association.[36] In the book, she gave a famous example of a man who pumped water to a house and who continued to do so, in order to gain his normal wage, even after learning that it had been poisoned by someone wishing to kill the inhabitants. While originally saying that she would agree with the man's claim not to intend their death,[37] she suggests a case in her Medalist's address which also presents a "side-effect" death. It is a variation on the pot-holer case where the opening of an escape path would certainly dislodge a rock crushing the leader's head. She comments: "it is at best a dubious business to say 'We don't intend that result'."[38]

Clearly, then, effort must be made to distinguish intentional actions which are as good as intended from those that are merely foreseen.[39] It may appear that the difference is not so important since all are agreed that foreseen consequences are morally relevant. It can be argued that we should not be afraid to call something an unintended consequence, as long as we maintain that the agent is responsible for it. However, there are at least two reasons to pursue our quest to see if there are not grounds to ascribe intentionality to some of these consequences. The first is that there must be some *reason* for claiming that the agent is responsible for the consequences he foresees. A notion of imputability divorced from intentionality is vague at best. Second, if negative consequences are held to be in no way intended, they will be permitted for a sufficient reason; if there is some intentionality, they may fall under absolute moral norms and be forbidden in all cases. This we recall is what is at stake in the question of cooperation with evil: discovering whether causing the foreseen consequence of facilitation contains some intentionality or not. Upon that depends its status as formal or material cooperation.

2. The notion of means

It bears emphasizing that there is a sort of will act, appropriately described by Duff as "paradigmatically intended", which everyone recognizes as an instance of the term "intention". This strong sense of intention implies that the agent is knowingly and willingly pursuing a goal. The attainment of this goal will count as a success for his project. He has a "pro-attitude" towards the object. From this point of view, desire appears as constitutive of intention.[40] The problem lies in assessing responsibility for various other consequences of our free choices, whether or not one wishes to extend the term "intention" to them.

For instance, there is the injury that may occur from risky behavior, such as playing "chicken" on a lonely stretch of road.[41] The agent chooses to play, intentionally, but does not intend to kill or maim himself. Still, such tragic outcomes are a long way from "unintended".

Negligent action is similarly problematic. Some authors will consider it "voluntary" if not "intentional" and therefore subject to praise and blame.[42] J. L. Austin demonstrated in regard to "voluntary" what we have observed in regard to "intentional"; namely, a comparison of the meaning of the term with the meaning of its grammatical opposite reveals how treacherous and unintuitive this territory is.[43] Eric D'Arcy argues that negligent omissions are not described naturally as "voluntary" in ordinary language and concludes that "what is required for moral blame is not the intention or the will or the desire to do what is wrong, but the ability not to do it."[44]

At the risk of complicating matters rather than clarifying them, several authors favor the use of the term "consent"[45] in contrast to intention. This term seems to cover what we have referred to as "oblique intention". As Annette Baier describes it: "The things I consent to are said to be those things I knowingly bring about by doing what I do intentionally."[46] Baier takes the notion from Chisholm who uses Bentham's scenario of an agent hunting with the King for stag. If "he acted with the intention of killing a stag and he had no other goal than that, but he knew that by killing the stag he would kill the King,"[47] would he intend the King's death as well? While admitting that it is "not clear", Chisholm comments that "it is tempting to say, however, that the death of the King was at least a *part* of what he intended."[48]

The debate can seem merely a matter of nomenclature: what does it matter if this member of the court is jailed for murderous carelessness or for a somehow intentional assassination? Perhaps for most legal theorists, no more is at stake. However, for those who maintain the existence of moral absolutes, the difference is critical.[49] If such an action is essentially not assassination, but merely foreseeing the death, then it could be permitted for certain reasons, graver, of course, than the desire to kill a deer.

In an effort to uncover the true nature of the situation, it is helpful to examine the notion of "means". Elizabeth Anscombe remarks that the idea that one can intend an end and not the means is "obvious bosh".[50] Doubtless, she is correct, but it is sometimes far from obvious what constitutes a means to an end. In the stag hunting case, the deadly arrow might pass through the King first, or through the stag first; would the King's death change from a means to a consequence as a result?

A helpful beginning to the analysis of what is meant by "means" was made by Nancy Davis. In her effort to evaluate the principle of double effect she noted: "Until the notions of means, ends, and intention are more carefully scrutinized, and their various strands untangled, their application to cases cannot yield verdicts that are authoritative."[51] In that same study she distinguished two main versions of the "means-end" relationship, which she describes as the agent-interpretation and the event-interpretation,[52] as well as two commonly used tests to confirm or deny the existence of a means-end relation: the conceptual connection and counterfactual analysis.[53] Let us begin with the agent-interpretation view.

Agent-interpretation of means

As we have already had occasion to mention, the agent-interpretation of intention, or of the means-end relation, is attractive because everybody will admit that what the agent aims at in order to attain some further goal is a means falling under his intention. What is at issue, however, is *what other features* of his action, if any, are also means in some sense. Still, it may be instructive to probe even the more common notion. Is it sufficient that the agent think or believe something to be necessary for the attainment of his goal, that it qualify as a means? The feasibility of the agent's proposal is certainly relevant to the applicability of the concept "intention". Baier notes that, if we are to intend something, "we must be able both to do it and not to do it."[54] What shall we say if someone propose to do something extremely difficult, such as, an amateur basketball player trying to sink a shot from half-court?[55] While the individual throws the ball at the basket intentionally and wishes that it go in, chance has much to do with it. The claim "I intended to sink that" might well be met with the retort "You just got lucky." Apparently, the degree of likelihood of success has something to do with distinguishing between our "reason for acting" and our intention. At least the agent's belief that success is possible seems necessary to genuine trying or intending. Similarly, an inveterate gambler might claim "providing for his family" as his reason for patronizing the casino, but a truer description of his action would be "squandering his money". If we suppose that the agent could and should know the true nature of what he is doing, and the implausibility of making a living at the gaming table, then his claim to intending that end becomes untenable. As many authors point out, a desire that is completely impossible, which no available means will attain, cannot be intended at all, but is classified as a "velleity".[56] So, one can desire, and have as a reason for action, objects which cannot properly be intended.

Contrariwise, the distinction between "reason for action" and intention can be used to show that one can intend what one does not desire. Glanville Williams first suggested the oft referenced case of an unscrupulous business man who wishes to destroy a plane so as to collect the insurance money on the cargo. Now, if this destruction of property requires the death of the pilot and perhaps others on board, shall we say that he has intended to kill them? Would the following description of a prosecuting attorney be accurate or misleading: "You willfully chose to kill an innocent young pilot and deprive his family of a father so as to satisfy your greed"? Is the death a means of some sort, and not merely a side-effect? R. A. Duff appears to answer affirmatively:

> One who intends to destroy a plane which will, he knows, be in mid-air and full of passengers at the time, surely intends not merely 'to destroy a plane', but to 'destroy a plane which is full of people'; our description of what he intends will include that circumstance, even if it is no part of his reason for action (if his aim is just to get the insurance money on the cargo).[57]

Yet according to Duff's distinction between "intend" and "acting intentionally", he usually identifies the agent-interpretation, the reason for acting, with "intend", although causing an effect intentionally may be morally and legally the same as intending it. This will depend, according to Duff, upon the judgment that third parties make regarding the suitability of the agent's "reason for action".

> Whether an agent *intends* to bring an effect about depends on *her* view of the relevance of that effect to her action; she acts with the intention of bringing it about only if it provides part of *her* reason for action. But whether we say that she *intentionally* brings about an expected side-effect of her action depends not on whether *she* thinks it is relevant to her action, but on whether *we* think it is something to which she should attend as a reason against acting thus; and we may disagree with her about this.[58]

The agent's interpretation of his action and of what counts as a means can, therefore, differ from the interpretation of other parties. We will have to return to Duff to see what might provide a legitimate basis for third parties to tell an agent what he actually is doing, intending, or choosing as means. While none of the writers we are considering use classic theological terminology, in the context of our study it is worth pointing out the similarity between this binomial (agent-view / third party-view) and the binomial, *finis operantis* / *finis operis*. Traditionally, there has been an end or goal which no one but the agent can identify with certainty (*finis operantis*), as well as an end which can be established objectively at least in theory (*finis operis*).[59]

   In the context of recent Anglo-Saxon moral philosophy, the agent-view is more akin to the category of "motive" (a word hardly used by St Thomas Aquinas).[60] Does not this term pick out the reason for acting that an agent has in mind? We can easily imagine that the investigators of the Glanville Williams air tragedy could establish the fact that a certain individual did willfully kill the pilot and passengers with a bomb, while remaining at a loss for the motive until they discovered that the accused was the owner of insured cargo. The eccentric nature of this example should not lead to the conclusion that such an assessment does violence to ordinary language. Many murders occur in conjunction with robberies in circumstances where the robber does everything possible to avoid the necessity of having to kill so as to steal. In the typical case, however, unlike Williams's scenario, the robbery and the killing are done in two separate acts.

This observation relates to the distinction that Elizabeth Anscombe made between motive and intention in her seminal work back in 1957. According to Anscombe, motive could be either "backward-looking" or "forward-looking", and only in the latter case would it be identified with intention. "If I kill a man as an act of revenge I may say I do it in order to be revenged, or that revenge is my object; but revenge is not some further thing obtained by killing him, it is rather that killing him is revenge. Asked why I killed him, I reply 'Because he killed my brother.'"[61] Soon after she adds, "I call a motive forward-looking if it is an intention." Similarly, blowing up the plane was not "some further thing" in the future, which required the killing of the pilot, but this murderous act just was "blowing up the plane" or "doing what was needed to secure the insurance money." It appears from the foregoing that the word "intention" is frequently restricted to a subset of motive that does not capture the whole of intentional action.

In the context of motive, D'Arcy returns to the idea of negligence. He wishes to maintain both that negligent acts are genuine voluntary actions and that they have no motive.[62] We would urge caution in claiming that there are voluntary actions that lack a motive, since it is easy to extend this to the claim that the negligence is unintended. The question of negligence is closely related to that of omissions, which allows us to recall what Gonzalez de Santalla argued four centuries earlier: there is no such thing as a "pure" omission.[63] Thus, the ship captain who lets the boat run aground because he was engrossed in a novel, makes a deliberate choice to pursue his literary whims at the risk of the integrity of the boat.[64] He is motivated by his desire to enjoy himself. The issue of negligence also leads D'Arcy to make a useful connection between motivation and explanation.[65] He shows that motive is one of various explanations for an action. In this light, perhaps, the ship captain's action could be explained in terms of a backward-looking motive. In answer to the question "Why did you let the ship run aground?" he might plausibly answer "Because I wanted to finish my book" (even though he had not adverted to the immediacy of the danger). Just as, in Anscombe's example, revenge was, under the circumstances, one and the same as killing a certain man, and not something else to be obtained by the killing, so also, enjoying the book was, under the circumstances, the same as letting the ship go aground, and not a future goal obtained by this event.

Therefore, only forward-looking motives, or intentions, involve means. Other kinds of acts may be intentional, however, even if they do not fit the means-end pattern. Anthony Kenny makes this point in connection with the concept of "choice." "Choice is concerned only with means and not with ends. This fits 'intention' but not 'intentional': acts done for their own sake are not done with any intention; but they are intentional *par excellence*."[66] Revenge would be a perfect example.[67]

Acts done for their own sake are also actions for which a motive is not expected. We might assume that all human acts, all moral acts, must have at least an implicit motive, something which moves the agent to act. However, D'Arcy makes yet another subtle but convincing distinction. For every human action there must indeed be a "reason for action"; but not every human action will have a motive.[68]

> We ask, or say, 'Why' only when there is or may be, a peculiar reason: something not built into the act-term: something therefore, 'ulterior' to it. Many of our regular act-terms already connote the reasons for making the arm- or leg-movements, or tongue-movements: compare, 'why is he planting potatoes?' with 'Why is he dropping those things into holes in the ground?'[69]

This observation is of great importance, for it reveals that the partisans of the agent-interpretation of "means-end" relations tend to forget that human action is naturally directed to an end.[70] It is not possible to drop those things into holes in the ground in order to please your mother, without also intending to plant potatoes. Even if the action concerns an activity that has nothing to do with nature, as planting does, the activity will have its own nature and teleology (cooking, watch-making, etc.); if it is undertaken for an ulterior reason, a motive will be demanded.

This brings us full circle to where this chapter began: the woman lying on her bed. If she were to answer "Resting" instead of "Lying on my bed", she would be giving a reason for lying on the bed, but not a motive, not an ulterior intention, not an item of information that is by nature knowable only to herself. The question is only asked because the questioner, apparently, just walked in.

If he were to wait a few minutes, it would become obvious whether this lying on a bed was resting or doing yoga or something else.[71] Nor would lying on a bed be a means to her end of resting, properly speaking. Motive, for D'Arcy, is not to be applied to "naturally or normally associated"[72] reasons for action, but to results that provide reasons for *this particular* agent to act. He writes:

> Most important, it is inappropriate to say that Q is a person's motive for doing X when Q is the natural *objective* or result of the action X: to say that an undergraduate is taking Schools in order to obtain a degree, or that a person shot a testator in order to kill him, or that the Government is creating work in a distressed area to provide jobs for the unemployed, is not to give the motives that prompted these actions...[73]

Now if a person detonates a bomb in an airplane which is in flight, the death of the people on board is a "naturally or normally associated" result of that action. It will remain to be seen whether or when a special motive (I just wanted to collect on the insurance) can cancel or outweigh this natural reason for acting, or, as Duff has put it,[74] this reason for not acting.

Two tests of means

We continue our search for a correct understanding of the notion of "means". In the chapters to come it will be of great importance to know if a given negative result of a choice is properly described as an effect, a means, an aspect, or the object chosen itself.

Returning to Nancy Davis, we consider the first of the means-end relations tests she offers, since it concerns the agent-interpretation. This is the logical or conceptual connection test. The idea here is that, if there is no necessary connection requiring that a putative means be connected to an intended end, then it will only be a means if the agent chooses it as such. Thus, in the case used by Davis as an illustration, the doctor who performs a craniotomy to save the mother's life would not, according to the conceptual connection test, necessarily have to intend the baby's death. It is conceivable, although not practically possible in the current state of medicine (so the argument goes) to narrow the baby's head sufficiently to remove him without killing him. "The survival of the fetus will be inconceivable," explains Davis, "just in case the woman cannot be saved unless the fetus dies, just in case the doctor cannot intelligibly be thought to be trying to save the woman if he is not regarded as trying to bring about the death of the fetus."[75] Davis easily demonstrates that this notion of means is entirely too restrictive. Indeed, she points out with some ingenuity that it is rather difficult to imagine a case where there really is a conceptual connection between a means and an end.[76] One might also seek an example of a means that is conceptually connected to an end in the Oedipus case that we have just considered. Suppose that Oedipus is planning to marry Jocasta, when he is apprised of her true identity. Now, no one in their right mind would say that he could go ahead with the marriage without intending to marry his mother. His desired end, "marry Jocasta", and the only way of accomplishing this, "marry mother", are logically connected. Since they are one and the same object, one can neither say that he would have to marry his mother (means) in order to marry Jocasta or that, if he married Jocasta, he would as a result have to marry his mother (consequence). In such an ideal case of "conceptual connection", we see that to marry Jocasta *just is* to marry his mother. Clearly, a claim to be "directing his intention", by insisting that he only intends to marry Jocasta, would convince no one.

Likewise, those who in some fashion propose a conceptual connection test of intended means, will freely admit that to intend an end *just is* to intend whatever is logically connected with it. However, the difficulty Davis notes in finding examples of logical connection stems from the fact that, as we saw with Oedipus, what is claimed as "means" and "ends" are really one and the same. No genuine means can be identified by this test. George Pitcher of Princeton University makes this point, for instance, in criticizing an example of the non-divisiveness principle given by Chisholm. Chisholm had claimed that, when one wills to drive off in a car belonging to someone else, one was bound to intend depriving the rightful owner of it. Observes Pitcher: "the (allegedly) two states of affairs—driving off in the car parked on the corner and driving off in the car that belongs to another man—are surely only one."[77] Here, it may be argued that one can intend this one state of affairs under the first description but not under the second. If one takes this route, one must explain how this "directing of intention" differs from that in the examples just given of Oedipus and craniotomy. Obviously, all will agree that you can deprive the rightful owner of his car for certain urgent reasons, even foreseeing that it will be impossible to return it in one piece; the problem is how properly to describe and justify such an action.

Another example of mistaking a conceptual connection for a "means-end" relationship can be found in an article applying the double effect to affirmative action. The author states that "to include members of one group entails that non-members are excluded, given both an oversupply of applicants and a limited number of openings." [78] In the opinion of the author, the bad effect, the exclusion of some, is "causally linked" with the intended effect, the promotion of others. He sees this as a violation of the third condition of the principle of double effect, namely, that the bad effect must not cause the good effect. From our point of view, the giving of a place to A rather than B *just is* depriving B of his place, not a logically distinct cause of his deprivation. We note, in passing, that several "classic" moral conundrums may resist solution because a "conceptual connection" is treated as a "means-end" relation. One thinks, for instance, of the choice to cut a rope holding a suspended climber in order to keep several from being pulled down. Also, there are the thankfully rare cases of conjoined twins, in which it may happen that the saving of one *just is* the killing of the other.

Let us now turn to the second sort of test for the evaluation of means: the counterfactual test. Duff admits that distinguishing between conceptual connection or entailment and consequences that are empirically certain is not always easy.[79] As a clear example of the former, he suggests that the hiding of a body logically entails preventing its burial. A hangover, however, while sure to follow from excessive drinking of whiskey is not logically entailed by it. As a more obscure example of logical entailment, he suggests firing upon a soldier to prevent his escape. The consequence of shooting him, causing him bodily harm, *just is* preventing his escape because only if he is hurt will his escape be stopped. In so arguing, Duff is using the counterfactual test, the second test of means-end relation brought up by Davis. If shooting the soldier did not (contrary to fact) injure him, the guard would not have bothered firing. Therefore, Duff argues, the guard must aim at injuring the soldier if he aims at stopping the escape, and the two are logically connected. We may do well to object to this conclusion. Under the circumstances, injuring the man may have been the only way to prevent his escape, but there appears to be a causal connection, not a logical one. The stopping of the escape is an effect of the injury to the legs, which seems like a genuine means to this end. The appropriate counterfactual would be rather: "If the guard could have stopped the soldier without hurting his legs, would he have?" Since the answer is presumably "yes", the counterfactual test would seem to show that he did not intend to hurt the soldier, a conclusion which Duff rightly finds unconvincing.

Clearly counterfactuals have some intuitive force and a long history of use. Francisco de Vitoria uses the method to defend Samson from the charge of suicide after pulling down the building upon himself. Contrary to Augustine, who felt that a special permission from God was needed to justify the action, de Vitoria writes: "He did not indeed kill himself intentionally, but he wanted to crush and kill the enemy, from which followed his own death. Indeed, he would have chosen willingly to kill the others preserving himself, if that had been possible."[80]

What in fact is the purpose served by a counterfactual test? In the soldier case, the counterfactual test seems to show the insufficiency of the agent-interpretation of means. Clearly the injury to the legs caused the escape to fail, and, furthermore, it was the only means that could. Yet, the supporter of the agent-interpretation of means would claim, that, if—*per impossibile*—the escape could have been foiled otherwise, the guard would have chosen it, and therefore should not be said to have intended the injury.

The Samson case differs in that the self-inflicted death did not cause the defeat of the enemy, whereas the injury to the soldier did impede his escape. Since Samson's death was not a means it would seem to be a pure side effect, as defined by Duff: "*pure* side-effects [are those] whose occurrence is *wholly* irrelevant to the success or failure of the action."[81] However, if the counterfactual test only tells us what is causally relevant to the agent's primary end, we might question whether it is really telling us anything useful at all.

James Sterba suggests an amended version of the counterfactual test[82] which asks: "Does the bringing about of the evil consequences help explain why the agent undertook the action as a means to the good consequences?" Still, it is difficult to see how this test gets at the issue of moral responsibility for consequences "of whose occurrence the agent is 'almost certain' or 'has no substantial doubt'."[83] As we have noted in various authors—from Duff to Searle to D'Arcy—these consequences seem sometimes to be "obliquely intended" and sometimes not. Even when the bad effect is not causally required for the production of the end sought by the agent, it can seem that we must admit that it is necessarily intended by the agent. This might be described as the "Portia argument". As much as Shylock maintains that he only seeks a pound of flesh, who would deny that he intends to kill Antonio? The taking of this quantity of flesh from a man's breast is, to use Foot's term, too "close" to the effect of his death,[84] to claim plausibly that one is intended and not the other. Shylock might have claimed, however, like the owner of the cargo in Williams's plane example,[85] that, if there had been another way of obtaining his end, he would have done it without causing death.

Eric D'Arcy proposes the notion of "cost", which might help sort things out. Speaking of side-effects, he notes, "in the language of accountancy, they are a realized but unwanted cost."[86] Unwanted cost seems to describe well, for instance, a situation Kenny proffers: "A man who rises in the night for a drink may know that he will wake the baby without intending to wake the baby."[87] There is no natural "cause-effect" relation between the baby's waking and the man satisfying his thirst, as there is in the case of the merchant saving his boat by throwing his cargo into the sea. In physical terms, the baby's waking is, on the contrary, an effect of getting the water. Yet, conceived as a "cost", this bad effect has something of the nature of a means: under the circumstances, he had to wake the baby in order to get the drink. Similarly, there is no natural connection between paying money and receiving a meal in a restaurant, but, in the circumstances of civil society, the payment (before or after eating) is the means to obtain such food.

The notion of cost does not imply that a simple utilitarian calculus will solve the ethical issues at stake. In the merchant case, he could not throw a passenger overboard, even to save twenty. Likewise, one wonders what goal, if any, the man getting up at night might legitimately pursue, if, instead of waking the baby, it would cause the baby's death. What criterion would make that result *praeter intentionem* in the requisite sense? To pursue the answer, we must look more deeply into what Davis called the "event-interpretation" of the means-end relationship.

Event-interpretation of means

In essence, Nancy Davis's concept of "event-interpretation" is yet another way of packaging Bentham's idea of "oblique intention". There are foreseeable consequences that are not directly aimed at which are in some manner intended by the agent. Davis's example concerns Harold's killing of Jane, who happens to be the fastest runner in town.[88] This fact may be irrelevant to his end (say, gaining an inheritance), but, we are still loathe to abandon entirely "the belief that the means-end relation is a species of

causal relation, and one that is—on a plausible interpretation of event-causation—extensional. If my doing *a* realizes *b* and *b* is also describable as *c*, then my doing *a*
realizes *c*."[89] If Harold knows that Jane is the fastest runner
in town, then we can hardly deny he intends to kill the
fastest runner in town. To this extent, this is territory we
have covered before, in reference to Oedipus and Jocasta.
However, Davis understands the "event-interpretation" of
the means-end relation in a broad, consequentialist sense.
That is, she maintains that from this perspective a hysterectomy that results in the death of the fetus will be
indistinguishable from a craniotomy that results in the
death of the fetus. Since the agent-interpretation would
appear to allow both operations and the event-interpretation forbid both, she concludes that the supporters of
double-effect reasoning, who generally agree that their
principle should distinguish between these cases, are in
trouble. We believe that Davis has now erred. She has not
adequately examined what "*b* is describable as *c*" should
mean. When is an explicitly intended end [b] accurately
described, in a moral sense, as another somehow intended
end [c]? When is it correct to say "causing *b*" *just is*
"causing *c*"? We have seen that this is easy when *b* logically
entails *c*, but what are we to say when they are causally
connected or perhaps connected in some other manner?[90]
As Anscombe pointed out in the context of her example
of the water pumper, "the mark of practical reasoning is
that the thing wanted is *at a distance* from the immediate
action, and the immediate action is calculated as the way
of getting or doing or securing the thing wanted."[91] We
have noted that some kind of assurance or likelihood that
doing *a* will effect *b* is required to claim that *b* is intended;
likewise, some kind of inevitability or probability that
doing *a* will also bring about *c* seems to require us to say

that it is as equally intended as *b*. Note that the phrase "some kind" is meant to allow for some other kind of certainly foreseen effects to remain unintended.

The use of the term "describable" by Davis remands us to Anscombe's celebrated discussion of moral descriptions of actions.[92] In fact, some authors use the title "Anscombe thesis" to refer to her claim that, for instance, working the pump, sending water, and poisoning the inhabitants is but one act under various descriptions. Donald Davidson, who accepts this thesis, applies it to the case of a prowler. He argues that "flipping a switch", "turning on the light", "illuminating the room", and "alerting a prowler" are four descriptions of the selfsame act. Our question is whether "alerting the prowler" is a moral description of the act in question. When the homeowner decided to flip the switch (knowing, of course, that it would also scare the prowler), was it a correct moral description of his act to say "you *just are* alerting a prowler"? Or could he have cogently replied: "I am not, although I foresee that he will be alerted when I illuminate the house"?

R. A. Duff, as was indicated earlier, is not satisfied with allowing the agent to determine completely the adequate moral description of his act by identifying his personal goal. Nor, however, will he say that all foreseeable consequences are intended. Duff tries to distinguish those consequences which must be considered in a moral description of the act by appealing to societal expectations.

> A crucial role in determining the logical and moral constraints on such descriptions [of a man's intentional action] is played by the moral perspectives within which the actions are both described and assessed: these determine the duties which we have with regard to our own lives and those of others, and thus the aspects of our actions, insofar as they affect these lives, to which we have a duty to attend

and of which we are accordingly held to be the intentional agents.[93]

He adduces several examples from actual legal cases in which the only apparent explanation for the court's decision appears to hinge upon the expectations of society.[94] In this manner, Duff explains when a person is liable for an omission: "Whether I am *morally* responsible for her death (whether I 'let her die', or 'fail to save her') depends on the scope of our moral responsibilities towards others..."[95] Duff's solution is certainly appealing in its simplicity. Nonetheless, it seems merely to balance the subjective view of the agent with that of the community. Ultimately, it seems to lead to a negative answer to Anscombe's question: "Let us ask: is there any description which is *the* description of an intentional action, given that an intentional action occurs?"[96]

The search for *the* moral description of a given act that both agent and observer should agree upon seems to require distinguishing the act from the circumstances in which it is performed. The "circumstance" that Davidson's light switch was connected to a working bulb is hardly unexpected. Thus when he flipped the switch, the natural consequence of illuminating the room, followed so "closely" that one could hardly intend the first but not the second. Now the presence of a prowler was certainly unusual, but given his presence, alerting him naturally followed flipping the switch. Does this circumstance enter into the act description? D'Arcy, in contrast to Bentham,[97] avers that distinguishing act and circumstance admits no easy solution: "I would suggest, there is no general, rigorous distinction to be drawn between 'act' and 'circumstance'."[98] The mature Anscombe seems to argue that the act description will only be found by analyzing the concretely given situation: "Circumstances, and the immediate facts about the means you are choosing to your ends, dictate what descriptions of your intention you must admit. *Nota bene* that here 'intention' relates to the intentionalness of the action you are performing as a means."[99]

3. The search for a basic act

Let us pause for a short review before proceeding. We have seen that an intentional action is either done for its own sake or for the sake of some consequence "at a distance". In this latter case, the action performed has the character of a means to an end. The consequence at which the agent aims is the content of his intention with which he performs the action. The difficulty consists in distinguishing clearly this consequence from the action itself. This is important, for there will be other consequences of the action per-formed which must likewise be distinguished from the action if they are not to fall within the "intentionalness of the action you are performing as a means", in the words of Anscombe just quoted. This action, isolated both from unintended side-effects and intended consequences, needs to be described morally. It is a description that Anscombe says the agent "must admit" as "dictated" to him by the concrete situation.

The action, so conceived, can be called "basic". Now many authors are eager to find a kind of action that is somehow basic. As D'Arcy points out at the beginning of *Human Acts*, the extreme positions on this matter have well known proponents. On the one hand, there is the view, argued for by J. J. C. Smart, that the ultimate consequence of an act can be considered as basic as the act itself.[100] A sheriff who saved four lives by executing an innocent man could say, according to Smart, that, in so acting, he "just was" saving lives. On the opposite extreme, D'Arcy points to John Austin's view that an action properly stops at the muscular movements of the agent. All else must be considered consequences. Donald Davidson supports such a view: "Our primitive actions ... mere movements of the body—these are all the actions there are. We never do more than move our bodies; the rest is up to nature."[101] It may seem that the term "basic action", originally coined by Arthur Danto as part of a rather ingenious argument,[102] implies such a physicalist view of basic acts. For him, the concept is necessary to avoid an infinite regress:

> That is, if there are any actions at all, there must be two distinct *kinds* of actions: Those performed by an individual *M*, which he may be said to have *caused* to happen; and those actions, also performed by *M*, which he cannot be said to have caused to happen. The latter I shall designate as *basic actions.*[103]

Julia Annas, in the process of trying to deflate the usefulness of any concept of basic action, admits its intuitive appeal. She describes it in terms of "by-locutions": "a non-basic action of agent *A* is an action *A* performs *by* performing some other action; a basic action of *A* is an action *A* does *not* perform *by* performing some other action."[104] She argues convincingly against the Davidsonian view that a bodily movement could serve as a basic action. She seems less successful in examining basic action as an interior act or volition. Only in this perspective, however, so uncomfortable to modern thinkers, can an agent originate an action without any apparent prior cause (excluding divine agency). Danto tries to avoid admitting internal causes of our exterior actions: "That there are actions, like moving an arm, which do not really require any other action as cause (and so no 'inner' action as a cause) entails, I believe, no refutation of dualism."[105] He maintains that it makes no sense to say that one "try" to perform a basic action.[106] John Searle, for his part, can only see "basic action" applying to any action that an agent can intend without intending something else first, as when a good skier turns left without thinking how he does it.[107] Yet he holds that "all actions consist of an Intentional component and a 'physical' (or other sort of) Intentional object component."[108] This seems to mean that even the action (turning left) undertaken for some further end (to get to the bottom of the hill) contains an intentional component (to go left), which would tend to an infinite regress. In any case, as Annas had warned, it does not seem to help us understand human agency any better.

In this light, Danto's notion of "acts that M cannot be said to have caused to happen" might be usefully amended. Annette Baier leads us to focus not on acts that cannot be said to have been caused, but that cannot be said to have been caused *in significantly different ways*. When we ask someone what he is doing, we seek a description "in terms of activities we understand, activities where we don't need to be told how he will do them, because we know how they are done."[109] We recall that the answer "lying on my bed" is indeed more basic than "resting" in some sense, but it does not qualify as a "basic action" description. We know how "resting" is done, namely "by lying on a bed" or by some morally indistinguishable physical process.[110] Thus, Baier claims to have identified a "vital" distinction "between things I can intend to do somehow, and the things I must intend to do as they are done."[111]

This suggestion of ignoring the physical movements that make up a "basic action" agrees entirely with trenchant observations made by Anscombe and D'Arcy. Anscombe points out that certain act descriptions can be "swallowed up" by others, or in D'Arcy's terminology "elided".[112] When certain act descriptions are not elided, the result can be misleading. If I say that "I flipped the switch" instead of "I turned on the light," my interlocutor might wonder if the light worked. Or, perhaps, the two can be used interchangeably, when the normal consequence of switch flipping is taken for granted. Anscombe gets at the same point with the example of making tea. Someone who is boiling water can answer the question "What are you doing?" with "Making tea" (indeed, the answer "Boiling water" would only make sense in a special context, such as a class on tea-making). "But the less normal it would be to take the achievement of the objective as a matter of course, the more the objective gets expressed only by 'in order to'. E.g. 'I am going to London in order to make my uncle change his will'; not 'I am making my uncle change his will'."[113] In another essay, Anscombe dubs the physical elements of an act that determine or "dictate" the basic action description "brute facts".[114]

Here it may be useful to mention a distinction in "by-locutions" brought up by Jonathan Bennett.[115] He distinguishes a "time-spanning" variety ("She doused the fire by throwing water on it") from "synchronous" ("By losing his temper, he fulfilled her prediction"). This latter sort of by-locution seems to correspond to Anscombe's backward-looking motives: by killing the man, he took revenge. We would suspect common language of imprecision if "in order to" were to be used in place of "synchronous" by-locutions, whereas "she threw water on the fire in order to douse it" makes perfect sense. We wish to know "how" she extinguished the fire, what basic action she performed as a means. Synchronous by-locutions can answer the question "how" and provide useful information, but they would not be providing "basic moral action" descriptions. "She made tea by boiling water, scooping in tea leaves, pouring in the water and letting it steep" tells you how tea is made, but these more elementary descriptions are not basic act descriptions in the given context. That is just how tea is usually made. In this light, making tea would not be a consequence of those actions so much as a simpler way of describing the process.

Duff attempts to solve the question of basic action[116] by denying, as he did in the matter of intention, the possibility of an objective answer. Actions are not "objectively individuated, in advance of our descriptions of them" he argues. "Which of [the] possible descriptions we offer depends not on some objective truth about what 'the action' really is (since there is no such truth), but on our own interests..."[117] This is a hasty and unfortunate abandonment of the search for objective structures to which ordinary language bears witness. D'Arcy shows clearly that at a certain point in the "accordion"[118] of act descriptions we can no longer continue the eliding process. Macbeth cannot simply describe his stabbing Duncan as "succeeding to the throne",[119] and this is surely not just because society has an "interest" in preventing murder.

Anscombe draws our attention to another distinction in act descriptions that demands inclusion in a comprehensive theory of action. Some action verbs can only be "intentional" while others can be performed either "intentionally" or not.[120] One cannot drive a car unintentionally, but one can drive it too fast unintentionally. One cannot punch someone in the nose unintentionally, but one can offend him some other way and beg that excuse. Certain act descriptions seem to be so basic that the agent, in undertaking them, must intend them. Other descriptions include an ascription of moral intent (to drive faster than allowed, to breach expected rules of respect) which the agent may have grounds to deny.

We can agree with Duff that there is a point at which analyzing intentional action will cause us to lose sight of the intention in question. "What I see is an intentional action ... Person and actions, that is, are logically basic categories; these concepts cannot be explained by an analysis which seeks to reduce them to supposedly simpler elements."[121] Let us place this comment in the context of the tripartite division of intention made by Hart: (1) bare intentions (2) intentional actions, and (3) further intentions.[122] Before the agent decides by what means to pursue his end (when he has but a "bare intention") an outside observer cannot identify his intention. Likewise, if he has particular motives ("further intentions") for performing an act, they also will be hidden in a private domain. However, there is an intention which is incarnated in the action, and for which the observer, in grasping the nature of the act, can ascribe responsibility to the agent choosing that act. In this sense, "What I see is an intentional action."

Has this attempt to identify a "basic moral act" or an objective moral act description brought us closer to our goal of distinguishing between consequences which are necessarily intended and those which are not? It can certainly seem that among the welter of positions and arguments there is fairly little consensus. We believe, however, that the British analytic tradition provides strong reasons to look beyond the agent's own goal to discover "what he is doing." Also, it leads us to believe that an objective judgment on the nature of an agent's action has some grounding other than the interests of the observer. Imagine a variation on the pot-holer example. Suppose the group had the option of pulling the leader out of the hole by the legs but were virtually certain that this rough treatment would result in his death by heart attack. As difficult as it may be to pinpoint, there is clearly a distinct structure to this act, in comparison to the other pot-holer cases, even though the goals of the group and the resulting states of affairs are the same as if dynamite had been used. The group causes the leader's death in the sense that he would have survived if they had not treated him roughly, but we are inclined to say that the man's weak heart was "responsible" for his death in an important sense.[123] In explaining the untoward consequences of an action, we may find, after correctly delimiting the primary agent's basic action, that other factors explain the bad effect. When a policeman kills a bystander while pursuing a criminal, we would usually blame that death on the criminal, not the policeman.[124] Duff provides the excellent example of a professor who gives a student a bad grade, foreseeing that this will harm the young man's career. Nonetheless, the responsibility for this consequence should be on the student not the professor.[125] It appears, then, that the search for a basic action needs to be complemented by a consideration of the natural tendency of an action to its effects, that is to say, a consideration of its metaphysical structure. Only then can one hope to determine the responsibility for those consequences which result from circumstances or the actions of others intersecting with the basic action to produce consequences not willed for their own sake by the agent. An exploration of causality will be required, as Joseph Pilsner indicates in his work on the specification of acts in St Thomas Aquinas:

> An essential relation [between actions] occurs where one end is necessary for the achievement of another; an accidental relation occurs when a proximate end creates some condition or removes some impediment which can permit the remote end to be pursued.[126]

The absolution of an agent, who wants to deny responsibility for a foreseen effect of his action, will depend then not only on the probity of his personal objective but on an analysis of the entire situation from a metaphysical point of view.

Notes

1   Steven Brock gives much more attention to British analytic philosophers than most Catholic authors, although his study "in no way pretends to be a 'dialogue' between Thomism and analytical philosophy, whatever such a thing would or ought to be." S. Brock, *Action and Conduct* (Edinburgh: T&T Clark, 1998), 2. John Haldane stands out as one who does promote such a dialogue with, for example, the book which he edited, *Mind, Metaphysics and Value in the Thomistic and Analytic Traditions* (Notre Dame, IN: University of Notre Dame Press, 2002).

2   "In the broad meaning of 'naturalism' most of the ethics that has been developed by Roman Catholic thinkers in recent times is 'naturalistic'. That is to say, they do feel that one may derive an 'ought' from an 'is'." V. J. Bourke, *History of Ethics* (Garden City, NY: Doubleday, 1968), p. 272.

3   Not all agree; Bourke quotes Jacques Maritain as saying of analytic philosophy, "Je la tiens pour absurde." *Ibid.*, p. 280.

4   Any effort to order our presentation categorically will be imperfect. Some of the representatives of "secular" thought are, of course, good Christians or Catholics such as Elizabeth Anscombe. Eric D'Arcy was the Catholic Archbishop of Hobart, Australia, but he argues very much in the tradition of British analytic thought which he studied at Oxford. As is well-known, Anthony Kenny, while currently an agnostic, was ordained a Roman Catholic priest after studies in Rome.

5   G. E. M. Anscombe, *Intention* (Oxford: Blackwell, 1963), p. 35.

6   *Ibid.*, p. 9.

7   H. L. A. Hart, "Problems in Philosophy of Law," in *Encyclopedia of Philosophy*, ed. P. Edwards, VI, pp. 267–8 (New York: Macmillan, 1967), p. 268.

8   "I think it plausible to suggest that *this* move on the part of

Sidgwick [denying *any* distinction between foreseen and intended consequences, as far as responsibility is concerned] explains the difference between old-fashioned Utilitarianism and that *consequentialism*, as I name it, which marks him and every English academic moral philosopher since him." G. E. M. Anscombe, "Modern Moral Philosophy," *Philosophy* 33 (1958), pp. 1–19, at p. 12.

[9] A. Kenny, "History of Intention in Ethics," in *The Anatomy of the Soul: Historical Essays on the Philosophy of Mind* (Oxford: Blackwell, 1973), p. 145.

[10] Anscombe, *Intention*, p. 88.

[11] *Ibid.*, p. 89. One recalls the hesitation that Aristotle manifested before "actions done through fear of a worse alternative" concluding "it is open to question whether such actions are voluntary or involuntary." Aristotle, *Nichomachean Ethics*, III, i, 2, tr. H. Rackham (Cambridge, MA: Harvard University Press, 1982), XIX, 117.

[12] J. C. Smith, "Comment on *Gillick*," *Criminal Law Review*, 1986, 114, cited by R. A. Duff, *Intention, Agency and Criminal Liability* (Oxford: Blackwell, 1990), p. 62.

[13] Duff, *Intention Agency*, p. 81.

[14] *Ibid.*, p. 78.

[15] P. Foot, "The Problem of Abortion and the Doctrine of the Double Effect," in *The Doctrine of Double Effect: Philosophers Debate a Controversial Moral Principle*, ed. P. A. Woodward, pp. 143–155 (Notre Dame, IN: University of Notre Dame Press, 2001), p. 146.

[16] G. E. M. Anscombe, "War and Murder," in Woodward, *Doctrine of Double Effect*, pp. 247–260, at p. 251.

[17] S. Theron, "Two criticisms of Double Effect," *New Scholasticism* 58 (1984), pp. 67–83 at p. 80. "[Foot's] conception of intention is to a large extent responsible for these illicit conclusions. Our suspicions are raised at once by her adoption of Bentham's tendentious (oblique?) terminology and speaking of 'oblique intentions' for foreseen but undesired consequences of actions, even calling them 'indirect intentions'."

[18] "According to the principle of double effect, the agent is sometimes morally responsible for unintended foreseeable effects. This is made clear by the last criterion [of proportionality]." G. Beabout "Morphine Use for Terminal Cancer Patients: An Application of the Principle of Double Effect," in Woodward, *Doctrine of Double Effect*, pp. 298–311, at p. 305.

[19]   Brock, *Action and Conduct*, p. 213.

[20]   *Ibid.*, p. 209, commenting on II *Phys.* lect. viii, § 215.

[21]   E. D'Arcy, *Human Acts: An essay in their Moral Evaluation* (Oxford: Clarendon Press, 1963), p. 171.

[22]   *Ibid.*, p. 172. Woodward, while apparently agreeing with D'Arcy in this matter, uses a terminology that may be simpler and clearer. Reminding us of Duff, Woodward considers "intentional" what D'Arcy calls "obliquely intended" and simply calls "intended" what for D'Arcy is "directly intentional." See P. A. Woodward, "Nancy Davis and the Means-End Relation: toward a defense of the doctrine of double effect," *American Catholic Philosophical Quarterly* 77 (2003), pp. 437–457, at p. 455 and p. 457. Philippa Foot brought up the case of the pot-holers as well expecting, like D'Arcy, that defenders of the double effect would see that the dynamiting of the stout leader could not be justified, as if his death were purely unintentional. "Problem of Abortion and the Doctrine of the Double Effect," in Woodward, *Doctrine of Double Effect*, pp. 143–155, at pp. 145–146. This is not obvious to all, however, as we shall see in Chapter 8 (for example p. 244).

[23]   R. M. Chisholm, "Structure of Intention," *Journal of Philosophy* 67 (1970), pp. 633–647, at p. 636.

[24]   This, the so-called "principle of nondivisiveness of intention," prevents the absurdity of claiming that someone who intends to visit Paris (p) when General de Gaulle is there (q) is acting with the intention of bringing it about that de Gaulle be in Paris (q). Cf. Chisholm, "Structure of Intention," p. 636.

[25]   J. Meiland, *The Nature of Intention* (London: Methuen, 1970), p. 7. This apparently self-contradictory term and the one like it used by Searle ("unintentional action") should not make us think that the concept they are trying to describe is nonsensical. The problem that we are wrestling with concerns actions (or aspects of actions) that are neither clearly intended nor unintended, but are somehow mixed. The felicity of the term is not so important.

[26]   *Ibid.*, p. 15.

[27]   Cf. *Ibid.*, p. 31.

[28]   *Ibid.*, p. 17.

[29]   J. Searle, *Intentionality: an essay in the philosophy of mind* (Cambridge: Cambridge University Press, 1983), p. 108. What Searle considers "unintentional actions" are still human acts, in classic terms, while mere "acts of man" he considers "not an action at all."

30   For Searle, contrary to the position we sustain, intention is a much more restrictive category than responsibility. He says that it would be "a mistake to suppose there is some close connection, perhaps even identity between intention and responsibility." *Ibid.*, p. 103.

31   *Ibid.*, p. 102.

32   *Ibid.*, p. 102.

33   *Ibid.*, p. 102.

34   T. Cavanaugh, *Double-Effect Reasoning: Doing Good and Avoiding Evil* (New York: Oxford University Press, 2006), pp. 95–96.

35   Cf. A. Baier, "Act and Intent," *Journal of Philosophy* 67 (1970), pp. 648–658, at p. 649.

36   Her "Medalist's address" is entitled "Action, Intention, and 'Double Effect,'" in Woodward, *Doctrine of Double Effect*, pp. 50–66. Also noting this change in Anscombe's thinking is John Finnis in "Intention and side-effects," in *Liability and Responsibility: essays in law and morals*, ed. R. Frey and C. Morris, pp. 32–64 (Cambridge: Cambridge University Press, 1991), at p. 58.

37   "In that case, although he knows concerning an intentional act of his—for it, namely, replenishing the house water supply, is intentional by our criteria—that it is *also* an act of replenishing the house water supply with *poisoned* water, it would be incorrect, by our criteria, to say that his act of replenishing the house water supply with poisoned water was intentional. And I do not doubt the correctness of the conclusion…" Anscombe, *Intention*, p. 42.

38   Anscombe, "Medalist's address," pp. 62–63.

39   Jean Porter suggests yet another case which demonstrates, in her view, that this sort of "side-effect" must be considered intentional. "If the actor [who ordinarily fired a gun with blanks] knew that her gun was loaded with live ammunition [by someone else], her act would be an intentional act of murder, even if it had been the case that she did not especially *want* to bring about the death of her unfortunate colleague. (She may just have said to herself, 'Well, this is hard luck for Fred, but the show must go on')." J. Porter, "The Moral Act in *Veritatis Splendor* and Aquinas's *Summa Theologiae*: A Comparative Analysis," in *The Historical Development of Fundamental Moral Theology in the United States*, ed. C. Curran and R. McCormick, pp. 219–241. Readings in Moral Theology, vol. 11 (New York: Paulist Press, 1999), at p. 232.

40   John Finnis observes that "[legal thinkers of the mid-twentieth century] almost unanimously … adopted *desire* as the middle or fundamental term of their explanation of intention." Finnis,

"Intention and side-effects," p. 34.

41 Cf. D'Arcy, *Human Acts*, p. 96.

42 Kenny, "History of Intention in Ethics," p. 134.

43 J. L. Austin, "A Plea for Excuses," in *The Philosophy of Action*, ed. A. White, pp. 19–42, (London: Oxford University Press, 1968), at pp. 31–32.

44 D'Arcy, *Human Acts*, p. 103.

45 Cf. Duff, *Intention Agency*, pp. 74–76.

46 Baier, "Act and Intent," p. 651. Note, however, that consent can cover much more than intention. "The objects of my intending are my doings, but the objects of my consenting, what I consent to, are states of affairs, including your doings and our doings" (p. 652).

47 Chisholm, "Structure of Intention," p. 634.

48 *Ibid.*, p. 640. Baier agrees: "In the case of the king-and-stag-killer, the agent did have the King's life in his hands, he could intend his death, and, I would say did intend it" (Baier, "Act and Intent," p. 658).

49 As Nancy Davis puts it: "For the deontologist who holds that there are limits on what agents may do to one another that function as constraints on the agents' pursuit of the optimal outcome, it is essential to distinguish the things that agents are said to *do* from the things that agents merely cause, or allow to happen, or fail to prevent." N. Davis, "The Doctrine of Double Effect: Problems of Interpretation," in Woodward, *Doctrine of Double Effect*, pp. 119–142, at p. 120.

50 Anscombe, *Intention*, p. 42.

51 Davis, "Problems of Interpretation," p. 138.

52 Cf. *Ibid.*, pp. 129–130.

53 Cf. *Ibid.*, p. 126 and p. 133, respectively.

54 Baier, "Act and Intent," p. 657.

55 The example is not terribly original, as Christopher Kutz also alludes to an author who speaks of free throws. Kutz, *Complicity*, p. 277.

56 For example, J. de Finance, *Essai sur l'agir humain* (Rome: Culture et Vérité, 1997), p. 35: "I can desire that which I know to be in no way in my power: for example not to die, to regain lost time, etc. But, whether I realize it or not, I am incapable of truly *willing* it."

57 Duff, *Intention Agency*, p. 89.

58 Duff, *Intention Agency*, p. 84.

[59] We add "at least in theory" because circumstances may be imagined which hinder the observation of what the agent is really doing, especially if the agent is attempting to mislead onlookers.

[60] "'Motive' is used infrequently by Aquinas, and when it does appear, it is often irrelevant to ethical concerns." J. Pilsner, *Specification of Human Acts in St Thomas Aquinas* (Oxford: Oxford Theological Monographs, 2006), p. 199.

[61] Anscombe, *Intention*, p. 20. Anthony Kenny makes a helpful comment: "Something familiar in recent philosophy [is the idea] that what appears under one description as a means may appear under another description as an end; as the killing of an enemy may be done *for* revenge and yet be itself the revenge." A. Kenny, "Happiness," in *Moral Concepts*, ed. J. Feinberg, pp. 43–52 (London: Oxford University Press, 1969), at p. 51.

[62] "Now for one thing, we have found that many acts done through negligence are done without the person's deciding to do them; but they are his acts, and he is held responsible and blamed for them. It is true that they are not done for a motive..." D'Arcy, *Human Acts*, p. 132.

[63] The interesting example, in which Gonzalez reveals his sensitivity to the issue of implicit intentionality, relates to the impeccability of Christ. The third tome of his *Selectarum disputationum* begins with the question "Whether a sinful pure omission is possible" (An sit possibilis pura omissio peccaminosa?). T. Gonzalez de Santalla, *Selectarum disputationum ex universa theologia scholastica*, (Salamanca: apud Lucam Perez, 1680–1686), tom. III, disp. I, sect. I, n.1. All sides agree that the issue is mainly of academic interest, as, in practice, one nearly always omits an act that one is obliged to perform for the sake of doing something else. Nonetheless, Cajetan adopted the position that it is theoretically possible to omit a prescribed act, such as attending Holy Mass, without fault, as long as one does not make a positive choice to do something incompatible with it, such as hunting (Cajetan, *Commentary* on *ST* I, q. 63, a. 5. cited by Gonzalez). Cajetan saw this position as necessary for maintaining Christ's freedom and impeccability; Our Lord would not have sinned by not saving us, even though this was His Father's will. In Gonzalez's refusal to accept Cajetan's solution to the Christological problem, we can discern his care to protect the truth of human action, specifically, the implicit intention present in concrete choices. One would not omit a prescribed act but for a reason, Gonzalez argues, "moved by a desired good". "Si

quis omittit rem praeceptam motus a bono delectabili, hoc ipso per ipsum exercitium omittendi respicit bonum illud, ut finem, illudque amat ... non omittit pure rem praeceptam, sed potius mediante actu respiciente intrinsecem illum finem." Gonzalez, *Selectarum disputationum*, tom. III, disp. I., sec. 2., n. 8. Even if one does not positively choose to pursue this good, the act of omitting the duty required is only accomplished by means of the desiring of some other good as an end.

64   St Thomas uses this example (*ST* I–II, q. 6, a. 3) as an example of indirect voluntary. He is showing that there can be voluntariness without any act, even any interior act, as regards the omission, but not as regards whatever other activity the agent chooses to perform.

65   D'Arcy, *Human Acts*, pp. 135–136.

66   Kenny, "History of Intention in Ethics," p. 134.

67   Other examples would seem to be acts where the *finis operis* and *finis operantis* appear simultaneous (such as "Giving alms in order to help the poor"). These are what Stephen Long will call "simple acts". S. A. Long, *The Teleological Grammar of the Moral Act* (Naples, FL: Ave Maria University, 2007), pp. 26–31.

68   D'Arcy, *Human Acts*, pp. 139–141.

69   *Ibid.*, p. 141.

70   In P. A. Woodward's analysis of Davis's article, he seems to treat, as in his example of a pool tournament, all ends as equally set by the agent (cf. "Nancy Davis," p. 448). This would seem to explain why, in his conclusion, he is unable to explain satisfactorily what is the significant difference between the two cases (hysterectomy vs. craniotomy), even though he suspects that the difference could be appropriately described as "intentionally" causing death in the latter case but not the former (p. 457).

71   As mentioned earlier (note 59), the possibility of deception does not affect the truth that actions have an objective meaning. Analogously, the possibility of mirages does not change the fact that an oasis either is or is not present.

72   D'Arcy, *Human Acts*, p. 142.

73   *Ibid.*, p. 142.

74   Duff, *Intention Agency*, p. 84 (see quotation at note 58).

75   Davis, "Doctrine of Double Effect," p. 126.

76   She suggests, for example, that a person wishes to inherit a kingdom and wishes to do so with an eccentric respect for the laws of the kingdom, necessitating the death of the present king.

Otherwise, in the case of a typical usurper, a kidnapping made to look like death could, conceivably, have attained the same results. Cf. *Ibid.*, p. 127.

77 G. Pitcher, "'In Intending' and Side Effects," *Journal of Philosophy* (1970), pp. 659–668, at p. 665.

78 J. Jordan, "The Doctrine of Double Effect and Affirmative Action," in Woodward, *Doctrine of Double Effect*, pp. 234–238, at p. 237.

79 Duff, *Intention Agency*, p. 90.

80 "Non enim interfecit se ex intentione, sed voluit hostes opprimere et interficere, ad quod secuta est mors ipsius. Ipse enim bene optasset alios perdere se salvo, si fieri potuisset." F. de Vitoria, *Relecciones teologicas*, in *Obras*, vol. 198 (Madrid: La Editorial Catolica, 1960), pp. 1129–1130.

81 Duff, *Intention Agency*, pp. 97–98.

82 J. Sterba, "Reconciling Pacifists and Just War Theorists," *Social Theory and Practice* 18 (1992), pp. 21–37, at p. 26, cited by Cavanaugh, *Doing Good*, p. 89.

83 Duff, *Intention Agency*, p. 27.

84 Foot, "Problem of Abortion," p. 146.

85 Duff says of this case: "Even if their deaths form no part of his reason for action, he surely intends not just to destroy the plane, or to destroy a plane which is full of people, but to *kill* the passengers: but the connection between the intended explosion and their deaths is surely empirical, not logical … he cannot claim that his action is aimed at the plane *as distinct from* its passengers; the destruction which he intends encompasses them all." Duff, *Intention Agency*, p. 91.

86 D'Arcy, *Human Acts*, p. 173.

87 Kenny, "History of Intention in Ethics," p. 146.

88 Davis, "Doctrine of Double Effect," p. 129.

89 *Ibid.*, p. 129.

90 Annette Baier maintains that many actions do not seem to fit a Humeian cause-effect pattern (for a similar comment see Luke Gormally's view in note 83, p. 256). "In this case [examining a definition to test the adequacy of its assumptions], and in many others, such as handing over money to pay my debts, raising my hand to salute, arguing to prove something, what we rely on to achieve our ends are not just causal laws but other sorts of connection" for sometimes "conventions, not causal laws, connect our means with our ends" (Baier, "Act and Intent," p. 649).

[91] Anscombe, *Intention*, p. 78.

[92] Cf. G. E. M. Anscombe, "Under a Description," *Nous* 13 (1979), pp. 219–233.

[93] R. A. Duff, "Absolute Principles and Double Effect," *Analysis* 36 (1976), pp. 68–80, at p. 79.

[94] Cf. Duff, *Intention Agency*, pp. 85–87, pp. 92–94.

[95] *Ibid.*, p. 85.

[96] Anscombe, *Intention*, p. 37.

[97] D'Arcy notes Bentham's "frequent insistence that acts and consequences alone are intentional, and circumstances not: since the former two alone are objects of the will, the latter of the understanding only" (*Human Acts*, p. 97).

[98] D'Arcy, *Human Acts*, p. 68.

[99] Anscombe, "Medallist's Address," p. 63.

[100] Cf. D'Arcy, *Human Acts*, pp. 2–3.

[101] D. Davidson, "Agency," in *Essays on Actions and Events*, pp. 43–62 (Oxford: Oxford University Press, 1980), at p. 59.

[102] A. C. Danto, "Basic Actions," *American Philosophical Quarterly* 2 (1965), pp. 141–148.

[103] *Ibid.*, p. 144.

[104] J. Annas, "How Basic are Basic Actions?" *Proceedings of the Aristotelian Society* 78 (1977–78), pp. 195–213, at p. 195.

[105] Danto, "Basic Actions," p. 57.

[106] *Ibid.*, 56. See also Meiland, *Nature of Intention*, 67, n. 1.

[107] Cf. Searle, *Intentionality*, p. 100.

[108] *Ibid.*, p. 106.

[109] Baier, "Act and Intent," p. 654.

[110] Martin Rhonheimer seems to be making a similar point when he writes: "Likewise it is indifferent if I rest lying on a bed or sitting in a chair. 'Lying on a bed' and 'sitting in a chair' both belong to the same type of action: they are the same type of basic intentional action and therefore have the same object of action (unless, for example, for some reason one doesn't have a right to sit in the chair: this would be a circumstance that is relevant as a modification of the structure of the object of action)." ("Così è anche indifferente se io mi riposo mettendomi sul letto o sedendomi in poltrona. 'Stare sul letto' e 'stare in poltrona' appartengono ambedue allo stesso tipo d'azione: sono lo stesso tipo di un'azione base intenzionale e hanno perciò anche lo stesso oggetto dell'azione (a meno che p. es. per un qualche motivo non

si ha il diritto di stare in poltrona: ciò sarebbe una circonstanza che è rilevante per la modificazione della struttura d'oggetto dell'azione.") M. Rhonheimer, *La prospettiva della morale: fondamenti dell'etica filosofica* (Rome: Armando, 1994), p. 126.

[111] Baier, "Act and Intent," pp. 654–655.

[112] D'Arcy, *Human Acts*, p. 30, citing Anscombe, *Intention*, pp. 45–47.

[113] Anscombe, *Intention*, p. 40.

[114] Cf. G. E. M. Anscombe, "On Brute Facts," *Analysis* 18 (1958), pp. 69–72.

[115] J. F. Bennett, *Events and their Names*, (New York: Oxford University Press, 1988), pp. 194–195.

[116] As Duff puts it "What is it that I really *do* when I shoot Pat, and what are really circumstances or consequences, rather than part of what I do?" (*Intention Agency*, p. 41).

[117] *Ibid.*, p. 41.

[118] Searle refers to this term, in *Intentionality*, p. 99.

[119] Cf. D'Arcy, *Human Acts*, p. 2.

[120] Cf. Anscombe, *Intention*, p. 84.

[121] Duff, *Intention Agency*, p. 130.

[122] H. L. A. Hart, "Intention and Punishment," in *Punishment and Responsibility: two essays in the philosophy of law* (Oxford: Oxford University Press, 1968), pp. 117–118.

[123] We are also reminded of the familiar example of Captain Oakes who, in walking away from camp to certain death, for the sake of freeing his comrades of a dangerous burden, was certainly killed by the cold and not by his own hand in a way that seems morally significant.

[124] Alan Donagan gives a similar explanation for the death of non-combatants in a just war. "It is the enemy's fault that non-combatants are [in the targeted military installations]" (*The Theory of Morality*, [Chicago: Chicago University Press, 1977], p. 87).

[125] Duff, *Intention Agency*, pp. 83–84.

[126] Pilsner, *Specification*, p. 236.

CHAPTER 5

MANUALISTS OF THE XIX AND XX CENTURIES

T HE GREAT HOLINESS and apostolic dynamism of St Alphonsus did not remain unrecognized for long by the Church. In addition to his moral works, he had published many devotional books and sermons, exercised his episcopal role admirably, and founded a major missionary order. After his death in 1787, his reputation for sanctity was rapidly confirmed by the Holy See. Beatified in 1816, he was canonized in 1839 and declared a Doctor of the Church by Pius IX in 1871.[1] Many of the positions taken by St Alphonsus became standard among moral theologians, although the intention of the Holy See in honoring the holy doctor was not to impose uniformity. This was clearly stated under Gregory XVI in 1831. In response to a query from the Archbishop of Besançon, the Sacred Penitentiary explained that while one could safely follow the teaching of St Alphonsus, without even seeking other opinions, other opinions were not thereby rejected as erroneous.[2] As Pius IX was later to state, St Alphonsus "showed the safe path, by which directors of Christian souls could with unhindered step proceed,"[3] but this did not mean that other authors did not or would not provide improved guidance at least on certain points.[4]

1. Gustave J. Waffelaert (1847–1931)

One author who set out to grapple with difficult issues in moral theology, inspired but not constrained by St Alphonsus, was Gustave Joseph Waffelaert. As a young professor at Louvain, the future bishop of Bruges published a work consisting of two studies, one on cooperation and the other on scandal. His thorough treatment provides a critical bridge in the development of Catholic moral thinking between St Alphonsus and the fairly settled doctrines of the later Manualist era.

To begin with, his side-by-side treatment of cooperation and scandal succeeds in distinguishing them still more clearly one from the other. He divides all forms of cooperation into three groups: cooperation in the wide sense, the strict sense and negative cooperation.[5] Negative cooperation, which refers to a passive stance before the evil of another, is usually a simple offence against the duty of fraternal correction.[6] Cooperation in the widest sense, indicating moral influence on the one carrying out the sin, is more properly called scandal.[7] The one provoking another into sin is to be considered a "total" cause of the sin on a moral plane. Thus, for Waffelaert, the problem of cooperation with evil is restricted to positive cooperation in the strict sense. While this can be mixed with scandal, if the one being assisted is not already fully determined to sin, cooperation proper assumes that he is so determined of his own doing.

Waffelaert's delineation of the notion of cooperation proper invites further investigation. Referring by way of example to a servant's cooperation, he restricts cooperation properly so-called to "furnishing, causing a means which is by its nature or under the circumstances a partial *cause* of the evil act of the master."[8] The essential note of cooperation is causality: "it remains true that there is no cooperation where there is no causality."[9] Otherwise, the servant is merely providing an occasion for sin which would count as scandal; and, if done solely to save his job, as indirect scandal. We recall, however, that St Alphonsus insisted on describing material cooperation as simply providing an occasion for sin to one who is determined to abuse it,[10] something which sounds like pharisaic scandal. Thus, it seems that what was formerly considered material cooperation may not, in Waffelaert's view, be called cooperation at all. In order to untangle the matter, we must delve into Waffelaert's essay on scandal.

Indirect scandal

If Waffelaert's essay achieves nothing else, it proves that those who claim that "what St Thomas thought appears clearer than the noonday sun"[11] are quite deluded at least in regards to the topic of scandal. Waffelaert surveys a host of theologians who, in interpreting Aquinas, disagree about what virtue is violated by a scandalizer, when scandal is given not for the sake of causing the other to sin (that is, "diabolical" scandal) but simply "part and parcel" with the goal of committing adultery, for instance, or in doing some benign but easily misinterpreted action. There are three positions on the matter: those who believe that this "indirect" scandal is a sin against the virtue violated by the one scandalized (chastity, in the case involving adultery); those (like Waffelaert) who think it is a sin against charity; and those (like Alphonsus) who think it is a sin against both. Were the goal simply to determine what sort of analysis should be made by a confessor, the vigorous debate generated by this question would seem excessive. However, the solution involves clarifying key concepts of action theory, such as: the nature of moral norms, the specifying role of circumstances, the notion of indirect voluntary. In particular, precisely what kind of end specifies the object of an act?[12]

The most obvious reading of St Thomas (II-II, q. 43, a. 3) is that scandal which is not caused precisely for the sake of leading another into sin cannot be a "special sin," that is, here, a sin against charity. Since it is the end that gives the species, and the scandal *qua* scandal was *per accidens*, even in the case of the adulterer, it cannot be a sin against charity *per se*. While agreeing with his conclusion, Waffelaert considers St Alphonsus's argument for the contrary view to be a misunderstanding of the issue at hand.[13] The key, for Waffelaert, is to observe that scandal can be a sin against charity either formally or materially.[14] In the latter case, the scandalous aspect of the agent's sin is a circumstance *addens speciem* to his action.[15] It is analogous to the thief who, only wishing to steal a gold cup, is indifferent to the fact that it is a chalice; nonetheless, this circumstance will make his action a sacrilege as well as a theft.[16] Although St Thomas refutes an objection (ad 3) that makes an argument based upon circumstances affecting the species, commentators with impeccable Thomist reputations, from Waffelaert to Reginald Garrigou-Lagrange, interpret him as meaning that diabolical scandal alone is "primarily and directly" a sin against charity.[17] They still maintain that indirect scandal is a sin against charity, since the foreseeable effect is a circumstance *addens speciem*.[18]

The point that is being safeguarded is of great significance. The agent's subjective goal, his *finis operantis*, does not determine the species of his act. He may be completely indifferent to whether his action will scandalize another or not, and yet, if he ought to foresee this result, he will be committing scandal.[19] Scandal is not to be defined, or understood to be defined, as "*intending* to cause another ruin by an unfitting word or deed" but simply as "[*positing*] an unfitting word or deed that provides occasion for the ruin of another."[20] This doctrine has application in relation to other vices as well. Waffelaert discusses the question of disobedience.[21] A Catholic who is indifferent to the fact that eating meat is forbidden on Fridays in Lent but merely seeks the enjoyment of eating meat, will still commit the sin of disobedience simply should he know that the prohibition exists.[22] Certainly this bears upon the matter of cooperation: cannot the circumstance of facilitating another's sin change the species of the act posited, and, if so, when? (We will assume that it is understood that in such a case, the "circumstance" would no longer be properly so called).

An attentive examination of the authors who agree that indirect scandal constitutes a sin against charity reveals another controversy emerging from the attempt to understand the mind of St Thomas, a controversy which also pertains to our investigation. St Thomas does not use the binomial "direct/indirect" in relation to scandal. If we consider only the act of the scandalizer, Thomas distinguishes (II-II q. 43, a. 1, ad 4) between active scandal and an act which is not properly called scandal at all, even if someone may take scandal from it.[23] He divides active scandal into two sorts—those actions which are done expressly to cause the fall of another, and those which are "of such a nature as to lead others to sin."[24] Both are considered to be always sinful.[25] We have noted in passing that this latter category—actions which cause scandal *praeter intentionem agentis* (thus excluding "diabolical" scandal) but only *ex conditione operis*—can be of two sorts: the act can be sinful itself or have only the *speciem mali*. St Thomas lumps them together, saying that both are to be avoided,[26] but subsequent commentators sought to expand on this point. They introduced a category of scandal which would contain an act that is good in itself, or at least not evil, from which the giving of scandal could be foreseen and yet the positing of which might be justified by a proportionate reason.[27] Such actions would be justified by appeal to the principle of double effect.[28] Such scandal is termed "indirecte volitum". Thus, into the category of active scandal, which Thomas had considered always wrong either by express intent or by the nature of the act, is inserted a caveat: some of the acts which are scandalous by their nature may not imply an evil will on the part of the one who posits them.

The most immediate result of this refinement is terminological confusion. Dominic Prümmer represents the majority position by classifying unintended scandal that results from a sinful act (the example of an adulterer) as "direct", but "materialiter or simpliciter" direct not "formaliter" which would be diabolical.[29] "Indirect scandal" would describe an act which appears evil, either given the circumstances or due to a defect in the one who takes scandal. Garrigou-Lagrange, on the other hand, seems to classify the scandal caused by an adulterer as "indirect" because not intended, but as sinful because the act posited which causes the scandal is evil.[30] He also adds a category of active scandal which is "omnino" *per accidens* because neither directly nor indirectly willed. At the root of the confusion seems to be the question of whether the scandalous act is a means towards a goal,[31] and thus intended *in se* but not *propter se*, or whether the scandal given is considered an effect, although perhaps logically entailed by the action performed. Here we see the matters discussed in the previous chapter resurfacing.

Once again, what seems to be mere technical quibbling concerns a serious issue. As we shall see, moral theologians following Thomas dramatically developed his idea of "indirect voluntary", making it a pillar of casuistry. The cost of this process needs to be assessed. In the case of scandal, Thomas determines first whether the action itself, be it evil or only bearing the appearance of evil, tends "de sui ratione" to lead others to sin. It may be foreseen to lead to sin even though it is not of a nature to do so, but then the passive scandal taken would be wholly attributable to the defect of the one scandalized. Perhaps in this case, Thomas would demand a proportionate reason for positing the act. However, there clearly appears to be a transformation of St Thomas's position on the part of the Manualists: Thomas gives no indication that a good or indifferent act, which, under the circumstances, is likely to lead a *reasonable* person into sin, can be done for any reason. Again, although this may seem like a technicality, it should be clear that the putative liberty to consider the liklihood that my action will lead another to sin as a circumstance which, unfortunate though it may be, can be "tolerated" or "permitted" sets a dangerous precedent. As in the previous controversy, the point at issue is that the subjective intention of the agent (his reason for acting) does not make an action to be scandalous; the nature and circumstances of the deed he performs do.[32]

Let us conclude this foray into the question of scandal by drawing a comparison between this debate and the kernel of controversy in the topic of cooperation with evil. Assuming St Thomas's original division, the two issues—scandal and cooperation—appear completely analogous, differing only in that scandal concerns "moral" influence and cooperation proper, "physical" assistance.

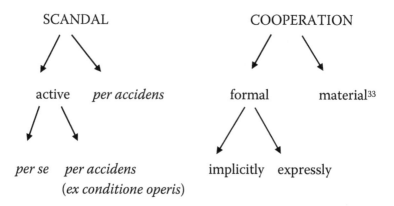

In essence, the controversial aspect of scandal is: when an act is of a nature to provoke another to sin (*ex conditione operis*), yet the agent has no interest in leading the other person to sin, what is the species of his act? Likewise, the aspect of cooperation with evil that is the subject of our study amounts to the following: when an act is of a nature to facilitate the sin of another, yet the agent has no interest in helping the other person to sin, what is the species of his act? We turn now to Waffelaert's study of cooperation to seek his further contributions.

Waffelaert on cooperation

Waffelaert appears to take the distinction between formal and material cooperation, straight from St Alphonsus. Formal cooperation obtains when "the one who cooperates has the same intention of producing the effect, the evil act, as the principal agent"; while material cooperation exists in absence of this intention.[34] We are alerted to the fact that he will interpret this intention strictly, that is, as an express intention, by his comment: "the whole question comes down then to *material* cooperation."[35]

In other words, Waffelaert accepts without discussion the notion that the species of the cooperator's act can be ascertained in isolation from the circumstance of its role in facilitating the sin of another. When breaking down the steps by which one is to evaluate given cases, he asks under the second heading "Is there in him, who participates in the evil effect, the same evil intention as in the principal agent?" and only later, under the third heading, does he suggest we ask "Is the act of cooperation by its formal object, its very intrinsic end, evil, in such a way that no extrinsic reason for acting could justify it ...?"[36] Waffelaert even allows that the cooperator could in some instances cooperate *immediately*, that is, "participating in the very action of the principal agent,"[37] when circumstances are such that the formal object of the cooperator's act is changed.[38] Thus, the idea of circumstances *mutans speciem* has not been altogether forgotten; here, however, it serves to allow rather than prohibit the positing of an action.

Waffelaert does not ignore the difficulty that some may have in trying to "understand how it can happen that such and such a reason or necessity of acting can legitimize cooperation in an evil act." He stops for several pages to present his argument.[39] Firstly, he explicitly states that one must examine the act "abstraction made from the cooperation" to assess whether it is intrinsically evil and then, in a second moment, consider it as an act of cooperation to assess whether it is legitimately posited. It seems that here a logical fallacy is committed when he states: "[Considered as an act of cooperation] it must be said that considered *secundum speciem*, it is not intrinsically evil, since a cooperation in an evil act can be licit."[40] This seems to amount to the following: since some acts of cooperation are licit, no acts of cooperation are intrinsically evil in virtue of their being acts of cooperation. But, there may be different kinds of acts of cooperation, some of which might be intrinsically evil as a result of a circumstance *addens speciem*.

Waffelaert continues his argument by acknowledging that there certainly is something troublesome about this circumstance of facilitating another's sin. In order to classify it, he recurs here and elsewhere to a class of action described by St Thomas as "*male sonantes*".[41] Such actions, for example, "to kill or beat a man," imply some deformity but, in certain circumstances they could be rendered legitimate. It should be noted, to begin with, that Waffelaert makes more use of this concept in his 75-page essay than does St Thomas in his entire extant corpus.[42] It seems rather like a first attempt of the Angelic Doctor to wrestle with these complex situations. As St Thomas notes in other places[43] an act description such as "occidere hominem" is not a moral act description at all. It would be wrong to think that such a description, in combination with a subjective intention, would adequately describe an act. Yet this seems to be the error made by Waffelaert when, for instance, he justifies proximate and even immediate cooperation in something considered intrinsically evil in the following manner:

> Even considered as cooperation, but abstracted from circumstances, in particular from the end of the agent who cooperates (*finis operantis*), these very acts of selling land which is to serve for the construction of a temple, of a bad school, etc, or the construction of these places themselves, are not intrinsically evil, but *male sonantes*, such that they can only be justified by the exterior reason for acting of the cooperator.[44]

In other words, he seems at times to reduce the cooperator's act to a purely physical description, such as when he justifies voting for a candidate who has declared in advance his intention to persecute religion on the grounds that casting a vote is not bad in itself.[45] He concludes that such electors are not cooperating formally from the fact that they are under compulsion.[46] Similarly, Waffelaert considers a Catholic minister's vote to subsidize the exercise of heretical cults as material cooperation, simply because his "personal" intention is to favor the Catholic cause, "which in the present circumstances he cannot do without cooperating at the same time with the exercise of false cults."[47]

Another element of Waffelaert's position that needs more precision regards the order of causation. We recall that his definition of cooperation was made in terms of causality.[48] He appeals explicitly to the principle of double effect[49] in order to justify material cooperation, but he does not have the principle worked out as neatly as was done in the classic formulation of Jean-Pierre Gury.[50] For this reason, perhaps, Waffelaert's justifications of material cooperation do not grapple with the issue of the good effect seeming at times to follow from the bad, a point to which we will return (see p. pp. 197–199).

In conclusion, it seems clear that Gustave Waffelaert arrived at divergent conclusions on two issues that are in many regards parallel: indirect scandal and implicit cooperation. Apparently, the fact that the latter theme involves physical causation plays a role in his asymmetrical conclusion. Whether this conclusion follows legitimately or fails to rise above an inherited physicalism, is a question that we will take with us as we look at subsequent generations of Catholic moral thinkers.

2. Subsequent adjustments of the Manualists

At first glance the treatment of cooperation in the manuals is limited to repeating that given by St Alphonsus. Usually, the subject is covered in two places, as it was by the saint:

under "sins against charity" and under "restitution". Often St Alphonsus's arguments for defining formal and material cooperation are quoted verbatim. Certainly, his judgment on Proposition 51 is maintained, even if the contrary position is sometimes mentioned as possible. Here follows an example from one collection of "Cases of Conscience":

> Thus it is illicit for Quirinus to hold a ladder to a house and help his master ascend, [it is justified] neither by reason of his role as servant, nor by reason of ills that may ensue, even very grave ones, provided the case of having to undergo death is excluded, because this cooperation is extremely proximate. Indeed, according to many, such cooperation is not to be permitted even so as to avoid death. The opposite opinion, however, which St Alphonsus maintained, is not only probable, but more probable.[51]

Nonetheless, even in a period when moral theology has been criticized for lacking creative impulse,[52] one can see that the desire to understand and explain such complex matters better was not wholly absent. Attempts to adjust and improve the received doctrine caused the tradition to be considerably less monolithic than it may appear.

Introduction of implicitly formal cooperation

While it is commonplace to describe cooperation as the most vexing of all areas of moral theology, some authors continued to think, as did Waffelaert, that the difficulties were confined to judgments in *material* cooperation.[53] Other authors, however, by pointing out how difficult it is in practice to distinguish formal from material cooperation intimate that St Alphonsus's categories call for further elaboration. Thus, in Aloysius Sabetti's manual, following an Alphonsian definition of the terms, we read:

"Practically speaking there is nothing more difficult [than the application of this principle] in the whole of moral theology. For often it is hardly possible to determine, whether cooperation is formal or material..."[54]

The difficulty of making this judgment soon became expressed by certain authors in a twofold division of formal cooperation. This dramatic development does not seem to have received the attention it deserves.[55] While formal cooperation remains "consenting to the evil intention of the principal agent",[56] many authors clearly state that this consent can be either implicit or explicit. Some, such as Joseph Aertnys, identify this division with the *finis operis* / *finis operantis* binomial.[57] Augustine Lehmkuhl divides the modalities of formal cooperation into three: 1) by intention, 2) by positing an action which contains approval by its nature or from the circumstances, and 3) positing an action which is by its intrinsic nature in the same evil genus as the principal agent's sin.[58] (This last category anticipates our discussion of immediate cooperation). John McHugh and Charles Callan combine the foregoing in their clear statement:

> Formal cooperation is implicit, when the cooperator does not directly intend to associate himself with the sin of the principle [sic] agent, but the end of the external act (*finis operis*), which for the sake of some advantage or interest the cooperator does intend, includes from its nature or from circumstances the guilt of the sin of the principle [sic] agent.[59]

Arthur Vermeersch had his own way of including implicitly formal cooperation in his definition of formal cooperation: "cooperation which in itself, that is, by its nature or from its necessary signification, contains the goodness or evil of the same genus as the principal action."[60] Marcellino Zalba, whom Ronald Fabbro highlights as singularly

intent upon maintaining the relevance of the circumstances of the particular situation for detecting the presence of implicitly formal cooperation, offers a nuanced
definition of formal cooperation:

> In *formal* cooperation assistance to the action of
> another is offered knowingly and willingly insofar
> as it has a determined morality; thus, it participates
> in its goodness or evil, at least implicitly by exer-
> cising a work which is so ordered to good or evil
> that it has no other end and effect but the good or
> evil of the other.[61]

Finally, we reproduce Bernard Häring's definition of
formal cooperation, which is instructively read in light of
Waffelaert:[62] "By contrast (to material), in formal cooperation one's action of itself is to be characterized as an
influence, as partial cause of an evil effect which must be
avoided. Wherefore, it is evil even when the agent himself
may deplore the evil effect."[63]

Worth noting is the fact that an analogous debate to
that which we examined in reference to indirect scandal
took place in regards to cooperation: when material
cooperation is illicit, is only charity offended or other
virtues as well, namely those virtues that are opposed by
the sin of the principal agent?[64] It appears that the opinions of authors coalesced relatively easily upon the conclusion that only charity is offended, because the
cooperator does not do anything evil in itself, but only by
extrinsic circumstance, "ex mala alterius voluntate".[65] For
our purposes, however, the significance of the debate lies
in the fact that it centered upon *material* cooperation
which is not the aspect of cooperation analogous to active
scandal *ex conditione operis*. The category of implicitly
formal cooperation appears to have been too underdevel-
oped to figure in this debate.

Immediate cooperation

As authors sought to make room in the definition of formal cooperation for acts which are implicitly formal, they had to contend with the classification of actions that assist in the very execution of the evil deed.[66] Is such cooperation necessarily formal? A few authors, such as Lehmkuhl and Aertnys, do not speak of "immediate cooperation" apart from formal cooperation, but they must find ways to explain difficult cases of immediate cooperation that are intuitively justifiable. Most prominently, the desire to explain why a clerk, held at gunpoint, could assist in a robbery, makes the inclusion of immediate cooperation in the formal category problematic. Charles Billuart, however, stalwartly embraces what appears to be the logical consequence: since immediate cooperation in theft is to commit a theft, it cannot be rendered licit even to save one's life.[67]

Most authors prefer instead to divide material cooperation into immediate and mediate, maintaining that immediate material cooperation, in contrast to formal, is only *almost* always to be considered illicit. Merkelbach, for instance, declares that immediate material cooperation is always illicit, except in cases having to do with the removal of material goods.[68] Ugorji remarks that there is no agreement on a "*principium divisionis*" between implicitly formal and immediate material.[69]

Fabbro notes the two directions[70] taken in dealing with immediate cooperation (calling it formal while making exceptions vs. calling it material while nearly always forbidding it) but seems to ignore the significance of the debate. He asserts: "By maintaining that immediate cooperation is formal these moralists tend to confuse this distinction [between formal and material] and imply that a moral determination can be made independently of the agent's intention."[71] However, these authors are not ignoring the agent's intention or its defining role for formal cooperation; rather they are resisting what appears to be a separation of proximate intention from the external action. How can it be that an agent choose to participate in the very execution of a crime without intending to commit the crime? Surely this stretches the ordinary understanding of "intend".[72]

A further problem arises when the evil deed is not theft, but a graver evil such as abortion or, as in the case of Proposition 51, rape. Here, immediate cooperation cannot be justified by the method of regarding material goods as a special case. Those wishing to justify such cooperation have recourse to a distinction between immediate and "omnino proxima".[73] The moral significance of such a distinction is not, however, obvious; what makes a slight distance from the actual execution of the deed capable of removing the need for refusal, even at the cost of martyrdom if need be?[74] And how would one apply this distinction? Objective criteria for measuring this distance are nowhere provided.[75]

The effort to grapple with difficult cooperation cases not only led to these refinements of the notion of cooperation; it induced moral theologians to expand their investigation of certain concepts of fundamental moral theology, as well. This aspect of the question we take up in the next chapter.

Notes

[1]   St Alphonsus was only declared the Patron of Moral Theologians and Confessors by Pius XII in 1950.

[2]   "Utrum sacrae theologiae professor opiniones, quas in sua Theologia morali profitetur B. Alphonsus a L., sequi tuto possit ac

profiteri? Affirmative, quin tamen inde reprehendendi censeantur qui opiniones ab aliis probatis auctoribus traditas sequuntur." Reply of Sacred Penitentiary to Archbishop of Besançon, 1831, cited by Deman, "Probabilisme," p. 587.

3   "[Alphonsus] tutam straverit viam, per quam christifidelium animarum moderatores inoffenso pede incedere possint." Pius IX, March 23, 1871, in elevating St Alphonsus to the status of Doctor of the Church, cited by Deman. *Ibid.*, p. 588.

4   Deman comments, in 1926, on the words of Pius IX: "Il y apparaît [in the texts of Church authorities] que l'église apprécie par-dessus tout le juste milieu où s'est tenu le moraliste, entre les extrêmes contraires du laxisme et du rigorisme. Cette position est en effet celle de saint Alphonse. Ainsi définie, elle lui est commune avec d'autres auteurs, notamment Patuzzi et Concina, qu'on ne taxe de rigorisme, nous l'avons dit, que par un abus de ce mot." *Ibid.*, p. 589.

5   These three divisions also correspond roughly to a tripartite division of the classic nine modes of cooperation: command, counsel, consent, coaxing (moral influence); sheltering, participating (causal influence); keeping silence, not impeding, not manifesting (negative cooperation). For some details concerning these categories, see p. 34.

6   G. J. Waffelaert, *Ètude sur la coopération et sur l'Espèce morale du Scandale* (Bruges: Vandenberghe-Denaux, 1883), p. 5. Although the two essays were published as one book, we will refer to them separately.

7   Waffelaert, *Coopération*, p. 7.

8   "Fournir, causer un moyen qui soit par sa nature ou par les circonstances *cause* partielle de l'acte mauvais du maître." Waffelaert, *Coopération*, p. 10.

9   "Il reste vrai qu'il n'y a pas de coopération, où il n'y a pas de causalité." *Ibid.*, p. 11.

10   "La cooperazione è materiale, cioè quando si coopera ad un'azione, di cui il prossimo potrebbe servirsi senza peccato, ma quegli per sua malizia se ne abusa a peccare." A. de Liguori, *Il confessore diretto*, IV, n. 17, cited by Roy, *"La coopération,"* p. 428.

11   "Quod luce meridiana clarius appareat quid ipse (S. Thomas) senserit." Vasquez, cited in Waffelaert, *Scandale*, p. 92.

12   "Finis enim dat speciem in moralibus." *ST* II–II q. 43, a. 3.

13   Alphonsus appeals to what is said in *ST* II–II, q. 43, a. 1, which admittedly is confused by St Thomas's use of the *per se / per*

accidens distinction in two different senses in the same question. Waffelaert comments: "Nous ne voulons pas insister sur cet argument, car il nous semble dépourvu de valeur. La question en effet n'est pas de savoir quand il y a scandale actif, mais quand le scandale actif est un péché contre la charité." Waffelaert, *Scandale*, p. 92.

[14]   Waffelaert supports this view convincingly with other texts from the Thomistic corpus, especially from the *Commentary on the Sentences*: "Sed activum scandalum potest accipi dupliciter. Uno modo formaliter; quando scilicet est speciale peccatum, ex hoc quod intendit alium scandalizare; et sic si intendat proximum inducere in peccatum mortale, mortaliter peccat; si autem intendat inducere ad aliquod veniale, peccat venialiter, quantum pertinet ad rationem scandali; quia si intenderet ducere in peccatum veniale per actum mortalis peccati, peccaret mortaliter; sed hoc accideret scandalo. Alio modo materialiter, quando est circumstantia peccati, quia non intenditur proximi nocumentum; et tunc idem judicium est de scandalo et de actu quo aliquis scandalizat; qui quandoque est veniale, quandoque mortale peccatum; nisi forte esset veniale aut indifferens habens similitudinem mortalis peccati; tunc enim scandalum activum esset peccatum mortale, cum ex aliquibus circumstantiis concurrentibus existimari probabiliter posset quod infirmi aspicientes peccarent mortaliter." *Super Sent.*, lib. IV, d. 38, q. 2, a. 2, qc. 2, cited by Waffelaert, *Scandale*, p. 100.

[15]   The most relevant text of Thomas is *ST* I–II, q. 18, a. 10: "Sed contra, locus est circumstantia quaedam. Sed locus constituit actum moralem in quadam specie mali, furari enim aliquid de loco sacro est sacrilegium. Ergo circumstantia constituit actum moralem in aliqua specie boni vel mali... Sicut tollere alienum habet speciem ex ratione alieni, ex hoc enim constituitur in specie furti, et si consideretur super hoc ratio loci vel temporis, se habebit in ratione circumstantiae. Sed quia ratio etiam de loco vel de tempore, et aliis huiusmodi, ordinare potest; contingit conditionem loci circa obiectum accipi ut contrariam ordini rationis; puta quod ratio ordinat non esse iniuriam faciendam loco sacro. Unde tollere aliquid alienum de loco sacro addit specialem repugnantiam ad ordinem rationis. Et ideo locus, qui prius considerabatur ut circumstantia, nunc consideratur ut principalis conditio obiecti rationi repugnans. Et per hunc modum, quandocumque aliqua circumstantia respicit specialem ordinem rationis vel pro vel contra, oportet quod circumstantia det speciem actui

morali vel bono vel malo."

16 Defending his position that the thief wills to commit sacrilege against an objector, Thomas says: "licet principaliter voluntas furantis non feratur ad rem sacram, sed ad aurum, fertur tamen super rem sacram ex consequenti; magis enim vult rem sacram accipere quam auro carere." *De Malo*, q. 2, a. 6, ad 6.

17 R. Garrigou-Lagrange, *De virtutibus theologicis* (Turin: Berruti, 1949), p. 515.

18 J. P. Gury called this view "communis … contra nonnullos veteres," a judgment which Waffelaert accepts with some hesitation. Cf. Waffelaert, *Scandale*, p. 102. He later expresses skepticism about the value of probabilistic judgments, based upon the degree of acceptance of an opinion; he says that the claim that an opinion is more common usually means "plus commune parmi les Auteurs de ma bibliothèque, ou qui pis est, parmi ceux que j'ai vu cités, à tort ou à raison, en sa faveur." *Ibid.*, p. 151.

19 Theo Belmans also makes this point. Cf. T. Belmans, *Le sens objectif de l'agir humain: Pour relire la morale conjugale de Saint Thomas*, Studi Tomistici, vol. 8. (Vatican City: Vatican Press, 1980), p. 76.

20 "Utrum scandalum convenienter definiatur quod est 'dictum vel factum minus rectum praebens occasionem ruinae." *ST* II–II, q. 43, a. 1.

21 Waffelaert, *Scandale*, p. 114.

22 Recall the similarity of this matter to some of the condemned laxist propositions, e.g. Prop. 52 of Innocent XI, and Prop. 2 of Alexander VIII. See pp. 21–22.

23 This taking of scandal would be called passive scandal, classified in the manuals as "acceptum" as opposed to "datum" which results from active scandal.

24 "Per se quidem, quando aliquis suo malo verbo vel facto intendit alium ad peccandum inducere; vel, etiam si ipse hoc non intendat, ipsum factum est tale quod de sui ratione habet ut sit inductivum ad peccandum, puta quod aliquis publice facit peccatum vel quod habet similitudinem peccati. Et tunc ille qui huiusmodi actum facit proprie dat occasionem ruinae, unde vocatur scandalum activum. Per accidens autem aliquod verbum vel factum unius est alteri causa peccandi, quando etiam praeter intentionem operantis, et praeter conditionem operis, aliquis male dispositus ex huiusmodi opere inducitur ad peccandum, puta cum aliquis invidet bonis aliorum." *ST* II–II, q. 43, a. 1 ad 4.

[25] "Similiter etiam scandalum activum semper est peccatum in eo qui scandalizat." *ST* II–II, q. 42, a. 2.

[26] *ST* II–II, q. 43, a. 2.

[27] Cf. D. Prümmer, *Manuale theologiae moralis secundum principia S. Thomae Aquinatis*, 6th ed. (Fribourg: Herder, 1931), I, 437, footnote 108.

[28] Cf. N. Hendriks, *Le moyen mauvais pour obtenir une fin bonne. Essai sur la troisième condition du principe de l'acte à double effet.* Studia Universitatis S. Thomae in Urbe, v. 12. (Rome: Herder, 1981), pp. 118–127.

[29] Cf. Prümmer, *Manuale theologiae moralis*, I, 438, n. 606. This is the view described by Hendriks, *Moyen mauvais*, p. 124. Note that in G. J. Waffelaert, while the "direct/indirect" distinction is applied to scandal, it is specifically not in reference to the intention of the agent, but rather in reference to the mode by which the scandal occurs. "Scandale peut être *direct*, quand on induit directement et immédiatement le prochain en péché; ou *indirect* quand on pose un acte d'où le prochain prendra occasion de péché, ou sera excité au mal." Waffelaert, *Scandale*, p. 87.

[30] Garrigou-Lagrange, *De virtutibus theologicis*, p. 515.

[31] Prümmer describes materially direct scandal as that which occurs when the agent pursues a goal that cannot be attained without the sin of the other. Thus the agent "indirectly" intends that sin. "[Scandalum] directum simpliciter…est quando homo actione sua non quidem directe intendit peccatum formale alterius, sed aliquid aliud quocum coniunctum est peccatum…Cum autem istum finem assequi nequeat sine peccato alterius, indirecte etiam intendit hoc peccatum." Prümmer, *Manuale theo. mor.*, I, p. 437.

[32] We can mention here Bruno Schüller's idiosyncratic view on scandal, cooperation and the principle of double effect. Viewing the effects of inducing another to sin and facilitating another's sin as *moral* evils, he agrees that in these two cases, but only in these cases, the doctrine of indirect voluntary has a meaningful role. Schüller writes: "As far as I know, there are only two cases where traditional theology makes use of the principle [of double effect] in a context of purely teleological considerations. These cases are: (1) actions apt to induce other people to a morally wrong behavior (*scandalum activum*), (2) actions of cooperating with other people in morally wrong behavior (*cooperatio cum peccato alterius*). Strikingly enough, in the recent past scarcely anyone has made an attempt at clarifying the principle of double effect through a thorough analysis

of its application to these cases. Admittedly these two sorts of action are of a very peculiar structure and, therefore, difficult to analyze. I assume, however, that theologians would not shrink from this difficulty if they found the traditional doctrine on *"scandalum activum"* and *"cooperatio"* implausible or somehow problematic in its practical consequences." B. Schüller, "The Double Effect in Catholic Thought: a reevaluation," in *Doing Evil to Achieve Good*, ed. R. McCormick and P. Ramsey, pp. 185–191 (New York: University Press of America, 1985), at p. 171.

[33] Recall that material cooperation, conceived as merely providing an occasion for the sin of another, would not really be considered cooperation properly speaking by Waffelaert. This would correspond to the per accidens scandal paired with active scandal, which is not, properly speaking, scandal at all.

[34] "Coopération *formelle*, quand celui qui coopère a la même intention de produire l'effet, l'acte mauvais, que l'agent principal... *matérielle*, quand le coopérateur n'a pas l'intention mauvaise de l'agent principal, mais une autre." Waffelaert, *Coopération*, pp. 8–9.

[35] "Toute la question se reporte donc sur la coopération *matérielle*." *Ibid.*, p. 8.

[36] "L'acte de coopération est-il, par son objet formel, sa fin intrinsèque même, mauvais, de manière qu'aucune raison d'agir extrinsèque ne puisse le légitimer?" *Ibid.*, p. 14.

[37] "en participant à l'action même de l'agent principal." *Ibid.*, p. 10.

[38] The mechanism by which this occurs is termed, by the theologians of the time, *per substractionem materiae*. It seeks to explain how someone could directly damage the temporal goods of another so as to save his life (cf. *Ibid.*, p. 10).

[39] "comprendre comment il se peut que telle ou telle raison ou nécessité d'agir, puisse légitimer la coopération à un acte mauvais." *Ibid.*, pp. 22–25.

[40] "[En tant qu'acte de coopération] il faut dire que considéré *secundum speciem*, il n'est pas intrinsèquement mauvais, puisqu'une coopération à un acte mauvais peut être licite." *Ibid.*, p. 23.

[41] "Sunt vero quaedam actiones quae absolute consideratae, deformitatem vel inordinationem quamdam important, quae tamen aliquibus circumstantiis advenientibus bonae efficiuntur; sicut occidere hominem vel percutere, in se deformitatem quamdam importat, sed si addatur, occidere malefactorem propter iustitiam, vel percutere delinquentem causa disciplinae, non erit peccatum,

sed virtuosum. In numero harum actionum videtur esse habere plures praebendas. Quamvis enim aliquas inordinationes contineat; tamen aliae circumstantiae possunt supervenire ita honestantes actum, quod praedictae inordinationes totaliter evacuantur." *Quodlib.* IX, q. 7, art. 2, c. (cited by Waffelaert with a different reference, *Coopération*, pp. 23–4).

[42] The actual phrase seems to appear only once in the relevant sense: "prima [obiectio] sumitur ex his actibus qui mox nominati in malum sonant, ut homicidium et cetera." *Super Sent.*, lib. II, d. 35, q. 2, pr.

[43] *ST* I–II, q. 1, a. 3, ad 3.

[44] "Même considérés comme coopération, mais abstraction faite des circonstances, en particulier de la fin de l'agent qui coopère (*finis operantis*), ces mêmes actes de vendre un terrain qui doit servir à la construction d'un temple, d'une mauvaise école, etc., ou la construction même de semblables locaux, ne sont pas intrinsèquement mauvais, mais *male sonantes*, de manière qu'ils ne peuvent se légitimer que par la raison d'agir extrinsèque du coopérateur." Waffelaert, *Coopération*, p. 40.

[45] *Ibid.*, p. 57.

[46] *Ibid.*, p. 53.

[47] "leur intention personnelle ... n'est pas du tout de favoriser ces cultes, mais bien plutôt de favoriser la religion catholique, ce que, dans les circonstances présentes, ils ne sauraient faire sans coopérer en même temps à l'exercice des cultes faux." *Ibid.*, p. 49.

[48] Cooperation proper would be "causer un moyen qui soit par sa nature ou par les circonstances *cause* partielle de l'acte mauvais ..." *Ibid.*, p. 10.

[49] *Ibid.*, p. 9.

[50] Jean-Pierre Gury, s.j. had presented the now classic formulation just a few years earlier. "Quatuor autem conditiones, quae in hoc principio enuntiantur, omnino requiruntur, scilicet (1) ut honestus sit finis agentis; (2) ut causa sit bona, vel saltem indifferens; (3) ut effectus bonus sit immediatus, et (4) adsit ratio gravis ponendi..." J.-P. Gury, *Compendium theologiae moralis* (Rome: Polyglotta, 1878), I, p. 8.

[51] J. Ferreres, *Casus conscientiae* (Barcelona: Eugenii Subirana, 1908), I, p. 126. "Illicitum est prorsus Quirino applicare scalam domui, et dominum ascendentem adjuvare, neque ratione famulatus, neque ratione incommodi etiam valde gravis, si casus mortis subeundae excipiatur, quia cooperatio haec est omnino proxima.

Imo, juxta multos, huiusmodi cooperatio ne ad mortem quidem vitandum permittenda foret. Opposita tamen sententia, quam tuetur S. Alphonsus, non solum probabile, sed etiam probabilius est."

52   Relevant is the observation of Thomas J. Bouquillon made in 1899: "We could give an almost endless list of problems, in the solution of which there has been no advance for two centuries, and no attempt at anything new is being made. One would almost think that we had fallen into skepticism or that we are afraid of the truth. This is particularly the case where an opinion is recognized as probable by a high authority." T. J. Bouquillon, "Moral Theology at the End of the Nineteenth Century," in *The Historical Development of Fundamental Moral Theology in the United States*, ed. C. Curran and R. McCormick, pp. 91–114. Readings in Moral Theology, vol. 11. (New York: Paulist Press, 1999), p. 109.

53   For example, Henry Davis writes: "So many factors enter into all questions of material cooperation, that only the most general principles can be laid down. Great varieties of opinion, therefore, on any given case except the most obvious, are inevitable, and there is no more difficult question than this in the whole range of Moral Theology." Davis, *Moral and Pastoral Theology*, I, p. 341.

54   "Practice loquendo, nihil est in tota theologia morali difficilius. Nam saepe vix determinari potest, utrum cooperatio formalis sit an materialis..." A. Sabetti and T. Barrett. *Compendium theologiae moralis*, 24th ed. (Regensburg: Frederick Pustet, 1916), p. 170, n. 194. Likewise, Dominic Prümmer writes: "Fatendum est, non raro esse difficillium discernere, utrum adsit cooperatio formalis necne; neque diversi theologi semper in hac re concordant." Prümmer, *Manuale theologiae moralis*, I, p. 447.

55   Ronald Fabbro has written the most helpful and thorough discussion of cooperation with evil in recent years: *Cooperation in evil: a Consideration of the Traditional Doctrine from the Point of View of the Contemporary Discussion About the Moral Act* (Rome: Pontifical Gregorian University, 1989). Regarding this point he sedately observes: "The definition offered by Alphonsus does undergo a further development in the manuals in at least one respect. Most Manualists will state that formal cooperation can occur in two ways" (p. 25). He unconvincingly describes this development as "recogniz[ing] that what Alphonsus meant by formal cooperation, namely, direct concurrence in the other's evil will, can in fact come about in two ways" (p. 26).

[56] "[Cooperation is formal] quando cooperans consentit malae voluntati principaliter agentis." B. H. Merkelbach, *Summa theologiae moralis ad mentem D. Thomae*, 10th ed. (Bruges: Desclée Brouwer, 1956), I, p. 401. He adds that "[Formal cooperation] peccatum principaliter agentis intendit ... tamquam consensus in illud eiusque approbatio."

[57] "*Cooperatio formalis ea est quae concurrit ad formale peccati alterius, seu ad ipsius malam voluntatem*, ita ut necessario includat consensum in ipsum peccatum. Hoc autem contingere potest dupliciter: a) *ex fine operis*, quando quis operam praestat, quae ex natura sua ad solum peccatum ordinatur; tunc enim necessario implicite dat consensum in peccatum; nam finis operis intrat in essentiam rei; qui ergo vult rem, necessario vult finem operis. b) *ex fine operantis*, quando quis operam praestat, esto in se indifferentem, ea praecise intentione, ut alter pravam voluntatem suam exsequatur seu facilius exsequatur." J. Aertnys and C. Damen, *Theologia moralis secundum doctrinam S. Alfonsi de Ligorio Doctoris Ecclesiae*, 17th ed. (Rome: Marietti, 1956), Lib. II, pp. 377–378. Likewise D. Prümmer says that formal cooperation occurs "sive ex ipso obiecto morali seu fine operis, sive ex fine operantis." Prümmer, *Manuale theo. mor.*, I, p. 447.

[58] A. Lehmkuhl, *Theologia moralis* (Freiburg: Herder, 1887), I, pp. 443–444. P. Palazzini and A. Jorio also speak of implicitly formal cooperation when the act is "*ex natura sua*" ordered to sin, while distinguishing this from immediate cooperation. See P. Palazzini—A. Jorio, *Casus conscientiae propositi ac resoluti a pluribus theologicis ac canonistis urbis* (Rome: Marietti, 1958), at pp. 304–305.

[59] J. McHugh and C. J. Callan, *Moral Theology: a complete course* (London: Herder, 1929), p. 618.

[60] "Formalis quoque dicitur cooperatio quae *in se*, sive natura sua sive ex ncessaria sua significatione, *bonitatem vel malitiam eiusdem generis continet atque actio principalis*." A. Vermeersch, *Theologiae moralis* (Rome: Pontifical Gregorian University, 1947), II, p. 86. Others, he adds, call this immediate material cooperation.

[61] M. Zalba, *Theologiae moralis compendium* (Madrid: Biblioteca autores cristianos, 1958), I, p. 155. Fabbro commends Zalba for reminding us that the meaning of the cooperator's act may well depend upon the use to which it will be put: "Zalba, as we have already pointed out, emphasizes that this determination [whether the act of cooperation is intrinsically evil or indifferent] involves

a consideration of the act, not in the abstract, but in the concrete circumstances. The meaning of the act on the moral level is not revealed by the external phenomenon alone, but by the whole context in which the cooperator finds himself or herself. In the moral evaluation one can never ignore the relationship which exists between the cooperator's action and the evil effect brought about along with the principal agent." Fabbro, *Cooperation in Evil*, p. 34. This certainly sounds more like Concina than St Alphonsus. See p. 72.

[62] Waffelaert considered *material* cooperation to be providing a partial cause of the evil effect.

[63] Häring, *Law of Christ*, I, p. 293. Bishop Anthony Fisher refers to Häring as a "rigorist" on this point. He adds that "the later Häring would undoubtedly repudiate this [position]." A. Fisher, "Cooperation in Evil," *Catholic Medical Quarterly 44 (Feb.* 1994), pp. 15–22, at p. 22.

[64] See Vermeersch, *Theologiae moralis*, II, pp. 87–88 for a summary of this debate.

[65] *Ibid.*, p. 87.

[66] Note well, this problem should not be confused with committing a sin together (e.g. adultery) as then the specific question of cooperation disappears.

[67] C. R. Billuart, *Summa Sancti Thomae*, 9th ed. (Paris: apud Victorem Palmé, 1847), VI, p. 6.

[68] Merkelbach, *Summa theo. mor.*, I, p. 402. Vermeersch makes the same exception, but equates the two categories: "Further, this must be said [that it is never licit] about *formal cooperation* which some call *immediate material*, if you except injustice alone in material goods." Vermeersch, *Theologiae moralis*, II, p. 87.

[69] Ugorji, *Principle of Double Effect*, p. 66.

[70] There is also a third direction taken by some authors: to list the immediate/mediate distinction *beside* the formal/material distinction, not as a subgroup of either. This is the approach taken by Gury, Noldin, and Marc (cf. Hendriks, *Moyen mauvais*, p. 142 n. 55).

[71] Fabbro, *Cooperation in Evil*, p. 51.

[72] Philosophical realists are put on alert by a statement such as: "it is necessary to get beyond one-sided 'common-sense' accounts of 'what is being done'..." J. Finnis, G. Grisez, and J. M. Boyle, "*Direct* and *Indirect*: A Reply to Critics of our Action Theory," *Thomist*

65 (2001), pp. 1–44, at p. 23.

[73] "Ut alias cooperatio *omnino proxima* licita evadat, praecipue si ad peccatum alterius est necessaria, aut tertio innocenti graviter damnosa: causa seu incommodum grave omnino, immo pro circumstantiis gravissimum requiritur, ut metus mortis alteriusve fere similis mali." Lehmkuhl, *Theologia moralis*, I, p. 446.

[74] We recall the implausibility of the claim, repeated, for instance, by Merkelbach, that assisting a rape by holding the ladder could be envisioned as *"omnino proxima"* cooperation, while writing and delivering love letters to a mistress is *"intrinsece malum."* Merkelbach, *Summ. theo. mor.*, I, p. 405.

[75] Hendriks cites several examples offered by one author as "immediate" and by another as "mediate" cooperation. In particular, the "putting a ladder in place" for a thief is considered mediate cooperation by Lottin, but immediate by Mausbach. Cf. Hendriks, *Moyen mauvais*, pp. 142–143, n. 57.

CHAPTER 6

DEVELOPMENTS IN FUNDAMENTAL MORAL CONCEPTS

AS NOTED IN the previous chapter, moral theologians came to realize that the available categories were not adequate to explain their intuitions about difficult cases of cooperation. With regard to basic concepts, greater precision and more general agreement was needed. The process to achieve this goal moved in two directions. The first, having to do more with behavior, is a deeper study of the *external* act of the will, and the related concept of direct/indirect causality. The second aspect, having to do with attitude, called for a closer look at the *internal* act of the will, and the question of direct/indirect voluntariness.[1] Much of the difficulty of moral analysis lies in the interdependency of these strands; in treating them separately, we must not separate them. With this caution in mind, we begin our look at the objective aspect of the problem.

1. Objective aspect: Intrinsic evil

A subtle shift in focus in the discussion of cooperation with evil can be discerned by the fact that we no longer refer to the topic as "cooperation in another's sin" as the manuals generally did, but as "cooperation in evil". The pioneers of this new nomenclature were Dominic Prümmer and Adolphe Alfred Tanquerey.[2] This would seem to herald the definitive end to the confusion caused by the emergence of the issue of cooperation from reflection on scandal. Gradually, the significance of the fact that the principal agent is presumed to be determined to sin was assimilated; the problematic aspect of cooperation lies not in its contribution to the action of the other *qua* sin, but *qua* disordered or damage causing. Can it be morally good for me, the cooperator, to contribute to that disorder or damage? Thus, the question of the objective nature of the cooperator's act took on increasing prominence.

Conditional intrinsic evil

We have grown so accustomed to thinking of intrinsically evil acts as evil *"always and per se*, in other words on account of their very object, and quite apart from the ulterior intentions of the one acting and the circumstances"[3] that it may surprise the reader to hear that the concept of *conditionally* intrinsic evil ever existed. Nonetheless, the study of the concept of intrinsic evil by James Murtagh indicates that a majority of Manualists favored this concept as they attempted to elucidate the notion of intrinsic evil.[4] Essentially, this category of conditionally intrinsic evil—envisioned as containing actions that are evil except in certain exceptional circumstances—is nothing new. We have seen it in Waffelaert's interpretation of *male sonantes* actions, in Genet's reference to actions which can "cohonestari" (be made licit) by circumstances, in Sanchez's category of quasi-intrinsic evil. Several Manualists divide the category of intrinsic evil into *three* parts: absolutely and in every case, conditionally depending upon ownership rights, and by reason of danger of sin ordinarily involved (e.g. the reading of obscene literature).[5] While maintaining the notion of absolutely intrinsically evil actions, these authors restricted it to sins such as blasphemy, for which no redeeming circumstances could be imagined.

From the perspective of half a century, this view of intrinsic evil seems to be an unsuccessful attempt to solve, among other things, the problem of immediate cooperation. It amounts to saying that extreme circumstances, such as the hold-up of a bank, reveal the fact that genuine intrinsic evil is not involved in theft. One wonders by what argument these authors would counter those who try to show that *no* acts are absolutely evil by pointing to other cases of extreme circumstances, such as that of a woman who might gain freedom from prison in return for committing adultery. The position of the Magisterium tends not to restrict the field of intrinsic evil to certain sins like blasphemy, but rather to offer an open-ended list:

> The Second Vatican Council itself, in discussing the respect due to the human person, gives a number of examples of such acts [which *per se* and in themselves, independently of circumstances, are always seriously wrong by reason of their object]: "Whatever is hostile to life itself, such as any kind of homicide, genocide, abortion, euthanasia and voluntary suicide; whatever violates the integrity of the human person, such as mutilation, physical and mental torture and attempts to coerce the spirit; whatever is offensive to human dignity, such as subhuman living conditions, arbitrary imprisonment, deportation, slavery, prostitution and trafficking in women and children; degrading conditions of work which treat labourers as mere instruments of profit, and not as free responsible persons: all these and the like are a disgrace, and so long as they infect human civilization they contaminate those who inflict them more than those who suffer injustice, and they are a negation of the honour due to the Creator."[6]

The failure of the graduated version of intrinsic evil, and also its disappearance in recent decades, appears to be linked to its dependence upon an insufficient understanding of the object of the act. Edouard Genicot, a representative of this position, defines the object of the act separately from the *finis operis* of the agent,[7] although these notions are now commonly identified with one another. In a footnote, Thomas Jorio does mention the term *finis operis*, saying that it is to be identified with the object of the act. Nonetheless, the notion of object as end is otherwise ignored by him, and his example of moral object is "the sum of money stolen".[8]

This "physicalist" understanding of object is usually presented as mistaking a physical object for a verbal noun phrase, which alone can be a moral object: in the case of theft, *res aliena* instead of *ablatio rei alienae*.[9] Yet it is interesting to note that Genicot is indifferent as to whether the object is described in one way or the other: "The *material* object of the act is that about which the act is concerned, either the thing, e.g. the money of another that is desired; or the action, e.g. the taking of what belongs to another."[10] What makes the object to be a moral object in the proper or formal sense is the agent's advertence to a norm governing the material object.[11] In other words, besides failing to bring out the distinctively moral aspect of the object, Genicot introduces the terms "material/formal" into the discussion in a manner that confuses the issue with the question of imputability. We shall return to this common pitfall in the next section, dealing with the subjective aspect of human action (p. ***).

Those moralists who maintain the absolute concept of intrinsic evil develop the notion of object *qua* moral object more clearly. Says Prümmer:

> The object, however, as principle of morality, is not
> the very *physical* object, which the human act
> concerns, but the moral object, insofar as it is
> *subject to the norm of morality*... Thus, e.g. in the
> action of stealing the moral object is not the very
> thing belonging to another that is taken considered
> in itself, but insofar as reason forbids that it be
> taken, its owner being rationally opposed.[12]

This requires defining the object of theft more narrowly:
"Theft is the stealthy reception or removal of another's
goods, whose owner is reasonably unwilling."[13] Likewise,
Davis, another representative of absolute intrinsic evil,
writes: "Thus, the object as here understood of the theft
of money is not the taking of money, but the taking of it
from its rightful owner against his reasonable will..."[14]

Such an understanding of the moral object requires that
significant elements of the situation be included in the
object and not among the circumstances. Murtagh comments: "The question is what criterion can we use to
determine what circumstance to include and to exclude
[as part of the object]: it seems here that there is a certain
ambiguity in the manuals..."[15] Some of the Manualists
themselves admit as much: "Often it depends upon the
formation of concepts or the framing of the question
under examination if one wishes to consider an element
as belonging to the object or as a mere circumstance."[16]

Two dangers threaten in the face of this difficulty. First,
if the object description is made more complex, one can
begin to include so many details that one can appear to be
essentially describing an action *in concreto*. There is virtual
unanimity today that individual actions are either good or
evil, but the notion of intrinsic evil claims that a class of
actions (e.g. theft) can be defined *in abstracto* and designated morally. If one must consider all morally relevant
circumstances before rendering a moral judgment, each

act will be "absolutely" good or bad, but the concept of intrinsically evil actions will be evacuated of its sense. This is the only understanding of intrinsic evil admitted by some authors today.[17]

If, on the other extreme, insufficient situational elements are provided, one appears to have an action that is indifferent with regard to species. It then seems necessary for the circumstances to determine the moral quality of the action in the given case. Often, the circumstance playing this role is the ulterior motive of the agent (traditionally, the circumstance answering the question *cur?*). This error easily occurs in the case of cooperation with evil, for the aspect of cooperation is ripe to be considered a mere circumstance. When one prescinds from the aspect of cooperation, an act description remains that often has no moral meaning other than the reason for which it is done. An example from Benedict Merkelbach will make this clear: he proposes the case of a bartender pouring a drink for a customer. Clearly, this seems good or indifferent if the circumstance of the customer's intoxication level is not included. If that is studiously ignored, the only way of determining the morality of the act is to consider the *finis operantis*. Thus, he concludes: "if a bartender gives someone drink for the purpose of inebriating him, the cooperation is formal; but only material if he serves him drinks to make a profit, foreseeing that he will get drunk."[18]

For this reason, the question of indifferent acts assumes a great importance.[19] Are "pouring a drink" and "handing over keys" indifferent moral act descriptions or act descriptions of the natural order? As we observed with Waffelaert's analysis of "casting a vote", it is misleading to treat such act descriptions, shorn of context which would make them morally appreciable, as good or indifferent actions. Merkelbach introduces his assessment of the bartender's behavior by recalling the position of St Alphonsus that "the same act can be either formal or material cooperation on account of a different intention."[20] No one will disagree that an act of material cooperation would become formal cooperation upon the presupposition of an evil *finis operantis*. In this sense the statement is clearly true.[21] However, what is in question is the existence of a great number of actions that have been adequately described as actions in the moral order, yet which are morally indifferent in species. This is particularly doubtful when the actions in question (giving a tipsy person a drink) are very similar to intrinsically evil actions (making someone drunk).[22]

Just what kind of action, if any, should be deemed indifferent according to species? It seems highly significant that the examples of indifferent acts given by Prümmer— "walking, painting, eating, etc."[23]—differ so radically from the well known example given by St Thomas: lifting a straw from the ground.[24] In that same article, St Thomas gives "tollere alienum" as an example of an act that is of an evil species. Certainly, Thomas is not writing with the express purpose of clarifying the controversies of our day, for in another place he gives a similarly brief act description—"occidere hominem"—as an example of a merely *physical* description.[25] We shall return to the task of interpreting this passage of St Thomas (*ST* I-II, q. 1 a. 3 ad 3), for it continues to fuel debate among moral theologians. For now, we must continue to follow the development of thought among the Manualists on intrinsic evil.

The "directly intended" equivocation

Another approach to intrinsic evil is identified in an article by Nicholas Hendriks: "certain moralists seem to qualify an evil act as 'intrinsecus malus' because the evil is direct.

D. M. Prümmer, for example, has written in his manual of moral theology that direct abortion, which is the direct putting to death of an innocent human being, is an intrinsically evil act."[26] This notion of intrinsic evil attempts to surpass the now outdated manner of speaking of Aertnys—Damen, which describes the object of an intrinsically evil act in purely physical terms: "Thus the taking of another's possessions, homicide, injuring someone's reputation are intrinsically evil; sometimes, however, they turn out to be licit."[27] This approach to intrinsic evil, which was, we recall, dominant, corresponded with the widespread definition of abortion as simply "the expulsion of a non-viable fetus".[28] Defined in this way, the death of the fetus, which naturally follows its expulsion, could be considered indirect.[29] H. G. Kramer even interprets the strong condemnation of abortion by Pius XI in *Casti connubii* in this manner.[30] Thus, in Kramer's view, the Pontiff would be condemning abortions done to preserve the life or health of the mother as *indirect* but unjustified (he calls them "therapeutic" abortions[31]), while abortions done for eugenic reasons would be condemned as *direct* abortions, because in this case the elimination of the child is sought as a means to improving society. Effectively, only these latter abortions, direct in the sense of "willed for their own sake", would be intrinsically evil.

Erroneously, Kramer claims that the condemnations by the Holy Office of various forms of abortion to save the life of the mother, including craniotomy, do not show that these forms of abortion are "directly willed killing".[32] Rather, in calling these "directe occisivam" the Holy See would only be saying that "the operation, by its nature, leads to death, but not that death is necessarily directly willed."[33] Kramer would maintain that the Holy See is merely demanding a much more substantial justification for willing indirectly something that directly causes the death of a fetus.

Notwithstanding this opinion, it seemed clear to Prümmer, as it was to the Holy Office, that the intentional expulsion of a non-viable fetus from the womb is a morally evil action for whatever reason it is done. The killing of the child is not an effect of the abortion, but abortion *just is* killing a child. To choose abortion directly is direct killing. Thus, it would be absurd to describe, as Kramer does,[34] abortions procured to preserve a career, prevent infamy, or promote the upbringing of existing children, as "indirect abortions" which are only evil on account of a lack of proportionate reason.

Yet there is a potential equivocation here that Hendriks has picked up on. If the term "directly intended" means that the agent's direct willing of evil is the *cause* of an action's being "intrinsically" evil, one doubts the appositeness of the word "intrinsic". Moreover, the traditional sense of the term would be lost: intrinsic evil denotes a moral object which makes the agent's will evil should he choose it, not vice-versa. Intrinsically evil acts must never be directly chosen, and thus one would confuse matters by defining intrinsically evil acts themselves as directly chosen. Presumably Prümmer and certainly magisterial documents today[35] have something else in mind (other than "directly willed") when they include the word "direct" in the definition of abortion. Or more precisely, there must be a relationship between "directly caused" and "directly willed". In order to define what acts are of their very nature intrinsically evil, the sense of "direct" that applies relates not primarily to the intention of the agent but to the causal structure of the case. The idea that some effects are so closely (intrinsically) tied to a cause led to the effort to discern what acts are intrinsically evil because they cause a bad effect, like the death of a baby, *directly*. This is the significance of the discussion concerning the *per se* effects of an act to which we now turn.

The "no other purpose" definition

Not a few authors describe intrinsic evil as "that which could not but serve an evil end."[36] This description, too, is not unambiguous. If all that is meant is that the agent will not be committing an intrinsically evil action provided he has some legitimate purpose in mind, we have nothing but Kramer's error just discussed: namely, provided there is some goal other than the death of the fetus in mind, abortion will not be direct killing in a moral sense. However, the "no other purpose" definition might also mean that the act is such that one choosing it *must* have an evil intention, because the nature of the act admits of no other purpose. This may be what Noldin was trying to get at with the following precision: "Therefore, a thing or action is not intrinsically evil in as much as it serves precisely and uniquely an evil end but in as much as it neither has nor could have an honest end."[37] This calls for a consideration of the relation between the *per se* effects of a human act and the end which specifies it as a moral act.

Two opinions developed on the issue over the centuries and were inherited by the Manualists.[38] The majority of thinkers held that only in natural causes is there a *per se* effect that determines the species of the cause. In so far as a human act is a natural cause (the act of adultery, for instance, can also be considered in its purely physical dimension as intercourse between a man and a woman), it will also be ordered to a unique *per se* effect, but this effect will not determine the species of the act *qua* moral act. Other thinkers, including Cajetan and Suarez, insisted that free actions also have a unique *per se* effect which is the *finis operis.*[39] Modern day supporters of this latter view are fewer[40] but include Prümmer and Vermeersch. Clearly, there is a danger that this position could lead to an unacceptable physicalism and rigorism. Perhaps to show that this is not necessarily so, Vermeersch took advantage of a controversial case to defend his position as authentically Catholic.

The issue that invited exploration of the moral relevance of direct causality was a doubt concerning the liceity of the removal of the cancerous uterus of an expectant mother. Vermeersch engaged in a debate with Agostino Gemelli, who maintained that the removal of the uterus in such a circumstance amounted to a direct abortion (directly willed) because the evil effect comes about inevitably and necessarily (directly caused). While trying to maintain the position that human actions have a single *per se* effect, Vermeersch disagreed with Gemelli and sought to justify such an operation. He denied that the certainty of an effect distinguishes it as willed *per se.*[41] Rather, he argued that there is a certain "direction of action", in relation to which such effects as the death of the child will be "accidental". If an effect is neither the end sought nor a means to the end (non quaeritur *propter se* [neque] *in se*), as determined by this "direction of action", it cannot specify the moral quality of the act.[42] In the hysterectomy case, Vermeersch argued rightly that the presence of the child in the womb was accidental to the therapeutic action being performed. The sign of this, he continued, is the fact that the hysterectomy would be performed even if the woman had not been expecting. This conclusion seems clear enough today. Yet, efforts to improve upon Vermeersch's argumentation must continue. For one thing, it does not provide a clear answer to the problem of ectopic pregnancy. He calls Lehmkuhl's support of the intervention known as salpinjectomy "plus discutable" (more debatable).[43] Yet the logic of Vermeersch's position would seem to forbid it, as such an operation would obviously not be undertaken if there were no fetus present.

As far as cooperation with evil is concerned, conclusions in reference to implicitly formal cooperation are difficult to draw from these debates. On the one hand, it seems that the bad effect in cooperation cases cannot be considered a natural *per se* effect, since it depends upon the decision of the principal agent. Kramer argues that free causes must be considered accidental.[44] On the other hand, many cases of cooperation, including that in Proposition 51 would fail Vermeersch's test: if the ladder were not going to be used to commit a crime, the servant would not have placed it. He was not "doing it anyway" as is the woman who has her infected uterus removed. Thus, on these accounts of direct causality, it is not clear whether or when cooperation would be intrinsically evil by reason of the object of the cooperator's act.

2. Subjective aspect: Indirect voluntary

We now turn our attention to developments made during the Manualist period concerning the subjective aspect of the moral act. As we have mentioned, it would be an error to separate artificially the subjective and objective aspects of moral analysis. At the same time, a failure to distinguish where necessary has lead to unnecessary confusion.

Duress

During our review of tendencies characterizing the casuist period preceding the condemnations of Innocent XI, we noted that one way of lessening the burden of the law upon the subject was to raise up *incommoditas* as a sort of balance to the demands of the law. While it is beyond question that a positive law (attending Sunday Mass, helping the poor) does not bind under grave inconvenience, no amount of hardship is supposed to justify the infraction of a negative precept. At times, however, even during the Manualist period, pressure upon the agent, usually called "duress", became a tool to excuse the agent from objective violations of the law. Again, this tendency is of great relevance to our study, because the most difficult cases of cooperation with evil—immediate material cooperation and Proposition 51 in particular—are usually presented as involving duress, even the threat of death.

In our examination of Genet, we were exposed to the traditional approach to the question of duress: threat or pressure cannot justify doing evil, nor make evil good and choice-worthy. However, fear in an agent might reach such a point as to render him no longer responsible for his actions. Then his actions, if lacking freedom entirely, would not be truly human, nor his crimes imputable to him.

This teaching appears consonant with what we find in St Thomas, although the latter's precision adds clarity. Firstly, Thomas distinguishes between the questions of whether "violence"[45] can cause an act to be involuntary and whether "fear" [46] can do so. Ordinarily, as in the case of the Servant and the Ladder, "duress" refers to fear of a future evil; the subject is not, however, being physically forced. In answering the question, "Whether fear makes an act simply involuntary?", St Thomas uses the famous example of a merchant throwing his goods into the sea for fear of sinking. Although his action is obviously involuntary in some sense (he regrets "having" to ruin his goods), it is "more voluntary than involuntary".[47] Indeed, contrary to our expectations, Thomas points out that it is precisely the circumstance of the fear that makes the destruction of goods "simply voluntary". Were it not for this circumstance, the destruction would be completely involuntary (and therefore would not take place), but in the *hic et nunc* of the threatening storm, the act is essentially voluntary. Thomas points out that morality concerns acts which occur in concrete circumstances and in these circumstances it must be assessed.[48] The result is counter-intuitive: although the circumstance of fear certainly tends to excuse or mitigate the guilt of the agent on a level of subjective imputability, it simultaneously constitutes the action as one for which the agent is objectively responsible.

This received teaching is difficult to accept. One way in which it was developed so as to excuse or justify behavior in extreme situations was by a distinction between voluntary and free. Gury, for instance, presents the traditional definition of voluntary (an act proceeding from the will with knowledge of the end) and distinguishes a subclass of voluntary acts, which proceed from the will "with the power of not acting".[49] Only these would be designated as "free" and capable of founding a human act. With an understanding of freedom thus detached from the voluntary, it became possible to conceive of choosing (voluntarily) an evil without (freely) willing it. Only in such a way could authors speak of choosing the lesser evil in a conflict situation.[50] Robert Morlino explains:

> For [Catholic Manualists], to choose evil that good may come of it presumes that the 'instrumental' evil is an authentic moral object: a strictly conditioned and freely chosen act. The Manualists have made it clear that lesser of evils reasoning applies only when the coercion factor is present, so that when the lesser of evils *is* chosen, a freedom-deficiency *is* operative, i.e. the evil chosen is rendered a non-moral evil.[51]

K. Peschke implies that this logic is at work in those Manualists—the majority, as we have seen—who classify implicit formal cooperation as immediate material. Noting that this classification allows for the possibility of exceptions in extreme situations, such as the threat of death, he adds, "this kind of cooperation is ... not performed with real consent."[52] Thus, he fails to distinguish objectively bad behavior that we should be very gentle in reproving from objectively good behavior that is choice-worthy and to be recommended.

Another contemporary author, Joseph Boyle, actually uses the very example that St Thomas proposed as evidence that voluntariness remains under duress to claim that coercion removes obligation to follow the law. Referring to the merchant throwing his goods into the sea, Boyle writes that duress makes "some chosen behaviors, wrong in most circumstances ... morally justified."[53] The problem of explaining what coercion justifies what behaviors, and why some are never to be justified will, of course, remain. He continues: "It is often not clear even to the conscientious when this happens and how it affects the obligation not to contribute to wrongdoing."

Practitioners of law are not infrequently faced with actual cases in which a person is moved by hunger or threats to commit a serious breach of the law. Duff cites a case from British law in which a man, under duress and fearing for his life, drove IRA killers to and from the murder of a policeman. One of the judges commented soberly: "The result [of duress] will be that what is done will be done most unwillingly but yet intentionally."[54] Extenuating circumstances call for merciful punishment not the denial of objective rights and duties.

Nonetheless, among Catholic theologians, the passage from formal cooperation to material in situations of duress is commonplace. In regard to the participation of judges in divorce cases, John Coughlin appears to say that otherwise formal cooperation ceases to be such under duress: "when refusal of a case is not a practical option, the doctrine of necessary material cooperation applies."[55] Pope John Paul II[56] noted the fact that judges are often faced with fewer options than lawyers, but his words are better understood to mean that the judge is justified in cooperating materially where a lawyer would not be, not that what would be formal cooperation ceases to be such for lack of good options. In another well known example to be discussed in Chapter 11 (***), the United States Conference of Catholic Bishops was asked to remove an appendix from the 1994 edition of the *Ethical and Religious Directives for Catholic Health Care Services* (ERD's) which had explicitly claimed that duress could convert implicitly formal into immediate material cooperation.[57]

Development of the indirect voluntary

The concept of duress can be seen as a special case of a much larger phenomenon, usually referred to as the "indirect voluntary". In the case of duress, an agent is acting so as to avoid a significant harm, but he might also be moved to act in order to attain a significant good. Indeed, it seems only a matter of style and not ethics whether one says that a person is acting to avoid the danger of death or to promote the good of a long life. In both cases—acting under duress and acting for some good end which also requires causing a negative consequence—freedom is in some way compromised. More precisely, in both cases the agent acts unwillingly, or with "mixed" voluntariness.

The sustained effort to discern when action is licit under such conditions caused "the celebrated *voluntaria in causa*", in the words of Thomas Gilby, "to loom large in casuistry."[58] This concept looms so large that it had better be solidly founded. Thus it is disconcerting to learn that, while the doctrine can be traced to St Thomas, his terminology has been changed and its meaning developed to such a degree that it ceases to qualify as a Thomistic doctrine.[59] To begin with, the *voluntaria in causa* is equated by the Manualists with a different Thomistic notion, the "indirect voluntary". Commonly, this hybrid notion refers to the will's relation to "side-effects": foreseen but unwanted effects of either actions or omissions. Additionally, it is employed by them for the purpose of exculpating the agent for such effects. While he is still held responsible for them, they can be "allowed" for a proportionate reason.[60] This doctrine of the indirect voluntary underlies the principle of double effect, which we will treat in the next chapter. For now, let it suffice to observe that the concept allowed effects such as the injury to the virgin in Proposition 51 to be considered as side-effects to be tolerated by the servant acting under pressure.

St Thomas, by contrast, understood two very different things by *voluntaria in causa* and *voluntaria indirecte*.[61] The former refers to *positively* willed acts which have the foreseeable effect of allowing or inducing the agent to do some harm (e.g. getting drunk and then crashing his car as a result).[62] The latter term refers to *negatively* willed acts, or even the absence of any interior act at all, when the agent could and should have acted (e.g a shipwreck caused by a negligent helmsman).[63] Both terms are used by St Thomas in the context of *bad* actions to indicate that voluntariness and responsibility remain in these cases.[64] Only centuries later were these terms conflated by the Manualists and used to show that evil effects need *not* be imputed to the agent, but rather may be considered as merely permitted.[65] Certainly, this period of theological reflection is not without enduring fruits, indicated by the use of the direct/indirect distinction by the Church's Magisterium today. Nonetheless, a critical examination of the process of development may serve to understand better and delimit properly the use of the "indirect voluntary" or as it is sometimes called "the intention/foresight distinction".

Evidence of the new thinking on this matter is already visible in Cajetan, whether or not he be the origin of it. In various places he simply applies the indirect voluntary to positive acts, thus identifying it with *voluntarium in alio* (or *in causa*). A clear example cited by Hendriks is that of a runner: "For example, when one willingly runs and from it gets tired, the running is willed directly and in itself: the consequent fatigue, however, is willed indirectly and in another, that is, in the willed running, from which it follows, and not in itself nor directly..."[66] Clearly there is something indisputably true about this analysis; the fatigue is sought neither as an end nor as a means. On the other hand, as we saw in our review of probabilism, the introduction of principles can lead to unexpected results. In particular, attention must be paid to the resulting category of "actively or positively permitted effects". Very easily a negative precept would become a positive obligation to impede a material (not directly intended) sin, an obligation which would not bind under proportionate *incommoditas*.[67] Then, the only negative precepts which bind *semper et pro semper* would be those forbidding the commission of some evil for its own sake. The number of absolutely intrinsically evil acts decreases, and Pascal's accusation (that only "sinning for the sake of sinning" is forbidden) takes on relevance once again.

This shift in thinking merits a detailed study. Here, we can suggest as a very tentative hypothesis a link with the Ockhamist approach in moral theology to which we alluded earlier (see pp. ***). Freedom had come to be conceived as sheer autonomy, disengaged from its object which is the good. For this reason it was viewed in opposition to the law, which only burdened and limited its exercise. From this background two impulses might have arisen that could have resulted in the new doctrine of "indirect voluntary". First, there is the inclination to analyze the agent's responsibility prescinding from the goodness or badness of the act involved. One is not most free or authentically free when choosing the good, but one is equally free to choose good or evil. Yet it is critical to note that St Thomas would apply the *voluntaria in causa* to a case which, like that of striking a pregnant woman, was known to be illicit so as to determine the imputability of the effect. Later, the concept is employed *before* a moral judgment on the act has been made, with the goal of determining whether the act itself can be posited. Billuart still maintained that effects only qualify as indirectly voluntary when they are forbidden, but this was to change.[68]

Second, in light of the Ockhamist view of "freedom as indifference",[69] we can understand the tendency to merge and confound action and omission. This seems to be what caused the two terms, *voluntaria in causa* and *voluntaria indirecte* to be used interchangeably; the very notions of positive and negative action gradually merged. A person is naturally understood to be free not to act, unless some duty compels him to act; thus, he understandably is not said to omit an action unless he could and should do it. This is really just common sense: one is not supposed to have "omitted" wishing someone "Happy Birthday" unless it is the person's birthday, and one is a close enough acquaintance to know it. Still, some authors began to argue that omissions are voluntary regardless of their being forbidden, that is, regardless of the omitted act being one that a person should do.[70] This step, taken by Billuart in opposition to Cajetan, is significant. Kramer says that "[it] may offer a key to the solution of the whole question of the indirect voluntary ... We find in Billuart's principles an argument for considering the voluntary character of effects to consist in their being negatively willed."[71] While this transformation, whereby side-effects were equated with omissions, took centuries, it does seem that one can see even Cajetan treating positive action in a parallel fashion to omissions: a person should be presumed free to do whatever he wishes, unless the law forbids him. For instance, commenting on the case of accidental death, he describes the reason for imputability of accidental homicide in the same terms as an omission: "for [an accidental] homicide to be imputed to someone, it is required not only that he could remove that from which death follows, e.g. the stone thrown, the sword girded, etc., but also that he should remove it, that is, that he be obliged positively, e.g. to remove the girded sword, or negatively, e.g. to abstain from throwing the stone."[72]

To conclude, it seems that these two related tendencies—(1) focusing on the question of voluntariness with a mind to discovering whether a proposed act could be posited and (2) likening, for the purpose of moral evaluation, the causing of side-effects with omissions—came to be combined. An example of the result has already been seen: Kramer's skewed reading of *Casti connubii*. We saw that he considered "therapeutic abortion" (including, improperly, under this rubric the removal of the fetus with the health of the mother in mind) to be "wrong because there is not sufficient reason for permitting the death of the innocent."[73] This transformation of categories was not played out when Kramer was writing in 1935. If one brackets the morality of acts and omissions, and equates the causing of bad side effects with the bad effects that result from not acting, one turns difficult moral problems into full-fledged conflicts of duty. The next chapter will show how these conflicts came to be resolved.

Another inconvenient result of this manner of dealing with foreseen effects—lumping them all together as *praeter intentionem* if they are willed neither *in se* nor *propter se*, and considering them negatively willed—is that the distinction between excuse and justification gets blurred. Even if these terms are frequently used interchangeably, there are two different situations that can be encountered, which the terms tend to pick out: an action can be good and choice-worthy despite bad effects (justified), or it can be bad and yet the agent escape blame for subjective reasons or extenuating circumstances (excused). The trends outlined above tended to shift the focus of morality away from identifying the good to be pursued, towards demonstrating that the agent is not responsible for the evil that he causes. Some authors, such as P. Palazzini, even insist that a foreseen evil effect of one's action is a sin but only a material sin, that is, a sin for which there is an excuse: "the evil effect joined to the action of the agent, though it be *praeter intentionem*, remains a material sin: indeed, far from rarely it leads to a grave danger of formal sin."[74] Ordinarily, material sin refers to deeds committed by a subject lacking in knowledge or the possession of his faculties; consequently, he will not be held responsible for the effects of his actions. However, in the case of an agent acting with indirect voluntariness, everyone acknowledges that he has a responsibility for the evil effects caused; for this reason a compensatory reason is required to cause them licitly. Treating *praeter intentionem* effects implicitly or, as Palazzini does, explicitly as material sin causes the following paradox to arise. Intention is part of the definition of imputability, as Vermeersch notes: "Actio vel omissio propria *imputatur secundum omnes notas quae intenduntur.*"[75] If the bad side-effects are described as *praeter intentionem*, it is hard to see how the agent could still be held responsible for them.[76] Likewise, when cooperation is classified as material, due to the fact that the evil effects are not intended as means or end,[77] the cooperating agent is still considered responsible for the evil caused. Having acted with full deliberation and consent, it still seems ambiguous if his action is justified (good) or excused (bad), and thus his relatioship to the harm caused remains unclear.

Notes

[1]   Our source for this division of the issues is S. Privitera, "Principi morali tradizionali," in *Nuovo dizionario morali*, eds. F. Compagnoni, G. Piana and S. Privitera, pp. 986–994 (Milan: Edizioni San Paolo, 1990), at pp. 993–994.

[2]   Cf. Fabbro, *Cooperation in Evil*, p. 9.

[3]   John Paul II, *Veritatis Splendor*, 80.

[4]   Murtagh, *Intrinsic Evil*, pp. 17–23. Hendriks goes so far as to state: "In fact, all moralists considered as licit certain acts which, without any doubt, are not evil only '*ex lege positiva*' but also '*ex propria natura*' (that is, intrinsically) ..." N. Hendriks, "La contraception artificielle: conflit de devoirs ou acte à double effet," *Nouvelle revue théologique* 104 (1982), pp. 396–413, at p. 409.

[5]   For example, Thomas Jorio writes: "*absolute* et in omni casu... eo quod ex se semper rectae rationi repugnant, ut odium Dei, blasphemia, oppressio innocentium... *conditionate* ratione *adiuncti* quod pendet a *dominativa potestate* Dei vel hominis, ut ablatio rei alienae, laesio corporis vel famae, quae aliquando licita evadunt... alia ratione *periculi* quod ordinarie involvunt." T. Jorio, *Theologia moralis*, 4ᵗʰ ed. (Naples: M. D'Auria Editore Pontificia, 1953), I, p. 47.

[6]   John Paul II, *Veritatis splendor*, 80, citing the Pastoral Constitution on the Church in the Modern World *Gaudium et Spes*, 27.

[7] E. Genicot, *Theologiae moralis institutiones*, 3rd ed. (Louvain: Polleunis et Ceuterick, 1900), I, pp. 38–39.

[8] Jorio, *Theologia moralis*, I, pp. 47–48.

[9] Chad Ripperger notes: "These two [Thomistic] traditions are clearly divided into those who say the object of the moral act is an object, i.e., the exterior thing about which the exterior action concerns itself, and those who say it is the exterior act itself." C. Ripperger, *"The Species and Unity of the Moral Act," Thomist* 59 (1995), pp. 69–90, at p. 74.

[10] "Objectum actus *materiale* est id circa quod actus versatur, sive res, ex. gr. pecunia aliena quae concupiscitur; sive actio, ex. gr. rei alienae ablatio." Genicot, *Theologiae moralis institutiones*, I, p. 38. Aquinas also "believes that both ways of considering an end are completely acceptable," as Joseph Pilsner amply explains. Pilsner, *Specification*, p. 88.

[11] "Objectum *formale* est istud idem prout cum advertentia ad normam honestatis attingitur ab agente… Manifestum est actum desumere moralitatem ex objecto formaliter inspecto…" Genicot, *Theologiae moralis institutiones*, I, p. 38.

[12] "Obiectum autem, prout est principium moralitatis, non est ipsum obiectum *physicum*, quod actus humanus attingit, sed obiectum morale, *prout subest normae moralitatis…* Hinc ex. gr. in actione furandi obiectum morale non est ipsa res aliena ablata in se considerata, sed quatenus ratio vetat ne auferatur, domino rationabiliter invito." Prümmer, *Manuale theologiae moralis*, I, p. 73. Januarius Bucceroni uses almost the same terms. Cf. J. Bucceroni, *Institutiones theologiae moralis secundum doctrinam S. Thomae et S. Alfonsi* (Rome: Pontifical Institute of Pius IX, 1914), I, p. 72.

[13] Prümmer, *Manuale theologiae moralis*, II, p. 74.

[14] Davis, *Moral and Pastoral Theology*, I, p. 55.

[15] Murtagh, *Intrinsic Evil*, p. 54.

[16] J. Mausbach and G. Ermecke, *Teología moral católica*, 2d ed. (Pamplona: Ediciones Universidad de Navarra, 1971); orig. *Katholische Moraltheologie*, 9th ed. (Münster: Aschendorffshche Verlagsbuchchandlung, 1959), cited by H. Boelaars, "Riflessioni sull'atto umano effettivo," *Studia Moralia* 13 (1975), pp. 109–142, at p. 117.

[17] For example, E. V. Vacek, "Proportionalism: One View of the Debate," *Theological Studies* 46 (1985), pp. 287–314, at p. 294.

18   Merkelbach, *Summa theologiae moralis*, I, p. 401. M. Zalba, in a
     similar vein treats the "giving of keys" as an indifferent act that can
     only be evaluated by looking at the servant's motive: "[in cooper-
     atione formali] sic accidit cum famulus tradit claves arcae pecuni-
     ariae furi *ut* is possit facilius pecuniam arripere;... In cooperatione
     materiali concursus praestatur actioni alterius quatenus physica
     est, sine ulla intentione participandi et sine ulla participatione
     neque implicita in eius moralitate.... Sic famulus qui sub minis
     mortis invitus tradit claves domus furi, materialiter cooperatur ad
     furtum istius, minime vero formaliter." Zalba, *Theologiae moralis
     compendium*, II, p. 282.

19   In this connection, the entire footnote 24 of Chapter 10 of Martin
     Rhonheimer's book, *Natural Law and Practical Reason* is worth
     quoting: "[The unfortunate tradition of abstracting an object from
     the context of the *genus moris*] can often be seen in the inability
     to distinguish objectively *indifferent* acts from acts considered in
     their *genus naturae*. For example, Merkelbach uses 'giving money'
     (*dare pecuniam*) as an illustration of an *actio indifferens* (*Summa
     theologiae moralis*, 2nd ed., vol. 1 [Paris, 1935], p. 142). But this is
     not an indifferent action; it is an action like 'giving alms' or 'paying
     a reward,' but treated in respect to its *genus naturae*. 'Giving
     money' as such does not exist, because 'giving money' as such is
     already and *always* a *proportio ad rationem*, and thus has the moral
     species of 'good' or 'evil.' An action is morally indifferent only when
     such a *proportio* is not found in it, but only in the circumstances
     or the intention. The standard examples Thomas uses are 'scratch-
     ing one's beard,' or 'going for a walk,' and so on. The difference
     between this kind of action and 'giving money' should be obvious."
     M. Rhonheimer, *Natural Law and Practical Reason: a Thomistic
     View of Moral Autonomy*, trans. G. Malsbary (New York: Fordham
     University Press, 2000), p. 532; original title, *Natur als Grundlage
     der Moral*, (Innsbruck: Tyrolia-Verlag, 1987).

20   "Eadem igitur actio potest pro diversa intentione esse cooperatio
     formalis vel materialis..." Merkelbach, *Summa theologiae moralis*,
     I, p. 401.

21   So, a comment such as the following remains ambiguous and
     unhelpful: "In other words, formal and material cooperation
     cannot be distinguished if one remains solely on the physical,
     material level. He who stands guard for the thief so that he will be
     able to steal with more security cooperates formally in the theft.
     Exactly the same physical action, for example, standing guard for

a thief, can be material cooperation if the one cooperating does it to save his life. The difference between the two can only be determined by examining the intention of the one cooperating." Fabbro, *Cooperation in Evil*, p. 168.

22 We will return later to the question of how to justify the use of intoxicating beverages as an anesthetic (pp. 338–339).

23 Prümmer, *Manuale theologiae moralis*, I, p. 87.

24 *De Malo*, q. 2, a. 5.

25 *ST* I–II, q. 1, a. 3, ad 3.

26 Hendriks, "La contraception artificielle," p. 407, citing Prümmer: "Numquam autem licet *directe* procurare abortum, cum hoc sit directa occisio hominis innocentis ideoque actio intrinsecus mala." Prümmer, *Manuale theologiae moralis*, I, p. 48. However, Prümmer actually defines abortion as "eiectio immaturi foetus viventis ex utero materno" (II, p. 127). Cf. W. E. May, *Catholic Bioethics and the Gift of Human Life,* 2ⁿᵈ ed., (Huntington, IN: Our Sunday Visitor, 2008), p. 203, fn. 1. Merkelbach seems to equate "directa procuratio abortus" and "directa occisio innocentis." Merkelbach, *Summa theologiae moralis*, II, p. 360.

27 "Sic ablatio rei alienae, homicidium, famae laesio, sunt intrinsece mala; aliquando tamen licita evadunt." Aertnys—Damen, *Theologia moralis*, I, p. 64.

28 "*Abortus* communiter definitur: *eiectio foetus immaturi*." Bucceroni, *Institutiones theologiae moralis*, I, p. 555. Likewise, see Vermeersch, *Theologiae moralis*, II, p. 449; also H. Noldin and A. Schmitt, *Summa theologiae moralis iuxta codicem iuris canonici* (Regensburg: Oeniponte/Lipsiae, 1941), II, p. 313.

29 This understanding of abortion has returned even amongst non-dissenting theologians, who follow the action theory of Grisez and Rhonheimer. Cf. P. Lee, *Abortion and Unborn Human Life* (Washington, DC: Catholic University of America, 1997), Chapter 4; May, *Catholic Bioethics*, pp. 192-202. It should be noted that these thinkers are more careful than Kramer to limit the scope of indirect abortions. The majority of abortions, according to Lee (p. 115), are intentional or direct, because the goal of the mother is to be rid of the responsibility of the child, which, in the absence of adoption, can only be attained by means of his death.

30 H. G. Kramer, *The Indirect Voluntary or Voluntarium in Causa* (Washington DC: Catholic University of America, 1935), p. 51. Kramer's argument relies heavily upon an ambiguous statement, in which Pius XI makes reference to "what is called the *law of*

extreme necessity, which could even extend to the direct killing of the innocent." Pius XI, *Casti connubii*, December 31, 1930, *Acta Apostolicae Sedis* 22 (1930), pp. 539–592, at pp. 562–564. Kramer interprets the Holy Father to be saying that such a "law" exists but does not apply to the case of abortion. He would, in Kramer's estimation, be using the word "direct" to mean directly caused but not directly willed (p. 51). In this view, Pius XI would be subscribing to the now outmoded terminology of conditional intrinsic evil. A. Vermeersch, on the other hand, interprets the Pontiff to be denying that such a "law of extreme necessity" exists: "Bene praeterea tenendum est principium a S. Pontifice enuntiatum: nullum necessitatis ius ad directam innocentis occisionem pertingere posse." A. Vermeersch, "Encyclical *Casti connubii* annotationes," *Periodica de re morali, canonica, liturgica* 20 (1931), pp. 42–68, at p. 57.

[31] Elio Sgreccia explains that the term "therapeutic" is not properly used in these cases, because the intervention is primarily focused upon the fetus not upon a disease of the mother, and thus they are not truly indirect. Cf. E. Sgreccia, *Manuale di bioetica*, 3rd ed. (Milan: Vita e Pensiero, 1999), I, pp. 466–467.

[32] Kramer, *Indirect Voluntary*, p. 49.

[33] John Connery comments: "Ultimately, to support his position [Grisez] falls back on an argument used by some nineteenth-century moralists to justify medical abortion to save the life of the mother. This opinion, which makes a distinction between direct abortion and direct killing, does not consider the death of the fetus in any sense the means to saving the life of the mother. It is the removal of the fetus from the uterus, not precisely its death, that saves the mother... It should be remarked here, however, that the Holy Office did not accept the distinction between direct abortion and direct killing." J. Connery, "Grisez on Abortion," *Theological Studies* 31(1970), pp. 170–176, at p. 175.

[34] Kramer, *Indirect Voluntary*, p. 52.

[35] Pope John Paul II in *Evangelium Vitae*, defines procured abortion as "the deliberate and direct killing, by whatever means it is carried out, of a human being in the initial phase of his or her existence, from conception to birth" (58).

[36] For example, Klueg, "Sin, cooperation in," p. 246, cited in Chapter 11, p. 342; also, Livio Melina's definition of "implicitly determined" formal cooperation: "quella implicitamente determinata per il fatto che nessun altro significato può ragionevolmente connotare

l'identità dell'azione e distinguere l'oggetto dell'atto di chi coopera dall'oggetto dell'atto di chi intende fare l'azione cattiva." Melina, "La cooperazione," p. 478.

[37] Noldin—Schmitt, *Summa theologiae moralis*, II, p. 120.

[38] For a treatment of this debate see Kramer, *Indirect Voluntary*, pp. 34-39; Ugorji, *Principle of Double Effect*, pp. 92-100; and Hendriks, *Moyen mauvais*, pp. 108-112.

[39] The key text of St Thomas in this regard is another assertion found in the same controversial response mentioned earlier: "Ad tertium dicendum quod idem actus numero, secundum quod semel egreditur ab agente, non ordinatur nisi ad unum finem proximum, a quo habet speciem, sed potest ordinari ad plures fines remotos, quorum unus est finis alterius." *ST* I-II, q. 1, a. 3 ad 3.

[40] At least up to the time that Kramer was writing, in 1935.

[41] Hendriks makes the point that many negative effects, such as in this case the sterility of the woman, are also certain to follow yet are not necessarily willed *per se*. Cf. Hendriks, *Moyen mauvais*, p. 195.

[42] A. Vermeersch, "De causalitate per se et per accidens, seu directa et indirecta," *Periodica de re morali, canonica, liturgica* 21 (1932), pp. 101*-116*, at pp. 115*–116*.

[43] A. Vermeersch, "Avortement direct ou indirect: réponse au T.R.P. Gemelli, O.F.M.," *Nouvelle revue théologique* 60 (1933), pp. 599-620, at p. 601. Salpingectomy is the current medical term for cutting out the part of the Fallopian tube to which the embryo is attached. Those who support this procedure as compatible with Christian morality would see the child growing out of place as a pathology analogous to the cancerous womb and the excising of the relevant part of the tube as an operation performed on the mother. For this reason, the procedure appears distinct from a salpingostomy, in which the embryo only is removed, as this appears to be an intervention performed on the fetus himself.

[44] "But there is another class of accidental causes, that are undetermined by their very nature, and therefore always and objectively accidental, abstracting from divine foreknowledge. These are the free causes, human wills. In reference to these another person can never be more than an accidental cause, for the manner of response can never be certainly foreknown." Kramer, *Indirect Voluntary*, p. 26.

[45] Cf. *ST* I-II, q. 6, a. 5. Thomas further distinguishes, in response to the first objection, pointing out that violence can only render the

external act (*actus a voluntate imperatus*) involuntary, while the immediate act of the will remains free.

46 Cf. *ST* I-II, q. 6, a. 6.

47 "Magis sunt huiusmodi voluntaria quam involuntaria." *Ibid.*

48 "Hoc autem quod per metum agitur, secundum hoc est in actu, secundum quod fit: cum enim actus in singularibus sint, singulare autem, inquantum huiusmodi, est hic et nunc; secundum hoc id quod fit est in actu, secundum quod est hic et nunc et sub aliis conditionibus individualibus." *Ibid.*

49 "Voluntarium, seu actus voluntarius dicitur, qui procedit a voluntate cum intellectuali finis cognitione ... Liberum dicitur, quod procedit a voluntate seipsam determinante cum potentia non agendi ... hinc omne liberum est voluntarium, sed non viceversa." J. P. Gury, *Compendium theologiae moralis*, I, p. 311. Note, this seems to be a bending of a legitimate distinction between voluntary and free that is made, for instance, by Billuart. Here voluntary is divided into "free" (*liberum*), which applies to people, and "necessary" (*necessarium*), which applies to animals and human actions done without deliberation (*in brutis et in motibus humanis praevenientibus deliberationem rationis*). Cf. Billuart, *Summa Sancti Thomae*, II, p. 202.

50 Note that the term "minus malum" is associated with a number of different notions in moral theology. Here we are speaking of the idea that one might find oneself in a situation, or imagine oneself to be in a situation, in which one cannot but sin. In this case of "perplexed conscience" some authors speak of the need to choose a lesser *moral* evil. There are at least three other occasions when the term *minus malum* arises: (1) in reference to a choice between *non-moral* evils, or burdens vs. benefits (2) in reference to the *toleration* by society of certain moral evils, such as prostitution or slavery, and (3) in reference to *counseling* a person determined to sin to do something less bad. Consequently, the term "the principle of the lesser evil" can cause considerable confusion.

51 R. C. Morlino, *The Principle of the Lesser of Evils in Today's Conflict Situations: new challenges to moral theology from a pluralistic society* (Rome: Pontifical Gregorian University, 1990), p. 104.

52 K. H. Peschke, *Christian Ethics: Moral Theology in the Light of Vatican II*, vol. 1, *General Ethics*, revised ed. (Alcester: Neale, 1986), p. 321. Remember that this is the imprecise assessment offered also by Russell Smith (p. xxi).

[53] J. M. Boyle, "Collaboration and Integrity: how to think clearly about moral problems of cooperation," in *Issues for a Catholic Bioethics*, ed. L. Gormally, pp. 187–199 (London: Linacre Centre, 1999), p. 191.

[54] Lord Morris (writing in Lynch 1975, A.C. 653), cited by R. A. Duff, *Intention Agency*, p. 19.

[55] J. J. Coughlin, "Lawyers and cooperation with evil in divorce cases," in *The Catholic Citizen: debating the issues of justice: proceedings from the 26th annual conference of the Fellowship of Catholic Scholars*, September 26-28, 2003, Arlington, Virginia, ed. K. D. Whitehead, pp. 151–164 (South Bend, IN: St Augustine's Press, 2004), at p. 158. His understanding of duress is itself quite relaxed: "Continued employment, financial security for family and opportunities to advance professionally may require that they be involved in divorce cases by necessity."

[56] After saying that "gli operatori del diritto in campo civile devono evitare di essere personalmente coinvolti in quanto possa implicare una cooperazione al divorzio," the Pope allows that "per gravi e proporzionati motivi [i giudici] possono pertanto agire secondo i principi tradizionali della cooperazione materiale al male." Lawyers, on the other hand, "devono sempre declinare l'uso della loro professione per una finalità contraria alla giustizia com'è il divorzio," which would not include divorce proceedings aimed solely at procuring legitimate protections. John Paul II, "Allocution to Officials of the Roman Rota," 28 January 2002, *Acta Apostolicae Sedis* 93 (2002) I, pp. 340–346, at p. 346.

[57] Cf. Catholic Health Association of the United States, "Report on a Theological Dialogue on the Principle of Cooperation," *Health Progress* 88 (2007), pp. 68–69 [Summary with link to full text at www. chausa.org/coopdialogue] Executive Summary, p. 2.

[58] T. Gilby, *Summa Theologiae* (London: Blackfriars, 1970), XVII, p. 15, note "c".

[59] Cf. Hendriks, *Moyen mauvais*, pp. 95-117, where he devotes the first chapter of his study to cataloguing and comparing the various conflicting uses and definitions of these and related terms. Hendriks examines four pairs of terms with overlapping usage: (1) *voluntarium directum / indirectum*, (2) *voluntarium in se / in causa (in alio)*, (3) *causa (vel effectus) per se / per accidens*, and (4) *effectus intentus (in intentione, ex intentione) / praeter intentionem*. After twenty pages of disentangling definitions, only with striking reserve does he conclude: "cette terminologie est assez multiforme

et ambiguë" (p. 116).

[60] Certain authors, such as Thomas Cavanaugh, point out that finding the right verb to describe the agent's relationship to these effects (e.g. allow, permit, tolerate) is not easy. Here lies a clue to the problematic nature of the doctrine: none of these verbs capture the fact that the agent is undeniably, if unwillingly, "voluntarily causing harm". Cavanaugh, *Double-Effect Reasoning*, p. 79.

[61] In *ST* I-II, q. 77, a. 7, St Thomas mentions the two concepts together, which makes contrasting them easy. Explaining the effect of passion on guilt, he says that passion, like drunkenness, can be caused by the agent, in which case the resulting actions are "voluntaria in causa" and imputed to him as "quasi voluntaria". The passions may also have originated apart from the agent willing it, but, if he omitted to do all he could and should do to resist them, the actions resulting from passion are "indirectly voluntary".

[62] In *ST* II-II, q. 150, a. 4, he explicitly asks whether drunkenness excludes from sin. Here the moral quality of the preceding act (the drinking) and not just its voluntariness is held to be relevant. If getting drunk occurred without sin, then the actions committed when drunk would have as well. If the drinking was, however, culpable, then "[peccatum sequens] redditur voluntarium ex voluntate praecedentis actus, inquantum scilicet aliquis dans operam rei illicitae incidit in sequens peccatum."

[63] Cf. *ST* I-II, q. 6, a. 3.

[64] Although he does not mention the terms themselves, he appears to employ the concepts side by side in *ST* II-II, q. 64, a. 8, when he identifies the two ways in which causing a death accidentally may be imputable to the agent: (1) when it is a result of some illicit act (e.g. the death of a fetus caused by striking a pregnant woman); and (2) when due care is not taken in a legitimate activity (e.g. Lamech killing a man thinking it was a beast). Although he does not say so, it would seem that (1) corresponds to *voluntaria in causa*, and (2) to *indirecte voluntaria*. Viewing the hunting case in this manner requires seeing the negligence as a constituitive element of the moral object, as in the case of the helmsman. Shooting at rustling bushes is a bad kind of action, much like steering ships while reading a novel or acting under the influence of passions that could have been put in order.

[65] Hendriks concludes (*Moyen mauvais*, pp. 103 and 108) that both terms are used today to signify the contrary of their original sense.

[66] "Verbi gratia, cum quis sponte currit et inde fatigatur, cursus est

directe et in seipso volitus: lassatio autem consequens est indirecte et in alio, hoc est in cursu, ad quem consequitur, volita, et non in seipsa nec directe..." Cajetan, *Commentary* on *ST* I-II, q. 150, a. 1, cited by Hendriks, *Moyen mauvais*, pp. 100-101.

[67] For example, Vermeersch, *Theologiae moralis*, I, p. 106: "Positiva obligatio impediendi materiale peccatum nos *non urget cum gravi incommodo.*"

[68] "Ad hoc voluntarium indirectum seu in causa theologi communiter requirunt tres conditiones. Prima est ut effectus fuerit praevisus, aut debuerit ac potuerit humano modo praevideri secuturus ex tali causa. ... Secunda, quod possit. Tertia, quod debeat auferre hanc causam et hunc effectum impedire; si enim nulla lege tenear hanc causam amovere, sed e contra habeam justam rationem illam ponendi, non est cur mihi imputetur, saltem moraliter, quod ex illa contra meam intentionem sequitur." Billuart, *Summa Sancti Thomae*, II, p. 203. Note that, if the reference to a law forbidding certain side effects be removed, some other way must be discovered to prevent foreseeable but trivial side effects from being called voluntary. This, we recall, was the problem with which John Searle was struggling (Cf. pp. 92–93).

[69] Pinckaers, *Sources*, passim.

[70] This leads to a great inconvenience noted by Hendriks. If an omission is considered voluntary *before* an objective moral judgment is made (that is, before it is determined to be something that the agent could and should do), then one must admit that a disaster occurring in China be considered voluntary *in causa* vis à vis a person on the other side of the world, who only subsequently and paradoxically is exculpated for what he voluntarily permitted on the grounds that he could not have prevented it. Hendriks, *Moyen mauvais*, p. 106. See also H. G. Kramer's treatment of this question (*Indirect Voluntary*, p. 23).

[71] Kramer, *Indirect Voluntary*, pp. 23–24.

[72] "Ad hoc quod alicui imputetur homicidium, requiritur quod non solum potuerit removere illud ex quo mors sequitur, puta iactum lapidis, gladium accinctum, etc., sed etiam quod debuerit illum auferre, hoc est quod obligatus fuerit divino vel naturali vel humani iure ad removendum illud; vel positive, puta auferendo accinctum gladium, vel negative, puta abstinendo a iactu lapidis." Cajetan, *Commentary* on *ST* II-II, q. 64, a. 8, cited by Hendriks, *Moyen mauvais*, p. 105.

[73] Kramer, *Indirect Voluntary*, p. 52.

[74] "Malus enim effectus, licet sit praeter intentionem coniunctus cum opere agentis semper remanet peccatum materiale: immo, haud raro inducit grave periculum peccati formalis." P. Palazzini, *Dictionarium morale et canonicum* (Rome: Officium libri catholici, 1966), p. 111.

[75] Vermeersch, *Theologiae moralis*, I, p. 103.

[76] The explanation that Cajetan gives for the responsibility of a drunkard for his actions would seem to mean that such evil effects remain somehow intended: "Et si quaeretur: quando iste committit illud sequens peccatum? Respondetur quod committit illud, actu quidem interiori, quando inebriatur, quoniam tunc vult ebrietatem et sequens peccatum: actu vero exteriori, quando, iam ebrius, peccatum illlud exercet." Cajetan, *Commentary* on *ST* II-II q. 150, a. 4, cited by Hendriks, *Moyen mauvais*, p. 107.

[77] The linking of material cooperation and indirect voluntariness seems to be the common view. Only T. Jorio's taxonomy of cooperation presents them separately: cooperation can be "*formalis* vel *materialis*, prout et *intentione* concurrit ad peccatum alterius, vel *opere* tantum seu *sine intentione* cooperandi ad alterius peccatum. Datur etiam cooperatio *physica* vel *moralis*, *directa* vel *indirecta*." Jorio, *Theologia moralis*, II, p. 204.

CHAPTER 7

THE RISE OF PROPORTIONALISM

I N OUR REVIEW of the development of fundamental concepts in moral theology during the Manualist period, we noted certain ambiguities that arose in trying to handle difficult moral situations, namely, those in which compelling reasons both to perform an action and to avoid it obtain. Many questions seemed to hang in the air. What is the relation between act and effect? How are we to distinguish an act described in *genus naturae* from a moral act of indifferent value? What determines the limits of a subject's proximate intention? What makes causing a physical evil to be a moral evil? When is an act to be considered intrinsically evil? With the ambiguities inherited from casuistry concerning the nature of moral evil and the responsibility of the subject still not fully resolved, Manualist authors tended to focus more and more upon the consequences of acts in order to evaluate their permissibility.

1. Increasing prominence of the principle of double effect

The principle of the double effect[1] (PDE) can be seen as a tool for analyzing difficult cases; it is ordinarily used to render explicit the ways that an agent could sin when faced with multiple consequences, both good and bad. The four conditions correspond, it seems, to an exhaustive listing of the ways that one could intend evil: by choosing an act with an evil object (intrinsic evil), by choosing a good or indifferent act[2] for the sake of an evil effect, by choosing to cause an evil effect for the sake of a good effect which will result, and, finally, by choosing to cause a good effect in a way that also results in an evil effect which is not compensated by the good effect sought.[3] If the agent is not intending evil in any of these ways, the act is considered licit.

Ambiguity concerning the third condition

While the PDE appears at first sight to clarify the aspects of a problem case, enabling objective analysis, attempts to make use of the principle reveal that it also stands in need of clarification. This is particularly apparent in regard to the third condition which appears ambiguous in three different ways. Ultimately, these three ways are intimately related.

Firstly, it is frequently asked whether the third condition is not contained in the first or vice-versa. Hendriks calls the first condition "secondary" citing Prümmer as saying: "Besides this [third] condition seems to coincide with the first. For if the first effect is morally evil, the act, which produces this effect, will be morally evil *in se*."[4] Hendriks notes that both conditions are frequently justified by the same argument,[5] namely, that "non sunt facienda mala, ut veniant bona," with the authority of St Paul in support.[6] Peschke remarks that the requirement that the good effect proceed at least as immediately as the bad effect is "in the last analysis, the same as the demand of the first condition that the act may not be evil in itself. For the immediate effect of an action is its object, and if this is evil, then the act is evil in itself."[7]

A second reason for apprehension regarding this condition of the principle of the double effect constitutes the subject of Hendriks's extended study.[8] It appears that the consensus of moral theologians and common sense allow the violation of this condition in a number of cases. The examples considered by Hendriks include mutilation, legitimate defense and cooperation with evil, each of which we will look at more closely in subsequent sections. Hendriks concludes:

> The concrete cases of certain acts with double effect which are considered licit despite the fact that the evil effect is the means for obtaining the good effect show that the importance of the distinction between means (direct effect) and consequence (indirect effect) for the moral judgment of an act with double effect is at least debatable.[9]

Thirdly, the depths of confusion over the third condition, and the PDE generally, is revealed by the uncertainty in authors over the nature of the evil of the "bad" effect. Is it a physical or moral evil? Most authors, such as Hendriks,[10] assume that the bad effect must be a physical evil, since causing a moral evil could not possibly be licit. To consider the bad effect a moral evil, would be, for these authors, committing the logical error of presupposing the conclusion which the principle is designed to discern. Some, however, such as Ugorji, insist that the bad effect is a moral evil, even an "intrinsic (moral) evil."[11] This point of view becomes comprehensible if the evil in question is not considered to be directly willed. A mere physical evil can be directly willed as a means, *in se*, if not *propter se*. Thus, if an evil cannot be willed even as a means, it seems to be because it is an evil of a different sort. In this light, Ugorji explains his position: "Catholic moralists consider the existence of proportionate reason a justification for the causing of physical (non-moral) evil. On the other hand, for the causation of an intrinsic (moral) evil, it demands more than a proportionate reason, it requires the fulfillment of the prescriptions of the principle of double effect."[12] This approach seems to see the PDE as excusing a sin, rendering it a material sin, while the other point of view assumes the evil is not moral, unless it fails to pass the "test" of the PDE, in which case, one would no longer be justified to cause it.

The ambiguity surrounding the third condition of the PDE highlights the importance of a thoroughgoing action theory. What is a basic human act description as opposed to a description of an act of man? Is a phrase such as "to kill non-combatants" sufficient as a moral act description? Certainly, we can imagine someone killing non-combatants by pure accident, in which case the phrase cannot but have the significance of killing in only a physical sense. Yet, this possibility should be excluded from the meaning of the phrase since the context is that of deliberate action. Moreover, would we not err in the opposite direction by defining this intrinsic evil as "to choose to kill non-combatants" or "to kill non-combatants directly"? Very easily, these qualifiers can be interpreted as importing a negative moral value into the definition of the sin, rendering the concept of intrinsic evil tautological and the rebuke of Pascal relevant ("sin for the sake of sinning"). This difficulty must be born in mind as we examine attempts to refine action theory in the next part of this book. For now we note Jean Porter's interesting insight, that at the heart of the problem lies the inability of describing an act without evaluating it.[13]

Amputation and transplantation

As is to be expected, new moral quandaries led to a deeper testing of principles, in this case, of the PDE. Certainly the possibility of amputating a limb for medical purposes is not wholly new (it is mentioned by St Thomas), but advances in surgical techniques made amputation a more viable option in modern times. Forms of "mutilation" such as hysterectomy were certainly unknown even to early

Manualists.[14] Moreover, excising an organ to replace it in another person was not something formerly even dreamed of. These medical developments, which common ethical intuition applauds, constitute one of Hendriks's prime examples of violations of the third condition.

To begin with, we are not surprised to find that some Manualists even describe auto-mutilation as "intrinsically illicit" although potentially justifiable. What does surprise, however, is that it is not only considered justifiable when indirectly willed for a proportionate reason, but when it is *directly* willed as an "end or a means".[15] Appeal is made to what is known as "the principle of totality" enunciated by St Thomas[16] and sustained in modern form by Pope Pius XII.[17] For our purposes, however, it still must be explained why this is not a case of doing something evil that good may come. It is a difficult problem with which, for instance, Elizabeth Anscombe struggles, ending by appealing to the principle of totality.[18] The trouble is now familiar to us: "cutting off a limb" seems to be a moral act description, and an evil one at that. Anscombe observes, apparently without alluding to the obscure Thomistic category, that it "sounds awful",[19] but appears to be justified by the end for which it is done. Ultimately, she concludes that the original description was indeterminate. Yet, even if we take "cutting off a limb" to be an indifferent action, the loss of the limb is certainly an evil effect, and it would appear to be a means, if the goal is, for instance, to stop the spread of gangrene.

Apparently, the way to avoid this violation of the third condition is to avoid the PDE altogether. This is what Gerald Kelly proposed in 1951. The loss of limb is simply a physical evil that one has a right to inflict upon oneself as part of a cure.[20] In this way the act of amputation seems to qualify as a lesser evil[21] that can be chosen for a greater good, like cutting into the body as part of any operation.[22] This approach is undoubtedly promising, but it does not solve all the difficulties. Kelly speaks of a "right" to cause this harm to oneself, which is surely begging the question. One would not have a right if it were evil, and that is what we are trying to discern. If the solution is to see the causing of the disvalue as "part and parcel" of the medical act and not a means to an end, thus avoiding the PDE altogether, then we will need criteria for determining when the PDE applies and when it does not. Ugorji makes a valid point in connection with the debate about whether or not St Thomas is to be interpreted as instituting what we call the PDE in his treatment of private self-defense.[23] He challenges those who claim that St Thomas is introducing the PDE to explain why so many of his commentators do not consider the principle necessary in order to justify private self-defense.[24] In both cases, denying that the PDE is applicable avoids the violation of the third condition, but fails to elucidate the matter. The arbitrary application of the principle of lesser evil to bad effects would amount to proportionalism: which is exactly what Richard McCormick sees anticipated in the opinion of Kelly on this point.[25] The resolution of the matter—that is, whether the loss of limb can be considered a mere physical evil or not—seems to depend upon whether it forms part of a medical act or is a consequence thereof. Ugorji maintains, in a manner reminiscent of Duff (pp. 111-112) that it is not possible to overcome an inherent ambiguity on this point.[26] We will try to show, in Chapter 10, that more attention to the natural teleology of human action should lead to satisfactory results.

From another perspective, the problem can be seen as setting limits to the use of the principle of totality. Pius XII noted that it would be simplistic to justify deutero-transplantation by this principle, as if one could sacrifice parts of one's body for others in just the same way as one does for oneself. "One neglects here the essential difference between a physical organism and a moral organism," noted Pope Pacelli.[27] Nonetheless, the Manualists did not find a justification for the growing consensus on the liceity of certain transplants of this type (from one living donor to another) other than a rather unconvincing variation on the principle of totality, which appealed to the donor as a composition of body and soul, who benefits his own person by sacrificing a physical part.[28] Certainly, further attempts to stretch the principle to include contracepted acts between husband and wife in the greater context of their conjugal life show how open to abuse is the principle of totality, unless it is carefully grounded.

Cooperation and the PDE

With regard to the application of the PDE to cooperation with evil, there are two points of interest. First, there is disagreement here, as in the case of self-defense, whether or not the PDE applies at all. Secondly, it is far from clear that cooperation routinely satisfies the third condition.

Concerning the applicability of the PDE to cooperation, most authors do assume that this is how material cooperation should be justified. This seems to follow naturally from the description of material cooperation made classic by St Alphonsus: the cooperator foresees that his good act will be abused, but he is not bound to forego it, if sufficient reason exists for positing it. Thus we have a bad effect (the facilitation of the principal agent's design) that is not intended and a proportionately weighty good effect that is intended: a clear invitation for the PDE. Yet, even if dissenting voices are few, their position is worth considering. L. J. Fanfani maintains:

> Which question [whether it is ever permitted to cooperate with another] is different from the previous one, about the *indirect voluntary*, that is, about *double effect*, good and evil, resulting from the same cause. There, indeed, the question is: 'whether it is licit to posit a cause, from which follow two effects, one good and the other evil'; while here it is precisely asked: 'whether it is licit to cooperate *in the evil action itself*, which is carried on by another.'[29]

At first glance, it may appear that Fanfani must be thinking only of immediate cooperation, which is ordinarily defined as cooperation in the evil act itself. However, this is not the case. Rather, he is calling our attention to the very meaning of the word cooperation, which indicates performing some (single) action together. In this light, the cooperator cannot simply claim that he is performing some other act which only happens to have a bad effect unrelated to the goal of his own act. Still Fanfani draws the same practical conclusions as the majority of Manualists, by emphasizing that the cooperator's role should not be viewed as *causing* the bad effect: "the action of the cooperator is only an *occasion*, rather than a cause of the sin of the other."[30] Hendriks also notes that there seem to be cases when the bad effect is not properly an effect of the cooperator's act, unless one considers the providing an occasion as itself a bad effect. Thus, in the case of a doctor who saves the life a dictator with the result that a persecution is continued, the continued persecution is not "the proper effect of the act of the doctor"; only the *possibility* of continuing it is.[31]

The position that the cooperator's act does not cause any negative effect clearly contradicts Waffelaert's understanding of cooperation as causal by definition, which is the same as the view of Billuart. This latter distinguishes cooperators, who provide help or instruments,[32] from immediate cooperators who he says are better called "co-executors" (*coexsequentes*). Both, however, "efficaciously influence" the evil deed, and thus bear responsibility "even if without their help the harm would have been committed" anyway. Contrary to the majority of authors, Billuart denies that immediate material cooperation could satisfy the PDE. To those who would liken such cooperation under duress to lethal self-defense against an unjust aggressor or to destroying a tower housing both innocents and enemies, Billuart replies:

> There is a disparity here, for in both of these cases, my defense or safety follows as equally immediately from my action as the death of the aggressor or of the innocents. But in our case [of immediate cooperation] my safety does not follow immediately from my harmful action, but from the altered will of the one threatening me: whence the evil is done before the good follows, which is precisely to do evil that good will come, which is wrong.[33]

Billuart remains uncompromising with regard to immediate cooperation but allows providing help before or after the crime, arguing that such aid would not be intrinsically evil. In sum, Billuart rejects immediate cooperation as evil in itself (violating the first condition) but his argument, which concerns the order of effects, pertains to the third condition.

If the cooperation is not evil by its object, which would mean *implicitly* sharing in the intention of the principal agent, it would seem to satisfy the first condition of the PDE. Only *express* formal cooperation would violate the second condition, which prohibits intending the bad effect for its own sake. The requirement of a substantial reason for permitting the foreseen evil of abuse by the principal agent (fourth condition) is mentioned by all. There remains, then, just the matter of the third condition. We have already had occasion to note that this third condition seems to get regularly overlooked by authors trying to explain why material cooperation may be licit.[34] Another example of this tendency follows:

> Material cooperation, on the other hand, is considered permissible under certain conditions, namely, that the action of the material cooperator is not evil in itself, that his intention is good, and that he has a proportionately grave reason for doing something that may contribute in some way to the sin of another… if the aforesaid conditions are verified, the Principle of Double Effect is applicable…[35]

This presentation seems to subsume under the proviso, "that his intention is good," both the second and third conditions, which can appear to be satisfied by the very definition of material cooperation. This is the approach taken by Fabbro, whose reasoning we will cite in its entirety:

> By the very fact that the cooperation is material and not formal, two of the conditions are satisfied by the very nature of the cooperation, namely, the effects caused are immediate [=condition 3] and only the good effect is intended [=condition 2]. One verifies that the good effect follows equally immediately from the act of cooperation by the fact that the good effect is not achieved by means of the evil effect. If the opposite were true, namely, the cooperator intended the other's sin as a means to his own good end, then the cooperation would not be material but formal. The other condition is also verified by the very definition of material cooperation, which excludes the intention of the other's sin.[36]

In other words: the fact that the cooperation is material implies that the third condition is not violated, which in turn is "verified" by recalling that the cooperation is material. Surely, any case in which the cooperator would not have posited his act unless it were going to be abused presents a problem for Fabbro's argument. As Billuart indicated, this is what makes the case of duress so difficult. Here it would seem that the agent is facilitating the sin of the other *precisely so as* to save his job, life, etc. We can imagine the one who is coercing an employee saying: "Do this, or else." The employee would characterize his cooperation as the only available *means* of saving his job.[37] Correctly, in our view, Billuart admits that there is a problem here needing to be resolved. He resolutely refuses to permit immediate material cooperation, and, as if to justify his lack of a cogent argument to support his general allowance of mediate cooperation under duress, he laments that there appears to be no other way to handle the myriad extreme situations in which people may find themselves. He also notes that this question is "extremely complicated" and "tortures theologians to no small degree"![38]

2. The dominance of proportionate reason

If any article merits the description "seminal", it is Peter Knauer's 1965 essay, "La détermination du bien et du mal moral par le principe du double effet".[39] It is universally acknowledged as the first crocus in the springtime now known as "proportionalism". This movement in Catholic moral theology can still claim the majority of theologians as adherents even if its promise of new life seems to have already wilted in the heat of "the Splendor of Truth".[40] The new season in moral theology inaugurated by Pope John Paul II will be the subject of Part III of this work. Knauer's interpretation of the PDE is generally regarded by non-proportionalist theologians as an abuse of the terminology developed by the Catholic tradition. In the words of Germain Grisez: "[Knauer] is carrying through a revolution in principle while pretending only a clarification of traditional ideas."[41] Yet these same contemporary non-proportionalist theologians tend to tax both the proportionalists and their predecessors, the Manualists, with making the same error of physicalism, an assessment with which we agree. However, this observation implies a more accurate image by which to describe proportionalism: not so much a revolution caused by forcing a heterogeneous viewpoint into traditional terminology, as the boiling over of an intellectual crisis that had been simmering and sputtering for decades if not centuries.

The nature of moral evil

Peter Knauer's achievement can best be understood as carrying the imperfect solutions of the Manualists to their logical and radical conclusion. Thus, for instance, the PDE, which had been growing in prominence for centuries, gaining a set form and name at the end of the XIX century, becomes finally, in Knauer's article, the fundamental pivot upon which all moral reasoning turns. Even before the explosive moment of the summer of 1968, when, following the appearance of *Humanae Vitae*, moral theologians would demand, practically in unison, a proof of what makes contraception evil, the sense was growing that the fundamental question of what makes actions evil had long gone ignored. The legalism which followed the high Middle Ages, developing especially after the Reformation, had trapped Catholic theology in a deontological perspective that was foreign to it and in need of being jettisoned. Most sins were considered bad either for lack of a right to act in the agent (suicide, homicide, mutilation) or because they frustrated a natural faculty (contraception, mastur-bation).[42] The deeper questions—"why is there no right to act?" and "when is frustrating a natural faculty wrong?"—were not sufficiently explored. Knauer believed that he had found the key to the matter, and so also a firm foundation for moral theology, in the fourth condition of the PDE: proportionate reason.[43]

What other answers to this question were available? In explaining why the third condition was considered essen-tial to the PDE, Hendriks observes that, if the evil effect were a means, it would be willed, and "to will evil is precisely sin."[44] This would seem to be a reference to the ancient dictum: *Voluntas volenda malum fit mala.*[45] Yet, the true import of this statement is to indicate the objec-tive "direction" of morality: choosing an evil object makes the will evil, not vice versa. It does not tell us what makes the object (morally) evil in the first place. It does not indicate that choosing a physical evil *in se* is a moral evil. Of course, it could not mean this as our discussion of medical acts made clear.[46] Kramer also touches briefly upon this question: "But what is meant by saying that an act is good? It means only that the act produces or acquires for the agent some perfection that is in conformity to his nature (*ST* I-II, q. 18, a. 2, ad 3). In other words, we judge the moral character of an act from the moral character of the object or effects that it produces."[47] It appears as though Kramer begins in the right direction, pointing to a metaphysical analysis of the act as perfective of the agent, but ends heading towards a weighing of effects.[48]

Interestingly, the early proportionalist thinkers noticed that in two areas only—scandal and cooperation with evil—did the Manualist tradition seem to appeal not to a legalist/physicalist (deontological) explanation of moral evil but to a balancing of effects (teleological).[49] This observation provided Knauer with what he took to be the key to justifying all moral acts in what he considered a non-physicalist manner.

Intention and proportionalism

Proportionalism was to alter the role of intention in moral analysis, a fact also presaged by the Manualists' treatment of cooperation. It is significant that in analyzing cooperation with evil, the tradition has been loath to see intrinsic evil in the cooperation itself. The agent is seen as essentially causing only a physical evil unless he also seeks to bring about this evil for its own sake. We recall that all authors, including St Alphonsus, recognized that the cooperator's act could be evil in itself, considered apart from its connection to the principal agent's project. But in the majority of cases, where the fact of cooperation is what renders the cooperator's action morally dubious, most theologians of the Manualist period presumed the cooperator's moral object was good or indifferent. Essentially, the role of *finis proximus* dropped out in favor of the *finis operantis*. This is what Knauer now proposed for all human acts.

Moreover, we have noted that the notion of absolute intrinsic evil had become difficult for Manualists to fit into their system. This difficulty seems to have followed from a lack of attention to the metaphysical basis of moral goodness, only against which can moral evil be defined. The proportionalists simply radicalized this tendency, alleging that there are no acts that can be considered evil *in specie*, that is, without a consideration of the circumstances and intention. Once the good and bad effects in the *hic et nunc* are assessed, an agent intending to bring about a preponderance of good will act morally, they alleged. In this way, the subjective intention of the agent, the goal at which he aims, took on the role of founding the morality of the act: "The question of intention—because this only determines the content of the human act—must evidently precede the question of good and evil."[50]

This expanded role of intention was to be criticized, notably by Theo Belmans, as a return to Peter Abelard. For Abelard, the ultimate intention provided the sole morally determining feature of human action. For instance, he described stealing in order to give the money to the poor as "giving other people's money to the poor".[51] In this way, the need to evaluate the means adopted so as to insure that one is not doing evil to achieve good evaporates. Another proportionalist, C. J. Van der Poel, makes this position his own arguing that an agent only wills the means insofar as they are conducive to the end. There is consequently no need to evaluate the means separately.

> [The agent] wants the means of the intermediate stages only insofar as the final goal is *contained in these means*... The fatigue and the danger of the mountain climb are not willed for themselves, but only insofar as the satisfaction of the vision of the landscape is contained in it. It seems, therefore, to be incorrect to speak of a double object of the will, the climbing and the vision.[52] There is only one object, the vision, which communicates its meaning to all the intermediate stages of the one *human* act.[53]

Many proportionalists do not see themselves as departing from St Thomas's teaching. In regard to this exaggerated role of the intention, Louis Janssens sees it as a faithful rendering of the Thomistic division of the human act into formal and material.[54]

Still, even proponents of this view must admit that the intermediate stages of moral action are intended in *some* sense. Our experience tells us as much. Surely the doctor performing an amputation intends to remove the limb, and even adopts appropriate means to do so. To explain this fact, proportionalists, beginning with Knauer, have introduced the notion of "psychological" intention as opposed to "moral". "For Knauer, what one psychologically intends differs from what one morally intends. If the agent has a proportionate reason, the evil caused, even as a means, though psychologically intended, remains outside of the agent's moral intention."[55] These authors are right to admit that there is a proximate intentionality in every action, but wrong to deny it status as a moral category.[56] In short, the notion of the proximate end, decisive for specifying the moral object in Aquinas, yet only tenuously present in some of the Manualists, is explicitly excluded in the "New Morality".

Defining the human act

The result of allowing the intention to define, in Abelardian style, *what* the agent is doing, means that the contours of the act will be defined by the ultimate goal. One commentator explains: "These authors [a group including Knauer] prefer to treat the posited act or means as a constitutive part or stage of a larger whole, which whole is the primary object of one's intentions, and this is the only true unit of moral significance."[57] Indeed, ultimately the intention by which the acts of an agent are to be assessed is his ultimate goal in life, wherefore Janssens has been attributed with developing the notion of "fundamental option". Writes Janssens: "In the actualization of a good end and the deliberation about the means to this end, the genuinely important question is what place this end has in the totality of human existence."[58] For Janssens the overarching goal of the acting subject is the formal element which specifies the act, for which reason he tells us, "Thomas carefully avoids the use of the expression *'finis operis'* in his *De actibus humanis*."[59] Other proportionalist authors make the same point in their own fashion. H. Boelaars speaks of a *"noema"*, a sort of super object of which the *finis operis* is but a part. In this way, there are always circumstances which could be included in the big picture, or *noema*, such that no *finis operis* could be said to be always unworthy of choice. This result, which is clearly contrary to the subsequent teaching of *Veritatis Splendor*, reveals that the *finis operis* is being regarded as a merely physical reality, devoid of an intentional component. This explains why Van der Poel thinks, erroneously, that he must reprove the tradition for dissecting acts and for imposing a body/soul dualism on them. He argues that an act must be viewed with all its effects as a whole,[60] for from his perspective there is no moral object apart from the agent's subjective goals and purposes.

Pre-moral evil

The proportionalist school reacts vehemently to the tradition's calling some acts evil by their very object, because they see this as attributing a moral value to what is only a physical reality. In consequence, they accuse their predecessors of "physicalism". However, the real physicalism of which they, the proportionalists, are guilty, and which they have inherited to some degree from the Manualists, is to consider the external act to be a mere physical reality. It is central to the proportionalist approach to bracket the moral question until the whole act with all its effects can be assessed. Evils caused by the agent are considered merely physical until such an assessment can be made; they will remain in the physical category in the case due proportion obtains. The need to describe this class of evils has spawned a number of new terms that are more or less interchangeable, especially "pre-moral" or "ontic" evil.

Christopher Kaczor observes perspicaciously that "once the distinction between pre-moral and moral evil is made, the first condition [of the PDE] drops out as begging the question."[61] Whether the act is wrong in itself has been bracketed, until the particular circumstances are assessed. From this perspective all disvalues are of an equal status. No foreseen effect can be judged *a priori* wrong to cause, unless it is itself a sin. For this reason, it appears to Bruno Schüller that the only cases in which the intention/foresight distinction, or the indirect voluntary, has a role to play are the cases of scandal and cooperation with evil.[62] It is surely not coincidental that it is in connection with cooperation that the Manualists came closest to speaking in terms nearly identical to those of "pre-moral" versus "moral" evil. A typical rendering of the distinction between formal and material cooperation follows: "[That cooperation is] *formal*, which cooperates in the sinful action of the other *insofar as it is a sin*; *material*, which cooperates in such an action, *insofar as it is a physical action*, not a sin."[63] The cooperator's contribution is considered a mere disvalue, a premoral evil, until his ultimate intention is known, and then only is it classified as a sinful action or not. Knauer simply generalized this formula to obtain proportionalism: the agent's act can be considered as causing a physical evil only, unless it be shown that his intention was to cause harm. In truth, physicalism will only be avoided when it is recognized that the only non-moral evils are those that are not yet *chosen*, not those which are not yet assessed in terms of effects. A certain moral evaluation is possible in the abstract, antecedent to the choice of the agent, and it becomes actual moral evil upon being elected.

Due proportion

As has already become apparent, the fourth condition plays the role of a hinge in this system. The first condition was eliminated on the basis that there was no way yet to judge the external action morally. The second condition (one must not seek evil as an end) maintains its force,[64] but whether the evil is sought or is merely the least ontic evil that can be produced under the circumstances cannot yet be decided. Finally, the third condition, regarding the intention/foresight distinction, no longer has significance if the goodness of the agent's intention depends upon causing the least ontic harm possible. In this way, only the fourth condition remains as the decisive factor in determining moral value.

This assertion of Knauer's was all the more persuasive as the tradition was reluctant to call the side-effects intended in any sense. As we noted (p. 178), an explanation was wanting to connect them to the agent in some convincing manner. Hendriks makes this point in the following way:

> If the evil of the evil consequence is greater than the good of the good end, it does not seem possible any longer to say that the consequence is *praeter intentionem*. The fourth condition offers then in some sense, as does the third condition, an objective criterion which is determining for the intention independently of the subjective intention.[65]

Perhaps, if *praeter intentionem* effects had been more closely considered by the tradition, and not all lumped together, be they *per se* or not, partially caused or fully, they would not have been so easily pressed into service by Peter Knauer.

By way of review, we would do well to recall the difficult issues with which the Manualists were struggling that seemed to be resolved by this new emphasis on proportionality. First, we recall the legalist framework that paid insufficient attention to what made moral evils evil. Next there was a restriction of absolute intrinsic evil to such a degree that doing away with the concept altogether began to seem plausible. Thirdly, there was difficulty in explaining the difference between an act and an effect, and so in identifying when the principle of lesser evil applied[66] and when the PDE was needed. Fourthly, as the third condition became contested, attention naturally focused all the more on the role of the fourth condition. In all these ways, the traditional view was straining, and the suggestion of Peter Knauer appeared most attractive. Once again, it was a solution which the Manualists themselves had prepared. They had begun to view the object of the act apart from the proximate intention of the agent. The *per se* effects of an action were not considered by most to be determinative of the agent's intention. No distinction remained between effects that were clearly foreseen and caused, and those which are accidental in the fullest sense of the word. The doctrine of indirect voluntary had become such as to consider a great many evils caused as "bracketed" until the consideration of effects would determine if the evils were "permitted" or "intended". Thus, the Manualists themselves prepared the potion that Knauer would promote as a panacea.[67] Genuine medicine was, however, on the way, in the form of the Second Vatican Council's call to renew the study of moral theology, and nearly thirty years later, in the decisive contribution of Pope John Paul II through *Veritatis Splendor*.

Notes

[1] While the PDE has been presented in a variety of forms over the last century and a half, we will follow the most common arrangement of four conditions, under which it would be licit to posit a cause of two foreseen effects, one of which is good and the other evil, only if: (1) the action *in itself* is good or at least indifferent; (2) the evil effect is not intended, but only the good one; (3) the good effect follows at least equally immediately as the evil effect, that is, not by means of the evil effect; and (4) there is a relatively grave reason for permitting the evil effect. This rendering of the four conditions, is based upon that of Lehmkuhl (cf. *Theologia moralis*, I, p. 20).

[2] The typical presentation of the first condition of the PDE usually speaks of the act having two effects as being good or at least indifferent. As will become clear, this seems to us evidence of a physicalist understanding of the act. Also relevant was our discussion of act descriptions such as "giving a key" on pages 162 and 180.

[3] The first three ways of intending evil would normally be qualified as "directly willed" or intended. Many authors would consider the fourth condition to refer to an "indirectly willed" effect that is in no way intended. It only qualifies as a manner of intending the evil effect in the sense of "oblique" intention for those who use that terminology, for it also qualifies as *praeter intentionem*. (cf. pp. 195–199).

[4] Prümmer, *Manuale theologiae moralis*, I, p. 46, cited by Hendriks, *Moyen mauvais*, p. 19.

[5] Hendriks, *Moyen mauvais*, p. 19.

[6] The reference is always to the Apostle asking rhetorically whether we should do evil that good may come: "And why not do evil that good may come?—as some people slanderously charge us with saying. Their condemnation is just" (Rm 3:8).

[7] Peschke, *General Ethics*, p. 267.

[8] N. Hendriks, *Le moyen mauvais pour obtenir une fin bonne. Essai sur la troisième condition du principe de l'acte à double effet*, in Studia Universitatis S. Thomae in Urbe, vol. 12., (Rome: Herder, 1981).

[9] *Ibid.*, p. 303.

[10] *Ibid.*, p. 28.

[11] Ugorji, *Principle of Double Effect*, pp. 28, 30, 37, 45, etc.

[12]   *Ibid.*, p. 28.

[13]   "In order to draw out a methodology for moral decision-making from the criteria of object, circumstances, and aim, we would first need to be able to identify which component of a particular action is which, *prior to* forming a moral evaluation of the action. Yet as Aquinas recognizes, this is just what we cannot do ... Description is not prior to evaluation; to the contrary, to describe an action from the moral point of view is to form a moral evaluation of the action." Porter, "The Moral Act," p. 223. See also p. 341.

[14]   The very nomenclature, "actus mutilativus", in reference to medical acts jars. This is a warning against a physicalist perspective: the description of an act includes some intentionality, which in these cases is not to mutilate.

[15]   "Directa mutilatio intrinsece illicita est ... *Directa* tamen mutilatio licebit ad corpus totum vel humanam vitam salvandam." Vermeersch, *Theologia moralis*, II, p. 261.

[16]   *ST* II–II, q. 65, a.1.

[17]   Pius XII, "Allocution to the Participants in the XXIV congress of the Italian Association of Urologists," 8 October 1953, *Acta Apostolicae Sedis* 45 (1953), pp. 673–679, at p. 674.

[18]   Cf. Anscombe, "Medalist's Address," p. 58.

[19]   *male sonantes*, cf. p. 140. Anscombe, "Medalist's Address," p. 58.

[20]   Cf. R. McCormick, "Moral Theology 1940–1989: an Overview" in *The Historical Development of Fundamental Moral Theology in the United States*, ed. C. Curran and R. McCormick, pp. 46–72. *Readings in Moral Theology*, vol. 11 (New York: Paulist Press, 1999), at p. 53. McCormick also cites this passage from Kelly in his article "Ambiguity in Moral Choice," in *Doing Evil to Achieve Good*, ed. R. McCormick and P. Ramsey, pp. 7–53 (Chicago: Loyola University Press, 1973), at pp. 10–11. Here he charges, as we shall see in the next section of this chapter, that the underlying question of what constitutes moral evil was being ignored before the proportionalists: "This explanation of Kelly is absolutely correct. What is not clear is what is to count (and why) for *moral* evil. Kelly clearly regarded contraceptive interventions and directly sterilizing interventions, for example, as falling into this category. Knauer has questioned—and I believe rightly—just that type of conclusion and insisted that what is morally evil can only be determined after we have examined the reason for the procedure."

[21]   Recall the ambiguity of the term "lesser evil" (pp. 170–171). Here we are referring to a lesser evil in the sense of causing a lesser harm

or a lighter burden.

22 The description given by Palazzini of choosing the lesser evil (in the sense of lesser harm) is the following: "It is licit to choose a lesser evil, when this lesser evil is not a moral evil (sin) in itself, but is either a purely physical evil or an act or omission that is good in itself or indifferent, from which, however, in the concrete case will follow an accidentally evil effect, which is less evil that would be produced by choice of another means." F. Roberti and P. Palazzini (ed.), *Dizionario di teologia morale* (Rome: Studium, 1968), II, p. 1047.

23 *ST* II–II, q. 64, a. 7.

24 Cf. Ugorji, *Principle of Double Effect*, p. 42. The denial that PDE is employed to justify self-defense may also be motivated by the fact that it is not obvious that the death of the assailant is not a means. M. Zalba, for instance, rejected the use of PDE in this case because "the preservation of one's own life is achieved *through* the wounding of another life rather than as a concomitant of this wounding." Zalba, *Theologia Moralis Compendium*, II, p. 278, cited by McCormick, "Ambiguity in Moral Choice," p. 41.

25 Cf. McCormick, "Moral Theology 1940–1989: an Overview," p. 53: "Unless I am mistaken, I detect the general shape of this *Denkform* [of proportionalism] as early as 1951 in the work of Gerald Kelly."

26 He considers the following remark "enlightening": "There is … no rigid distinction between action and consequences, and we are free to construe many characteristics either as results or as constitutive of an expanded version." A. Oldenquist, "Choosing, Deciding, Doing," in *The Encyclopedia of Philosophy*, II, p. 101, cited by Ugorji, *Principle of Double Effect*, p. 48.

27 Pius XII, "Allocution to the directors and members of the Italian Association of Cornea Donors," 14 May 1956, *Acta Apostolicae Sedis* 48 (1956), pp. 459–466, at p. 461.

28 For instance, Zalba is cited in this vein by Hendriks, *Moyen mauvais*, p. 175.

29 "Quae quidem quaestio [utrum unquam liceat alteri cooperari] diversa est a praecedenti de *voluntario indirecto*, idest de *duplici effectu*, bono et malo, ex eadem causa procedenti. Ibi enim quaesitum est: 'utrum liceat ponere causam, ex qua sequuntur duo effectus, unus bonus et alter malus'; hic quaeritur praecise: 'utrum liceat cooperari *in ipsa actione mala*, quae ab alio producitur'." L. J. Fanfani, *Manuale theorico-practicum theologiae moralis ad*

mentem D. Thomae (Rome: Ferrari, 1950), I, p. 150, cited by Hendriks, *Moyen mauvais*, p. 138.

30 "unde fit quod actio cooperantis potius quam causa peccati alterius, sit tantum *occasio.*" Fanfani, *Manuale theoretico-practicum*, I, p. 136.

31 Hendriks, *Moyen mauvais*, p. 81, commenting on a case raised by W. Conway.

32 His first example of such cooperators concerns those who "furnish, set up, hold or maintain a ladder for a thief to climb up." Billuart, *Summa Sancti Thomae*, t.VI, diss.viii, a. xiii, §5, I.

33 *Ibid.*, II.

34 We have noted this oversight in Laymann (p. 38) and in Waffelaert (p. 41), as well as alluding to Hendriks's treatment (pp. 190–191). To show the consistency of the tradition on this matter we could also mention Dominicus Viva (*Damnatae theses*, p. 299) and Dominic Prümmer (*Manuale theologiae moralis, I*, p. 448). They both provide the same three conditions needing to be met if one is to provide material cooperation licitly. These three conditions correspond clearly to the first, second and fourth conditions of the PDE: the cooperator's action must not be intrinsically evil; it must not be given with intention to help the other accomplish the sin; and there must be a proportionate reason. The fact that the cooperation seems to be a means to a goal is simply ignored.

35 Klueg, "Sin, cooperation in," p. 156.

36 Fabbro, *Cooperation in Evil*, pp. 32–33, contents of brackets added by me.

37 Peter Cataldo tries to explain why providing insurance coverage that pays for immoral services does not violate the third condition of the PDE. Inexplicably, he remarks that this condition presumes "that [all] reasonable means of avoiding the cooperation have been attempted and that there is no reasonable way in which assistance in evil ... can be avoided." Why the lack of options should render the contemplated cooperation no longer an (evil) means to a (good) end is not explained. It is true that the PDE presupposes that the agent does not have a way of achieving the good effect without causing the bad, but this has no obvious relevance for the evaluation of the means-end relationship which the third condition proscribes. Cf. P. J. Cataldo, "Compliance with contraceptive insurance mandates: licit or illicit cooperation in evil?" *National Catholic Bioethics Quarterly* 4, no. 1 (Spr 2004), pp. 103–130, at p. 126.

[38] "Sed quaestio valde implexa est et quae non parum torquet theologos, utrum qui haec agunt metu mortis aut alterius gravis mali, ut contingit v.g. in captivis apud Turcas remigantibus adversus Christianos, in rusticis avehentibus praedas furtivas militum, etc. peccent et teneantur ad restitutionem". Billuart, *Summa Sancti Thomae*, t.VI, diss.viii, a. xiii, §5, II.

[39] "La détermination du bien et du mal moral par le principe du double effet," *Nouvelle revue théologique* 87 (1965), pp. 356–376.

[40] That is, the Encyclical Letter *Veritatis Splendor*, of Pope John Paul II, 6 August 1993.

[41] G. Grisez, *Abortion: The Myths, the Realities, and the Arguments* (New York: Corpus Books, 1970), p. 331.

[42] Cf. Ugorji, *Principle of Double Effect*, pp. 54–55.

[43] Janet Smith also argues that "the deepest divide between proportionalists and the magisterium is on what standard one uses to determine what is evil and, of course, what constitutes moral evil." J. Smith, "*Veritatis Splendor*, Proportionalism, and Contraception," *Irish Theological Quarterly* 63 (1998), pp. 307–326, at p. 316.

[44] Hendriks, *Moyen mauvais*, p. 17.

[45] also *ST* I–II, q. 19, a. 1.

[46] Here, also, St Thomas's teaching should be recalled that all agents act for a good end, at least an end that they perceive as good. Moral evil consists properly in acting for this end without due order. "Sed peccatum proprie consistit in actu qui agitur propter finem aliquem, cum non habet debitum ordinem ad finem illum." *ST* I–II, q. 21, a. 1.

[47] Kramer, *Indirect Voluntary*, p. 76.

[48] Kramer sums up the PDE as follows: "evil may be indirectly willed (i.e. permitted) for a sufficient reason." *Ibid.*, p. 77. This is frightening if we recall that he describes any abortion except those done for eugenic reasons as "permitting the death of the innocent" (p. 52).

[49] Bruno Schüller states: "The analytical propositions—one may not lead another into nor cooperate in the sin of another—have forced us to make the distinction between the direct and the indirect consequence of an act because the result of the prohibition seems to consist in the absolute disvalue of sin." B. Schüller, "Direct Killing/Indirect Killing," in *Moral Norms and Catholic Tradition*, ed. C. Curran and R. McCormick, pp. 138–157, *Readings in Moral Theology*, No. 1. (New York: Ramsey, 1979), p. 146. Despite his

evolution in dialogue with McCormick, this article and his "Double-Effect in Catholic Thought: a reevaluation" (esp. at p. 188) capitalize upon the Manualists' alteration of the Thomistic teaching on scandal. In this regard, see also L. Janssens, "Ontic Evil and Moral Evil," in *Moral Norms*, pp. 40–93, at pp. 57–58. Peter Knauer focuses on cooperation with evil in his "La détermination du bien et du mal moral par le principe du double effet," *Nouvelle revue théologique* 87 (1965), pp. 356–376, at pp. 362–363.

50   W. van der Mark, "Régulation de la fécondité," 402 (sections translated by and cited in Hendricks, *Moyen Mauvais*, p. 260).

51   *Super Sent.*, lib. 2, d. 4., cited by Kenny, *Anatomy of the Soul*, p. 138.

52   Note the similarity of this example to that of Cajetan's runner (p. 174).

53   C. J. Van der Poel, "The Principle of Double Effect," in *Absolutes in Moral Theology*, ed. Charles Curran, pp. 186–210 (Washington: Corpus Books, 1968), at p. 200.

54   Janssens, "Ontic Evil," p. 74; this point is made by Ana Marta Gonzalez in her book, *Moral, razón y naturaleza: una investigación sobre Tomás de Aquino* (Pamplona: Eunsa, 1998), p. 429. It is interesting to note that, in total contradiction to the view of Belmans, Janssens places Thomas squarely in Abelard's camp: "The second [current of thought, in comparison with Peter Lombard], which had already been advocated by Anselm of Canterbury and had been elaborated by Abaelardus and his followers, was adopted by St Thomas who thoroughly systematized it. It ties the definition of the structure and the morality of the human action to the agent." Janssens, "Ontic Evil," p. 40.

55   C. R. Kaczor, "Double Effect Reasoning from Jean Pierre Gury to Peter Knauer," *Theological Studies* 59 (1998), pp. 297–316, at p. 304.

56   Elizabeth Anscombe pauses in her Medalist's address to take Richard McCormick to task on this point: "While I am speaking of Fr McCormick, I will also remark on his curious use of 'intention in a psychological sense.' With respect, there is no other relevant sense." Anscombe, "Medalist's Address," p. 62.

57   A. DiIanni, "The Direct/Indirect Distinction in Morals," in *Moral Norms*, pp. 215–243, at p. 206.

58   Janssens, "Ontic Evil," p. 81. Janssens (1908–2001) was noted for his attempt to incorporate the perspective of personalist philosophers, both French and German, into moral theology. Cf. M. Fahey, "Janssens, Louis 1908–2001," *Theological Studies* 63 (2002),

pp. 1–2, at p. 2.

59 Janssens, "Ontic Evil," p. 81.

60 Cf. C. J. Van der Poel, "The Principle of Double Effect," pp. 189–190, cited in Hendriks, *Moyen mauvais*, p. 272.

61 Kaczor, "Double Effect Reasoning," p. 304.

62 C. Kaczor describes Schüller's position: "The distinction [between intended and foreseen consequences] is morally relevant only with respect to intending the sin of another person (a *moral* evil)." *Ibid.*, p. 305.

63 "*Formalis*, quae ad actionem peccaminosam alterius, *ut peccatum est*, cooperatur; *materialis*, quae cooperatur ad eiusmodi actionem, *ut actio quaedam physica est*, non ut peccatum est," Lehmkuhl, *Theologia moralis*, p. 386.

64 Cf. Janssens, "Ontic Evil," p. 69. This proviso becomes the first in his list of steps to act morally in a world in which every choice causes some ontic evil.

65 Hendriks, *Moyen mauvais*, p. 20.

66 In the sense of burdens and benefits (again, see p. 184).

67 Martin Rhonheimer also notes that proportionalists, despite their protestations to the contrary, seem to be "entangled in the categories of the strongly legalistic and casuistic manual tradition." Rhonheimer, "Intentional Actions," p. 280. He goes on to explain: "I have always conceded that proportionalism and consequentialism in Catholic moral theology have aspired to overcome the limitations and flaws of a traditional understanding of the 'moral object'... [but] I have contended that they have not succeeded because they have overlooked, and thus conserved, the basic error inherent in this tradition: to fail to understand human acts as embedded in an intentional process, that is, to fail to understand them from the perspective of the acting person" (p. 286).

PART III

A NEW PERSPECTIVE

CHAPTER 8

CATHOLIC AUTHORS AFTER *VERITATIS SPLENDOR*: GERMAIN GRISEZ

IN A BRIEF but significant statement, the Second Vatican Council called for the renewal of Catholic moral theology.[1] The new movement known as Proportionalism, which broke upon Catholic academia immediately following, was surely not what the Council Fathers had in mind. Certainly not all Catholic moral theologians welcomed the "new morality". Among the voices raised in immediate opposition, those of Servais Pinckaers, Theo Belmans, and Germain Grisez stand out. Yet, for their criticism to bear fruit a whole work of analysis and rethinking had to be done. Virtually everyone agreed that St Thomas remained the outstanding, sure guide but that his teaching would have to be recovered from the subtle distortions of the Manualists and the outright manhandling of the proportionalists. This work has progressed during the last forty years and is not yet finished. Before treating the leaders of this effort still active today, we will note some interventions of the Holy See. For, throughout this difficult period, the Magisterium has continued to treat moral issues authoritatively, examining contraception, euthanasia and abortion, among other issues, and providing theologians with precise definitions of these sins. Most interesting for our purposes is the analysis of the moral act and intrinsic evil found in *Veritatis Splendor*, and the new definition of formal cooperation given by Pope John Paul II two years later in *Evangelium Vitae.*

1. Contribution of the Magisterium: Three definitions

Clues for ulterior refinement of the notion of the object of the act are naturally to be sought in the Magisterium's definition of certain sins. The one that has generated the most interest is the definition of contraception given by Paul VI in *Humane Vitae.* "Similarly excluded is any action which either before, at the moment of, or after sexual intercourse, is specifically intended to prevent procreation—whether as an end or as a means."[2] While a great number of commentators saw in this statement only a preoccupation with physical or biological factors, some see an effort to move away from a physicalism alleged to be present in earlier Church teaching. In contrast to Pius XI's formulation, Martin Rhonheimer tells us, Paul VI gives us a "more precise definition of the contraceptive choice": "*Humanae Vitae* defined contraception in a new way—not in terms of frustrating natural processes and patterns, but in terms of its intentional opposition to the *bonum prolis*, the specific marital 'good of offspring'."[3] The idea is that a conscious effort was made to move away from the language of Pius XI which spoke of acting "against nature," by "artificially [*de industria*] depriving the act of its natural power and virtue."[4] Joseph Boyle also emphasizes the interior attitude of the agent as opposed to his exterior behavior. "The proscribed kind of act, is not, therefore, defined in behavioral terms... but in terms of what the agents will in acting."[5] About this two comments are in order.

Firstly, those who seek to make this point ignore the texts in *Humanae Vitae* that speak of contraception as a kind of behavior that is not defined solely by the intention of the agent. The Pope speaks, for instance, of "the inseparable connection, established by God... between the unitive significance and the procreative significance which are both inherent to the marriage act"[6] and of "limits expressly imposed because of the reverence due to the whole human organism and its natural functions."[7] Likewise, in distinguishing periodic continence from contraception, the Pope notes: "In the former, married couples rightly use a faculty provided them by nature. In the latter, they obstruct the natural development of the generative process."[8] Obviously, the inclusion of the natural or behavioral aspect of the act of contraception in its definition does not mean that the Pope has forgotten that we are speaking of an intentional act. How else could it be a sinful one?[9]

Secondly, it is worth noting that the original text of *Humane Vitae* 14 speaks not of the agent's intent but of the *tendency* of the act itself. "Item quivis respuendus est actus, qui, cum coniugale commercium vel praevidetur vel efficitur vel ad suos naturales exitus ducit, id tamquam finem obtinendum aut viam adhibendam intendat, ut procreatio impediatur."[10] In the English version "intendat" is translated with the passive "is intended" (likewise the Romance language versions, e.g. "toute action, qui... se proposerait comme but ou comme moyen..."), which give more prominence to the agent than the original Latin. There is no problem with the translations themselves,[11] as long as an interpreter does not seek to divorce the act with its natural tendency or *per se* effects from the proximate intention of the agent choosing that act.

A second definition which provides an opportunity to ponder the roles of intention and behavior in a human act is the definition of euthanasia. In a document issued by the Sacred Congregation for the Doctrine of the Faith in 1980, euthanasia is defined as "an action or omission which of itself or by intention causes death, in order that all suffering may in this way be eliminated."[12] Bishop Anthony Fisher accurately observes[13] that this definition, and the sentence following, is nearly quoted verbatim by Pope John Paul II in *Evangelium Vitae* with one interesting alteration: the definition now says "of itself *and* by intention". Fisher's explanation for this adjustment, however, is not at all satisfying. He writes:

> [the original version] seemed to suggest that an action could be euthanasia 'of itself' without any intention of causing death—which would make nonsense of the distinctions between withdrawal of burdensome life-sustaining treatments and/or the giving of appropriate but life-endangering pain-relief on the one hand, and euthanasia or other homicide on the other.[14]

On the contrary, the near interchangeability of the two versions indicates that an agent who chooses to perform a behavior that "of itself" causes death must have a euthanistic intent (proximate intention). One could also commit euthanasia by performing a good behavior, for example, administering a dosage adequate only to relieve pain, but with a superadded intention of speeding death (further intention). In his eagerness to prevent anyone from interpreting the original definition to mean that a physical behavior devoid of intentionality is a moral act, Bishop Fisher interprets the definition to be saying this very thing. In fact, if there were not a need to forestall such misreadings, the former definition would seem preferable. This is not a minor point, especially for our purposes, as *Evangelium Vitae* contains a definition of formal cooperation which makes use of "or" in much the same way as the former definition of euthanasia.[15] This definition will be explored in Chapter 11.

The third definition made by the Magisterium which we must mention here regards the object of a human act itself. The key text, which is by now well known, should be cited at length for future reference:

> *The morality of the human act depends primarily and fundamentally on the 'object' rationally chosen by the deliberate will,* as is borne out by the insightful analysis, still valid today, made by Saint Thomas. In order to be able to grasp the object of an act which specifies that act morally, it is therefore necessary to place oneself *in the perspective of the acting person.* The object of the act of willing is in fact a freely chosen kind of behaviour. To the extent that it is in conformity with the order of reason, it is the cause of the goodness of the will; it perfects us morally, and disposes us to recognize our ultimate end in the perfect good, primordial love. By the object of a given moral act, then, one cannot mean a process or an event of the merely physical order, to be assessed on the basis of its ability to bring about a given state of affairs in the outside world. Rather, that object is the proximate end of a deliberate decision which determines the act of willing on the part of the acting person. Consequently, as the *Catechism of the Catholic Church* teaches, 'there are certain specific kinds of behaviour that are always wrong to choose, because choosing them involves a disorder of the will, that is, a moral evil.'[16]

Bishop Fisher's commentary on this passage in light of cooperation with evil seems to us most insightful.[17] First he points out that there are two major avenues of interpretation of this passage, and especially of its reference to the "perspective of the acting person": a "natural meanings" account and an "intended acts" account. The former emphasizes the limitation placed upon the proximate intention of the agent by the nature of the external act itself, while the latter recalls the primacy of the contribution of the subject which makes the external act to be a moral act in the first place. Both appear compatible with the text of the passage itself, according to Fisher. He then notes that the interpretation chosen dramatically affects a person's estimates of formal and material cooperation:

> Some acts that, on the natural meanings account, are implicit formal cooperation in evil, whatever the agent says or believes he/she intends, are only material cooperation on the intended acts account; likewise some acts that are only immediate material cooperation on the natural meanings account are formal cooperation on the intended acts account. To advocates of the natural meanings account those who support an intended acts account look subjectivist, and the encyclical's warnings against intentionalism seem very telling; to the second group the first look physicalist, and the encyclical's insistence on the perspective of the acting subject seems most telling.[18]

It is in the light of this impasse that we now turn to a closer examination of three leading contemporary Catholic thinkers. The first two would count as representatives of "intended acts" accounts, while the third is a promoter of "natural meanings".

2. The subject-centered approach of Germain Grisez

In his overview of the recent history of moral theology, Richard McCormick lists a slew of proportionalist authors ("the best known names in moral theology") and only five opponents of the "new morality": "Germain Grisez, John Finnis, Joseph Boyle, William May and the late John R. Connery, S.J."[19] Written in 1999, six years after *Veritatis Splendor*, McCormick's observation shows how meager was the immediate response to the moral theology crisis. Not only does he mention only five non-proportionalist authors, but the first four can in many respects be treated as one. They have often collaborated on their writings and are even referred to at times by a shorthand acronym "GBMF". As Grisez is both the originating source of this group's common approach to human action and the one who has written most explicitly on cooperation with evil, we will focus primarily on him.

Dr. Germain Grisez, a metaphysician by training, gradually became a leading thinker in ethics and moral theology, especially as a result of the controversies surrounding the publication of *Humanae Vitae*.[20] Seeking to defend the Church's teaching on contraception, abortion, and nuclear deterrence, subjects about which he has written book-length treatments, Grisez became convinced that a significant updating of natural law theory would be needed to achieve this. He found the arguments against contraception offered by the Manualists, at least as they were expressed and generally interpreted, to be no more convincing than did the rising tide of dissenting theologians. Largely in an attempt to provide a better explanation of the evil of contraception than the "perverted faculty argument", he developed his theory of basic goods. It is often referred to as the "new natural law theory". For having initiated a line of renewal of Catholic thought that is intellectually rigorous and fundamentally in accord with tradition, he is rightly admired and studied by many. Our treatment of his ideas, which focuses only on the degree to which Dr. Grisez's work is helpful in furthering our understanding of the formal/material distinction in cooperation, would seem excessively critical if considered an appraisal of his entire work.

Cooperation with evil

Grisez makes frequent reference to the doctrine of cooperation with evil throughout his major three-volume work, *The Way of the Lord Jesus*, devoting several pages specifically to it in both the first and second volumes. Still, he considers the 25-page second appendix of the third volume to contain his fullest treatment of the matter.[21] Regarding the formal/material distinction that is our primary concern, Grisez claims to distinguish "formal from material cooperation precisely as Alphonsus did."[22] His original contribution regards material cooperation where he attempts to expand on the tradition's analysis of proportionate reasons. Grisez does, however, claim that his manner of understanding the moral act, which he summarizes in the preceding Appendix 1, "facilitates distinguishing in practice between formal and material cooperation."[23] We will examine this analysis of the moral act in more detail after considering his interpretation of the traditional doctrine of cooperation and his application of it to certain cases.

Grisez begins by listing four restrictions on the concept of cooperation in evil.[24] He reasonably notes that the type of action with which this issue of moral theology is concerned is (1) to be distinguished from scandal, (2) concerns a helping action, not a co-execution of an evil deed, (3) is ordinarily an action and not an omission, and finally (4) is usually not wrong in itself. In explicating this last point, Grisez makes an intriguing observation:

> Problems about cooperation usually do not arise if
> the action is recognized as sinful even apart from

the agent's involvement in another's wrongdoing. So, *cooperator* usually refers to someone whose act seems morally acceptable in itself—though, as will be explained, the formal cooperator's act, when accurately analyzed, turns out to be wrong, and often gravely so, in itself.[25]

In our review of the history of the discussion of cooperation, we have seen that one of the chief difficulties has been determining if and when the cooperator's action is "wrong it itself". Indeed, this really is a way of restating the problem of identifying implicitly formal cooperation. Abstracting from the circumstance of cooperation, cooperation generally is not wrong in itself (e.g. "holding a ladder" in the case of Proposition 51). It could be evil in itself apart from the issue of cooperation (e.g. if the servant were asked to kill the night watchman so the master could enter the house), but that has nothing to do with the evaluation of cooperation. Thus, Grisez correctly notes in this fourth point that cooperation cases properly involve an action that would only be sinful because of the context of involvement with the sin of another. Grisez continues, however, to say that all formal cooperation will be "wrong in itself", but this seems to portend a blurring of the distinction between *finis operis* and *finis operantis*. Ordinarily, the former term corresponds to "wrong in itself", while formal cooperation by virtue of the *finis operantis* would be wrong because of this superadded intention. The problem lies in identifying the former case. Certainly there will be a wrong intention (otherwise it would not be formal cooperation), but it will be "wrong in itself" because the cooperative act is such that it cannot be chosen *without* this wrong intention. Grisez, on the other hand, wants to identify the presence of this evil immediate intention from the side of the subject, by identifying the willingness of the cooperator to bring about the sin as a means. Thus, while he makes a two-fold division of formal cooperation (see p. 229: "purpose" and "proposal" indicating *finis operantis* and *finis operis*, respectively), he maintains that *all* formal cooperation is "wrong in itself". This seems to make this phrase otiose; formal cooperation only occurs when the cooperator intends the evil of the other, and intending evil is "wrong in itself." But the key question is: how do we know whether the cooperator intends the evil of the principal agent when the actual completion of the latter's plan is irrelevant to him? The answer should be: if he has done something "wrong in itself". "Wrong in itself" should be a reference to the *finis operis*, but, we will argue, Grisez's identification of *finis operis*, or object of the act, with the agent's proposal tends to blurr this concept with that of the *finis operantis*.

This claim of ours finds expression on the following page in an example that Grisez provides. He observes that "sometimes the moral act carried out by a certain outward behavior can be either formal or material cooperation, depending on what the cooperator intends."[26] He gives the example of two police officers asked to intervene in prolife workers' activities; one does it so as to facilitate more abortions, and the other simply to comply with the orders received. So, "intervening in prolife workers activities" is not *wrong in itself*, according to Grisez, but this is so only because it is not yet considered a moral act but "outward behavior". Grisez recognizes, of course, that there can be no moral act without an intention on the part of the agent. However, he does not recognize an immediate intention that *both* policemen in the example must share if they choose "to intervene in prolife workers activities." He deems the intention "to comply with the orders received" an immediate intention, while we would argue that it corresponds to a further intention. This is a confusion between proximate and further intentions to which we must continue to attend (see pp. 344–347).

In his first volume, subtitled *Christian Moral Principles*, Grisez elucidates Alphonsus's notion of "formal" cooperation by identifying two ways in which it can occur. "Cooperation is formal and is altogether excluded in the following two cases: (1) one's purpose is or includes that another commit sin; (2) one's proposal—what one chooses—is identical with or includes the immoral proposal of the person with whom one is cooperating."[27] In his second volume, *Living a Christian Life*, Grisez expands this second reason into a third: "(3) one's proposal includes the other's successfully carrying out an objectively wrong choice."[28] Grisez has introduced the language of proposal to indicate the proximate intention of the cooperator. Although he means to describe the object of the act with this term, it is not clear why "proposal" does not correspond better to the traditional category of *finis operantis*. In this manner, a separation is inadvertently created between the cooperator's intention and his "outward acts". As a result, the notion of implicitly formal cooperation drops out entirely, even in the case of immediate cooperation. This can be seen in the following conclusion of Joseph Boyle:

> Most of the simple behaviours people choose to carry out in response to constraining circumstances in the knowledge that they contribute to wrongdoing can be material cooperation only, just as long as they are not actually carrying out the wrongdoing itself. So nurses can choose behaviours very closely and immediately related to abortion for the sake of keeping their jobs and be cooperating with abortion only materially (though not necessarily justifiably)...[29]

Emphasizing the fact that formal cooperation consists in making the principal agent's evil intention one's own may appear to lead Grisez to the position taken by Charles Curran. Curran claimed that "there can be no formal cooperation when the individual involved [the presumed wrongdoer] does not have a bad will."[30] Grisez does not agree with Curran, but in responding he seems to miss the mark by claiming that "Curran's conclusion could be correct only if one could rightly choose to act contrary to one's own conscience."[31] To this Curran would surely reply that one must first determine whether the proposed cooperation (with someone who does not recognize the evil he is pursuing) is morally acceptable and if, as Curran claims, it is, then the cooperator would not be "choosing contrary to his own conscience" should he cooperate. Grisez needs to explain *why* the cooperator is acting contrary to his own conscience, if formal cooperation only occurs when the cooperator adopts as his own the proposal of the principal agent.

In the next paragraph Grisez says that the "fundamental flaw" in Curran's argument is failing to recognize that "formal cooperation is absolutely excluded because it involves bad intending *by the cooperator*." This is correct, but Grisez does not explain why an act of cooperation would involve bad intending even if performed by the cooperator solely for the sake of, say, not embarrassing the principal agent, or not compromising his ethical autonomy. Since it is the objective evil of the deed in question, and not the recognition of the evil by the principal agent, that matters, the possibility remains that cooperating with an objectively bad act may be as indicative of a bad intention as initiating it oneself. It is the doing of a bad act that manifests a bad intention, as Grisez admits in the next paragraph:

> Moreover, another's possible good faith is one
> thing; whether his or her act includes bad intend-
> ing is another... While others' judgments of con-
> science never are directly accessible, the intentions
> that shape their actions, though sometimes hidden
> or obscure, often are obvious ... from the intrinsic
> connection between their evident deeds and
> entirely credible words. Therefore, though the
> common teaching of the manualists on coopera-
> tion presupposed that one can recognize others'
> wrongdoing by identifying their bad intentions, it
> did not assume that one can know anyone to be in
> bad faith.[32]

These are excellent points made by Grisez to show that
the cooperator cannot base his decision on the principal
agent's good faith. However, these same points would
appear to apply equally to the cooperator. Cannot cooperators "in good faith" perform actions, such as the holding
of a ladder for a master bent on evil, which allow others
to "identify their [the cooperators'] bad intentions," "intentions that shape their actions"? To apply this to Proposition 51, it would mean the servant holding the ladder for
the vicious master with the proviso *"scienter"* removed. In
other words, if the servant holds the ladder, he would be
guilty of bad intending, unless he were invincibly ignorant,
and so "in good faith", something that the proposition's
inclusion of *scienter* seems intended to exclude.

Grisez wishes to show that St Alphonsus also taught
that "formal cooperation ... involves bad intending *by the
cooperator,*"[33] and that it therefore does not depend upon
whether the principal agent commits sin or not. However,
as Grisez notes, even Alphonsus's ardent defender, Roger
Roy, understood the holy doctor to be claiming that
cooperation is not formal "unless the cooperator not only
concurs in the wrongdoer's bad intending but positively

influences it—somehow incites or encourages the bad will."[34] The contested passage (Tom. II, Lib. III, tr.v, n. 571) is an important one, in which Alphonsus confronts the difficult question of a servant forced to help thieves steal from his master. Grisez interprets Alphonsus's statement—"Nor is it true that you concur formally in the sin of the thief, for this would be the case, if you positively influenced his evil will"[35]—to mean that Alphonsus is only talking about scandal, that is, bringing about the sin of the thief *qua* sin. However, this interpretation fails to recognize how long cooperation with evil was treated as "cooperation in the sin" of another. Grisez shows that he himself is completely free of this legacy by pointing out that one could formally cooperate in the act of theft "by doing anything that involves intending that someone already determined to steal carry out the plan successfully—for example, choose to provide a tool needed to do the theft in exchange for a share in the proceeds."[36] Still, to apply this distinction (between cooperating in the *act* and cooperating in the *sin*) to Alphonsus would be anachronistic. The saint's separate discussion of the servant's act *"respectu domini"* does not make any mention of a formal/material distinction. Rather, he is only establishing that the servant has a proportionate reason to help the thief, if the harm he would cause is of a lower level than that which he fears for himself. Then, in the event that the cooperation is deemed only material, the case will be decided. While it would be clearer to establish material cooperation first and then proportionality, the meaning of the passage is clear enough.[37]

Grisez's criticism of the ERD's

Most helpful for appreciating the stance of Germain Grisez on the formal/material distinction is his criticism of the treatment of cooperation in one edition of the *Ethical and Religious Directives for Catholic Health Care Services* (ERD's). Approved by the United States National Conference of Catholic Bishops in 1994, this appendix has since been removed at the request of the Holy See, presumably for its controversial treatment of implicitly formal cooperation. (See endnote,[38] where the relevant part of this appendix is reproduced.)

In addition to his desire to amend the notion of proportionality in the case of material cooperation, which does not concern us, Grisez has two criticisms of this appendix. The first criticism concerns the notion of "implicit cooperation". Let us quote Grisez's entire comment on the matter:

> In the first paragraph, the sentence concerning implicit cooperation is written from the perspective of an outside observer rather than of the acting person. I do not know what could be meant by *explicit* and *implicit*, used in reference to acts of the will. Since acting persons consciously intend both the objects of their acts—that is, the proximate ends of their choices—and their ends in view in making their choices, they are aware of all their own intending, though they may not reflexively focus on it, may not keep it in mind once a choice has been made, may not talk about it, and, if they do, may not speak accurately or truthfully about it. Used in reference to an intention underlying someone else's activity, *implicit* apparently refers to the status of an intention denied by the cooperator but inferred from the situation and his or her outward behavior.[39]

Grisez begins by bristling at the use of the word "implicit" in this context, but by the end of his commentary he shows that he understands the term as we have been using it: "an intention denied by the cooperator but inferred from the situation and his or her outward behavior." While he puts us on notice that this way of thinking arises "from the perspective of an outside observer rather than of the acting person," we do recall that in connection with the distinction between intention and good faith, Grisez allowed that an outside observer could identify the former although not the latter. This paragraph shows that Grisez's understanding of "first person" morality and of the moral object as choice or proposal will tend to exclude by definition the concept of implicitly formal cooperation.

The second criticism aimed by Grisez at the ERD appendix is that the identification of "implicit formal cooperation" and "immediate material cooperation without duress" is self-contradictory. Certainly, every reader, and doubtless the authors themselves, will have noticed that since formal and material cooperation are defined as contraries (intending the object of the wrongdoer's activity vs. not intending it), any overlap between implicit formal and immediate material cooperation will sound contradictory. However, it is obvious that the authors mean that the absence of duress makes what would *otherwise* be immediate material cooperation to be, in reality, formal. Whether this is correct is another question, but it would be persnickety simply to claim that the authors are contradicting themselves. Indeed, in the next section of his appendix, Grisez makes essentially the same kind of point in regard to duress. He writes that "[duress] can be a circumstance in which outward behavior that usually carries out a morally bad choice instead carries out a good one."[40] The ERD was essentially claiming that duress can cause an action that would otherwise be implicitly formal cooperation (a morally bad choice) to be immediately material (a good one). It would seem that the inconsistency that Grisez sees in the formulation of the ERD would be more accurately described as an illegitimate claim that duress can transform what would be an intrinsically evil action (say, stealing) into a matter where the loss of goods can be considered a side-effect to be weighed against the benefit of relief from duress.

Application to cases

The subtle distinctions at issue in evaluating Grisez's presentation of the traditional doctrine on cooperation may be illumined by considering some actual cases. We have a good opportunity to hear Grisez develop his thought with regard to the public funding of abortion as his position on this matter merited a critique by Richard A. McCormick[41] to which Grisez responded in print.[42]

McCormick's position is that supporting public funding of abortion, when one does not "want" or "approve" abortion, is material cooperation (in this case, he maintains, the material cooperation would be unjustified). He accuses Grisez of "collapsing the distinction between material and formal co-operation" by claiming that any supporter of public funding must necessarily cooperate formally, both "wanting" and "approving" of abortion.[43] Grisez responds that he only claimed that a supporter of public funding "wills that abortions be done"[44] and may, at the same time, disapprove, deplore, or regret their occurrence. All that is required for formal cooperation, Grisez implies, is that the cooperator will the evil as an end or as a means. Interestingly, however, while noting that "[people] can formally cooperate in wrongful acts of which they do not approve,"[45] Grisez does not accuse the public funder of abortion of cooperating formally. His first response to McCormick is that the topic of cooperation should not have been raised at all, since Grisez had maintained that public funders of abortion were primary agents of abortion. Grisez continues to maintain that the provision of funds for abortions "is a system of procuring abortions for poor women in order to reduce public welfare expenditures."[46] He notes that he would not have been surprised had McCormick attacked this factual premise,[47] and indeed, McCormick may well have. One could easily imagine a supporter of public funding, such as the religious sister concerned in the case at issue, who would deny intending that any abortion be performed with the funding. Rather, the goal might be simply to provide any woman with the resources to make this choice if she wished, while hoping all the while that all eligible women choose instead to carry their babies to term. Grisez, however, is determined that the death of a child must be an end or a means in the view of a supporter of public funding: "Those who advocate and support abortion funding may have various reasons for wanting abortions done. But whatever their ends in view, they choose to procure abortions by getting the government to procure them."[48] It is because of his certainty on this point that Grisez does not even consider supporters of funding to be cooperators in evil, but holds them to be primary agents. He draws a parallel with a Mafia boss who contracts someone to commit a murder. While admitting that the advocating of abortion funding "differs in various ways from that of the Mafia boss,"[49] he does not see that a typical case of abortion funding is adequately described as the provision of financial help to a woman so that she may do something that she has determined to do—a classic case of cooperation in evil. While it is indeed conceivable that institutional agents would help women to have abortions for ulterior motives (so that there be less welfare recipients, as Grisez suggests), this certainly is not necessarily the case. Indeed, democratically elected legislators may support abortion funding for the sole reason that their constituents favor it.

We have spent a fair amount of time presenting Grisez's position on this matter because it seems significant that he should not recognize the possibility of public funding for abortion qualifying as formal cooperation in evil. Grisez denies McCormick's claim that providing funding is material cooperation and argues instead that it is committing the evil itself. Perhaps the reason is that formal cooperation, conceived as it is by Grisez—as desiring that the abortion occur for some purpose—is hard to distinguish from acting as primary or co-executing agent. There surely seems to be a category of supporters of abortion funding for which Grisez cannot account without admitting something like "implicitly formal cooperation".[50] This term is intended to describe cooperation which is somehow inseparable from the evil deed intended by the principal agent, yet which is provided reluctantly *for some reason other* than that the evil deed be accomplished. Grisez, by contrast, seems to think that in formal cooperation the cooperator's objective must be an effect of the evil itself, making the evil—in this case the abortion—a willed means.[51]

To take another example, Grisez classifies as formal the cooperation of hospital administrators with sterilization, who nonetheless disapprove of the procedure. His judgement seems to hinge upon the claim that setting up the necessary procedures for the operation cannot be done without the procedure being carried out.

> Hospital administrators who, among other things, must see to it that sterilization procedures are carried out 'properly'—that is, with competent techniques to ensure that patients who undergo

> them will not get pregnant again—... might prefer
> that no sterilization be done in their hospitals, but
> they cannot commit themselves to ensuring that a
> sterilization be done properly without intending
> that sterility be achieved ...[52]

While we agree that such hospital administrators are
cooperating formally, we disagree with the logic that the
completed sterilization must be a "condition of satisfaction" (to use the popular term of moral philosophers) of
the agent's proposal in order for his choice to qualify as
formal cooperation. Consider another example suggested
by Grisez: a supplier of temporary workers is presented
with the possibility of entering into a contract with a
company on the condition that it, the temp firm, find an
escort service that will provide immoral services.[53] Grisez
sees here a case of formal cooperation, commenting,
"people can formally cooperate, especially in some subtle
fashion, in an action they abhor." While we agree that this
would be a case of formal cooperation, Grisez's reason—
that "[the owner of the temp firm] intends that [the escort
service] undertake and carry out its part of the
arrangement"—is questionable. The owner only intends
this in the sense that the fulfillment of its contract is a
likely or certainly foreseen consequence of the entering
into a contract, which the owner does intend. But the temp
firm's deal is not, according to the example, predicated
upon the fact that such business actually will take place.
The prostitution is not a means in the narrow sense. Why
is this important to note? The contracting of a provider
who will very likely fulfill the contract is analogous to a
nurse handing instruments to an abortionist who will very
likely use them to kill the baby. We cannot call one formal
cooperation and the other immediate material.[54]

In contrast to Grisez's position on public funding is his stance on the liceity of certifying that one has counseled a woman seeking an abortion.[55] Grisez considers the provision of such certificates, which can then be used to obtain an abortion, to be material cooperation, and he even maintained (before the intervention of Pope John Paul II the following year)[56] that such cooperation could be justified by the hope of dissuading many women from making this choice. Grisez's position follows logically from his premises: the actual abortion is not a means to the counselor's end in the paradigmatic sense of the word "means". While this is a notoriously difficult case, which we do not plan to analyze here, Grisez's reluctance to entertain the possibility that the situation may be one of implicitly formal cooperation is highlighted by his response to a still more drastic version of the dilemma. Would one be able to counsel suicide-prone people in the hope of dissuading some, on the condition that one would give a cyanide tablet to those who insist on carrying through? Grisez asserts: "The prolife counselor would give the capsule in order to keep his or her promise—a promise made in order to get suicidal people into counseling. So, the cooperation still would be only material."[57] In other words, for Grisez, the nature of the assistance given, even its immediacy, such as giving a suicidal person a cyanide pill, does not indicate formal cooperation. For Grisez, only the role that the person's death would play in the plans or "proposal" of the one providing the assistance could make it formal cooperation or wrong in itself. Even from this perspective, Grisez's conclusion is questionable for a reason to which we have adverted earlier: in some sense, a certain number of suicides seems to be a means to the end of saving future clients. Does the ethical reality really change when the suicides are viewed as a cost accepted for the good of saving others? While it may be pointed out that the death *as such* is not needed as a means to continuing in the role of counselor, how is it really different to say that only the *facilitation* of death is chosen as a means? This question highlights the need to examine the action theory held by Germain Grisez and his colleagues, Joseph Boyle, William May and John Finnis, the matter to which we now turn.

Grisez's theory of action

Grisez's theory of action is presented in contrast to the one supposed to underlie "scholastic natural law theory". He maintains that St Thomas's understanding of natural law was distorted by subsequent commentators, especially Suarez, who confuse fact and value; they make "a logically illicit step—from human nature as a given reality, to what ought and ought not to be chosen."[58] Grisez is most especially concerned to reject an argument against contraception that sees the evil in the fact that it "perverts the generative faculty by using it while frustrating its natural power to initiate new life."[59] He cannot see any difference between this argument and one that would claim chewing sugarless gum must be evil for a similar reason. Rather than seek to exclude a crude physicalism, Grisez tries to locate the determining moral factor entirely in the will, in making a "contra-life" choice.[60]

This eagerness to avoid committing a "naturalistic fallacy" has repercussions in action theory as well. Grisez's emphasis on the subject's will is what he and other authors sometimes refer to as a "first person perspective".[61] In Grisez's understanding, however, this leads to the inability to describe concrete behaviors without taking *this particular* agent's immediate goal (or "proposal") into consideration. As we have already had occasion to note, this can make the application of the traditional categories of *finis operis* and *finis operantis* arbitrary: what determines if a given end is "immediate" or "further"? Grisez does not think it possible to identify an act as belonging to a given moral species without knowing the immediate goal of the agent, whereas it is, in fact, impossible to know the immediate goal of the agent without having identified the moral species of his act.[62] Writes Grisez:

> The older moral theologians started out by thinking of human acts in a commonsense way, as chunks of behavior having some moral significance because of their inherent characteristics and their being done on purpose. If one takes this view, one literally never knows exactly what anyone is doing, and so one will not be able to deal with precision with difficult cases of the sort for which the principle of double effect was designed.[63]

In other words, in like manner to Duff, Grisez fails to show how we can objectively identify the object that a subject may or may not choose to execute. Admittedly, classifying even natural objects can be a metaphysical challenge. There is no way to evade the fact that the human act will be at least as mysterious. Grisez's solution—identifying the moral object with the agent's "proposal"—is not wrong, but it does not tell us how to distinguish between the agent's genuine proposal and a tendentious, self-serving description that he might give to his act.

This new approach, emphasizing choice not performance, may clarify, but only at a price. Let us observe, for instance, what happens when applied to the question of indirect voluntariness. Grisez contrasts the pain that is foreseen by a trip to the dentist or a voyage on the sea with the pain which might be sought by a masochist or a person needing sea-sickness as an alibi.[64] Certainly, everybody will see a difference in these pairs, but the question is how to analyze it. Grisez describes the agent in the first sort of case as only "bring[ing the pain] upon" himself, while the agent in the second sort of case intends it. This is not controversial. However, Grisez explains:

> Not every aspect of the behavior [in this case the pain] will be integrated in our action... When such effects are only accepted by us as incidental consequences and never ordained by us to any purpose, they seem to incur upon our world of human meaning, if they concern us at all, almost as if they arose from causes completely outside us.[65]

Note well: the identification of the object chosen depends upon whether the effect is "ordained by us to any purpose". Thus it appears that the *sole* difference in the cases presented is the intention of the agent. Indeed, the intention does differ, as we have admitted, but more differs than that. Consider the contrast between the case of a man going on vacation by ferry and the case of a man needing an alibi. Many conditions, which are, perhaps, relevant to defining the object, have changed. Only the barest natural description (man on boat on choppy water) remains the same. The question should be: does the choice of this behavior in the situation described shape or misshape the intention, or will, of the agent? What elements of the situation correspond to the agent's proximate intention? If the two cases in each pair were truly identical but for the alteration of the agent's goal, we would have only an evil *finis operantis* vitiating an otherwise good act.

Another remark of Dr Grisez indicates this tendency to overlook the essential parameters placed by reality on what the agent can or cannot intend:

> By contrast, the older approach tended to obscure what is morally relevant by focusing on features

> which are significant for common sense or legal or
> metaphysical reasons... [but] ... The work of moral
> analysis proceeds more easily if one first distin-
> guishes between choosing to kill and freely accept-
> ing death, and then examines the morality of
> each.[66]

The problem, however, is that one needs a basis, and
precisely a metaphysical one, by which to distinguish
between cases in which the subject is "choosing to kill"
and in which he is merely "accepting death". The result of
assuming that this distinction can be drawn with ease is
demonstrated by the position of Grisez, Finnis, and Boyle
on craniotomy.[67] They conclude, implausibly in our view,
that the "baby's death may be *accepted* to save the
mother."[68] According to these authors, a doctor performing a craniotomy can describe his proposal only as "alter-
ing the child's physical dimensions"[69] because he would
be delighted if the baby—*per impossibile*—survived (or,
contrary to fact, had already died). This emphasis on the
subject's goal is deemed necessary to avoid naturalism.
Grisez remarks that "when [classical moralists] said that
the object of the act is a determinant of its morality, they
seemed to be trying to ground morality directly in nature
considered physically and metaphysically, rather than in
human goods."[70] We agree with Grisez that it would be
physicalism to think that the moral object of an act can be
fully described or equated with its external aspects. Our
point is simply that the intentionality that is denoted by
"*finis operis*" or, for Grisez, "proposal", *corresponds* to
external aspects (*materia circa quam*) in such a way that
acts possessing the same moral object can be identified as
"kinds of behavior" (cf. *Veritatis Splendor*, 78).

Intention, in Grisez's theory of moral action, is given a
very specific definition. "'Intend' means more than 'fore-

see', more even than 'willingly cause'. To intend something is either to aim at it as at one's precise purpose in acting or to embrace it for its positive contribution to the achievement of that purpose."[71] The intuitive appeal of such a definition comes from the fact that we ordinarily think of intention only in the strict or proper sense, as aiming at a goal that is either desirable or useful, and not in its secondary sense of "proximate intention". Grisez illustrates his point by noting, "I realize that the drapery will fade if I close it against the sun, but I do not intend its fading."[72] Obviously, the agent's goal in drawing the curtains is not to make them fade but to prevent the sun from damaging the furniture or blinding the inhabitants. The fading of the curtains is not the *finis operantis*. Nonetheless, someone aware of the effect that keeping the curtains drawn will eventually produce, must say, in effect, "Let the curtains fade; it's worth it, to save the furniture."[73] It is surely not so farfetched to claim that he intends the ruination of the curtains *in some sense*—as a means to the preservation of the furniture—even though it is not the ruination, *per se*, that saves the furniture.[74] Under the circumstances, one would naturally say that there is no *means* of saving the furniture other than by sacrificing the curtains. Moreover, denying that an agent intends certain evils that are somehow inseparably connected with behaviors he chooses to carry out, can lead to alarming consequences such as the one found soon after in Grisez's treatment of abortion: "May the death of the child that is in fact brought about by aborting it actually be unintended in this case [of abortion after rape]? I believe that the answer must be yes."[75] Elizabeth Anscombe rightly alerted us to the dangers of such an approach. Commenting upon attempts to describe not only self-defense but even just war in such a way that the killing is not directly chosen but tolerated as a side-effect (attempts typified by Grisez[76] and Finnis[77]), Anscombe remarks: "The idea that they may lawfully do what they do, but should not *intend* the death of those they attack, has been put forward and, when suitably expressed, may seem high-minded. But someone who can fool himself into this twist of thought will fool himself into justifying anything, however atrocious, by means of it."[78]

Applied to cooperation with evil, Grisez's action theory will have dramatic effects. It does indeed eliminate much ambiguity regarding the formal/material distinction, but only, it seems, by eliminating much formal cooperation. His disciple, Joseph Boyle, writes: "The examples I have used tend to suggest that there are not likely to be difficult cases of formal cooperation: it will be obvious at least upon a moment's reflection when one's will concurs with another's wrongdoing, and so the hard cases arise only in the area of material cooperation."[79] In the area of material cooperation, the intuition of tradition that there is something very suspect about immediate cooperation is not maintained. Since the key point is always the role that the accomplishment of the evil deed may have in the cooperator's plan, Grisez will note: "Closeness of a material cooperator's involvement [is not] morally significant *of itself*."[80] Immediate material cooperation would be permissible if other factors such as the likelihood of impeding the duty to witness, being an occasion of sin, causing scandal, and so forth did not obtain (which, in fairness to Grisez, is not often).[81]

In a paper critical of the approach of Grisez and colleagues,[82] Luke Gormally indicates that the essential point is indeed a metaphysical one. He argues that the concept of intentionality in which only those consequences which are willed for their contribution to the end sought by the agent are "intended" depends, ultimately, upon an Humeian notion of causation, in which cause and effect are only contingently related. By contrast, the Aristotelian view recognizes that natural causes have a tendency to determine essentially certain effects.[83] Gormally argues that this notion of cause must apply to moral action as well: "Just as there are essential effects of natural causes so there are essential effects of intentional acts, effects that a particular kind of intentional act tends to produce. And such effects are part of the significance of what one chooses to do in choosing to do that type of act."[84] He denies that such an admission consigns one to a "third person perspective" or to a "physicalist" approach. He observes: "these are truths [about human causal activity and about the objects on which that activity is exerted] which properly enter the perspective of the acting person not by way of informing foresight of consequences but by way of characterizing intention."[85]

We should note a corollary of the basic tenet of Grisez's action theory, which also bears upon the topic of cooperation with evil. Certain results of an agent's choice which would formerly have been termed "effects" of his basic moral action, are, to Grisez's way of thinking better described as "aspects". In this he agrees with a wide range of authors from Peter Knauer to Theo Belmans. "[Knauer] rightly points out," writes Grisez, "that the 'effects' in Aquinas's example of self-defense are actually distinct aspects of the act rather than effects consequent upon it."[86] This position does not necessarily align these thinkers with Jozef Ghoos, who maintained against Joseph Mangan[87] that Aquinas's famous article 7 of the *Summa Theologiae* I-II, q. 64, does *not* employ what is now called the principle of double effect. Rather, it fits self-defense into the traditional PDE mould by bending the third condition and reducing the role of the first as well. As Belmans puts it: "In fact, the fact of escaping death does not constitute a simple effect but the authentic objective of the self-defense. It would be necessary then to speak rather of two aspects of a given act, one duly sought as we have just described, the other tolerated regretfully, in the case of the eventual death of the aggressor."[88] But this means that the subject's action is considered as morally unidentifiable until his immediate objective or "proposal" is known.[89]

Grisez introduces the new concept of "divisible" acts into the discussion of PDE with the stated goal of making the third condition, which prohibits the good effect from resulting from the evil effect, less restrictive.[90] This requirement of traditional PDE analysis has, as we have noted in alluding to the work on this issue of N. Hendriks,[91] given rise to considerable doubts particularly in connection with organ donation. Grisez seeks to bypass any sort of causal analysis of the relationship between the bad and good effect by speaking instead of "divisible" or "indivisible" processes. Since, according to Grisez, from an ethical perspective, the goodness of the will initiating the process determines its moral meaning, then it follows that:

> So long as no other human act intervenes or could intervene, the meaning (intention) of the behavior which initiates such a process is no less immediate to what is, from the point of view of physical causality, a proximate effect or a secondary or remote consequence. For on the hypothesis that no other human act intervenes or could intervene, the moral agent who posits a natural cause *simultaneously* (morally speaking) posits its foreseen effects. The fact that not everything in the behavior which is relevant to basic human goods equally affects the agent's moral standing arises not from

> the diverse physical dispositions of the elements of
> the behavioral aspect of the act, but from the
> diverse dispositions of the agent's intention with
> regard to the intelligible species of the act.[92]

By this development of PDE doctrine, Grisez would
explain how it is that a storekeeper can shoot to kill, if
necessary, without intending to kill: "[one can view] the
storekeeper's act as a killing not intended by him, because
the various aspects of the outward act are indivisible
(assuming, of course, that the storekeeper cannot otherwise defend himself)."[93] As Grisez applies this opinion to
certain kinds of therapeutic abortion (not certainly to
justify them), Belmans parts company with him.[94]

By way of conclusion, we might observe that Germain
Grisez's emphasis on the intentional "proposal" of the
subject has the effect of minimizing the helpful additions
to St Alphonsus's position made by some of the Manualists, namely, implicitly formal and immediately material
cooperation. This makes material cooperation the main
focus of interest, for which reason, perhaps, Grisez is
mainly concerned with improving upon the distinctions
traditionally made in this category. The central problem
of the Servant and Ladder case resides in the question
whether the behavior itself, undertaken by the servant, is
compatible with a good will or not. Grisez's desire to avoid
any semblance of physicalism and to locate all moral
meaning of an action in the subject's near and distant goals
essentially renders this a moot question. Since the success
of the master's crime is not necessary for the servant to
avoid punishment, it would not appear to Grisez to be a
means to the servant's end, and his action could in no way
be anything but material cooperation. Ironically, for one
who is so strong an opponent of physicalism, Grisez's
position shares in the error of his opponents to some

degree. For Grisez, the behavior chosen is morally neutral (what is called "ontic" or "pre-moral" by proportionalists) until the agent provides the moral specification, the most immediate reason for which he does it. Such a result leaves us no closer to discovering the *finis operis* of the servant described in Proposition 51 than we were in Chapter 3.[95]

Notes

[1] "Item ceterae theologicae disciplinae ex vividiore cum Mysterio Christi et historia salutis contactu instaurentur. Specialis cura impendatur theologiae morali perficiendae, cuius scientifica expositio, doctrina S. Scripturae magis nutrita, celsitudinem vocationis fidelium in Christo illustret eorumque obligationem in caritate pro mundi vita fructum ferendi." Vatican II, *Optatam totius*, 16.

[2] "Item quivis respuendus est actus, qui, cum coniugale commercium vel praevidetur vel efficitur vel ad suos naturales exitus ducit, id tamquam finem obtinendum aut viam adhibendam intendat, ut procreatio impediatur." Pope Paul VI, *Humanae Vitae*, 14.

[3] M. Rhonheimer, "The Contraceptive Choice, Condom Use, and Moral Arguments based on Nature: a reply to Christopher Oleson," *National Catholic Bioethics Quarterly* 7, no. 2 (Sum 2007), pp. 273–291, at p. 286. Rhonheimer's own definition of contraception further emphasizes the intentional aspect: "A contraceptive choice is the choice of an act that prevents freely consented performances of sexual intercourse, which are foreseen to have procreative consequences, from having these consequences, and which is a choice made just for this reason." M. Rhonheimer, "Contraception, Sexual Behavior, and Natural Law," *Linacre Quarterly* (1989), pp. 20–57, at p. 30.

[4] "Cum autem actus coniugii suapte natura proli generandae sit destinatus, qui, in eo exercendo, naturali hac eum vi atque virtute de industria destituunt, contra naturam agunt et turpe quid atque intrinsice inhonestum operantur." Pope Pius XI, *Casti connubii*, in *Acta Apostolicae Sedis* 22 (1930), pp. 539–592, at p. 559.

[5] J. M. Boyle, "Human Action, Natural Rhythms, and Contraception: a response to Noonan," *The American Journal of Jurisprudence* 25 (1980), pp. 32–46, at p. 35.

[6] Paul VI, *Humanae Vitae*, 12. Cf. Long, "*Veritatis Splendor* §78," p.

154.

[7]   *Ibid.*, 17.

[8]   *Ibid.*, 16.

[9]   Clearly, since a human act is at issue, the behavior must be intentionally chosen. This does not mean, however, that the definition of the act requires knowing the agent's reason for acting. Boyle appears to be confusing these issues when he says: "In explaining why it is morally legitimate to use therapeutic means necessary for curing disease even though these have the effect of impeding fertility, the Pope emphasizes the intentional character of the kind of act he proscribes. The impediment to procreation involved in such procedures may be foreseen but it may not be 'directly intended'." Boyle, "Human Action, Natural Rhythms, and Contraception," p. 35. Surely, there should be no more cause for emphasizing the "intentional" character of the act of contraception than of any other human act.

[10] Paul VI, *Humanae Vitae*, 14.

[11] The translations are natural and in keeping with Pius XII's summary of Pius XI's position: "che ogni attentato dei coniugi nel compimento dell'atto coniugale o nello sviluppo delle sue conseguenze naturali, attentato avente per scopo di privarlo della forza ad esso inerente e di impedire la procreazione di una nuova vita, è immorale... e che nessuna 'indicazione' o necessità può mutare un'azione intrinsecamente immorale in un atto morale e lecito." Pope Pius XII, "Allocution to the Meeting of Italian Catholic Obstetricians," (29 October 1951), in *Acta Apostolicae Sedis* 43 (1951), pp. 835–854, at p. 843. The trouble begins when an interpreter thinks that the "coniugi" (spouses) can determine the "scopo" (goal) of the "attentato" (behavior) chosen even when it does, of itself, deform the marriage act.

[12] "actio vel omissio quae suapte natura vel consilio mentis mortem affert ut hoc modo omnis dolor removeatur." Congregation for the Doctrine of the Faith, Declaration on Euthanasia *Iura et Bona*, in *Acta Apostolicae Sedis* 72 (1980), pp. 542–552, at p. 546.

[13] A. Fisher, "Cooperation in Evil: Understanding the Issues," in *Cooperation, Complicity and Conscience: Problems in Law and Public Policy*, ed. H. Watt (London: Linacre Centre, 2005), p. 51, fn. 75.

[14] *Ibid.*, p. 51, fn. 75.

[15] The "or" in question (Lat. "aut") is the second, which I have italicized: "from the moral standpoint, it is never licit to cooperate

formally in evil. Such cooperation occurs when an action, either by its very nature or by the form it takes in a concrete situation, can be defined as a direct participation in an act against innocent human life *or* a sharing in the immoral intention of the person committing it" (*Evangelium Vitae*, 74).

[16] John Paul II, *Veritatis Splendor*, 78, citing *Catechism of the Catholic Church*, n. 1761.

[17] Fisher, "Cooperation in Evil," p. 50.

[18] *Ibid.*, p. 51.

[19] McCormick, "Moral Theology 1940–1989: an Overview," p. 54.

[20] For an appreciation of Grisez's life and influence, see, for example, R. Shaw, "The Making of a Moral Theologian," *The Catholic World Report*, 6 (March 1996), pp. 46–53.

[21] G. Grisez, *The Way of the Lord Jesus, Vol. 1, Christian Moral Principles* (Chicago: Franciscan Herald Press, 1983), pp. 300–303; *Vol. 2, Living a Christian Life* (Quincy, IL: Franciscan Press, 1993), pp. 440–444; *Vol. 3, Difficult Moral Questions* (Quincy, IL: Franciscan Press, 1997), pp. 871–897. Joseph Boyle comments at the beginning of an article on cooperation that his analysis "is heavily indebted to Germain Grisez's recent work on cooperation, which I helped him develop." Cf. Boyle, "Collaboration and Integrity," p. 187.

[22] Grisez, *Difficult Moral Questions*, p. 889.

[23] *Ibid.*, p.889.

[24] *Ibid.*, p. 872.

[25] *Ibid.*, p. 872.

[26] *Ibid.*, p. 873.

[27] Grisez, *Christian Moral Principles*, p. 302.

[28] Grisez, *Living a Christian Life*, p. 440.

[29] Boyle, "Collaboration and Integrity," p. 195.

[30] C. Curran, "Cooperation: Toward a Revision of the Concept and Its Application," *Linacre Quarterly* 41 (Aug 1974), pp. 152–167, at p. 160.

[31] Grisez, *Difficult Moral Questions*, p. 892.

[32] *Ibid.*, pp. 892–893.

[33] *Ibid.*, p. 892.

[34] *Ibid.*, p. 891, n. 477. Roy has no doubts about this question writing: "Saint Alphonse insiste fortement dans ses descriptions de la coopération formelle sur cet influx que la coopération exerce." Roy, "Coopération," p. 427. He does not consider that the saint is

confusing cooperation with scandal, however, because this scandalous effect, although always present, is not the formal, essential element of formal cooperation; this remains the sharing of the evil will of the principal agent.

[35]   "Nec verum est, quod formaliter tunc concurris ad peccatum furis: nam hoc esset, si positive tu influeres in ejus malam voluntatem." Liguori, *Theologia moralis*, t. II, lib. 2, tr. 5, n. 571. Later in the passage, Alphonsus repeats that to guard the back of the thief, or tell him the best time to strike, or perform similar services would be formal cooperation because it is of a nature to influence his evil will, at least by making him bolder. "Quia in his in ipsam pravam voluntatem furis, eum saltem animosiorem reddendo; et sic formaliter cooperaretur ad illius peccatum: quod nunquam licet."

[36]   Grisez, *Difficult Moral Questions*, p. 891, n. 477. Notice that, for Grisez, the cooperation will be formal only because the reason— "for a share in the proceeds"—requires the successful completion of the principal agent's evil act. We maintain that this is an end more properly classified as *finis operantis*, corresponding to *explicit* formal cooperation. *Implicit* formal cooperation would occur when the same help is given for another end, namely, to avoid the threatened injury.

[37]   A commentary on St Alphonsus's teaching, written a century after the death of the saint, confirms Roy's interpretation: "Materialiter cooperatur, qui actione sua, sive proxime, sive remote ad executionem conducente, pravam dispositionem ad peccatum parati in statu quo relinquit." A. Ballerini, *Vindiciae alphonsianae seu Doctoris Ecclesiae s. Alphonsi M. de Ligorio doctrina moralis vindicata a plurimis oppugnationibus, cura et studio quorumdam theologorum e Congregatione SS. Redemptoris* (Propaganda Fide: Rome, 1873), Pars II, q. 5, a. 1, n. 6.

[38]   "The principles governing cooperation differentiate the action of the wrongdoer from the action of the cooperator through two major distinctions. The first is between formal and material cooperation. If the cooperator intends the object of the wrongdoer's activity, then the cooperation is formal and, therefore, morally wrong. Since intention is not simply an explicit act of the will, formal cooperation can also be implicit. Implicit formal cooperation is attributed when, even though the cooperator denies intending the wrongdoer's object, no other explanation can distinguish the cooperator's object from the wrongdoer's object. If the cooperator does not intend the object of the wrongdoer's

activity, the cooperation is material and can be morally licit. "The second distinction deals with the object of the action and is expressed by immediate and mediate material cooperation. Material cooperation is immediate when the object of the cooperator is the same as the object of the wrongdoer. Immediate material cooperation is wrong, except in some instances of duress. The matter of duress distinguishes immediate material cooperation from implicit formal cooperation. But immediate material cooperation—without duress—is equivalent to implicit formal cooperation and, therefore, is morally wrong. When the object of the cooperator's action remains distinguishable from that of the wrongdoer's, material cooperation is mediate and can be morally licit." National Conference of Catholic Bishops, *Ethical and Religious Directives for Catholic Health Care Services* (Washington, DC: United States Catholic Conference, 1995), 26, cited in Grisez, *Difficult Moral Questions*, p. 894.

[39] Grisez, *Difficult Moral Questions*, p. 895.

[40] *Ibid.*, p. 896.

[41] R. McCormick, "Medicaid and Abortion," *Theological Studies* 45 (1984), pp. 715–721.

[42] G. Grisez, "Public Funding of Abortion: a reply to Richard A. McCormick," *Homiletic and Pastoral Review*, 85 (June 1985), pp. 32–51.

[43] Cf. McCormick, "Medicaid and Abortion," p. 716.

[44] Grisez, "Public Funding of Abortion," p. 32.

[45] *Ibid.*, p. 47.

[46] *Ibid.*, p. 32.

[47] *Ibid.*, p. 46.

[48] *Ibid.*, p. 48.

[49] *Ibid.*, p. 46.

[50] It is interesting to compare Grisez's analysis of public funding for abortion with Peter Cataldo's treatment of an institution providing health insurance coverage for employees including contraceptives. The institution is "giving particular assistance to the contraceptive acts" (p. 107) that may occur, and the question is whether this assistance is material or formal, although admittedly repugnant to a Catholic employer. There is no question of the institution being the primary agent. Cf. Cataldo, "Compliance with contraceptive insurance mandates: licit or illicit cooperation in evil?" National Catholic Bioethics Quarterly, no. 1 (Spr 2004), pp. 103–130.

[51] In the "agent-interpretation" sense of means (see pp. 97–103).

[52] Grisez, *Difficult Moral Questions*, p. 892.

[53] *Ibid.*, pp. 874–875.

[54] In the next paragraph, Grisez suggests an example designed to
      show that cooperation is material when the evil facilitated is not
      a means to the cooperator's goal (pp. 875–876). He imagines a boy
      who, in order to cover up his absence from school, does not admit
      to the police that he has witnessed a murder. Grisez says that, since
      the boy does not need the murderer to get off in order to achieve
      his goal, this evil effect is not a means and so the cooperation with
      the murderer is only material. While the case is complicated by
      the fact that the boy's deed is an omission, he is doing something
      that may be described under the circumstances as directly ordered
      to facilitating the wrongdoing.

[55] *Ibid.*, pp. 380–385.

[56] Cf. John Paul II, "Letter to German Bishops", *Acta Apostolicae
      Sedis* 90 (1998), pp. 601–607. Incidentally, it should be noted that
      the phrases used by the Holy Father—"key role in carrying out"
      (Schlüsselfunktion fur die Durchführung) and "involved in carry-
      ing out" (in den Vollzug ... verwickelt)—do not seem apt for
      describing material cooperation, understood as an essentially good
      act that is abused by another. Admittedly, the Pope did not use
      the word "formal" either, or even the word "cooperation". None-
      theless, the phrases translated as "carrying out" seem to fit well
      with the notion of "direct participation" found in *Evangelium
      Vitae*, 74 (see p. 347).

[57] Grisez, *Difficult Moral Questions*, p. 384.

[58] Grisez, *Christian Moral Principles*, p. 105.

[59] *Ibid.*, p. 105.

[60] Cf. G. Grisez, J. M. Boyle, J. Finnis and W. E. May, "Every Marital
      Act Ought to be Open to New Life: Towards a Clearer Understand-
      ing," *Thomist* 52 (1988), pp. 365–426, at p. 372; G. Grisez, *Contra-
      ception and the Natural Law* (Milwaukee: Bruce, 1964), p. 20.

[61] For example, he writes, "As in appendix 1, the analysis will be from
      the point of view of the agent—that is, the acting person—not that
      of an outside observer. The latter perspective can be appropriate
      for law; but the cooperation treated here must be distinguished
      from legally defined ways of being involved in another's action,
      such as being an accessory to a crime." Grisez, *Difficult Moral
      Questions*, p. 871.

62 For example, if we define adultery as having sexual relations with a person to whom you are not married, then a person choosing to commit this behavior *must* intend to commit adultery.

63 *Ibid.*, p. 308. In fact, the first condition of the PDE supposes that the object is morally evaluable before asking about the agent's goal (second condition) or means to that goal (third condition).

64 Grisez, *Abortion*, p. 328.

65 *Ibid.*, p. 328.

66 Grisez, *Christian Moral Principles*, p. 230.

67 Finnis, "*Direct* and *Indirect,*" pp. 21–31

68 Grisez, *Way of the Lord Jesus*, p. 502. Emphasis added.

69 *Ibid.*, p. 502.

70 Grisez, *Christian Moral Principles*, pp. 233–234.

71 Grisez, *Abortion*, p. 327.

72 *Ibid.*, p. 327.

73 It may seem that this view destroys the intention/foresight distinction and any role for a principle of double effect. It will be recalled, however, that many of the philosophers discussed in Chapter 4, who argued for some notion of oblique intention, were not thereby denying the existence of side-effects. The problem of distinguishing genuine side-effects from undesired but directly caused effects returned in Chapter 6 (pp. 163-168). We will return to the matter as it relates to PDE later in Chapter 7 (pp. 195-199) and Chapter 11 (pp. 337–341).

74 This point of view seems to be that adopted by St Thomas regarding the merchant jettisoning his goods to save his ship. The destruction of the goods is a means, yet it is *praeter intentionem* in some sense as well. See the discussion of *Summa Contra Gentiles*, III, cap. 5, n. 13, later in Chapter 10 (pp. 299–301). Thomas's expression for means—"ea quae sunt ad finem"—seems better suited for a wider scope.

75 Grisez, *Abortion*, p. 343. Certainly, Grisez does not approve of abortion in such cases and hastens to add that the psychological benefits sought could never justify the loss of innocent life. Nonetheless, the claim that such an action does not constitute direct abortion is a dramatic concession, reminiscent of Kramer (see Chapter 6, p. 164).

76 Cf. Grisez, *Christian Moral Principles*, p. 226; also, J. Finnis, J. M. Boyle, and G. Grisez, *Nuclear Deterrence, Morality, and Realism* (Oxford: Clarendon, 1987), pp. 309–318.

[77] Finnis, "'Direct' and 'Indirect'," p. 43.

[78] Anscombe, "War and Murder," p. 250, fn. 2. Since she was writing in 1961, Anscombe did not direct this sharp remark at Grisez or Finnis.

[79] Boyle, "Collaboration and Integrity," p. 194. Boyle does not claim, however, that "there are no cases in which formal cooperation is difficult to detect," citing primarily contractual relationships made to provide immoral services by a third party (cf. pp. 195–196).

[80] Grisez, *Difficult Moral Questions*, p. 890.

[81] To support his claim that immediate material cooperation is not as problematic as one might think, Grisez provides a most unnerving example: Our Lord's carrying of his Cross (cf. Grisez, *Difficult Moral Questions*, p. 890). This example shows that even identifying a moral act of cooperation (let alone distinguishing formal from material) is not possible if one abandons a metaphysical approach (see pp. 331–332). An unjustly condemned man who walks down the hall, mounts a scaffold, etc. is *not* immediately materially cooperating with his own murder. He is not undertaking actions which contribute causally to his death, which is imminent no matter what he does. Indeed, if he were to struggle, break into a run and the like, he would be contributing in a more immediate and causally significant way.

[82] L. Gormally, "Personal and social responsibility in the context of the defence of human life: the question of cooperation in evil," in *Christian Conscience in Support of the Right to Life: Proceedings of the Thirteenth Assembly of the Pontifical Academy for Life, Vatican City, 23–25 February 2007*, eds. E. Sgreccia and J. Laffitte, pp. 92–111 (Vatican City State: Libreria editrice Vaticana, 2008).

[83] *Ibid.*, pp. 98–99: "For Hume, causal laws simply describe constant conjunctions of cause and effect, and cause and effect are conceptually unrelated. The connection is simply a contingent, empirical connection, and there can be no *a priori* reason for excluding the conjunction of any kind of cause with any kind of effect and no reason, therefore, to speak of essential causal effects. For Aristotle, by contrast, there is a logical or conceptual relation between a cause and its effect, it being part of the definition of a cause that it has a tendency to produce such-and-such kind of effect. It is because a cause is defined as a tendency to produce such-and-such an effect that we can distinguish between essential and accidental effects."

[84] *Ibid.*, p. 99.

85   *Ibid.*, p. 99.

86   Grisez, *Abortion*, p. 330.

87   J. Ghoos, "L'acte à double effet, Étude de théologie positive," *Ephemerides theologicae Lovanienses* 27 (1951), pp. 30–52; see also V. M. Alonso, *El principio del doble efecto en los commentadores de Santo Tomás desde Cayetano hasta los Salmanticenses* (Rome: Pontifical Gregorian University, 1937). This dissertation, which for the first time seriously challenged the received opinion on the matter (namely, that this article of St Thomas is the true parent of the PDE), resulted in Mangan's attempt to justify the dominant position (see J. T. Mangan, "A Historical Analysis of the Principle of Double Effect," *Theological Studies* 10 (1949), pp. 41–61). Mangan admits that "Alonso's presentation of arguments and conclusions is quite formidable" (p. 46) and that the opposing opinion is only "more or less traditional" (p. 47).

88   "En effet, le fait d'échapper à la mort constitue non pas un simple effet mais l'authentique objectif de l'autodéfense. Il faudrait donc parler plutôt de deux *aspects* d'un acte donné, l'un dûment visé que nous venons de relever, l'autre toléré à regret, en l'occurrence la mort éventuelle de l'agresseur." T. Belmans, "Saint Thomas et la notion de 'moindre mal'," *Revue Thomiste* 83 (1983), pp. 40–57, at p. 43.

89   For this reason, Joseph Boyle, in discussing the principle of double effect, remarks that "this way of understanding the second condition [the first in most other enumerations, namely, that 'the cause must be good or at least indifferent'] has the effect of rendering it, strictly speaking, superfluous." J. M. Boyle, "Toward Understanding the Principle of Double Effect," pp. 7–20, in Woodward, *The Doctrine of Double Effect: Philosophers Debate a Controversial Moral Principle*, at p. 11.

90   Grisez, *Abortion*, pp. 333–334.

91   N. Hendriks, *Le moyen mauvais pour obtenir une fin bonne. Essai sur la troisième condition du principe de l'acte à double effet*, Studia Universitatis S. Thomae in Urbe, v. 12 (Rome: Herder, 1981).

92   Grisez, *Abortion*, p. 333.

93   *Ibid.*, p. 335. A similar case in which the store-keeper's action would not initiate an indivisible process would be shooting the attacker's colleague in the expectation that this would make the attacker flee. In this case, another human intervention, the decision of the attacker, would make the death of the colleague qualify, on Grisez's terms, as a means to an end.

[94] "Regarding the objective malice of all procured abortion … it is impossible for us to share the surprising opinion of G. Grisez, who writes that such interventions [in the life-saving or therapeutic cases] hardly pose a problem once one has recognized, in the death of the expulsed fetus, an effect comparable to that of the death of the aggressor, that one tolerates rather than desires. The error of this assertion seems to us to be that, firstly, the author in his turn confuses the *effect* of the intervention with its *formal object*; then, that instead of adopting the eminently concrete optic of the Master for whom 'kill' clearly signifies 'kill in a deliberate manner', [Grisez] departs from an abstraction devoid of moral sense, that is, the fact that someone finds death *quocumque modo*." Belmans, "Le moindre mal," p. 45, (trans. mine).

[95] As noted, Grisez's main focus is on refining the conditions under which material cooperation is allowed. Since he wants these restrictions to be more stringent, he may well believe that the servant is not justified in cooperating. Still, we maintain that this is not sufficient. Proportionalists usually prohibit the same acts that the tradition condemns as intrinsically evil; but *theoretically* they could be justified. Likewise, classifying therapeutic abortion as "indirect" or the servant's action as "material" cooperation may not change Grisez's judgement on liceity, but these actions would no longer fall under the corresponding absolute moral norms.

CHAPTER 9

CATHOLIC AUTHORS AFTER *VERITATIS SPLENDOR:* MARTIN RHONHEIMER

T HE SECOND MAJOR non-proportionalist voice that we have chosen to help us interpret *Veritatis Splendor* and the current direction of Catholic moral action theory is Father Martin Rhonheimer of the Pontifical University of the Holy Cross in Rome. His major work, originally published in 1987, *Natural Law and Practical Reason,*[1] joins the effort begun even before the Second Vatican Council, especially by Servais Pinckaers,[2] to reestablish a convincing, non-legalistic understanding of natural law. In his postscript to the English edition, Rhonheimer acknowledges that he, like Grisez, was stimulated by the controversy surrounding *Humanae Vitae* to improve upon arguments against contraception that were easily confused with "biologism". He acknowledges his debt to Grisez although the position regarding the natural law that he develops "is by no means identical with that of Grisez."[3] Rhonheimer's efforts to explain the natural law depend upon lifting up the practical reason, as "the axis upon which the entire ethical-philosophical enterprise turns,"[4] in a role apart from speculative reason.[5] From Rhonheimer's study of natural law emerges his theory of action, with which we are most concerned. While there is a notable similarity with that of Grisez, there are also significant differences. Rhonheimer will not use the language of "proposal" that characterizes Grisez's approach[6] and will differ with him in some conclusions, but they are at one in supporting a "first person" approach. Rhonheimer mentions Theo Belmans[7] and Giuseppe Abbá[8] as the two thinkers who have led the way in this regard.

Choice vs. behavior

Just as Belmans had made his work a crusade against "chosisme" (thing-ism), so also Rhonheimer is chiefly concerned to combat a naturalistic version of ethics which results, in his view, from underestimating the true role and character of practical reason. In this he is not far from Grisez whom he quotes approvingly: "human acts have their structure from intelligence ... Action with a given structure and acts structured by intelligence differ as totally as nature differs from morality ... Morality has an order which reason institutes by guiding the acts of the will."[9] The distinction between the *genus naturae* and the *genus moris* must be constantly born in mind. As Rhonheimer laments, "over and over again it is the concept of the object—or the *finis operis*—that is being understood 'naturalistically'."[10] As did Grisez, Rhonheimer also finds this tendency present in Manualist authors, and he convincingly shows that proportionalist writers have not overcome the fundamental error of conceiving of the moral object devoid of an intentional element. This is what causes the proportionalists to locate the element that morally specifies an act in the intention to maximize goods and minimize evils; these values appear, from such a physicalist perspective, as "pre-moral".[11] Viewing moral choices as mere physical processes (Rhonheimer speaks of the "corpse"[12] of a moral act), the proportionalists cannot see how the object itself can contain moral value. This leads to the confusing result that they themselves, the proportionalists, level the charge of physicalism against those who see moral value inherent in objects of choice, apart from a consideration of consequences. The version of physicalism they decry is to let "mere behavior" dictate moral value; genuine physicalism, however, is to think of human acts as "mere behavior" in the first place.

Rightly then, in our view, Rhonheimer insists, in company with Grisez, that one cannot speak of a human action at all apart from some intention. For this reason, he writes that "the encyclical *Veritatis Splendor* refers moral evaluation not simply to 'kinds of behavior'… but to kinds of *choices* of behaviors: it is not the behavior that includes the moral evil (or good), but the *choice* of that behavior."[13] In this word "choice", however, lies an ambiguity around which our criticism of Rhonheimer will turn. Certainly the object, to be a moral object, must be chosen, but can the object itself be determined by the agent's choice? It would seem that the notion of object, and the related notion of objectivity in morality, would demand that the object is something which the subject may choose to do or not, but that his choosing determines who he is (a thief or an honest man) not what the moral quality of his choice shall be. Rhonheimer alludes to "this apparent puzzle", namely, "if it is said that the 'object' is a chosen act, describable only by referring to an intention, one might wonder how one can then simultaneously affirm— as does *Veritatis Splendor*, along with traditional moral theology—that the goodness of the (choosing) will depends on the object."[14] We might describe the puzzle as a chicken-and-egg problem: the agent chooses an object with moral value, yet there is no moral value present before the choice. Rhonheimer continues: "The solution of this apparent puzzle, however, is easy: The object, its intentional element included, is *first* an object of reason, and in this sense it is prior to choice, insofar as choice is an act of the will shaped by reason." The puzzle, however, seems not so easily dismissed. Reason, Rhonheimer tells us, determines what a person is choosing, and is the guarantor of objectivity. If so, it would seem that any subject presented with this situation, or any fully informed observer, would, in virtue of the reason common to us all, make the same assessment of the moral object in question. Yet this conclusion is one that Rhonheimer would resist, as it appears to violate his firm distinction between the realms of fact and value, speculative and practical reason. Thus, the "puzzle" remains to be solved: there is no moral value present in the action until practical reason constitutes it, yet reason must "find"[15] this moral truth in the action it anticipates.[16]

We have alluded earlier to a text of St Thomas, the interpretation of which is key to the resolution of this issue. The holy doctor states: "it should be said that each single act, inasmuch as it goes forth once from an agent, has but one proximate end, from which it has its species, but may be ordered to various remote ends, of which one is the end of another."[17] William Murphy, a thinker in the same line as Rhonheimer, explains this "central teaching" as follows:

> Thomas thinks a given act has only a single proximate end, although he grants that 'it can be ordained to several remote ends.' Therefore, although we can trace 'chains of means and ends'(13) up to our ultimate end, in order to determine whether a given act falls into the category of 'murder' or 'self-defense', for example, we must identify the proximate end that specifies its kind... this proximate end can be identified by determining the good for which the agent acts, and precisely the one that explains why he does what he does.[18]

Several questions emerge from such an explanation: (1) what is the significance of Thomas saying that an act can have but *one* proximate end, if what sets this end apart from remote ends is merely that it is first in a chain? (2) Is there only one proximate end because the act can be done but once, or because the same agent or another performing a like act in like circumstances must have the same proximate end? (3) What is it about the proximate end, as opposed to the remote ends, that enables it to specify the object? (4) How can "the good for which the agent acts... [which] explains why he does what he does" also determine *what* he does? (5) Why is this good less variable than are the remote ends referred to by Thomas, and so capable of determining a unique "proximate" end?

Another way of seeing the issue is in light of the Anscombian phrase: "under a description". Rhonheimer writes: "'What' we do is always a 'why' we do something *on purpose*. It is a 'material doing' ('*materia circa quam*') chosen *under a description*, while it is the 'description' which actually contains the intentional content of the action."[19] With this we can certainly concur, but the question remains: who chooses the description? Or, again, what limits the agent's ability to determine the description and to what extent is it limited?

Reason and objectivity

Rhonheimer devotes no less than three chapters of his major work to the task of explicating "the objectivity of human action". Ironically, it is in regard to this very point, this crucial point, that he indulges in uncharacteristic vagueness. "Objectivity," he writes, "is finally nothing other than the fundamentally human and personal meaning of behavior, as it emerges from the objectification achieved in the practical reason."[20] Or again, he says that it must not be "forgotten that the objective meaning of an action can be understood only in the context of its objectification through the will, on the basis of an ordering of the reason."[21] He clearly and correctly observes that the goodness or evil of the object will depend upon the "fittingness" (*convenientia*), which corresponds to "due matter" (*debita materia*),[22] yet he wants to deny that this fittingness is a sort of fact that is simply understood by the intellect. Rather, "the reason brings its own claim, which is in fact the claim of human 'existence' (as person and as the wholeness of the suppositum), *into the configuration of the object*."[23] He favors the verb "constituting"[24] to describe the role of practical reason in giving rise both to the natural law and to objects of moral action. He is at pains to distinguish this view of reason's role from that of merely "reading off", "translating", or "interpreting" facts of nature, as well as from the opposite view in which reason "creates"[25] moral truth out of thin air. He thinks that the former error has trapped the great majority of well known Thomists, including, for instance, Joseph Pieper.[26] The following passage shows Rhonheimer trying to explain his middle way, in reference to the constitution of the moral object:

> We have quite an extended power to organize our actions intentionally, and thus in a sense to consti-
> tute the moral properties of our acts. But there are what I would call *naturally given limits* to this. *Therefore*, (provided sound perception) I cannot shoot at a person's heart and truthfully say, "I love you," meaning that I am doing this with the intent of doing good to this person. What is crucial to recognize is that not every behavioral pattern fits for any intention.[27]

Rhonheimer cannot then dispense entirely with the idea that the limits upon reason are naturally given. Yet, he does not want those natural givens to determine completely the object that reason constitutes. This indeterminate area in establishing the moral object that is left to the subject would be the realm of prudence.[28] This seems to be one of the distinctive features of Rhonheimer's conception of virtue ethics.[29] Otherwise, he argues, one would be making the mistake of confusing the speculative and the practical realms, thinking that "what is required *here and now*" can be "derived" from universal principles.[30] It must be recalled, however, that we are not speaking of the wisdom of performing a certain action in these concrete circumstances—a question prudence rightly decides, but rather we are speaking of what enables us to identify the moral species of an action in the first place.

Rhonheimer has a two-fold response to the charge of subjectivism. On one hand, he will deny it on the grounds that reason is not arbitrary.

> These statements [of mine] can be misunderstood, unfairly, as subjectivism leading to arbitrariness, arguing that this perspective makes the moral value of any action depend on the arbitrariness of the person who acts, directing his intentions in each situation toward what he wants. In my opinion, however, this criticism misses the point, since it ignores the decisive fact that every act of the will necessarily depends on reason. Nothing can be willed unless reason presents it to the will as a good, and the judgments of reason regarding the good can be evaluated precisely according to criteria of reasonableness, that is, objectively and therefore not arbitrarily.[31]

One may wonder, however, how such an explanation is to be inserted into the "first person" framework. On another

occasion, Rhonheimer defends his position against subjectivism in a second way by arguing that a true theory of
human acts is both objective and subjective. "The opposition between 'subjective' and 'objective,' in fact, is coun-
terfeit coin in the realm of morality."[32] He continues: "the
object of an action is not constituted without relation to
the action of the agent, or to that agent's will and reason."
This is one of the rare occasions when Rhonheimer speaks
of reason explicitly as the reason of *this particular* agent.
This question—"Whose reason?"—has been constantly
haunting the discussion. Objectivity would seem to be
preserved only if this agent and *any reasonable person* in
his position or any reasonable person adequately informed
of the morally relevant circumstances facing the agent
would all discover (or constitute) the same *finis operis*.

Rhonheimer has been concerned to avoid a reductive
view of reason that merely "'scans' or 'reads off' or
'applies'"[33] the data gleaned from the real world. However,
perhaps this fear would be removed by substituting the
phrase "reads into" for "reads off". In other words, the role
of reason is neither negligible nor automatic, but rather
fully worthy of our spiritual dignity, if it consists in an
insight into the metaphysical reality of the situation.
Moreover, the complexity of moral questions is such that
a genuine autonomy remains, even without denying that
the objective reality determines what a person is doing
whenever an act "goes forth once from an agent,"[34] that is,
in given concrete circumstances. The analogy of mathematics seems particularly apt. Just as triangles and, still
less, mathematical formulae have no existence without
mathematicians to think of them, neither do moral norms
exist in nature before an agent applies his practical reason
to a situation. The truth now known as the Pythagorean
theorem is not "read off" of nature; it takes a certain

amount of creativity to discover and formulate it. Different authors have produced different proofs of this relation, each bearing personal traits, yet no one would deny that it is objectively true, in the sense that any man who wants to relate the three sides of a triangle must come to the same conclusion. Rhonheimer states that "this *debitum* lies neither in 'things' nor in the 'nature of the act' as objectified in the *genus naturae*. Rather, it is these that must be ordered by the reason...";[35] one wants to add that the "nature of the act" is reason*able* and order*able*, which fact alone can keep the objectification by the practical intellect objective.

Two kinds of intention

We noted earlier that there must be a reason why there can be but one proximate intention, besides the vacuous reason that it is the first in a series. It has some special character, which sets it off from remote intentions, and accounts for the objectivity of moral evaluations. Rhonheimer certainly recognizes this and seeks to defend this distinction, as, for instance, in his reply to his proportionalist critic, Richard McCormick:

> The expanded notion of object [a reference to McCormick's view that a moral object cannot be identified until all foreseeable consequences are assessed], however, in reality is equivalent to the abolition of the notion of object altogether, for the very notion of 'object' necessarily implies a distinction between the *basic* intention that characterizes the object and *further* intentions.[36]

Despite Rhonheimer's desire to preserve this distinctive role for the basic or proximate intention, his opinion that it is determined by the agent's choice seems to undermine this distinction in theory and generate confusion in practice. Rhonheimer is cautious in using the traditional terminology, *finis operis* and *finis operantis*, because "it must be said that the *finis operis* is always a *finis operantis*."[37] He explains that "the conventional neo-scholastic terminology that distinguished sharply between 'objects' and 'ends', or the *finis operis* and *finis operantis*, has led to a neglect of this truth [that the object is an end of the will]."[38] Murphy is still more emphatic in opposing "the casuist *finis operis*", which would refer to natural ends, and "Thomas's *finis proximus*", which would be the subject's reason for acting.[39] It would seem, however, that rather than pitting a disembodied *finis operis* (subsumed under the *finis operantis*) against a physicalist *finis operis* (devoid of intentionality), the goal should be to combine under the one rubric both of these elements.

As was the case with Grisez, Rhonheimer's approach to action theory seems to entail a counterintuitive explanation of morally permissible killings. In the matter of self-defense, to which we will return in our examination of Steven Long, Rhonheimer maintains that the difference between "self-defense" (that is foreseen to be lethal) and "the choice of killing in order to save one's life" can only be detected "if you look at the action not from outside, but from the acting person's perspective."[40] In the case of a soldier in a just war, this means that "it entirely depends on what is going on in my heart, i.e., whether I want the enemy soldier to be dead, or simply to stop his aggression and to win the battle."[41] In other words, Rhonheimer considers the act of firing a deadly weapon directly at someone as a behavior that does not determine a proximate intention to kill. Ordinary language, and ordinary soldiers, certainly testify to intending to kill the enemy in such a case, even when they later take care of the wounded. Our view is that such mercy does not show, as Rhonheimer believes, that there had been no intention to kill when they fired, but merely that now, after the immediate threat is passed and the guns are laid aside, there is no longer an intent to kill. If a soldier failed to care for enemy wounded, that would be a good indication that, in firing, he had had a superadded *finis operantis*, of say, revenge. That, however, can only be surmised, for that further intention, and not the *finis operis*, is "what is going on in [his] heart."

It should also be noted that Rhonheimer's approach forces him to identify "intention" and "desire". Of an executioner he writes, "he does not do what he does because he wants the executed to be dead (this could be a further motive, but a condemnable one)."[42] For Rhonheimer, the moral object of the executioner is "to punish"; he does not explain why the fact that the punishment is achieved "by killing" does not make killing a means. The problem stands out in greater relief if the execution was done not so much as an act of retributive justice but as a necessary way to defend society. In such a case, the elimination of any possibility of the dangerous individual committing crimes in the future seems to require encompassing his death as a means.[43]

Two kinds of circumstances

Rhonheimer is rightly concerned about the genuine danger represented by the loss or obscuring of the intention/foresight distinction. Writing against teleologists, he warns that this would mean "the concept of moral responsibility will disappear from view."[44] Although Glanville Williams's airplane case was devised to cast a shadow on this distinction, Rhonheimer does not consider it necessary, as do Grisez and associates,[45] to deny that the man blowing up the airplane for insurance money also intends to kill the passengers. This judgment of Rhonheimer surprises. On his terms it would seem to be clear that the response of the agent to "Why are you planting the bomb?" would *not* be "to kill the passengers". The bomber does not "want" them dead, and, as in the case of soldiers, if he should find any survivors he will likely care for them. Moreover, their death does not seem to be a "means" from the perspective of the acting subject, since he would plant the bomb were there no passengers on board (Rhonheimer does not distinguish between pilot and passengers).

The reason why Rhonheimer considers this a direct act of killing is that, *pace* Grisez, "we cannot define or redefine the objective significance of our actions in function of what we propose." He continues: "that which an agent can reasonably propose (and consequently choose) in a given situation is... subject to the concrete circumstances in which the choice is carried out." In a footnote, in which the airplane case is recalled, Rhonheimer avers that St Thomas would surely not have accepted Grisez's description of the bomber's choice. St Thomas, Rhonheimer explains, maintained that "specific circumstances can at times become a 'principalis conditio obiecti rationi repugnans' [causing] a 'differentia essentialis obiecti'."[46] He remarks that "the action theory of Grisez/Finnis/Boyle ignores this decisive aspect of Thomistic doctrine."

Certainly this position of Rhonheimer renders his action theory more complex and subtle than it might have first appeared. He employs the same reasoning to explain why one is not always bound to return a borrowed item, such as a weapon, to its owner. The fact that the owner is planning to use the weapon to commit murder would be an example of "circumstances [that] can change an action in its objective meaning."[47] To be precise, he notes that such a circumstance is "no longer *merely* a 'circumstance' but is in fact a 'principle [sic] condition of the object'."[48]

A glance at *Veritatis Splendor* shows just how tricky this issue is: "the foreseeable consequences are part of those circumstances of the act, which, while capable of lessening the gravity of an evil act, nonetheless cannot alter its moral species."[49] Grisez would call the death of the passengers a foreseeable consequence which does not alter the species of the act; Rhonheimer would call it a 'species determining circumstance,' not a *mere* circumstance. How is one to decide?[50]

Indeed, a very clear answer to this question is not evident in Rhonheimer's presentation. At least one critic, Janet Smith, seizes upon this ambiguity to accuse Rhonheimer of inconsistency:

> I agree with Rhonheimer's disagreement with Grisez [concerning the airplane case]. But I cannot see how the structure of the act of fertile hetero-sexuals using a condom to reduce the risk of transmitting the HIV is any different from the individual blowing up the plane to get an indemnity. They are intending a certain means to an end; the condomizers do not desire the infertility nor does the detonator desire the death of the passengers but they both choose those realities as means to their ends.[51]

Rhonheimer would not, of course, admit that the detonator is choosing the death of the passengers as a means. In fact, Rhonheimer's action theory appears to render dubious results precisely in the case of acts in which a foreseen effect that cannot be licitly chosen does not serve as a means in the traditional, causal sense. In addition to the HIV-infected couple case (in which the prevention of fertility resulting from condom use is not readily described as a means to the end of disease prevention), we can point to Rhonheimer's position on craniotomy[52] and masturbation to obtain a medical sample.[53] One cannot licitly choose to crush the skull to cause the death of the baby, but only to remove him from the womb, the argument in favor of permitting craniotomy goes. Since the death itself does not contribute to the removal, one can intend the crushing *qua* narrowing, not *qua* killing. By the same logic, a man cannot licitly choose to stimulate his sexual organs for the sake of pleasure, but he could do so to obtain a specimen for analysis.[54] In both cases, the foreseen effect (the death of the child, the pleasure experienced) would be side-effects for Rhonheimer, since they do not appear to be means to the ends sought. Rhonheimer asks, "why should simple 'solitary stimulation of genital organs as such' be the definition of the object and the intrinsical [sic] nature of a human act, when this contains absolutely no indication as to why one would do such a thing?"[55] An obvious rejoinder would be that neither does the act description of adultery—to unite sexually with a woman married to another—indicate *why* one chooses to do so. The inclusion of the purpose clause in the definition of masturbation contained in the *Catechism of the Catholic Church* to which Rhonheimer refers (n. 2352: "By *masturbation* is to be understood the deliberate stimulation of the genital organs in order to derive sexual pleasure") should not be understood as a tacit acceptance of deliberate sexual stimulation for other motives.[56]

Rhonheimer sees those circumstances that are conditions of the object as constituting a sort of background without which the intentionality inherent in the behavior chosen is incomprehensible.[57] This background he calls the "ethical context".[58] "I want to accentuate," writes Rhonheimer, "the fact that such a basic intentionality can be formulated and acquire its moral significance only in relation to what we can call the 'ethical context'."[59] Without this background of conditions, one cannot speak of a human action, but only the physical aspect of an action, abstracted from the context in which it alone can be an object of moral choice.[60] Another example provided by Rhonheimer is the circumstance that a woman with whom one chooses to unite sexually is married to another. "The fact that the woman is the wife of another is not the object, but a circumstance, relevant, however, for the constitution of the object and therefore to be included in its description."[61] This example serves to illuminate the distinction between *genus naturae* and *genus moris*. Rhonheimer means to say, and we agree, that "sexual union by a man with a woman" describes a natural phenomenon, but not a moral act which can be appraised morally without a more detailed description. Nonetheless, this point becomes extremely controversial when the relevant passage from St Thomas (*ST* I-II, q. 1, a. 3, ad 3) is interpreted as suggesting that acts which are the same in regard to their natural species can be different in regard to their moral species because, Rhonheimer and Murphy argue, the *proximate* intention could vary from agent to agent.[62] On the contrary, the details required to identify the moral species (that the woman is married to another, is a close relative, is unwilling, is requesting money, etc.) are objectively verifiable facts. One does not need to know *why* a person wants to engage in adultery, incest, rape or prostitution to know that he is doing so. Thus, as we just observed in regard to masturbation and adultery, one must exercise caution in demanding enough details to identify why the agent finds the act choice-worthy. The intention that will serve to identify the moral species must be built-in to the act and will not be specific to this particular agent, or else it will not serve the purpose it is traditionally held to serve.[63]

Two kinds of consequences

Related to the foregoing distinctions—between intentions (basic vs. further) and between circumstances (condition of object vs. "mere")—is what Rhonheimer calls the "anthropological differentiation of consequences".[64] He argues that authentic Christian ethics, which is often labeled "deontological" as if it had no concern for consequences, in reality considers consequences ethically relevant but distinguishes among them. It is the ability of an ethical system to distinguish certain consequences as inevitable and unredeemable that qualifies a system as teleological in the Aristotelian sense.[65] On the other hand,

> A 'teleological ethics' [in the proportionalist sense] that does not possess any means of distinguishing between (a) consequences that are constitutive of the action in a moral sense (since they specify the action as a human and moral action) and (b) consequences that are only contingent, circumstantial, and possible ... must necessarily define the object of action at a natural, physicalistic level.[66]

Teleologists "are only capable of judging any consequence in the context of *all* possible consequences."[67]

This distinction in consequences is helpful, but it is not so clear whether Rhonheimer can provide the criteria by which to apply it objectively in practice. Smith presents a list of actions with consequences that she would consider constitutive of the act in a moral sense and not "side-effects":

> If Joe ate hotdogs to win an eating contest, Joe would necessarily need to will absorbing the calories possessed by hotdogs; if Anne cut off Doug's leg to stop the spread of gangrene, Anne could not say she did not will that Doug be lame. If George stepped on the brakes of a car to send a signal to

> Alice—say there was danger ahead, George could
> not say that the slowing down or stopping of the
> car was a side-effect or double effect of his action;
> brakes are ordained by their nature to slow down
> or stop a car. If Sally threw a stone through a
> window to rescue Billy from a burning building,
> she could not claim that the broken window was a
> side effect of her action. In all of these cases the
> agents may not have desired the end of the object
> or the *finis operis / actus* but they cannot avoid
> choosing it as a part of the act since it is an intrinsic
> ordination of the act. They do not just 'tolerate' the
> calories, the amputation, the slowing-down, the
> broken window.[68]

In Smith's terminology "willing/choosing" is contrasted
with "desiring/intending"; a distinction that, as we saw,
Rhonheimer occasionally seems to confuse. The issue at
stake is whether and when an agent is permitted to
will/choose to cause consequences that he does not
desire/intend to cause (thus they are *praeter intentionem*
in some sense). If we were to attempt to apply the statements of Smith and Rhonheimer to the case of the hot dog
consumption, it would appear that neither would think
that the principle of double effect applies—but for different reasons. For Smith the unwanted effect (the intake of
calories) is to be included as part of the moral object
(eating hotdogs) and the winning of the contest is a further
intention. For Rhonheimer some intentionality (in this
case, the desired effect of winning the contest) is needed
to specify morally what would otherwise be a merely
physical process (eating hot dogs); since gaining calories
is neither his goal nor a means[69] to it, then getting fatter
is a side-effect or an unintended consequence.

Let us also take the more serious example of contraception. Rhonheimer makes a statement with which all of the

non-proportionalist authors that we are considering would agree: "Paul VI rejected such a view that focused entirely on 'nature' in the sense of physiological patterns, by teaching in *Humanae Vitae* that the sinfulness of contraception was ... the very purpose of having sex while simultaneously and intentionally trying to deprive it of its possible procreative effect."[70] This is not controversial. Rather, the following issue is in question: is it *possible* to engage in condomized sex voluntarily without "intentionally trying to deprive it of its possible procreative effect"?[71] Would this not be equivalent to eating a plate of hotdogs without "intentionally consuming many calories"? Rhonheimer is aware that a false move at this point can lead to all kinds of laxist abuses. Consider the case of a husband who makes use of such a device simply because his wife insists. Let us suppose that his goal is simply to stop his wife from complaining or nagging or refusing to have relations with him. He does not wish to avoid another pregnancy and the actual prevention of one is not a means to his goal. The use of a prophylactic, from the perspective of *this* agent, would seem intended to prevent nagging in a manner analogous to its prevention of the spread of HIV. As if to forestall such arguments, at one point in his major work, Rhonheimer states in italics: "*Certain things cannot be done without willing them also.*"[72] As if in answer to "what things?" Rhonheimer declares "whatever one wills to do *directly*, one also *wills* to do."

Direct/indirect

In this way we see that moral theology is again confronted with the matter of the elusive meaning of the term "direct". Not without reason did Elizabeth Anscombe say: "'Direct' and 'indirect' are dodgy terms."[73] Rhonheimer holds the position that a "direct" consequence, in a morally relevant sense, is one which is pursued as a means by the agent, however reluctant he may be to admit it. He employs the example of bombing Hiroshima at the end of the Second World War. "One could not maintain that not this [the death of civilians] was willed, but only the end of the war: the killing of the civilian population was a chosen *means* to an end ..."[74] No one will doubt this conclusion, but it does not provide the criterion by which Rhonheimer includes the downing of the airplane for insurance money as a "direct" killing, when the death of the passengers is not so obviously a chosen means. This "agent-interpretation" of means does not even explain why the husband in the example just adduced, whose goal of placating his wife does not depend upon the contraceptive device actually functioning, commits contraception directly.

Rhonheimer's action theory has been accused of "intuitionism"[75] because of his eagerness to avoid any resemblance to the physicalist perspective of years gone by. While Rhonheimer insists that "there are things which are directly morally significant, although they are not established by reason but determined by nature,"[76] he does not want to admit that *every* proximate intention is somehow determined for reason in advance. Consequently, an air of arbitrariness remains: for instance, he asserts "...genital acts between persons of the same sex [are not] apt to be an expression of friendship and love. But I think one can reasonably express marital love in sexual intercourse while using a condom to reduce the danger of infection."[77]

Rhonheimer insists on the non-observable character of an intentional action. Wishing to emphasize the fact that intentionality is integral to a human act, he asserts that "it will never be possible to observe such a differentiation [between ten killed persons and ten murdered persons] from the observer's viewpoint."[78] He wishes to make the point that a moral act description includes something more than a description of a physical event. Yet he fails to address the highly significant fact that observers *can* discern this intentional element quite readily.[79] It is actually quite difficult to imagine a case when an observer with sufficient time and resources could *not* distinguish the two cases he suggests. The entire legal system depends upon the possibility of third-party investigation being able to distinguish between accidents and murders. In the very rare cases when a well-informed third party cannot tell what the proximate intention is, it will also be hard for the agent himself to know with confidence what he is doing. Imagine a case of a doctor administering strong painkillers aware that he may shorten the life of the patient by doing so. Ordinarily the dosage required to relieve pain and the dosage required to cause death (not just weaken the patient and so shorten his life) are quite distinct. Were they less clearly distinct in this objective order due to the peculiarities of the case, it would be hard for the doctor himself to know "what he was doing" as he administered the drug.[80]

In a case such as craniotomy, we are not confronted merely with a narrowing of the distinction between the directly willed means and the directly caused consequence. Rather, the two are identical. One could imagine a world in which babies occasionally survived this means of extraction from the womb, and in such a world the moral object of the doctor would change accordingly. As it is, however, choosing to narrow the head *just is* killing the child. As Basil Cole points out in his article on the moral species of craniotomy, there is a sense of "direct" that moral theology cannot do without, which is not a result of the chosen intention but which determines the intention of one choosing. "I claim that this act of violence [a craniotomy] treads on the inviolable dignity and sanctity of human life because the direct action of its nature, apart from intentionality, efficiently causes a substantial change, the separation of soul from the body, and so, is not a mere side effect."[81] It should be noted that Cole's terminology can give the impression that he has fallen into physicalism. He speaks of the human act "apart from intentionality"[82] even apart from "immediate intention".[83] However, the fact that he does not conceive of the act as a pure physical process is revealed by his (too infrequent) use of the term "built-in intention": "I hope to show that ... craniotomy of its very nature has a built-in intention against human life, and, therefore, cannot be used to save the life of a mother."[84] Thus, he is arguing that the will of the agent must relate differently to effects which are directly caused than to those accidentally caused. In this sense, he asserts that "the reason for invoking the terms 'direct' and 'indirect' is that the kinds of physical causality of the act are what is in question. *Per se* and occasional / *per accidens* causes are clearly different in their influences on an effect."[85]

Evidence that this is the operative sense of the term "direct" for moral evaluation, can be found in the speech of Pius XII regarding masturbation already cited. After listing a number of "grave reasons" of a medical nature why someone might think that deliberate stimulation of the genitals would not constitute the sin of masturbation, he notes:

> Such a procuring of human seed, effected by masturbation, does not aim *directly* at anything other than the full exercise of the generative faculty natural to man; which full exercise, carried out outside the conjugal embrace, bears upon the *direct* and unduly usurped use of this same faculty. In this undue use of the faculty is properly located the intrinsic violation of the norm of morals.[86]

Again, we should not rush to interpret such a position as physicalism. The point is not that the proposed physical behavior has moral value apart from the intentionality of the agent, but that the basic intention of the agent is determined by his choice to engage in this physical behavior.

Conclusion

Before drawing our examination of Fr Rhonheimer's position to a close, we must emphasize that we have focused upon and criticized only one aspect of his wide ranging scholarship. While it is far from being a point of little consequence,[87] it would be misleading not to acknowledge as well the vast erudition and significant accomplishments of the author. Indeed, one often finds a fresh insight or deft articulation on every new page. Moreover, the main thrust of his theory of action, with the explicit recovery of the "perspective of the acting person", is most welcome. We heartily agree that the human act is not "only an event or a physical process" but must be "described from 'the perspective of the acting person'... as an act or behavior that is chosen, the 'proximate end' of an act of the will, informed by reason that orders the external behavior to this end, presenting it as a (practical) good to the will."[88] It is the nature of the link between this "proximate end" and the "external behavior" that is the bone of contention. Perhaps a key paragraph from Theo Belmans can provide needed illumination:

> The intention and the election, the distinction between these two moments of the volitive process helps us to resolve the antinomy opposing two affirmations: on one hand, the end is said to constitute the *proper object of the willing*, on the other, the external action finds itself ordinarily qualified simply as *object*. This difficulty disappears

> as soon as one recognizes in the end the *object of
> the intention* and in the external action *that of the
> deliberate choice*. The two formally distinct objects
> are called to join themselves in a concrete action,
> the agent being held to respect the sense of the
> action carried out by which he counts on attaining
> his goal.[89]

The key point is that the two objects are *formally* distinct,
only; in one, simple action, however, they are one. Where
the agent does not respect "the sense of the action carried
out", as Belmans puts it, the object of his action will not
be what he may think or claim it to be. In saying that "the
object of a given moral act [is not] a process or event of
the merely physical order,"[90] the Holy Father should not
be interpreted as saying that it is not a physical event at
all. To avoid the extremes of "naturalism" and "subjectivism", one must choose *both*, since the object of the act is
both the external action and an end sought by the will.

Unfortunately, Rhonheimer's aversion to combining
the givens of nature with the proximate intention makes
it impossible for him to read *Veritatis Splendor* and the
Catechism of the Catholic Church in full harmony, despite
the fact that they are virtually contemporaneous documents. He speaks of the *Catechism* taking "a somewhat
different approach on the matter [of the sources of moral-
ity]."[91] In particular, Rhonheimer questions the following
unequivocal reminder that the object is a given that the
agent must respect: "In contrast to the object, the intention resides in the acting subject."[92] He finds this to be a
possible source of "confusion" because "[it cannot be said
that] unlike the end followed by the intention, the object
is something that *does not* proceed from the acting person."[93] However, the distinction between object and
intention highlighted by the Catechism is critical; the

object can only be said to reside in the acting subject in a consequent sense, namely, that in choosing a given object, the acting person adopts the corresponding proximate intention as his own.

To put the key point in the strongest possible, even provocative, terms: Rhonheimer's position actually preserves a residue of the physicalism that he so convincingly and eloquently unmasks in his proportionalist opponents.[94] Rhonheimer strongly (and correctly) opposes the idea that a human action is a composite of a physical process (a causing of a consequence) and a good intention (a reason for causing such a consequence), maintaining that a murder is essentially an "act of intending P's death".[95] Yet, if this intentional act can only be identified from the viewpoint of the acting person, in the sense that "what he is doing" is a secret knowable only to himself, then the nexus between physical process and intentionality is again severed. Considered in the abstract from *this* agent and his immediate goal, there would be no moral value to the action. Moreover, moral absolutes would then still be subject to the accusation of tautology brought by proportionalists. What makes a universal negative norm meaningful is that it describes objective behavior that is always wrong when chosen by any agent for any reason. In other words, he *must* have a bad proximate intention if he chooses to engage in the designated behavior. If the bad proximate intention is *itself* part of the definition of the proscribed act, then it is hard to see how the accusation of tautology is to be countered.

What essential difference is there between the claim of the proportionalist that the intention to cause the least harm gives moral meaning to an otherwise merely "ontic" good or evil and the position of Rhonheimer and associates that the *immediate* intention of the agent imparts moral meaning to the physical, external act? Neither party is capturing the key point that behaviors, in and of themselves, imply a certain intentionality for any agent that willingly chooses them. In order to avoid a subtle "semi-proportionalism", the nature of the case must determine (or, if you like, co-determine) the unique object that any reasonable acting person must have in choosing this action. Indeed, how else is an infinite regress to be avoided? The "chain of means and ends" to which Murphy alluded can only have a beginning when there is some action (B) that is chosen for the sake of some goal (C), but which cannot itself be described as a more basic act (A) chosen for the sake of B. This basic action B is what one must intend if one chooses to act, and it is what informed observers can see that you intend to do.

Rhonheimer does not treat the issue of cooperation with evil in the detailed manner that we saw in Grisez. Nonetheless, the reader will recognize all of the issues that he does discuss as vitally relevant to determining the precise nature of the formal/material distinction. Can a servant help his master commit a crime (with a modicum of awareness and freedom), without *intending* to help him commit the crime? What is his proximate intention, and how are we to identify it? What are the *direct* consequences of the servant's holding the ladder? What circumstances of this case are constitutive conditions of the object? The master's evil purpose? The fear of retribution for refusing? These are the sorts of questions that our survey of post-*Veritatis Splendor* action theories is intended to illumine.

Notes

1   *Natural Law and Practical Reason: a Thomistic View of Moral Autonomy*, trans. G. Malsbary, (New York: Fordham University Press, 2000); original title, *Natur als Grundlage der Moral: Die personale Struktur des Naturgesetzes bei Thomas von Aquin: eine Auseinandersetzung mit autonomer und teleologischer Ethik*, (Innsbruck: Tyrolia-Verlag, 1987).

2   *Ibid.*, p. xv, n. 1. Rhonheimer highlights especially one essay by S. Pinckaers, "Le rôle de la fin dans l'action morale selon Saint Thomas Aquin," *Revue des sciences philosophiques et théologiques* 45 (1961), pp. 393–421.

3   *Ibid.*, p. 556.

4   *Ibid.*, p. 351.

5   In this regard he acknowledges a special debt to Wolfgang Kluxen, cf. *Ibid.*, p. xviii, n. 3.

6   This divergence from Grisez is seen in their definitions of contraception. "This view [that the evil of contraception lies in the contra-life intention] ... famously defended by Germain Grisez, John Finnis, Joseph Boyle, and William May—is one that I have constantly rejected and also extensively criticized." Rhonheimer, "The Contraceptive Choice," p. 274.

7   "I owe much to Belmans's studies" (p. 470). M. Rhonheimer, "The Perspective of the Acting Person and the Nature of Practical Reason: the Object of the Human Act in Thomistic Anthropology of Action," *Nova et Vetera* 2 (2004), pp. 461–516.

8   Rhonheimer, *Natural Law*, p. 562.

9   M. Rhonheimer, ""Intrinsically Evil Acts and the Moral Viewpoint: clarifying a central teaching of Veritatis Splendor," *Thomist* 58 (1994), pp. 1–39, at p. 6; citing G. Grisez, "A New Formulation of a Natural-Law Argument against Contraception," *Thomist*, 30 (1966), pp. 343–361, at p. 343.

10 Rhonheimer, *Natural Law*, p. 410.

11 In Rhonheimer's words: "In this way, we are presented [by proportionalists] with an action analysis in which 'acts' are simply physical events ('realizations of goods and evils' or of 'lesser evils') to be given a moral character by intentions that justify these performances on the ground of 'appropriate' (commensurate) reason." Rhonheimer, "Intentional Actions," p. 288. In a footnote, he remarks that proportionalists must hold this theory of action implicitly, "since it is obviously absurd."

[12] Rhonheimer, *Natural Law*, pp. 436, 519.
[13] Rhonheimer, "The Contraceptive Choice," p. 283, fn. 23.
[14] Rhonheimer, "Intentional Actions and the Meaning of Object," p. 284, fn. 12.
[15] "The Greek word for truth—*alethia*, "un-hiddenness"—brings out this aspect of knowing: a power that does not 'make,' but 'finds'." Rhonheimer, *Natural Law*, p. 261.
[16] Russell Hittinger would seem to go a bit far in the other direction saying: "Father McCormick holds that 'intention tells us what is going on,' whereas the Pope [in *Veritatis Splendor*] holds that the concrete nature of acts tells us whether an intention is morally good or bad. This dispute is not a chick-or-egg-first dilemma, or a puzzle of moral epistemology." R. Hittinger, "The Pope and the Theorists," *Crisis* 11 (1993), pp. 31–36, at p. 34.
[17] "Ad tertium dicendum quod idem actus numero, secundum quod semel egreditur ab agente, non ordinatur nisi ad unum finem proximum, a quo habet speciem, sed potest ordinari ad plures fines remotos, quorum unus est finis alterius. Possibile tamen est quod unus actus secundum speciem naturae, ordinetur ad diversos fines voluntatis, sicut hoc ipsum quod est occidere hominem, quod est idem secundum speciem naturae, potest ordinari sicut in finem ad conservationem iustitiae, et ad satisfaciendum irae. Et ex hoc erunt diversi actus secundum speciem moris, quia uno modo erit actus virtutis, alio modo erit actus vitii. Non enim motus recipit speciem ab eo quod est terminus per accidens, sed solum ab eo quod est terminus per se. Fines autem morales accidunt rei naturali; et e converso ratio naturalis finis accidit morali. Et ideo nihil prohibet actus qui sunt iidem secundum speciem naturae, esse diversos secundum speciem moris, et e converso."("In reply to the third objection, it should be said that each single act, inasmuch as it goes forth once from an agent, has but one proximate end, from which it has its species, but may be ordered to various remote ends, of which one is the end of another. However, it is possible that one act according to natural species is ordered to different ends of the will, such as that which is the killing of a man, which is the same according to natural species can be ordered to the end of conserving justice, and also to satisfying anger. And from this, they will be different acts according to moral species, because one way it will be an act of virtue, and in the other an act of vice. A movement does not takes its species from the *terminus per accidens* but only from the *terminus*

per se. Moral ends are accidental to the natural reality; and conversely, the natural meaning of an end is accidental to moral one. So, nothing prohibits acts which are the same according to natural species to be different according to moral species and vice-versa."), *ST* I–II, q. 1, a. 3, ad 3 (translation mine).

18 W. F. Murphy, "*Veritatis Splendor* and 'Traditionally Naturalistic' Thomism: the object as proximate end of the acting person as a test case," *Studia Moralia* 45 (2007), pp. 185–216, at p. 193. The internal note (13) acknowledges borrowing the phrase from David Gallagher.

19 Rhonheimer, "Moral Viewpoint," p. 30.

20 Rhonheimer, *Natural Law*, p. 539.

21 *Ibid.*, p. 502

22 Cf. *Ibid.*, pp. 491–493.

23 *Ibid.*, p. 493.

24 Thomas does indeed use this term. Notably, in *ST* I–II, q. 94, a. 1, we read: "lex naturalis est aliquid per rationem constitutum."

25 Rhonheimer, *Natural Law*, p. 535.

26 "In this conception of ethics, which has been most clearly formulated by Pieper, the function of the practical reason is in any case reduced to that of simply grasping and carrying out the objective regularities that are immanent in the world of things." *Ibid.*, p. 185.

27 Rhonheimer, "Intentional Actions and the Meaning of Object," p. 298. It should be noted, that husbands, who have shot their terminally ill wives to prevent a painful death, do indeed claim to do so out of love. Moreover, Murphy's explanation of how to identify the proximate intention—by determining "the good that explains why he does what he does"—would not seem at all helpful for identifying the moral object in such cases as euthanasia.

28 Another thinker in line with Rhonheimer writes: "what one is doing in the moral sense... must be answered in the first instance, not by the interpreter, but by the prudential judgment of the agent." E. Kravesac, "The Good that We Intend, and the Evil that We Do: a new look at *Praeter Intentionem* in Aquinas," *Angelicum* 79 (2002), pp. 833–854, at p. 853.

29 Rhonheimer, *Natural Law*, p. 574.

30 Cf. *Ibid.* p. 575.

31 Rhonheimer, "Acting Person," p. 488.

32 Rhonheimer, *Natural Law*, p. 436.

33 *Ibid.*, p. 70.

34 referring to *ST* I–II, q. 1, a. 3, ad 3.
35 Rhonheimer, *Natural Law*, p. 422.
36 Rhonheimer, "Intentional Actions," p. 291. See also p. 294.
37 Rhonheimer, *Natural Law*, p. 432.
38 *Ibid.*, p. 415.
39 Murphy, "'Traditionally Naturalistic' Thomism," p. 191.
40 Rhonheimer, "Intentional Actions," p. 302. Ana Marta Gonzalez, a theorist whose thinking parallels Rhonheimer's, seems to indicate that the cause-effect structure of our actions can somehow be reversed by adopting the agent's point of view. "In particular, the second point [a reference to the 'third condition' of the principle of double effect, that the good effect not be a consequence of the bad] lends itself to particular confusion because, by adopting a physical point of view rather than a moral one, one could come to think that, in the case of death in self-defense, the good effect—the preservation of one's life—is a consequence of the death of the aggressor, and not the reverse. Such a conclusion, nevertheless, would be an error derived from the adoption of a physical point of view—the point of view of an external observer—at the moment of examining human acts."("En particular, el punto 2 se presta a especial confusión porque, adoptando un punto de vista físico y no moral, podría llegarse a pensar que, en el caso de la muerte en defensa propia, el efecto bueno—la preservación de la vida propia—fuera una consecuencia de la muerte del agresor, y no a la inversa. Tal conclusión, no obstante, sería un error derivado de adoptar un punto de vista físico—el punto de vista del observador externo—a la hora de examinar los actos humanos.") Gonzalez, *Moral, razón y naturaleza*, p. 423.
41 Rhonheimer, "Intentional Actions," p. 303.
42 *Ibid.*, p. 306.
43 Note that even Patrick Lee who classifies certain procured abortions as indirect (e.g. if done to preserve the mother's figure) considered abortions done to avoid the burdens of child raising as direct because this end could only be attained by the elimination of the child. This would seem to be analogous to capital punishment for the protection of society, a goal that cannot be achieved without the elimination of the miscreant. Cf. Lee, *Abortion and Unborn Human Life*, Chapter 4.
44 Rhonheimer, *Natural Law*, p. 542.
45 For this discussion see Rhonheimer, "Acting Person," p. 473, in

which he refers to Finnis, "'Direct' and 'Indirect'," p. 30.

[46] "a principal condition of the object repugnant to reason" [causing] "an essential difference in the object." Cf. *ST* I–II, q. 18, a. 5, ad 4.

[47] Rhonheimer, *Natural Law*, p. 519.

[48] *Ibid.*, p. 520.

[49] John Paul II, *Veritatis Splendor*, 77.

[50] We recall that the difference is not merely terminological; if the object is evil (as Rhonheimer claims), no reason could allow it to be done; if the consequences are merely disproportionate (as Grisez maintains), then other foreseen effects could justify it. A partisan of Grisez's analysis might find support in the general approval of shooting down a hijacked passenger jet in order to protect a city (see note 57 and pp. 310–311).

[51] J. Smith, "The Morality of Condom Use by HIV-Infected Spouses," *Thomist* 70 (2006), pp. 27–69, at p. 59. The fact that Grisez, contrary to Rhonheimer, holds that a couple may *not* licitly make use of a condom in order to prevent the spread of HIV (cf. *Living a Christian Life*, p. 640) does not mean that he shares Smith's reasoning or action theory. He seems to be making a different, also valid, argument against Rhonheimer's position: namely, condomized sex does not qualify as a marital act, which is "the pattern of behavior which, in conjunction with other necessary conditions, would result in conception" (*Ibid.*, p. 634). Grisez is not alleging that there is necessarily present in such a couple a contraceptive intent.

[52] A position he takes in his forthcoming book, *Killing in Conflict Situations*, according to May, *Catholic Bioethics*, p. 199.

[53] Rhonheimer, "Intentional Actions," pp. 296 and 300. It is not at all obvious how Rhonheimer would distinguish his position from that of Richard McCormick: "Proportionalists would argue that this ('solitary sex act') is an inadequate description of the action. For self-stimulation for sperm testing is a different human act from self-pleasuring, much as self-defense is different from homicide during a robbery. They are different because of different reasons for the act, i.e., different goods sought and aimed at different intentions. Intention tells us what is going on." R. McCormick, "Document Begets Many Legitimate Moral Questions," *National Catholic Reporter*, 29 (Oct 15 1993), p. 17. Rather, the following observation of *Veritatis Splendor* would seem to apply equally to both: "*One must therefore reject the thesis,* characteristic of teleological and proportionalist theories, *which holds that it is impos-*

sible to qualify as morally evil according to its species—its
'object'—*the deliberate choice of certain kinds of behavior or
specific acts, apart from a consideration of the intention for which
the choice is made...*" John Paul II, *Veritatis Splendor*, 79 (Italics
in the original).

54   Pius XII explicitly rejects collecting semen in this manner. "Si actus
huiusmodi [vis. masturbation] ad explendam libidinem ponantur,
eos vel ipse naturalis hominis sensus sua sponte respuit, ac multo
magis mentis iudicium, quotiescumque rem mature recteque
considerat. Iidem actus tamen tunc quoque respuendi sunt, cum
graves rationes eos a culpa eximere videntur, uti sunt..." Pius XII,
"Allocution to the Second World Congress on Fertility and
Sterility", in *The Human Body*, ed. The Monks of Solesmes
(Boston: St Paul Editions, 1960), p. 391.

55   *Ibid.*, p. 300.

56   Compare with the definition of euthanasia: "an action or omission
which of itself and by intention causes death, with the purpose of
eliminating all suffering" (*Evangelium Vitae*, 65). The purpose
clause tells us what species of murder we are talking about, but the
first part of the definition already establishes the act as a sin against
life. Obviously, the stimulation of sexual organs for a purpose other
than sexual pleasure is not common enough to warrant a special
term other than masturbation.

57   This, we suspect, would be his way of justifying fighter pilots who
would shoot down hijacked airplanes to defend a city.

58   Cf. Rhonheimer, *Natural Law*, pp. 475–483; "Acting Person," pp.
493–500.

59   Rhonheimer, "Acting Person," p. 500.

60   "This 'ethical context' is always that of a particular virtue." *Ibid.*,
p. 501.

61   *Ibid.*, p. 500, fn. 106.

62   Rhonheimer cites this response of St Thomas in order to explain
his position on HIV-infected couples making use of condoms. Cf.
M. Rhonheimer, "On the Use of Condoms to Prevent Acquired
Immune Deficiency Syndrome," *National Catholic Bioethics
Quarterly* 5, no. 1 (Spr 2005), pp. 40–48, at p. 43.

63   Human freedom consists both in the ability to choose to do this
or that, and in the ability, having settled upon an option, to do it
or not. These aspects of freedom are discussed as "liberty of
specification" and "liberty of exercise", respectively, by Kevin
Flannery. See K. L. Flannery, *Acts amid Precepts: the Aristotelian*

Logical Structure of Thomas Aquinas's Moral Theory (Washington, DC: Catholic University of America, 2001) p. 112, and pp. 132–135. It is important not to confuse liberty of specification with the claim of Rhonheimer and Murphy being criticized here. Liberty of specification refers to the ability of a free agent to choose from among various objects of choice (to do a craniotomy or to attempt a risky C-section) while we interpret these authors as saying, in essence, that, having settled on one option (to do a craniotomy), the agent is still free to decide what the moral object will be (to narrow the skull or to kill the child). Of course, these two "moments" would occur simultaneously.

[64] Rhonheimer, *Natural Law*, pp. 361–2.

[65] *Ibid.*, p. 362.

[66] *Ibid.*, pp. 363–364.

[67] *Ibid.*, p. 362.

[68] Smith, "Morality of Condom Use," p. 57.

[69] Note the ambiguity of "means" again. It would not be a means for Rhonheimer because he would still be awarded the prize even if it were discovered that, by some miracle, he had gained no calories. But this is what was designated the "agent-interpretation" of means in Chapter 4.

[70] Rhonheimer, "Contraceptive Choice," p. 287.

[71] More precisely, to avoid the red-herring of whether the couple is fertile or not, one should ask whether it is *possible* to engage in condomized sex voluntarily without intentionally depriving it of its *per se* ordination to procreation. As Paul VI says: "Ecclesia … id docet necessarium esse, ut *quilibet matrimonii usus* ad vitam humanam procreandam per se destinatus permaneat." Paul VI, *Humanae Vitae*, 11. The fact that these acts are forseen to be infertile, by some illness or unknown cause, is not relevant.

[72] Rhonheimer, *Natural Law*, p. 464.

[73] Anscombe, "Medalist's Address," p. 62.

[74] *Ibid.*, p. 464.

[75] Long, *Teleological Grammar*, p. xi, fn. 1.

[76] M. Rhonheimer, "The Moral Significance of Pre-rational nature in Aquinas: a reply to Jean Porter (and Stanley Hauerwas)," *American Journal of Jurisprudence* 48 (2003), pp. 253–280, at p. 262.

[77] Rhonheimer, "On the Use of Condoms," p. 44.

[78] Rhonheimer, "The Moral Viewpoint," p. 13.

79   Anscombe observes: "Now as to 'intention can't be known, because
     it is something private,' that is in general absurd... you don't have
     to know what some private person killed his uncle for, in order to
     know he committed murder, so long as he was awake, *compos
     mentis*, and was doing the killing on purpose." Anscombe, "Medal-
     ist's Address," p. 57.

80   Steven Long rightly notes: "Although we may use a quantum of
     morphine that we judge likely to attrite lifespan—likely, let us say,
     to reduce the lifespan from three months to three weeks—we
     cannot reasonably use a dosage of morphine which we judge
     certainly to be immediately and proximately sufficient to kill."
     Long, *Teleological Grammar*, p. 16.

81   B. Cole, "Is the Moral Species of Craniotomy a Direct Killing or a
     Saving of Life?" *Nova et Vetera*, English edition , vol. 3, No.4 (2005),
     pp. 689–702, at p. 698.

82   *Ibid.*, p. 698.

83   *Ibid.*, p. 702.

84   *Ibid.*, p. 694.

85   *Ibid.*, p. 702.

86   "Eiusmodi procuratio humani seminis, per masturbationem
     effecta, ad nihil aliud *directe* spectat, nisi ad naturalem in homine
     generandi facultatem plene exercendam; quod quidem plenum
     exercitum, extra coniugalem copulam peractum, secum fert
     directum et indebite usurpatum eisudem facultatis usum. In hoc
     eiusmodi indebito facultatis usu proprie sita est intrinseca regulae
     morum violatio." Pius XII, "Allocution to the Second World
     Congress on Fertility and Sterility", in *The Human Body*, p. 391
     (Italics added).

87   Consider Steven Long's assessment: "Nor, finally, should it be said
     that the error of those who reduce the object of the moral act
     merely to an ideational or mental intention is of small import,
     because the number of spouses who would be affected by errone-
     ous teaching on this point is small. The error in question subverts
     the general integrity of the Church's teaching regarding the role
     of normative teleological order in specifying intention and choice,
     and so is dislocative with respect to the entire moral magisterium.
     It is in its fashion a more dangerous error than that of the
     proportionalists: for while the latter to a large degree forthrightly
     reject the magisterium of the Church in morals, the
     transcendentalist/logicist account as found within Catholic circles
     today putatively accepts the Church's teaching while interpreting

it in such a way as to render possible and indeed likely the entire deconstruction of its meaning. Thus, this error is rightly designated as 'angelist', 'logicist', 'a residue of Cartesian error', et cetera, and frankly deserves much more ill report besides." S. A. Long, "The False Theory Undergirding Condomitic Exceptionalism: A Response to William F. Murphy Jr. and Rev. Martin Rhonheimer," *National Catholic Bioethics Quarterly 8, no. 4* (Win 2008), pp. 709–731, at p. 731.

[88] Rhonheimer, "Acting Person," p. 492.

[89] "L'intention et l'élection, la distinction entre ces deux moments du procès volitif nous aide à résoudre l'antinomie opposant deux affirmations: d'une part, la fin est dite constituer le *propre object du vouloir*, d'autre part, l'agir externe se trouve d'ordinaire qualifié *objet* tout court. Cette difficulté se dissipe dès qu'on reconnaît dans la fin *l'objet de l'intention* et dans l'agir externe *celui du choix délibéré*. Les deux objets formellement distincts sont d'ailleurs appelés à se rejoindre dans l'agir concret, l'agent étant tenu de respecter le sens de l'agir effectué par où il compte atteindre son but." Belmans, *Sens obiectif*, p. 116.

[90] John Paul II, *Veritatis Splendor*, 78.

[91] Rhonheimer, "Acting Person," p. 493.

[92] *Catechism of the Catholic Church*, n. 1752.

[93] Rhonheimer, "Acting Person," p. 494.

[94] It should be noted that such labels can be quite misleading. We saw that the physicalism of the proportionalists means that the entire moral value of an act comes from the agent (wherefore they do not see themselves as physicalist). Likewise, the physicalist residue that I have mentioned in Rhonheimer, leads him to overemphasize the role of the subject, earning him the epithet of "angelism" as well (cf. note 87 above).

[95] Rhonheimer, "Moral Viewpoint," p. 12.

Chapter 10: Catholic Authors after *Veritatis Splendor*: Steven Long

1. Natural meanings theorists

A MONG NON-PROPORTIONALIST CATHOLIC moral theologians, the most noticeable voices belong to the defenders of "first person morality". Of these we have selected Germain Grisez and Martin Rhonheimer as the leading lights. As we have seen, these thinkers seize upon the phrase of *Veritatis Splendor* 78—"the perspective of the acting person"—as an authoritative confirmation of their action theory. We have indicated that they view proportionalism as a morbid consequence of a legalism and physicalism latent in Catholic moral thinking for centuries. In order to fully exorcise the demon, they have deemed it necessary to rethink some fundamental points. Practical reason must be seen as independent of speculative. Ethics should be seen as having a certain primacy over metaphysical questions. Natural law is not discovered by examining man, but he is understood by grasping natural law. One expects at any moment the announcement of another "Copernican revolution".[1]

With this tendency in contemporary Catholic scholarship, one must contrast another line of thought. Although it is less homogenous, less clearly comprised of leaders and disciples, it counts among its representatives a number of noteworthy names, including: Stephen Brock, Romanus Cessario, Kevin Flannery, Russell Hittinger, Steven Long, Ralph McInerney and Janet Smith. It will be recalled that the basic, underlying question which was being ignored by the legalism of the Manualists and which the proportionalists thought that they had resolved was: what is it that gives moral value to our actions? The advocates of a first person approach do not seem to have come to terms effectively with that fundamental demand of a moral theory. The prominence given to the practical reason in contradistinction to speculative gives the impression of intuitionism and the avoidance of the question of the ultimate grounding of right and wrong. In Theo Belmans, not just a vague impression is given, but a bold admission: "As soon as one clings to the physicalist optic, one sees oneself constrained to face the following question: whence comes the moral value of our actions?—an artificial problem, to our mind, which is to be imputed to a radical misunderstanding of the givens of ethical reasoning."[2] Such is the result of acceding to the accusation that Catholic theology had been committing a naturalistic fallacy all these years.

The proponents of action theories which emphasize the essential role of the nature of the case for determining the object of the act are essentially offering another answer to the question of "what determines the moral value of acts?": not conformity with a law (Manualist), nor proportionate reason based upon an assessment of foreseen consequences (proportionalism), nor the refusal to make a choice against a fundamental good or human virtue (first person moralists), but natural teleology. It will be important to evaluate the plausibility of these thinkers' claim to have avoided physicalism. Indeed, showing how intentionality distinguishes a human act from an event of the purely natural order is not without pitfalls. Anscombe and Rhonheimer each provide a pair of contrasting images (Anscombe: a person rolling down a hill "like a package" vs. intentionally dislodging a boulder, and, Rhonheimer: a tornado killing ten people vs. a murderer doing so) which can cause one to miss a subtle point. The point is raised by Eric D'Arcy regarding planting potatoes: namely, apparently physical action descriptions are very frequently not devoid of intentionality.[3] Hence, pretending a person is a package or a tornado for the sake of the argument is misleading. Only some physical descriptions ("she dropped her keys") leave one in doubt as to whether the action was done on purpose or not.

No one, it seems, would like to be classified as a "third person morality" theorist. The term "teleologist" has now been given a negative, proportionalist sense. Although the appellation suggested by Fisher, "natural meanings" theorists,[4] is rather close to the epithet, "natural ends" theorists, which carries the implication of physicalist tendencies, it will have to suffice when we must refer to this group of thinkers as a class. As our focus is on the action theory itself, which we plan to apply to the case of cooperation, we will not describe or defend the philosophical position underlying it, regarding the nature of practical reason and the character of natural law. As David S. Crawford indicates, the question of the relation between fact and value touches on many philosophical issues: "The strict division between 'is' and 'ought' presupposes a reduction of nature to dead matter, of reason to rationalism, of freedom to freedom of indifference, of causality to merely efficient causality, of order to mechanism, etc."[5] Such issues must only be raised insofar as they touch upon our specific topic.

2. Steven Long

From the chief representatives of "natural meanings" theorists, writers who recall and emphasize the objective, natural determinants of the moral object, we have chosen Steven Long for detailed examination. More than other writers of like mind, for instance, Stephen Brock and Kevin Flannery, Long has developed a complete theory of action[6] which can be compared with those of Grisez and Rhonheimer. Moreover, his succinct "primer", which has even recently been presented in the form of an article,[7] makes summarizing his complex position relatively easy.

Unified natural teleology

Long's starting point is the assertion of the existence of a unified natural teleology of human acts. Where Rhonheimer assigned a "normative" and "constitutive" role to the practical reason, Long applies these terms to "natural teleology". His use of the word "grammar" in this context indicates that the "language" of morality cannot be understood without a certain substratum, given before an agent even comes to choose. This substratum is an ordering, a hierarchy of ends—hence the adjective "unified"—which provides something analogous to rules that make the language of morality possible. An evil will not be classified as a "moral" evil because it is foreseen to cause a lesser amount of ontic good, or because it requires acting against a basic human good, but because it is of itself disproportioned to the ultimate good of man.

Long certainly does not deny the manifest Thomistic doctrine, emphasized by Rhonheimer, that "the species of moral actions are constituted by forms as conceived by the reason"[8] or that the decisive aspect of this constitution of the species is played by the end sought by a particular agent. Long willingly admits both these truths. Yet, he underlines that the object of the act is itself hylemorphically composed. While the most formal aspect of the object is "that which makes it choiceworthy to the agent," also included in the object is "the act itself and its integral nature".[9]

From this explanation of the object of the act, as containing both a formal and a material aspect, follows a critical conclusion. The most formal aspect of the act, the subject's goal, may or may not fit with the material aspect, the natural teleology or orientation of the act chosen. When this orientation corresponds with the end sought by the agent, that is to say, with the reason for which he considers this external action choice-worthy, one is dealing with a simple act. Long calls this simple case of a moral act "the fundamental *unit of currency* of St Thomas's entire treatment of the moral act."[10] The "correspondence" just mentioned (between the material and formal aspects of the object) is more accurately described as being "proportioned" or "*per se* ordered". For this reason, Long often refers to a simple act as "the *per se* instance of the human act" because the object is *per se* ordered to the end. It is, of course, essential to be able to identify when an object is *per se* ordered to an end, a point to which we shall return. Long tells us that it can happen in one of two ways: "For one thing is said to be *per se* ordered to the other if the achievement of one thing is absolutely required for the achievement of the other, or if one thing simply by its nature tends toward the achievement of another."[11]

The notion of *per se* ordering plays, in Long's estimation, an irreplaceable role in determining the object or moral species. When the agent's end corresponds to the natural teleology of the means chosen, the agent's end provides the species of the act; this is the simple case. However, when the agent's end does not correspond to the natural teleology of the means chosen, the agent is ordering a simple act *per accidens* to an ulterior goal. A classic example is stealing to give to the poor, or stealing in order to commit adultery. In such cases, the end of the agent remains the most formal aspect of the object, but there are really two acts of different species. Long describes the resulting "complex act" thus: "Yet, in truth, we have two simple acts, one of them further ordered in the mind of the agent to the other, which is 'more formal' inasmuch as it is, for the agent, the principal end sought."[12] For this reason St Thomas says that such conduct is both theft and adultery, but more the latter than the former.[13] So it appears that *per se* ordering plays a role in every human act, for which reason Long calls it "the fundamental currency" of an authentic action theory.

Long uses a precise set of vocabulary to which he adheres very closely. Nonetheless, it would seem that his terminology translates into the classical one in the following manner. The object of the external act is the means chosen to achieve an end. The end intended is the object of the internal act. The former, the means chosen, corresponds to the *finis operis* and the latter, the agent's intention or reason for acting, to the *finis operantis*. In the case of a simple act, where there is *per se* ordering of one to the other, the *finis operantis* overlaps with the *finis operis* (giving alms to the poor in order to help the needy). This does not happen where the means chosen is not naturally ordered to the agent's end (giving alms to the poor in order to impress your friends). In the latter case, the object chosen is really an act unto itself, ordered *per accidens* to another end. Of the two simple acts composing this complex act, one is more formal in regard to the other. In other words, this complex act is more an act of vanity than almsgiving, but it is still an act of almsgiving. Applying the traditional analysis, we will judge the action to be wrong not by defect of object, but by a wrong intention which vitiates the (complex) act.

Dr Long is far from finished with his explication of what he considers to be authentic Thomistic moral action theory. The foregoing points are necessary for understanding correctly the term "*praeter intentionem*". Corresponding to the two sorts of human act (simple and complex) there will be two senses of the term "*praeter intentionem*". The object can be *praeter intentionem* in the sense of not intended as an end in itself or in the sense of not intended as an end or as a means.[14] In the case of a simple act, the means chosen may be *per se* ordered to the end and yet repugnant to the agent for other reasons. This is the case of "mixed voluntary" and the first sense of *praeter intentionem*—not intended as an end. The other, broader sense of *praeter intentionem*, which refers to consequences that are willed neither as means nor end, can occur in both simple and complex acts. These consequences would be genuine side-effects.

One major advantage to this aspect of Long's presentation is that it helps makes sense of the usage of *praeter intentionem* by St Thomas. Boyle, who, as a disciple of Grisez, wishes to describe as a means only those elements which contribute to obtaining the end sought by the agent and so are included in his "proposal", finds it difficult to explain why Thomas sometimes describes as *praeter intentionem* elements which clearly serve as means. The chief example is the one borrowed from Aristotle of the merchant throwing goods into the sea so as to lighten his boat.[15] As Long sees the situation, the loss of merchandise is outside the intention only in the sense that it is not intended as an end, but it is willed as a means. Because the jettisoning of the cargo is *per se* ordered to the end of saving the boat, it can be included materially in the object and yet considered *praeter intentionem* inasmuch as it is not formally intended. Were the jettisoning not naturally ordered to the agent's end, it would not be contained in the species derived from the end and would have to be intended in its own right. Then there would be two simple acts. Other effects, such as the demise of the company that owned the merchandise, even if foreseen with absolute certainty, would be *praeter intentionem* in the sense of not being intended either as an end or as a means. With this Boyle would agree.

Another angle from which to describe the situation is the following. Both Boyle and Long admit that St Thomas uses the term "intention" in both a broad and a narrow sense. The narrow sense of intention seems to exclude the means, and the broad sense of intention applies to both end and means. Boyle, as a representative of "first person" moralists, would consider the narrow sense of intention *secondary*, even improper. "It should be noted, first of all," he writes, "that Aquinas's statement that one intends only the ultimate end is inconsistent with his teaching in *De Veritate* q. 22, a. 14 and *ST* I-II, q. 12, a. 1… perhaps [he] is simply using 'intend' in a stricter and narrower sense here [in reference to the merchant jettisoning goods] than in the *De Veritate* and the *Prima Secundae*."[16] Intention, for Boyle, is primarily of the end and means together, that is, the end as acquired by the means. Long, on the other hand, considers this narrower meaning of intention (and the corresponding broader sense of *praeter intentionem*) to be the *primary* meaning of the word for Thomas. Long points out that one can intend an end before any means are selected.[17] Applied to the means, intention, according to Long, is used in a "wholly secondary, derived, and analogical" way.[18] "Intention is not indifferently to be used, then, of end and means, and the more proper term is 'choice' with respect to means."[19]

This apparent quibble over the narrow or broad sense of intention only shows its full significance in light of Long's fundamental thesis regarding natural teleology. If the means chosen is *per se* ordered to the end, then only is the species of the object chosen defined by the end pursued by the agent. When the agent is actually ordering a simple act *per accidens* to an end, that simple act, now functioning as object of the complex act, possesses its own moral species. "In complex acts the end of the first simple act serving as a quasi-object is intended."[20] The dramatic practical difference between the two positions will become clear as we turn to a few cases.[21]

Private self-defense, ST II-II, q. 64, a. 7

The second chapter of Steven Long's book is an extended application of the foregoing analysis to the case of private self-defense. This is the "proving ground"[22] for any moral action theory, according to Long. Before considering his analysis of the article, we should stop to marvel that 800 years after the greatest of theological geniuses defended the permissibility of an action that all agree, intuitively, is permissible, the academic world remains unable to agree on what he is trying to say. Opinions fall into two main groups. The first group continues in the dominant Manualist tradition that sees this article as the origin of what is now called the principle of double effect.[23] Not all of these thinkers agree, however. There are those (the "weak" version)[24] who take St Thomas's clear statement that a private person cannot intend the death of an aggressor[25] to mean that he may only posit an action which *risks* resulting in the assailant's death.[26] Others (the "strong" version) claim that the agent can posit an act which he knows with certainty will be lethal to his attacker without thereby intending it. This latter faction, which includes Grisez and associates, predominates today. "Aquinas' discussion of self-defense clearly fits under the principle of double effect according to my understanding of it,"[27] writes Grisez. His understanding means that one should consider the good and evil effects "aspects" of the act. The overarching goal of self-defense specifies the act as defensive, and the lethal "aspect" need not be treated as a means to this end in light of his "indivisibility principle".[28] Defenders of the "strong" version argue that such a deed (even spearing the assailant's heart[29]) can be intended *qua* defensive but not *qua* lethal. Yet, many would ask incredulously, as does Gregory Reichberg: "Can one deliberately spear the heart of an assailant without intending to kill him?"[30] As if in answer, Boyle claims that, if the killing is not considered to be a means, an agent can "direct his intention to the good effect of his action and withhold it from the bad effect."[31]

The second main group does not consider private self-defense to be a situation suitable for double effect analysis. Yet, the reasons vary considerably. Rhonheimer resists applying PDE to this case. As he explains: "Here [in I-II, q. 64, a. 7], [Aquinas] simply makes a general point about the moral species of an act and intention: what is beside the intention does not form part of the moral species of an act; this means that what is *praeter intentionem* does not enter into its object."[32] For Rhonheimer, the physical action (spearing the assailant) cannot be evaluated as a human act without knowing the agent's reason for doing so, which, in the example, is presumed to be self-defensive.[33] As for Steven Long, we can anticipate, based upon our foregoing discussion of the jettisoning of cargo, that the ambiguity over *praeter intentionem* will enter into his explanation of the article. Contrary to Rhonheimer's assertion, in the case of "mixed voluntary" something that is *praeter intentionem* (broad sense) *can* enter into the object, but only as the material element.[34] If, and only if, this element is *per se* ordered to the end sought by the agent (defending his life), will this defensive aim specify the object of the act. It will be materially "homicide" but formally "defensive", or, as Long puts it, a "defensive homicide".[35] The killing will be deliberately chosen as a means, but not intended in the narrow (primary, for Long) sense of intention. Self-defense will be the *finis operis*; as a simple act, this *finis operis* either coincides with the *finis operantis* (according to the example given earlier of "Giving money to the poor so as to help them financially") or there is an unstated *finis operantis* (he defended his life, so that he could go on caring for his family).

By way of summary, one notes that the logic of the first group examined can be described essentially thus: one must intend the means one chooses to an end; but one cannot intend to kill the aggressor; therefore, the death of the aggressor is not a means, but a side-effect. This result does seem to jar against our natural intuition, that the death of the aggressor functions as a means. Taking this natural intuition as a premise and combining it with the same middle term—the death of the aggressor cannot be intended—we get the conclusion maintained by Long: the death of the aggressor is a means; one cannot intend to kill the aggressor; therefore, the means to an end is not always intended (in the sense of intention that specifies an act morally). On both accounts, it is essential to know whether the means to an end is always intended or not, or in what sense. Reichberg, who shares Long's view, explains the situation thus:

> Yet the claim that a private defender might, under conditions of grave necessity, be entitled to kill his assailant deliberately would nevertheless seem to be inconsistent with Aquinas's main point in ST II-II, q. 64, a. 7, namely, that self-defense will be

licit only when the lethal outcome stands outside of the agent's intention. It can be said, however, that this inconsistency would arise only if Aquinas were using *intentio*... in a manner akin to the English word *intention*, which broadly designates "a determination to act in a certain way," and hence as applicable to both ends and means. But, in light of the fact that article 7 clearly distinguishes between the act of self-defense and the end for the sake of which this act is done, there is little doubt that intention must here be taken in the more narrow, technical sense of 'aiming at an end'. Thus understood, Aquinas's purpose in the article was to distinguish between two different goals for the sake of which killing might be carried out by private individuals: strict necessity (protection from ongoing or imminent harm), on the one hand, and the desire to impose a penalty on the other. Only in the second case would harming have the character of an end; defensive harming, by contrast, would solely have the character of a means.[36]

There does seem to be a strong claim to this interpretation of intention in the tradition.[37] Long notes that Cajetan has had a strong influence in the opposite direction by "anomalously ... adopt[ing] a univocal account of intention ... an exception to the tradition's general treatment of the moral object."[38]

We should remember that the practical significance of this debate still does not yet appear because the action taken by the victim of the attack is presumed by all to be proportionate to the end of self-defense. Yet, when this is not the case, when, in Long's terms, the chosen means is not *per se* ordered to the end, then the practical conclusions may differ. In the HIV-infected couple case, for instance, Long sees, in the chosen means, a directly intended simple act (committing contraception) which is accidentally ordered to a good end (preventing the spread of disease). From Rhonheimer's point of view, as we saw, the moral object is not known until the action in *genus naturae* (having relations with a condom) is further described so that the intentionality present can be identified (preventing the spread of disease). Given the significance of the question, then, we must continue another step with Long's theory.

Effect on the principle of double effect

Long, like the other members of the second group, does not deny all merit to the notion of the principle of double effect, but he does wish to see its scope restricted. Long's position implies that it is confusing to speak of PDE in those cases when the evil is *praeter intentionem* in the sense of not willed *simpliciter* as an end, but is deliberately chosen as a means, *per se* ordered to the end. Often no one thinks to describe such cases as PDE, for example, the cutting into a patient's body in order to operate on his heart. Yet, often, as in the case of self-defense, they do. From Long's perspective, it would seem that the loss of understanding of natural teleology corresponded with an expansion of appeals to the PDE, and eventually to its elevation to ultimate guiding principle of morality by Peter Knauer. With Knauer it is clear that the loss of a metaphysical notion of an act as containing certain effects that are proper to it leads to the loss of the concept of absolute intrinsic evil. There is no longer any clear line dividing effects which truly are aspects of an act from further, accidental consequences.[39] Lacking this distinction, the loss of a leg resulting from a medically indicated amputation seems to violate the third condition of the PDE. In fact, the problem with the third condition, about which Hendriks wrote, seems to come from confusing deliberately chosen means with accidental side-effects. It is to these latter that the PDE properly pertains.

Long's restricted application of the PDE would seem to be a promising avenue of response to the strong and persistent criticisms of this doctrine from secular philosophers. In her particularly potent attack on PDE, Alison McIntyre points out that genuine means are often classified as *praeter intentionem* by "some sleight of hand".[40]

> It is correct to say that death or injury, if it occurs, is an unintended side effect of the protective effort, and one could truly say, 'I didn't intend to kill her, but only to save her from the fire,' if the child thrown out the window perishes from the fall. But it does not follow that what the agent chooses as her means, which involves exposing a person to a risk of harm from another source in an effort to protect that person, is itself unintended. One could not plausibly say, 'I did not intend to endanger the child, I only meant to throw it out the window.'[41]

Accordingly, she interprets 64.7 in a manner consonant with Long. "Aquinas's point here is that one may kill the attacker provided that one does not view that killing as an end to pursue for reasons unrelated to its instrumental value in self-defense, for this would show one to be acting out of anger or a desire to punish."[42] However, it is important to note that, although she sees Aquinas as giving permission to kill deliberately, she cannot see why this permission would not extend to therapeutic abortion.

Another unexpected source of support for Long's version of PDE comes from Denis Sullivan. This author, drawing a completely different conclusion regarding self-defense, supports the "weak" version of PDE. Nonetheless, his reasoning coincides with Long's position inasmuch as he views many alleged side-effects (including the certain death of an assailant) as means:

> I will argue that Aquinas is justified in holding that it is only those side effects that are less than certain that can be justified by the doctrine of double effect. There are many side effects that come to mind, like the pain that accompanies dental work or the discomfort one produces in returning a paper with a poor grade, that can be certain and still be justified as side-effects. But such examples are of effects, which, while they could not be justified as final ends, could be justified as intermediate ends. Hence they are irrelevant to the discussion of double effect.[43]

Despite his ambiguous use of the term "side-effect" in this passage (which reflects the ambiguity of *praeter intentionem*), Sullivan is, like Long, insisting that the PDE be restricted to evaluating the morality of causing effects that are outside the intention in the broad sense and that the PDE not be applied to those effects which are only outside the intention in the narrow sense and so are actually means. Sullivan seems to overstate the case, however, when he says that "For Aquinas ... we intend only the end, not some complex of end and means."[44] Yet, he does lend support to Long's view that a means would be a simple act if it were not naturally ordered to the end. He concludes a sustained and convincing argument thus: "What we ordinarily call means—for example, calling for a doctor, taking medicine, waving my arm—can all be picked out with a description that could also be used to identify some other act than the act by which some particular end is achieved."[45] Sullivan is aware of the danger of atomizing action into pieces which are no longer human acts, pieces which can then viewed in *genus naturae* until informed by the agent's subjective intention.[46]

Despite his embracing the "weak version" of PDE, Sullivan thinks that Thomas's "use of the term 'sometimes' [*quandoque*] does not relate to the question of whether the death is intended or not. The death of the assailant is not intended, for Aquinas, simply because it is not the end of the act."[47] This opinion agrees with Long as far as it goes, but Sullivan does not see the importance of assessing the natural teleology of the lethal action. If it were not *per se* ordered to defense, then, according to Long, it would be intended, even though the agent was not seeking the death for its own sake. This is the sense in which to understand Anscombe's remark, "It is nonsense to pretend that you do not intend to do what is the means you take to your chosen end."[48] This is not telling against Long's claim that we do not *intend*, say, the cutting open of a patient's chest, in the proper sense of the word; rather, it is telling against thinkers like Boyle who say that we do not intend to kill the child in a craniotomy, because they deny that such a death is a *means*. The notion of *per se* ordination seems essential in order to distinguish effects that "frequently or always follow"[49] an action yet are side-effects and from those which are means. This will be critical for judging whether effects caused under what Michel Therrien calls "circumstantial necessity",[50] that is, caused as necessary for an end under the circumstances, count as a means or a side-effect.

Evaluation of Long's position

We have already had occasion to indicate some promising aspects of Steven Long's presentation of Thomistic action theory. Not the least appealing aspect is that its key ideas do seem to be lifted whole cloth from Thomas.[51] The argument made in *ST* I-II, q. 18, a. 7 is either passed over in silence or noted, as by Belmans, without sufficient emphasis.[52] Belmans[53] does, however, seem to agree with Long in substance:

> One will remember the article I-II 18,7 which speaks of a commanded act being ordered *per se* or *per accidens* to a given end; if it is ordered *of itself* (as valiant combat is to victory), the end aimed at will be of the order of *finis operis*—in the contrary case (as theft is ordered on occasion to almsgiving), it will be a case of *finis operantis*.[54]

As Long points out, this same essential point about *per se* ordination is made by Thomas in one of the replies following the corpus of 64.7.[55] Yet, for all the ink spilled on the issue of self-defense this decisive aspect of the fourth reply occasions little of it.

Moreover, it seems that only the emphasizing of natural teleology keeps the *finis operis* from collapsing into the first in a series of *fines operantis*.[56] Without this distinction maintained in a meaningful way, it will be impossible to see the way forward in various puzzles that have arisen for moral theologians' consideration. Firstly, there is the puzzle, raised by Rhonheimer, of how the object can be both the proximate intention, which is an act of the will, and somehow antecedent to choice so as to determine the moral value of the choosing will.[57] If there is a natural teleology to be respected, basic actions will have a proximate intention simply by virtue of being apprehended and chosen.[58] Then there is a related enigma discussed by various authors: does an act receive its moral specification from the object or from the end?[59] Pinckaers demonstrates that St Thomas made a bold and decisive innovation with respect to his predecessors by placing the primary specifying role on intention.[60] Yet, this does not keep Thomas from being interpreted, as by *Veritatis Splendor*, as still assigning the first place to the object.[61] Long's explanation provides the needed key: the agent's end has the priority in specification when the object is *per se* ordered to it, but otherwise, his object is itself a simple act with its own moral species. It is still the agent's intention that is specifying the object, but his *proximate* intention, which he may detest and deny, not his further intention or goal. Finally, this perspective clarifies a third related issue: how can the agent's end be considered a circumstance, if it gives the act its species?[62] Again Pinckaers refers to the "apparent antinomy" of Thomistic texts, as recounted by Dom Lottin, which show the *finis operantis* now described as "the most important, the most formal element of morality" and now "relegated among the circumstances."[63] The explanation given by Pinckaers—that Thomas "conserves the traditional nomenclature" as a "vestige of respectable tradition"[64]—fails to convince. Once again, with the help of Long's "primer", it appears clear that the intention really only plays the role of circumstance when it is increasing or decreasing the moral value of an act already determined by the object (the case of a "complex act"). It plays the more central, specifying role in the case of a simple act, which is a basic building block essential to the comprehension of any moral act.[65]

We should also note that Long's description of the double sense of *praeter intentionem* opens up great possibilities for dissipating the skepticism of secular thinkers in regard to Catholic moral positions. Much of the antagonism towards the principle of double effect has been based upon a sense that supporters of the intention/foresight distinction include too much, too easily in the category of "merely permitted side-effects". Glanville Williams's airplane case and the other arguments in favor of some kind of "oblique intention" discussed in Chapter 4 are perhaps now more easily addressed. The widespread opinion that some consequences are obliquely intended (that is, neither aimed at as instrumental to a goal nor merely caused by accident) seems to be alleviated by underlining the narrow notion of "intention" and natural teleology. Such consequences would be deliberately chosen but, if *per se* ordered to the goal, not intended in a narrow sense. Thus, blowing up a plane full of passengers by military jets to stop hijackers from destroying a building would not require intending the deaths of the innocents (as the act of shooting down the jet is *per se* ordered to defense), while the man in Williams's example could not deny intending the passengers' deaths (narrow sense) as a means chosen and ordered *per accidens* to his collecting insurance money. If this analysis is correct, the solution to Philippa Foot's problem of "closeness" would depend not upon a sort of physical assessment, nor upon the instrumentality of the deaths *qua* deaths *vis à vis* the agent's goal, but upon an intrinsic proportionality of the basic action to the end sought.

Additionally, the reduced role of the principle of double effect, which Long restricts to the analysis of complex acts, seems to address two great weaknesses that PDE suffers even in the eyes of Catholic thinkers.[66] Firstly, the first condition which demands that the act be either good or neutral (apart from any of the considerations covered in the other three conditions) seems to imply a physicalist view of the object. As applied to self-defense, a PDE analysis begins by saying "shooting an assailant" is either good or indifferent, which either begs the question that the PDE is helping to discover or it means the object is considered "neutral" because only physically described. For this very reason, because the description of the object in question requires some intentionality, neither Long nor Rhonheimer sees a case of PDE in the question of self-defense. In complex acts, however, the quasi-object is a simple act which already has a moral value; therefore, as Long explains, the PDE can be of use in these cases. The second weakness of the PDE, as classically described, regards the third condition. There are occasions of permissible actions, such as self-defense, when the bad effect truly seems to serve as a means. We saw that Grisez and Rhonheimer both have their explanations for this, but Long's is more satisfying: these are not cases for PDE, but simple acts where the "bad effect" is a deliberately chosen means *per se* ordered to the end.

These observations are sufficient to indicate that Long's writings on action theory hold great promise not only for pointing the way out of the post-Manualist crisis but even for facing with some measure of confidence the vexing moral conundrums that the modern world seems daily to invent. Nonetheless, Long cannot be supposed to have solved all issues in a short primer and a handful of articles. The application of his action theory to difficult cases[67] does not remove all their obscurity; this serves as a warning to us that it will be difficult to apply his principles to cases of cooperation. We can also discern in his discussion of cases some potentially problematic points.

Firstly, as mentioned earlier, it is absolutely fundamental to be able to distinguish instances of *per se* ordination from *per accidens*. On several occasions Long provides two signs of the former. "There is such a *per se* order either when the object of itself naturally tends to the end, or where the end is such that it can in no other way be attained."[68] The latter manner of identifying *per se* ordination is also described in this way: "when attainment of an end *by the very nature of the end* requires a certain action, that action is also said to be naturally or *per se* ordered to the end."[69] The enunciation of these two signs is not accompanied by any specific reference to St Thomas. Rather, the understanding of *per se* ordering appears frequently in St Thomas and seems to be presumed by him.[70] However, a correct understanding of natural order-ing can certainly not be presumed for modern man, Catholic moral theologians included. The uncertainty in the Manualist period about the liceity of removing the cancerous uterus of a pregnant woman suffices to show that distinguishing *per se* effects from side-effects is not at all obvious. In fact, since the difficulty of isolating what aspects of the material action are morally decisive is so great, Long's casting aside of the accusation of "physical-ism" seems overly hasty. He writes: "the error of supposing that the relation to reason is irrelevant for a fully specific account of a moral act is a mistake which virtually no one makes. Yet it is the only error that would properly be worthy of the name of physicalist..."[71] Surely the vast majority of Catholic moral theologians, falling both under the proportionalist and the first-person moralist headings, are reacting to a real defect in moral analysis that they label "physicalism". Therefore, distinguishing his own position clearly from what was misconstrued by the Manualists, would seem to be for Long a worthwhile endeavor.

A related concept which Long presumes as a tool for his analysis of difficult questions is "partial cause".[72] Once again, distinguishing types or grades of causation is clearly necessary for analyzing these questions, but Long does not go into the issue very deeply. This leaves his explanations seeming at times rather arbitrary. For instance, he says that the soldier jumping on a hand-grenade is not com-mitting suicide to save his comrades, because he is only a *partial* cause of his own death.[73] Would he say the same about Captain Oakes? If so, a woman altruistically leaping out of an overloaded lifeboat would seem to be only a partial cause of her death. Why then would a man pushing her out for the same reason not be only a partial cause of her death? Similarly, regarding a suicide bomber, Long says that his action is suicidal even if his goal is just to wreak destruction, for *"its generic nature is such as to materially and directly include the planned acquisition of* [his] *own death."*[74] Now it would be difficult to distinguish the action of such a suicide bomber from Samson's pulling down the building on his own head, too, without further precisions.

At times, Long seems aware that some of his arguments are reminiscent of those of his opponents. For instance, those who defend craniotomy argue that this operation would be done even if the baby were known to be stillborn and that his death as such plays no instrumental role in saving the mother's life. Similarly, in explaining why the submerging of a submarine, when a crew member remains outside, is not unjust killing, Long mentions both that the submarine commander would have done the same even if the crew member were not outside, and that his death is not a means. Long tries to identify the difference between the two positions:

> The good effect which is the end of the act [in the submarine case] is not achieved *through the evil effect or consequence as a means* (it is not through the death of the crew member that the submarine is submerged and taken out of harm's way, there is no direct action against the crew member as such, and if the crew member lived the submarine would *still* have been submerged: the definition of submerging a submarine does not involve killing a crew member).[75]

Another way of putting the difficulty might be: when, if ever, does a circumstance render an action *per se* ordered to an end to which it otherwise would not be ordered? Pilsner notes that in the case of stealing to commit adultery "even if money were the only available means for adultery in a particular case, there is no necessary connection between them as kinds of action."[76] Yet, does not the *circumstance* that a lethal spear thrust is the *only* available means of stopping an assailant bear upon whether or not that action is *per se* ordered to self-defense? Does not the introduction of poison into Anscombe's water pumper's water supply constitute a circumstance that renders his action of pumping *per se* ordered to killing the inhabitants of the house?

What remains clear is that the key notion of *per se* ordination or natural teleology is bound up with types of causality, the indirect/direct distinction, and the relevance of counterfactuals (i.e. the morally specifying role of circumstances). While Long seems to be clearly on the right track, more elaboration and explanation are necessary.

––––––––––––

One way of recapitulating and comparing the action theories discussed in the last three chapters is by reference to the material element of the object of the moral act. No authentically Catholic author is going to ignore completely the physical reality of a human act. Grisez, for instance, chides one proportionalist thus:

> Van der Marck permits any purpose of the agent to determine the moral significance of the act, the implications of the physical behavior being ignored entirely. Thus, the operation normally called 'abortion' in medical circles is nonchalantly characterized by Van der Marck as that, or as 'removal of

the effects of rape', or as 'saving the life of the
mother'...[77]

Nonetheless, it is precisely the specter of this error (to a
greatly reduced degree) that haunts Grisez's own action
theory: in the case of craniotomy, for instance, is not the
physical behavior being overlooked by undue emphasis on
the doctor's "proposal", with the result that an abortion is
described as "narrowing a baby's head"?

Rhonheimer, like Grisez, notes that not any matter can
be ordered by the will to any end. As we saw, he believes
that his action theory includes relevant material considerations, such as those circumstances which are in fact
conditions of the object. Yet, his emphasis on identifying
the intentionality of a basic action leads him to overlook
the intentionality inherent in given behavior, which the
acting subject cannot deny having should he choose a
given act. Both Grisez and Rhonheimer would seem to
share Finnis's preoccupation that—absent "the perspective
of the acting person" (as understood by "first person"
moralists)—one cannot make sense of Anscombe's water-
pumper case. Writes Finnis: "the criteria for a sound
analysis of intention(ality) and thus of *action* require that
we distinguish knowingly pumping in poisoned water from
intentionally pumping in poisoned water (or: pumping
water with intent to contaminate the water supply)."[78] We
agree that there is a distinction to be made, but it is not,
as Finnis thinks, "that the water-supply be poisoned was,
for this man on this occasion, a side-effect." Rather, the
distinction is the classic one between *finis operis* and
operantis. The pumper might not only knowingly pump
in poisoned water (*finis operis*), but he might also do this
with the super-added intention of eliminating the inhabitants (*finis operantis*).

Long, finally, by making natural teleology fundamental to moral analysis maintains a morally relevant material element is present in *every* human action. Some thinkers seem to admit the limiting role of physical behavior *vis à vis* the agent's intention in matters relating to the body,[79] but not in every behavior that is intelligible as an object of choice. One of the primary tasks remaining to us is to evaluate the material element of cases of cooperation in light of natural teleology. What kind of cooperative behavior, materially considered, necessitates by its intrinsic ordination that an agent choosing it intends the evil of the principal agent? As four hundred years of debate indicate, this is not an easy question. In order to avoid physicalism, in the sense of a substitution of natural processes for freely chosen objects of the acting subject, it does not suffice to show that natural processes, insofar as they are natural, have a purpose (even stones have a direction they naturally tend). However, these purposes are not morally irrelevant when they become involved with human action, as the dictum "a purpose which is not a human purpose is simply no purpose at all" might indicate.[80] The question is: when does the agent, acting in a world full of meaning and purpose, necessarily make this natural teleology his own?

Notes

[1] For example, Rhonheimer writes "With this model [neo-scholastic naturalism], the relationship between the 'natural law' and its 'objective givenness' is put on its head. It is really the other way around: what is there 'to begin with' [*das Ursprüngliche*] is the very constituting of the natural law through the practical reason, and only secondarily, in reflection, is the order of reason (*ordo rationis*) recognized as an 'objective' natural law, as constituted through the preceptive act of the *ratio naturalis*; through the *reditio* it is likewise recognized as the 'ought' that arises from human nature itself." Rhonheimer, *Natural Law*, p. 140.

[2] "Dès qu'on adhère à l'optique chosiste, on se voit contraint d'affronter la question que voici: d'où vient alors la valeur morale de nos agirs?—problème artificiel, à notre sens, à imputer à une méconnaissance radicale des données de la raison éthique." Belmans, *Sens obiectif,* p. 291.

[3] See p. 102 above. Kevin Flannery gets at the same point when he argues that "the decisive ethical factor... [is] in the actualization of a *prosequendum* composed of practical form and matter... if the decisive factor does not subsist in the matter of the act itself, other matter must be pressed into service in order to be able to talk about one's 'intentions'." Flannery, *Acts amid Precepts,* p. 166.

[4] Fisher, "Cooperation in Evil," p. 50.

[5] D. Crawford, "Conjugal Love, Condoms, and HIV/AIDS," *Communio* (Fall 2006), pp. 502–512, at p. 508. Note that Crawford holds this view while still seeing physicalist argumentation at work in some of the "natural ends" thinkers: "Other moral theologians have expressed the wrongfulness of the use of condoms to prevent the passage of HIV/AIDS to a spouse in terms that also—it seems to me—ultimately imply an introduction of natural ordination into the determination of the moral object... And, of course, Rhonheimer has been quick to point out this implied dependency by way of criticism" (p. 512, fn. 17).

[6] Long himself says, in reference to the books of Brock (*Action and Conduct*) and Flannery (*Acts amid Precepts*) that, "neither of these fine works, with all their strengths, seem to me to carry the analysis of the teleological grammar that governs the constitution of the object and species of the moral act to its systematic completion." Long, *Teleological Grammar,* p. xii.

[7] S. A. Long, "*Veritatis Splendor* §78 and the Teleological Grammar of the Moral Act," *Nova et Vetera* 6 (Win 2008), pp. 139–156 is an effective summary of his *The Theological Grammar of the Moral Act.*

[8] Cf. *ST* I–II, q. 18, a. 10, resp., cited by Long, *Teleological Grammar,* p. 11, fn. 9.

[9] Cf. Long, *Teleological Grammar,* p. 12.

[10] *Ibid.,* p. 85.

[11] *Ibid.,* p. 28. See also pp. 70 and 84. Also, Long, "*Veritatis Splendor* §78," 178.

[12] Long, *Teleological Grammar,* p. 27. Also, on this point, see Flannery, *Acts amid Precepts,* pp. 159–161.

13 For example, *ST* I–II, q. 18, a. 6.
14 Cf. Long, *Teleological Grammar*, pp. 66–67. His description is a bit opaque here: "We have implicitly dealt with this view [that the element of homicide in self-defense cannot be materially included in the object of the defensive act] above by providing a contrary account of the actual teaching of St Thomas showing that the object is itself *praeter intentionem* in the most formal sense of *not being the end*, while not in the normative instance of the human act being *praeter intentionem* with respect to species (for when an object is naturally ordered to the end, the most formal, defining, and containing species is derived from the end)."
15 *Summa Contra Gentiles*, III, cap. 5, n. 13 (cited by Boyle as *SCG*, III, 6). J. M. Boyle, "*Praeter Intentionem* in Aquinas," *Thomist* 42 (1978), pp. 649–665, at p. 654–657. Gregory Reichberg comments usefully on Boyle's position in "Aquinas on Defensive Killing: A Case of Double Effect?" *Thomist* 69 (2005), pp. 341–70, at pp. 350–351. The commentary of Stephen Brock, however, should be cited at length: "What is in question is the status of the act of jettisoning as an object of intention. This act has various features, and Boyle has focused on one that is slightly different from the one considered by Aquinas. The two features have different relations to the sailor's intention. What the sailor directly intends is (Boyle's feature) to throw the cargo *overboard*, i.e. off the ship; he needs to lighten the ship. But, because the ship is surrounded by the sea, his throwing the cargo overboard is simultaneously a throwing it *into the sea* (St Thomas's feature); and this is *not* something the sailor is intending or trying to bring about, except indirectly. This is important, because it means that results not directly intended can be counted as falling somehow under one's intention even if one is not culpable for them. (Boyle seems to assume they cannot; this is why he rejects the comparison with the *deordinatio* of a sinful act)." This commentary brings out clearly the logic at work in Boyle's defense of craniotomy: just as the sailor would intend throwing the cargo overboard, but not into the sea (i.e. not ruining it), so also the doctor would intend the narrowing of the skull, but not the killing of the infant (cf. Brock, *Action and Conduct*, pp. 207–208).
16 J. M. Boyle, "*Praeter Intentionem* in Aquinas," *Thomist* 42 (1978), pp. 649–665, at p. 655.
17 Cf. Long, *Teleological Grammar*, p. 85. Both Boyle and Long point to *ST* I–II, q. 12, a. 4 in support of their positions. To a certain

degree, the difference is a matter of emphasis. "Sic igitur inquantum motus voluntatis fertur in id quod est ad finem, prout ordinatur ad finem, est electio. Motus autem voluntatis qui fertur in finem, secundum quod acquiritur per ea quae sunt ad finem, vocatur intentio. Cuius signum est quod intentio finis esse potest, etiam nondum determinatis his quae sunt ad finem, quorum est electio." *ST* I–II, q. 12, a. 4, ad 3.

[18]   Long, *Teleological Grammar*, p. 29.

[19]   *Ibid.*, p. 85.

[20]   *Ibid.*, p. 85.

[21]   Imagine, for instance, that the merchant wanted to lighten his boat by throwing a passenger off. If this action is considered neither a means nor an end (*praeter intentionem* in Boyle's sense), then how can it be prohibited if it is foreseen to save the lives of all others on board? One would need to appeal to some other principle such as justice, but the problem remains: why is it a violation of justice, if it is an indirect killing?

[22]   *Ibid.*, p. 39.

[23]   The first line of St Thomas's reply seems to favor this hypothesis: "Respondeo dicendum quod nihil prohibet unius actus esse duos effectus, quorum alter solum sit in intentione, alius vero sit praeter intentionem." Partisans of this interpretation can point to Cajetan as an early authority, and the classic historical review of the PDE favors this perspective. See, J. T. Mangan, "A Historical Analysis of the Principle of Double Effect," *Theological Studies* 10 (1949), pp. 41–61.

[24]   Denis Sullivan, who uses this terminology, has a thought provoking article on the subject. D. F. Sullivan, "The Doctrine of Double Effect and the Domains of Moral Responsibility," Thomist (2000), pp. 423–448.

[25]   "illicitum est quod homo intendat occidere hominem ut seipsum defendat," *ST* II–II, q. 64, a. 7.

[26]   These find support in the word *quandoque* in ad 4, where St Thomas is defending the permissibility of positing an "actus ex quo quandoque sequitur homicidium." However, the fact that the very next article treats of accidental killing seems to be a convincing argument against the weak version, which is essentially a special case of accidental killing. See Reichberg, "Aquinas on Defensive Killing," p. 347; Brock, *Act and Conduct*, 206, fn. 18.

[27]   Grisez, *Abortion*, 335.

28 The fact that another choice either of the agent or of another agent is not required (or even possible) in order to bring about the good effect (the preservation of life) makes the act "indivisible" for Grisez. Both effects become aspects of one act regardless of the causal relationship between them. Cf. Grisez, *Abortion*, p. 333.

29 John Finnis's "provocative example" recalled by Gregory Reichberg. See J. Finnis, *Aquinas: Moral, Political, and Legal Theory* (Oxford: Oxford University Press, 1998), p. 287; cited in Reichberg, "Aquinas on Defensive Killing," p. 348.

30 Reichberg, "Aquinas on Defensive Killing," p. 348. On the following page, Reichberg presents two reasons which make the idea that the killing is not a means highly doubtful. "The problem [in calling the death of the assailant a side-effect in contrast to clear PDE cases] arises because in this particular case the person against whom the defender deliberately directs his blows and the one who suffers death (purportedly as a side-effect harm) are the self-same subject. Moreover, and most importantly, the defender clearly stands to benefit from the harm he has done to the assailant, since this is precisely what stops the latter's wrongful attack."

31 Boyle, "*Praeter Intentionem*," pp. 649–650. While Boyle admits that the notion of "direction of intention" is open to abuse, he does make use of the phrase.

32 *Ibid.*, p. 43.

33 Rhonheimer, "On the Use of Condoms," pp. 42–43.

34 Presumably, this is the point at which even Kevin Flannery gets the impression that Long "conten[ds] that the object of an individual moral act is *praeter intentionem*." K. L. Flannery, "*The Teleological Grammar of the Moral Act* by Steven Long," *Thomist* 72 (2008), pp. 321–325, at p. 324. In fact Long is only pointing out that the object is intended (secondarily), *because* the end to which it is ordered is intended (primarily). "In the *per se* case, moral acts take their species according to what is intended—from the end." Long, *Teleological Grammar*, p. 43. When the object chosen is not *per se* ordered to the agent's end, it will be intended in its own right and accidentally ordered to the agent's further goal.

35 Long, *Teleological Grammar*, p. 67.

36 Reichberg, "Aquinas on Defensive Killing," pp. 363–364 (citing *Merriam-Webster Online Dictionary* for the definition of "intention"). Reichberg's excellent article also draws attention to Thomas's treatment of *rixa* (strife) in *ST* II–II, q. 41, a. 1, showing that the first group of thinkers would have to find a way to justify doing

any injury to an assailant. In regards to strife, Thomas writes that, if someone's "sole intention be to resist [*solo animo repellendi*] the injury done to him, and he defends himself with due moderation, there is no sin, and one cannot say that there is strife on his part." Now one could hardly argue that inflicting harm to repel attack is intended, but that all injuries inflicted thereby are beyond the intention.

[37] Alonso's ground breaking dissertation, reevaluating the tradition's understanding of 64.7, notes, "Si realmente ello es asi y el articulo septimo se ha de entender en el caso en que el daño es previsto aunque no pretendido, tendriamos que el Santo lo unico que niega es que sea licito pretender la muerte de suerte que ella constituya el fin total de la accion, a la cual todo lo demas se ordena, y no que sea licito elegir la muerte como medio para defenderse." Alonso, *El principio del doble efecto, p. 218.* Reichberg notes that Mangan seems to have misinterpreted de Vitoria in favor of PDE. Reichberg, "Aquinas on Defensive Killing," p. 348, fn. 17.

[38] S. A. Long, "St Thomas Aquinas through the Analytic Looking Glass," *Thomist* 65 (2001) pp. 259–300, at p. 261, fn.7. It is a cause for alarm that Cajetan expands upon his interpretation of killing in self-defense to claim that a judge ought to sentence a man to die when he knows him to be innocent through private sources (cf. Cavanaugh, *Double Effect Reasoning,* p. 18). Here Cajetan seems to stretch the point Thomas is making in *ST* II–II q. 62, a. 2 almost to the point of killing an innocent for the sake of the common good.

[39] Richard McCormick points out this pitfall in the work of another proportionalist. "Van der Marck should have attempted to show why in this instance we are not dealing with a true means at all... if one fails to do this, then eventually any intended effect can be grouped under title of end and be said to specify the act in its human meaning. In summary, there is a cutoff point between the physiological description of the action and the consequentialist (or intentional) description. It is this cutoff point that is not clear in Van der Marck. And it is this cutoff point, I think, that is precisely the practical problem." McCormick, "Ambiguity," p. 16. Noting the problem, however, does not mean McCormick resolves it successfully.

[40] A. McIntyre, "Doing Away with the Double Effect," *Ethics* 111 (2001), pp. 219–255, at p. 243.

[41] *Ibid.,* pp. 243–244.

42 *Ibid.*, p. 249.

43 Sullivan, "Doctrine of Double Effect," p. 441.

44 *Ibid.*, p. 424.

45 *Ibid.*, p. 428.

46 *Ibid.*, pp. 430–433.

47 *Ibid.*, p. 437.

48 Anscombe, "War and Murder," p. 257.

49 St Thomas reminds us: "Stultum est enim dicere quod aliquis intendat aliquid, et non velit illud quod ut frequenter vel semper adiungiter." *In Physic.* II, lect 8, n.8. Yet, "si aliquis frequenter aut semper madefacit sibi pedes, quando vadit ad locum lutosum, et hoc licet non intendat, tamen hoc non dicitur esse a fortuna." *Ibid.*, n. 9.

50 M. Therrien, "Did the Principle of Double Effect Justify the Separation?" National Catholic Bioethics Quarterly 1, no. 3 (Aut 2001), pp. 417–427, at p. 425–426.

51 One notes Long's exasperation at the failure of some to recognize his central argument as taken "virtually verbatim" from Thomas. "When Aquinas speaks of whether the object is per se ordained to the end, he quite clearly and undeniably means the object of the external act. He could not mean the object of the internal act of the will which is the end, because this would then be to ask whether the end is ordered to itself, which would be a remarkably silly and otiose question. It follows that the object can either be per se ordained to what the agent intends or not, and—since in either case the agent intends what the agent intends—whether the object is per se ordered to the end of the agent is not determined by the agent but by the objective natural ordering of the act in question. If the act is not per se ordered to the end principally sought by the agent, then the act has its own per se order to a distinct end that of itself is not ordered to the end of the agent, and for this reason it also has its own separate moral species that is not contained within the moral species derived from the end. This teaching is virtually verbatim from I–II, q. 18, a. 7. But clearly in that case the end of that distinct act, the *finis operis*, and what the agent intends as end, the *finis operantis*, not only differ one from another but have no essential order to each other. To say that this is not originally Thomistic is like saying that the metaphysics of esse, or the distinction of act and potency—or, for that matter, the existence of the Dominican Order—was an invention of perverse sixteenth century commentators." Long, "False Theory," pp.

718–719.

[52]   Edward Krasevac presents an instructive example. He quotes *ST*
        I–II, q. 18, a. 7 at length and seems to come the same conclusion
        as Long: "[Aquinas's] point is that *if a 'means' is duly proportioned*
        to the end or intention, it is subsumed under the species of that
        intention, and does not have the character of a separate moral
        object. In the case of legitimate self-defense, if the use of deadly
        force is the only way in which the life of the one unjustly attacked
        can be saved, it is indeed in 'due proportion' to the intention of
        self-defense, and does not constitute a separate moral object of
        murder." Krasevac, "The Good that We Intend," p. 843. However,
        the notion of "due proportion" or "*per se* ordination" does not
        depend for Krasevac on a notion of natural teleology. He seems to
        favor something like Grisez's notion of indivisibility to separate
        off acts that are not *per se* ordered to the end, such as "a terrorist
        who kills innocent civilians in order to force concessions from an
        unjust government" (p. 845, fn. 13). In the end, after throwing in
        his lot with Rhonheimer (pp. 850–851), he concludes, "Yet there
        will always be a question, in difficult and borderline cases [by
        which he refers to ectopic pregnancies], of concretely what one is
        doing in the moral sense. And that question must be answered in
        the first instance, not by the interpreter, but by the prudential
        judgement of the agent" (p. 853).

[53]   Belmans, *Sens obiectif,* pp. 102–106, 216.

[54]   "On se rappellera l'article I–II 18,7 qui parle d'un agir impéré
        s'ordonnant *per se* ou *per accidens* à une fin donnée; s'il s'y ordonne
        de soi (comme un vaillant combat à la victiore), la fin en cause sera
        de l'ordre du *finis operis*—dans le cas contraire (comme le vol
        s'ordonne parfois à l'aumône que l'on veut faire), il s'agira d'un
        finis operantis." Belmans, *Sens obiectif,* p. 216. And Belmans notes
        with approval that this means that "le *finis operis* implique
        forcément une certaine intention, alors que le *finis operantis*
        concerne une ultérieure intention venant modifier la première."

[55]   "If one may kill in defense, why then cannot one fornicate [to save
        one's life]?... [Thomas] answers: 'The act of fornication or adultery
        is not necessarily directed to the preservation of one's own life, as
        is the act from which sometimes homicide follows.'" Long, "*Ver-*
        itatis Splendor §78," p. 147.

[56]   A useful background for this delicate but essential point is the
        exchange between Belmans and Pinckaers. See Belmans, *Sens*
        Obiectif, 280–289; and S. Pinckaers, *Ce qu'on ne peut jamais faire:*

la question des actes intrinsèquement mauvais—histoire et discussion (Paris: Cerf, 1986), pp. 111–116. Belmans accuses Pinckaers quite forcefully of a certain voluntarism (p. 284) that comes from refusing to identify the *finis operis* with the object of the act (p. 282). Pinckaers, for his part, hopes to avoid both voluntarism and rationalism (p. 112) saying that, for Thomas, "*et* la raison *et* la volonté contribuent corrélativement à la formation du jugement et du choix moral" (p. 113).

[57]   Rhonheimer, "Intentional Actions," p. 284, fn. 12; also Belmans, *Sens obiectif*, p. 267.

[58]   For a clear comment on this point, also see S. L. Brock, "*Veritatis Splendor* §78, St Thomas, and (Not Merely) Physical Objects of Moral Action," *Nova et Vetera*, English Edition, 6 (2008), pp. 1–62, at p. 34.

[59]   Cf. Hendriks, *Le moyen mauvais*, p. 265; also, Gonzalez, *Moral, razón, y naturaleza*, p. 461: "A pesar de haber respondido anteriormente sin más precisiones que es el objeto—fin proximo—lo que da la especie a una acción, Santo Tomás examinará ahora también si el fin—remoto—especifica los actos. Y responde que sí." She goes on to discuss *ST* I–II, q. 18, a. 7, but without discovering there an essential key to understanding human action, such as would solve the problem of self-defense.

[60]   Pinckaers, "Le rôle de la fin," pp. 397–398.

[61]   "The morality of the human act depends primarily and fundamentally on the 'object' rationally chosen by the deliberate will, as is borne out by the insightful analysis, still valid today, made by Saint Thomas." John Paul II, *Veritatis Splendor*, 78, citing *ST* I–II, q. 18, a. 6. Joseph Pilsner (*Specification*, pp. 234–238) also provides an excellent explanation of the "apparently contradictory position" (p. 234) found in Thomas. Pilsner's explanation, while compatible with Long, places more emphasis on two ways of looking at an act: *secundum suam speciem* or *secundum individuum*.

[62]   Pinckaers laments: "Partout néamoins se retrouve la distinction entre le *'finis operis'*, qui rentre dans l'object, et le *'finis operantis'* que se range parmi les circonstances." S. Pinckaers, "*Le probléme de l'intrinsece malum,*" *Frieb. Zeitschrift für Phil. und Theol.* 29 (1982) pp. 373–388, at p. 386.

[63]   Pinckaers, "Le rôle de la fin," pp. 402–403; also, *Ce qu'on ne peut jamais faire*, p. 112.

[64]   "[Thomas] conserve la nomenclature traditionelle ... un vestige d'une tradition respectable..." Pinckaers, "Le rôle de la fin," pp.

402–403.

[65]   Cf. *ST* I–II, q. 7, a. 3, ad 3.

[66]   Grisez picks out these difficulties, along with a third—the determination of proportionately grave reasons—and proposes his
action theory as a solution. Cf. Grisez, *Christian Moral Principles*,
p. 308.

[67]   Cf. the extended appendix in Long, *Teleological Grammar*, pp.
89–137. He denies pretending to "infallibility in the application of
teleological analysis" (p. 90).

[68]   *Ibid.*, p. 70. Cf. also, pp. 28, 84; Long, "*Veritatis Splendor* §78," p.
147.

[69]   Long, *Teleological Grammar*, p. 84. Pilsner writes that "an essential
relation occurs where one end is necessary for the achievement of
another; an accidental relation occurs when a proximate end
creates some condition or removes some impediment which can
permit the remote end to be pursued." Pilsner, *Specification*, p.
236.

[70]   While he does analyze the notion in the *Posterior Analytics*
§§84–88, it is not clear how these various senses of *per se* correspond with Long's description. Cf. Flannery, *Acts amid Precepts*,
Appendix B, pp. 236–246.

[71]   Long, *Teleological Grammar*, p. 36.

[72]   In the context of the removal of a gravid cancerous uterus, Long
comments: "The agent would be the total cause of the effect if the
nature of the act directly were such as *per se* to bring about death
to a child in every such case (but it isn't) or if the killing of the
innocent child were indeed in some way a *means* to the end of
aiding the mother." *Ibid.*, p. 92.

[73]   *Ibid.*, p. 73. He introduces the notion of "risk" as evidence that only
a partial cause was posited. In light of the discussion of self–
defense, it seems better to assume the death is certain to isolate
the intentionality present. Similarly, the defenders of craniotomy
and the induced delivery of non–viable fetuses confuse the issue
by speaking of the possibility in the future of babies being able to
survive such actions. Yet, surely it is the certitude of death under
the circumstances that matters to analyzing a particular case.

[74]   Long, *Teleological Grammar*, p. 78.

[75]   *Ibid.*, p. 94.

[76]   Pilsner, *Specification*, p. 237, fn. 40.

[77]   Grisez, *Abortion*, p. 332.

78 Finnis, "Intention and Side-effects," p. 59.

79 H. Boelaars writes: "Fuori dell'esempio sopra esposto delle azioni sessuali complete intenzionalmente contraccettive o senza amore non ne conosco alcun altro [esempio di atti effettivi che devono necessariamente ricevere una deteminata intenzione]." Boellars, "Riflessioni sull'atto umano effettivo," p. 131. While Boelaars's position is extreme, even an author like Chris Oleson, who presents a strong argument against Rhonheimer on the HIV-infected couple question, seems quick to describe many non-sexual acts in neutral terms, without the conditions that would make *per se* ordination appear. He asks "… is contraception evil in the way that adultery and homosexuality are evil, or is it evil in the way that killing a man could be evil?" (p. 721). Perhaps for this reason, Oleson only has "minor quibbles" with Rhonheimer's action theory (p. 720). C. Oleson, "Nature, 'Naturalism', and the Immorality of Contraception: A Critique of Fr Rhonheimer on Condom Use and Contraceptive Intent," *National Catholic Bioethics Quarterly* 6, no. 4 (Win 2006), pp. 719–729.

80 James McEvoy says that this view is frequently attributed to A. J. Ayer. See J. McEvoy, "The Teleological Perspective upon Nature," in *Finalité et intentionnalité: doctrine thomiste et perspectives modernes, ed.* J. Follon and J. McEvoy, pp. 1–8 (Louvain-la-Neuve: Editions de l'Institut Supérieur de Philosophie, 1992), at p. 5.

CHAPTER 11

TOWARDS A MORE NUANCED NOTION OF FORMAL COOPERATION

1. Harmonizing views of cooperation

ALTHOUGH WE HAVE seen a number of opinions regarding our theme proposed over the centuries, we can identify three voices who demonstrate, by their disharmony, the complexity of the problem: Alphonsus, Waffelaert, and Häring. In brief, Alphonsus considered material cooperation to be providing an occasion for the sin of another; Waffelaert did not consider this to be cooperation at all, requiring even material cooperation to be a partial cause of the evil. Häring, for his part, seemed to return to the pre-Alphonsian position that to be a partial cause of the evil is to cooperate formally. These views come from serious thinkers[1] at intervals of approximately 90 years. We will consider our investigation a success, if we can suggest a plausible manner by which to integrate their points of view.

In our discussion of St Alphonsus's position, we noted that something certainly seemed deficient in his description of the servant's action as simply "providing an opportunity" for the master. The claim that the servant was performing a good act which he foresaw would be "abused" appeared forced.[2] The underlying error, reminiscent of what Alison McIntyre referred to as "sleight of hand",[3] is a confusion of act and omission. Although the servant is making a positive contribution to a crime, it is treated as a mere omission or negative agency, as not preventing harm or impeding the crime. Presumed to fall under a positive precept, the obligation to intervene (i.e. not hold the ladder) would not bind *semper et pro semper*, but only when an intervention (i.e. refusal to cooperate) could be made without serious *incommoditas*. By this method, extreme duress justifies the servant's acquiescence.

It should be recalled that St Alphonsus did not arrive at this conclusion moved by the desire to find any excuse whatever to save servants from the duty to suffer for righteousness's sake. The patron of moral theologians was obviously no laxist. He pointed to various actions a servant might be requested to perform which would be intrinsically evil and maintained that they should be forbidden regardless of the duress which might be applied. The difficulty for Alphonsus lay in identifying what cooperative actions ought to be considered intrinsically evil. As we saw, he included only actions which were scandalous, which were co-executions of an evil (e.g. fornication), and which were done for the express purpose of bringing about the evil. What is missing—because it would be missing generally for two centuries—is attention to the "proximate intention" of the cooperator. An evil "proximate intention" would make a given action formal cooperation; it would also make the action no longer "good or indifferent in itself". Saying, as St Alphonsus does, that "material cooperation is licit when the action is good or indifferent in itself..."[4] is, in this light, true but circular. If the action were not good or indifferent in itself, the agent would have a bad proximate intention, and it would not be material cooperation in the first place. The problem is precisely to discover what actions cannot qualify as material cooperation, even though the cooperator's reason for acting (*finis operantis*) differs from that of the principal agent.

The intention of the cooperator, understood only as his subjective goal or proposal, cannot suffice to identify all formal cooperation. In this connection, it has been important for us to highlight, throughout our investigation, examples of sins that are committed without the agent intending an evil *propter se*. This was the purpose of our examination of indirect scandal. One commits the sin of scandal by doing something scandalous for whatever purpose; if one did it so as to cause the spiritual ruin of another, then it would be diabolical scandal. Likewise, our discussion of omissions and the original Thomistic category of indirect voluntary had this aim. When one omits to do what one should and could have done, one is culpable, even if one did not omit it "on purpose". As Thomas pointed out, no internal act is required for an omission.[5] Moreover, when one disobeys a precept that one should and could have known about (e.g. abstinence on Fridays), one is guilty even if there was no desire to show disrespect but only a desire to eat meat. Again, when one becomes aware of certain significant (that is, act-specifying) circumstances like the sacred nature of a cup one plans to steal or the presence of passengers on a plane one wants to destroy, one cannot deny intending these evils in some sense if one proceeds with the original plan.

Overemphasis on the agent's intention *qua* proposal, to the exclusion of the actual behavior that is being chosen, can wreak havoc in moral analysis generally and in the understanding of cooperation in particular. The result is the inclusion within the spectrum of "cooperation" of everything from co-execution of crime to doing something entirely benign (like building roads or cars, even though someone is sure to drive recklessly),[6] followed by the removal into the formal category of those actions that are done *so as* to cause harm. Likewise excluded from being choice-worthy are those actions that seem to be virtually the same as that of the principal agent: co-execution and, for some authors, immediate cooperation. But what is the rationale for deciding that immediate cooperation should be treated as formal or, if not as formal, as something always to be forbidden? Why should another increment of physical removal away from co-execution indicate the absence of a bad proximate intention? The proper domain of cooperation—making some contribution (by act or omission) to an evil act principally committed by another—and the divisions within it cannot be identified by the cooperator's (subjective) intention; rather, his proximate intention must be identified by considering the type of contribution he is making.

Waffelaert makes a genuine advance by restricting cooperation proper to acts which contribute to the bringing about of an evil. The cooperator's role is not a passive one. Consequently, for Waffelaert, material cooperation, will be partially causing the evil. Clearly though, a cooperator is a partial, as opposed to total, cause by definition. We recall that Waffelaert saw the giving of scandal as being a "total" cause. Therefore, we need to divide the category of being a partial cause into unacceptable and acceptable varieties; the terms "direct" or "essential" cause for the former and "indirect" or "accidental" cause for the latter seem appropriate.[7]

Finally, we interpret Häring's position as pointing out that being a partial cause (in the sense of direct or essential cause) is to cooperate formally. When the cooperator only does so reluctantly, or under duress, the formal cooperation would be implicit. Thirty years later, Benedict Ashley and Kevin O'Rourke make this comment upon his position:

> Bernard Häring (1963) distinguishes two kinds of
> cooperation, formal and material. But instead of

describing two different forms of material cooperation, he describes two kinds of formal cooperation. Implicit formal cooperation indicates that a person who cooperates intimately in performing an evil act should know the evil he is helping to perform. We do not concur with this nomenclature because it involves an interpretation of another person's subjective state of mind. While we do not concur with the use of this distinction, we recognize it as legitimate. However, we would prefer to keep the analysis in the objective order.[8]

From our earlier discussions, it should appear that this claim of "keeping the analysis in the objective order" is rather questionable. If we admit implicitly formal cooperation, we are saying that in performing certain behaviors with awareness the agent *necessarily* intends and does certain things. Usually *this* position is viewed as "objectivist", even guilty of third person morality and physicalism. If, with Ashley and O'Rourke, we do not admit such behavior as implicitly formal, but say that the cooperator may be performing this very dubious behavior with a good intention which we cannot verify, as his proximate intention is knowable only by him, the first person … are we really keeping the discussion in the objective order at all? And on what grounds do we then say, as Ashley and O'Rourke would have us do, that the behavior is always to be forbidden?

The considerations made in this section can be tabulated in the following manner:

	Formal cooperation	Material cooperation		Not cooperation
St Alphonsus Liguori (1780)	Sharing goal of principal agent	Providing occasion, by contributing material/physical cause		
Gustave Waffelaert (1870)	"	Accidental cause (his term: partial)		Providing occasion
Bernard Häring (1960)	"	Essential cause (his term: partial)	Accidental cause	Providing occasion

Viewed in this way, theological reflection upon the problem of cooperation with evil appears to have progressed steadily over the centuries, by an albeit inelegant process. The distinctions that we have identified need to be further elucidated and defended. Then, it is devoutly hoped, we can apply them to the case of the Servant and the Ladder in a satisfactory manner.

2. Senses of "indirect"

The chief weakness in St Alphonsus's analysis of the case of the Servant and the Ladder is, we repeat, that of treating the cooperator's action as an omission. The saint is not responsible for originating this maneuver in moral theology but only for applying it to cooperation with evil. This confusion appears to be part of a larger melding of related pairs of concepts (causing/allowing, act/omission, direct/indirect, and *in intentione/praeter intentionem*) that developed over the Manualist period. José Rojas stands out by trying valiantly to remind contemporary thinkers of the subtle differences between these notions: "the [Thomistic] distinction between *in intentione* and *praeter intentionem*… is not quite the same as the direct/indirect distinction."[9] The latter has to do with the material substratum of the human act, as Rojas indicates earlier in his article: "St Thomas drew the distinction between *voluntarium secundum se* and *secundum suam causam* more on the basis of the *posture* or *attitude* of the will towards an object… in contrast, he drew the distinction between *voluntarium directe* and *indirecte* more on the basis of the *mode of physical causality*…"[10]

The various distinctions between the pairs act/omission, direct/indirect, and causing/allowing—cannot be reduced to the reason for acting of the agent.[11] The tendency to misconstrue the central role of the agent's intention has caused the confounding of these several binomials. We have criticized both Grisez and Rhonheimer for continuing in this line. Kramer, whom we noted making the same error earlier in the twentieth century, purports to trace the path by which the confusion of act and omission became institutionalized (for him, this was a positive development).[12] He argues that Billuart distinguished between omissions and their effects in the following manner: the former could be voluntary regardless of whether there existed a precept regarding it (i.e. whether or not it is something that *should* be done), while the effects would be voluntary (that is, imputable to the agent) *only* if there were a precept regarding them. This is a change from the definition of the omission itself as omitting what one could and should do. Billuart's development is predicated upon the idea that the effect of omissions comes about due to other causes. In one of his examples— the omitting to intervene in a street fight, which results in the death of a participant—this is clear enough: the death is primarily caused by the sword of the other fighter. However, other cases of omission, such as the helmsman running the ship aground, do not seem to admit so readily of attributing the evil effect to extraneous causes.[13] In this way, Billuart seems already to have confused act/omission with direct/indirect. Kramer sees it as a significant development that was soon taken further: "Dumas seems to approach one step closer [than Billuart] to the view that all indirectly willed effects are so willed in that they are negatively willed, that is, in that they are not impeded."[14] ("Indirectly" here means not aimed at as an end or a means, or the opposite of *in intentione*.)

In other words, the choice of the agent who omits to act is severed from the effect of that omission; the latter is imputable only if there is a prior obligation to impede the effect, or if it is brought about by the agent as a means to some end. This analysis of omissions is then transferred to commissions: the act itself may be voluntary but not morally evaluable until the effects are considered. They will be imputable (and the act, therefore, illicit) if there is a precept prohibiting their causation or if they are willed *in se* or *propter se*. Otherwise, the agent is treated as a mere "partial cause" of the bad effect, even if this flies in the face of common sense.

What risks being forgotten in this approach—the separation of the act from its effects combined with the exaggeration of the role of the intention of the acting subject in determining the moral value of the act—is a prior ordering of goods. This is what Long sought to emphasize with his insistence on "natural teleology".

There is a prior obligation to consider at the level of the agent's causing of an omission or an action, not at the level of deciding whether the effects of his act or omission are imputable. Failure to perceive the role of a prior obligation deriving from a natural ordering of goods makes the question of the source of moral evil appear to turn entirely on the agent's desire (or lack thereof) to cause physical harm as a means or as an end. This understanding of moral evil has, as we have seen repeatedly, two great inconveniences. First, some good moral actions (e.g. self-defense, organ donation) require the deliberate causing of physical evils. Second, it seems that some physical evils (e.g. the baby's death in craniontomy, the sterility for HIV infected couples) should not be caused even though they are neither a means nor an end from the agent's perspective, and even though they are proportionate harms.

Asymmetry of action

The importance of some moral evaluation occurring before the act is posited (that is, not simply as a posterior determination of imputability) is marvelously expressed by Anscombe thus: "I should contend that a man is responsible for the bad consequences of his bad actions, but get no credit for the good ones; and contrariwise is not responsible for the bad consequences of his good actions."[15] An action must be characterized morally *before* we can tell if the consequences are imputable. It is not bad *because* the negative consequences will be imputable to the agent. Gregory Reichberg makes the same point:

> PDE teaches that agents will be absolved from the liability which ordinarily attaches to the production of harmful side effects only if (at a minimum) the deliberate activity which gave rise to the said side effects *was itself not blameworthy*. By contrast,

the negative side effects that follow from the
commission of a *crime*... are ascribable to the agent
as an aggravating condition for which he will be
held accountable, regardless of the fact that these
were wholly undesired by the agent and in no way
contributed to the commission of his crime or the
enjoyment of its illicit gains.[16]

These authors are recalling us to the perspective of St
Thomas in which *voluntaria in causa* and *indirecte voluntaria* were discussed as ways of imputing bad effects to an
agent *in the context of bad actions*. Likewise, Kevin Flannery, in his book *Acts Amid Precepts*, tries to overcome
certain *aporia* associated with the PDE by asking whether
certain acts fall within an accepted craft or can be
described as "practicing one's own business".[17] This effort
can be interpreted as insisting upon knowing first if the
act itself is good in order to decide if the evil caused is
imputable.[18] For example, Flannery argues that the crushing of a baby's head does not fall within the craft of
medicine and therefore cannot be subsumed under the
species of health bringing, as can the cutting into a
patient's chest.

Only in this light does the true meaning of *male
sonantes* emerge. Actions such as striking, killing, stabbing, or getting drunk, "sound bad" because they are
ordinarily the material part of an evil object. But, circumstances may be such that the physical action, which sounds
bad before the entire situation is described, is later seen
to be the material part of a good object. For instance, it
sounds bad to get drunk, because the physical actions of
drinking too much alcohol and the moral act of "abusing
alcohol" usually go together. But, in the context of an
emergency operation when no other anesthetic is available, the moral object will be "anesthetizing oneself".

However, it is Steven Long's analysis that makes clear that this description is possible *not only because the agent intends to anesthetize himself*, but because drinking a certain quantity of alcohol is *per se* ordered to this end. This natural teleology is what enables the agent to choose deliberately, to cause directly, this physical evil of drunkenness. Thanks to this natural ordination, it can be a chosen means and yet, like the jettisoning of goods, *praeter intentionem*. An analysis which relies solely on intention, claiming that the agent is only intending the intoxication *qua* anesthetizing but not intending *in any sense* the drunkenness, simply because he is not interested in getting drunk *qua* drunkenness, only appears equivalent. Its deficiency is revealed when it is applied to cases in which the evil means is *not* naturally ordered to the end. For instance, the effect of death to the baby in craniotomy is separated from the effect of narrowing his skull, and the claim is made—illegitimately—that only the latter is intended.

We recall that Boyle and Long each emphasized a different sense of intention (Boyle: that both means and end are intended; Long: that intention is primarily of the end) while Thomas did not appear to make so clear a distinction. Perhaps the positions of Boyle and Long can be harmonized, and better assimilated to Thomas, by recalling the "asymmetry of action". When the act is good, the means will be subsumed by the species of the end and, therefore, will not be, properly speaking, intended. When the act is bad, the means will not be subsumable by the species of the end, but will become in Long's terms "a quasi-object", that is willed *propter se* and accidentally ordered to the end. In such complex acts, intention will refer both to the means and the end.

Perhaps, we would do well at this point to recall the extreme relevance of this discussion for the identification of formal cooperation. Bishop Fisher's observation gets to the heart of the matter:

> Some acts that, on the natural meanings account, are implicit formal cooperation in evil, whatever the agent says or believes he/she intends, are only material cooperation on the intended acts account; likewise some acts that are only immediate material cooperation on the natural meanings account are formal cooperation on the intended acts account.[19]

In other words, there are two possible disagreements. The first alluded to by Fisher occurs when intended acts theorists (what we called "subject-centered" theorists) make an illicit separation of act and effect (as in craniotomy). In this way, a formal act of cooperation (on the natural meanings account, because the bad effect is proximately intended) can appear to be but immediate material (on the intended acts account). The second disagreement occurs when natural meanings theorists subsume a chosen means under the end and therefore consider it *praeter intentionem*. In this way, an act of formal cooperation (on the intended acts account, because all means are intended) can appear to be but immediate material (on the natural meanings account).[20]

The notion of circumstance has emerged during our study as particularly critical. Which elements of the "moral context" are part of the object (act-specifying)? Which are integral to the act but subsumable under the species of the end? Which are truly accidental and only capable of increasing or decreasing the moral value of the act? One cannot be satisfied with Ugorji's throwing up of his hands: "notions of objects as well as circumstances are highly

indeterminate and elastic."[21] Likewise, we have rejected
the claim that only a particular agent's practical reason
can constitute a moral object from a given concrete
situation.[22] Rather, the correct identification of the elements of a moral act and their moral value can only come
from a true judgment based upon the intrinsic hierarchy
of goods, the natural teleology of actions, and the objective
causal relations between elements of an act. The reminder
that there is a moral truth *preceding* the acting person is
a common theme of natural meanings thinkers. For
instance, Brock quotes Flannery approvingly: "In determining what is and what is not within a person's intention,
we do indeed presume that certain things are to be
pursued, other things to be avoided."[23] In this sense, too,
we recall and approve Jean Porter's observation that to
describe a moral act is to evaluate it:

> In order to determine the object of an action,
> distinguishing it in the process from circumstances
> and from the agent's aim in acting, it is *first*
> necessary to arrive at a correct description of the
> act from the moral point of view. That process, in
> turn, depends upon prior evaluative judgments, in
> terms of which we determine what is morally
> relevant and what is not, and how the different
> components of the action should be interrelated
> to one another. Description is not prior to evalua-
> tion; to the contrary, to describe an action from
> the moral point of view is to form a moral evalua-
> tion of the action.[24]

Causation

The understanding of material cooperation common to
all participants in the discussion is that the material
cooperator's action is essentially good, and only accidentally involved in an evil act. Throughout this study we have

rejected the idea that this "accidental" relation rests entirely on the subjective intention (or goal, or *finis operantis*) of the cooperator. The goodness of the cooperator's action must be established in an objective manner. Only if there is a sufficient explanation for his action can the evil effect be truly accidental. This will establish his action as a *separate* action, with its own existence, and not only a taking part in an evil action. This seems to be the only legitimate interpretation of the "no other purpose" condition for identifying formal cooperation that is fairly frequently encountered, as in this excerpt from an encyclopedia article:

> He can do this [cooperate formally] by wanting the evil act performed and doing something to help bring it about or by making an unambiguous contribution to the performance of the act, that is, by contributing help that of its nature has no other purpose than to make the sin possible or to facilitate its commission.[25]

It is critical to note that this author rightly takes care to state that the existence or not of a legitimate purpose for the cooperator's act depends upon "its nature". Otherwise, the circumstance of duress immediately transfers cooperation into the material category, since the desire to avoid the threatened harm becomes the "other purpose" ("other" than the principal agent's) for which the cooperator acts. The demonstration of a legitimate purpose for acting, even when the unfortunate consequence of facilitating the crime of another is foreseen, will be necessary for rendering this causal relation accidental and not essential.

In addition to the inclusion of the clause "of its nature", some notion such as "in the concrete situation" should be understood in the explanation of formal cooperation just cited. We recall how authors in years gone by argued that idols, or the performance of lewd sketches, or rowing for the Turks might all be products or services that could conceivably be put to a good use. This attempt to deny that virtually anything is of its nature ordained to an evil purpose misses the point. If an agent performs an action that naturally tends to an evil purpose, his contribution to an eventual evil will be essential or direct; were the principal agent to surprise him subsequently by erratic behavior, the cooperator would be no less guilty. "In the concrete situation" the idol is not going to be put to good use; the fact that one could imagine a case when it might be bought so as to be destroyed does not change the nature of the cooperator's action.

If, in the concrete situation, there is a legitimate reason for the cooperator to posit his action, his contribution to the sin of another would appear to be accidental. He is simply going about his business. He would have done what he did "anyway", even if it were not contributing to a crime. One example in support of this view of formal cooperation may be drawn from a pronouncement of the Holy Office regarding dueling. The question was raised whether a doctor could assist at a duel if his intention was restricted only to caring for the wounded. The answer was that he would incur excommunication, if he were to offer his services *by prior agreement*. If, on the other hand, he were called upon simply because he happened to be nearby, he could help.[26] The point does not seem to be that his agreeing to help in advance would be some sort of encouragement to the duelers. Rather, his going to a lonely place by agreement with a vengeful man is not something that doctors do "anyway" (regardless of whether someone is going to have a duel); they do, however, rush to the side of a wounded man regardless of the liceity of the activity during which he was wounded.

Meaning of "perspective of the acting person"

In this light, the concrete situation primarily determines the meaning of the basic action of the cooperator. Our point is *not* that the cooperator's intention is not the key to formal cooperation; it is. Our point is that his *proximate* intention is equally key to formal cooperation. Consider two similar situations. In the first a fire company is called to an abortion clinic to remove a tree limb that has fallen in the previous night's storm and is preventing the access of clients. It may be that a member of the crew considers refusing to participate in the action because he foresees that his service will have the effect of facilitating the killing of innocent children. Nonetheless, should he cooperate, his cooperation in their deaths will be material, since he is only doing what firefighters do "anyway". The second case concerns policemen who are called to an abortion clinic to remove protesters who are blocking access. Here it would be tempting for a pro-life policeman desirous of avoiding likely censures to tell himself that he is only "removing trespassers," which is an ordinary part of a policeman's work. He admits that there are abortionists in the wings, waiting to "abuse" his "good" act. In reality, however, an accurate description of the relevant circumstances must include the fact that these are not just any trespassers. He is not doing something that he would do "anyway" (that is, if the crime of abortion were not about to occur), since, if no crime were being committed, there would be no protestors. Consequently, a counterfactual argument ("I would do this no matter who they were, strikers, for instance") fails. The "circumstance" that the trespassers are *pro-life* protesters is more than a circumstance; it is linked to the evil in question. In reality, the policeman is being asked to take part in opposing a very noble enterprise (the protest) and in perpetuating an iniquitous practice. The nature of the trespassing is integral to determining what the policeman does if he obeys his orders; what he is considering doing is neither morally indifferent nor "part of a policeman's job", adequately understood. He cannot deny that he is doing something bad so as to avoid censures or preserve his job.[27] His cooperation would be implicitly formal.[28]

Such a distinction is not possible if "the perspective of the acting person" of which *Veritatis Splendor* 78 speaks is interpreted as "intended acts" theorists would like. When this interpretation is expressed in an extreme fashion, its problematic nature becomes evident. Cathleen Kaveny, for instance, writes: "Catholic thought employs an intention-based action theory; it analyzes an action under the description provided by an agent's own account of what he or she is *doing*—that is, a description of this purposeful activity that situates it within a broader framework of the agent's near and distant goals."[29] Does she really think that asking John Wilkes Booth for a description of what he was doing in President Lincoln's box—in light of his near and distant goals—will be helpful, let alone necessary, for determining the object of his act? Thomas Cavanaugh is correct in denying, as part of his criticism of Grisez et al., the existence of an epistemological privilege belonging to the acting person.[30]

The authentic meaning of the phrase in question— "from the perspective of the acting person"—is neither new nor subtle. We must recall that the Holy Father is writing with proportionalists in mind; he is not trying to solve the debate we have discussed in the last chapters. As the footnote in the encyclical indicates (a reference to Thomas's teaching that the goodness of human acts is derived from the end), the point is primarily to remind ethicists that moral theology concerns the will of the acting person and not the best possible outcome. Joseph Pilsner indicates that the agent's viewpoint leads us to speak of the object as an action chosen, not a physical object.[31] As David Crawford observes: "The passage clearly points to the fact that the object is not only an event that can be observed from the outside, but is also—from the specifically moral point of view—an act of human freedom."[32] It is an object (a visible "kind of behavior") that is *chosen*, and it is precisely by deliberately deciding to choose it that "the act of willing on the part of the acting person" is determined. The agent does not determine a proximate intention *under which* or *with which* to choose a behavior; he determines his proximate intention *in* or *by* choosing the behavior in a given situation.

The "perspective of the acting person" also reminds us that no moral evaluation can be made without taking into account the knowledge and freedom of the acting person. Consequently, when knowledge is completely lacking, some authors even speak of the object changing. Traditionally, however, authors have preferred to speak, for instance, of *material* adultery, when, to use the traditional example, a man has relations with a woman whom he mistakes for his wife. Flannery argues that such ignorance "changes the very nature (the very species) of his basic act: his act is not an act of adultery."[33] Brock also wrestles with how to describe what is actually going on in such cases.[34] As usual, Anscombe may have the most penetrating assessment of the matter.[35] She observes that only certain actions have a neutral description (killing) as well as a designation that implies knowledge and freedom (murder). Adultery is not such a term, and so we might conclude from her observation that the awkward use of the qualifiers (material and formal) remains the best solution. It is important to note that, as the term "material sin" indicates, the husband may be *excused* of the evil that he has done, but the act is not *justified* by his good intention. This error is fostered by the attempt of proportionalists to introduce the terminological division between good/evil and right/wrong.[36] So, in view of legalist, consequentialist theories[37] that focus upon the "state of affairs" produced by an action, it is important to emphasize the fact that the subjective characteristics of this acting person will affect the moral evaluation of his choice. This is achieved by the reminder to view the moral object "from the perspective of the acting person".

3. Confirmation in Evangelium Vitae 74

As mentioned in Chapter 8, a most significant event in the history of our theme occurred in March 1995 when Pope John Paul II provided a definition of formal cooperation endowed with magisterial authority for the first time.

> Indeed, from the moral standpoint, it is never licit to cooperate formally in evil. Such cooperation occurs when an action, either by its very nature or by the form it takes in a concrete situation, can be defined as a direct participation in an act against innocent human life or a sharing in the immoral intention of the person committing it.[38]

If the inclusion of this definition in the encyclical was not a direct response to the controverted appendix to the ERD's (approved by the United States Bishops in November 1994), it was certainly a happy coincidence. It will be recalled that the appendix, withdrawn in June 2001, was especially remarkable for equating implicitly formal cooperation and immediate material cooperation without duress.[39] As a result of the controversy, the Catholic Health Association convened a gathering of theologians in December 1998 which met several times in subsequent years concluding with a report in May 2007. According to their report, one of the points of agreement between participants, who came from widely varying theological viewpoints, was that the magisterial definition made in 1995 "does not alter the traditional understanding of cooperation with evil."[40] While no one imagines that John Paul II wished to take up a wholly novel position on the matter, the "traditional understanding" is sufficiently varied and vague that a precise and nuanced statement such as we find in *Evangelium Vitae* 74 ought not to be summarily dismissed. While many authors seem to think that St Alphonsus's classic formulation can simply be repeated as is, John Paul II clearly does not. His definition offers three significant clarifications which, we believe, confirm the conclusions of our study.

First, the Pope indicates that formal cooperation can occur in two ways: by direct participation (*actum directo patratum*) in the evil act or (*aut*) by sharing in the immoral intention (*immorale propositum communicantem*) of the principal agent. Yet, he is definitely *not* saying that one who directly participates does not share the evil intention of the principal agent—that would indeed be a novel twist in the explication of formal cooperation, which has always meant a sharing in the principal agent's intention. In other words, the "aut" is an *inclusive* disjunction; it indicates that these are sometimes two ways of describing the same reality. The Holy Father should be interpreted as saying that one who directly participates shares the same moral object or proximate intention as the principal agent. Additionally, of course, one could formally cooperate by *explicitly* sharing the immoral goal of the principal agent, in which case formal cooperation could occur without direct participation. It would be a grave (physicalist) mistake to separate object from intention, and so distinguish immediate material cooperation from implicitly formal. One member of the CHA dialogue, Thomas Kopfensteiner, seems to do just this: "the second major distinction of the principle [of cooperation] excludes intention and instead, deals with the object of the action. It is expressed by immediate and mediate material cooperation."[41] He does not explain why the object should pertain only to material cooperation or why intention should not pertain to the object. The same author applies the definition given in *Evangelium Vitae* 74 to a case in a way that gives the impression that direct participation in the evil does not constitute formal cooperation at all: "It is clear from the case that the Catholic partner does not 'share in the immoral intention' of the foundation; there is no issue of formal cooperation here. Nor does the Catholic partner directly participate in the wrongdoing (EV 74)."[42] The first clarifying point of the Pope's definition has been altogether missed: you cannot assert that there is no formal cooperation present *until* it is shown that the cooperator is not directly participating.

A second point of interest in the definition proposed by the Holy Father is his use of the word "direct". Despite the fact that none of the theologians canvassed by the CHA seemed to see anything unusual here, this is not at all typical of Manualist definitions of implicitly formal cooperation. This is particularly remarkable as the direct/indirect distinction played a central role in the discussion of scandal. We noted that one would have expected an analogous treatment of cooperation. Of the Manualist authors that we reviewed, Thomas Jorio stood out for mentioning direct/indirect as a distinct division of cooperation.[43] When mentioned by other authors, as Fabbro notes, it is supposed to distinguish cooperation by positive contribution, from cooperation by non-intervention (the last three of the nine modes), which they said would be indirectly voluntary and improperly called cooperation.[44] The use of "direct" in the definition of John Paul II, however, describes a participation that cannot have any other meaning than that of bringing about the evil. It should be contrasted with a positive contribution that is, nonetheless, indirect (i.e. material cooperation). The Pope's use of "direct" appears to by-pass the division of positive vs. negative cooperation, as well as the gradations of immediate, mediate, proximate and remote. Language used by the Congregation of the Doctrine of the Faith in a review of the November 1993 draft of the ERD's provides the best gloss on this meaning of "direct":

> Formal cooperation is verified not only when somebody cooperates from conscious approval of what a principal agent wrongly does, but also when the collaborating agent acts in a fashion *directed* to the achievement of the primary agent's goal… [one implicitly cooperates when] what the collaborating agent chooses to do is only properly intelligible as *directed to achieving* the end/purpose of the principal agent.[45]

In sum, an act of cooperation is not direct participation because the cooperator wills the same evil as the principal agent. Rather, he wills the same evil as the principal agent because he chooses to cooperate directly.

The third important clarification contained in the definition confirms this understanding of "direct". The participation is known to be direct by its very nature (*suapte natura*) or (*vel*) by the form it takes in a concrete situation (*in certo quodam contextu*). We noted that Zalba stood out for emphasizing the importance of the circumstances for discerning the presence of implicitly formal cooperation.[46] The mention of the importance of the context for identifying the cooperator's object is certainly a long way from those explanations of cooperation which isolated a physical description ("holding a ladder") and declared it good or indifferent. In a note, Kopfensteiner remarks that "the tradition exemplified [implicit formal cooperation] as when a person boosts another through a window [of a house] so that it can be robbed... he cannot abstractly separate himself from the robbery by saying he only 'helped someone through the window of the house'."[47] On the contrary, most Manualist authors, such as Merkelbach,[48] would see here an example of proximate cooperation without any indication that it implies something about the intention of the cooperator. Moreover, we know what version of Proposition 51 is favored by the tradition. The emphasis of *Evangelium Vitae* 74 on the "concrete situation" is, then, far from being a mere rehearsal of a traditional view.

Given this authoritative description of "direct participation" as "formal cooperation", one might well ask whether the category of immediate material cooperation has been superseded. Surely, anyone but a trained theologian would smile at the suggestion that one could "immediately cooperate" if need be, but never "directly participate". While the participants in the CHA dialogue reported considerable progress in building bridges, analyzing their differences and proposing new language, the familiar points of controversy stubbornly remained: "*There remain significant differences among the participants, particularly with regard to the presence and role of duress in cooperation and whether substantial cooperation can ever be morally licit*, both very critical issues."[49] [Note that "substantial cooperation" is new language proposed by the group for immediate cooperation]. Perhaps no consensus will be found until the notion of "immediate material cooperation" is dropped altogether.

The ethicists at the National Catholic Bioethics Center did not take this step, but they do seem to get us closer to it.[50] They assert that formal cooperation is more than intending the same moral object as the principal agent; it includes intending "any one or more of the immoral components of the principal agent's act," namely, object, intention or circumstances.[51] The cooperation will be formal if the cooperator wills a component "either as an end in itself or as a means." The cooperation will be implicitly formal when the cooperator "intend[s] any one or more of the immoral components... as a means to something other than the principal agent's act."[52] So, intending an essential circumstance as a means *to some legitimate end* is implicitly formal cooperation. On the next page, immediate material cooperation is defined as contributing "to circumstances that are essential to the commission of the principal agent's act," when the cooperator does not intend the evil object. Such cooperation is deemed always illicit.[53] If there is an identifiable distinction here, it is exceedingly nice.[54]

Useful, however, is the distinction made by the ethicists of the National Catholic Bioethics Center between essential and non-essential circumstances. Contributing to circumstances that are "essential to the commission of the principal agent's act" recalls the notion of "necessary" cooperation—cooperation without which the evil could not take place. Moreover, it recalls Steven Long's explanation of *per se* ordering. One thing was *per se* ordered to another if it naturally tended to it, or if the latter required the former. It seems that this can help explicate the notion of "direct participation", which is so central to the magisterial definition.

The Servant and the Ladder

At this point in our study, it will doubtless not surprise the reader to learn that, in our view, the servant's action, as described in Proposition 51, must be considered implicitly formal cooperation with evil.

Several points must be made in support of this assertion. Firstly, the service requested of the servant is presented as necessary for the commission of the crime. "Necessary" does not mean only that the crime would have been prevented by his refusal, although this seems to be the case. This would be a very weak understanding of necessary cooperation. Rather, even if the master could have found any number of people willing to hold the ladder, it was necessary to his plan that someone hold the ladder. Yet, even if the servant's action were not necessary, we believe that it would still be direct participation. Even if the master might have managed to set up the ladder and ascend by it unaided, the fact that the holding of it facilitates the crime makes such an action *directed* to the evil end. We can assert that the holding of the ladder is directed to the evil end, and therefore is a direct participation (not an accidental one), because there is no *legitimate* reason why the servant should be holding it. One might object that holding ladders is the kind of thing that servants do. Yet, the circumstances—at night, under the window of a potential victim, knowing what the master seeks to do—are more than circumstances. They establish this request as something that is foreign to what servants do, unless being a servant is an evil craft. It is not something that a servant would do "anyway", even if no crime were likely to be facilitated. All commentators admit as much by saying that the "*ratio famuli*" (roughly, calling it his job) does not suffice to justify his compliance.

The lack of a legitimate reason (of a purpose other than that of the master) for holding the ladder leads to the attempt to locate a sufficient reason in the duress. Perhaps this argument has seemed so plausible over the centuries for a reason that now, with the help of Steven Long's analysis, can be made clear. Cooperation will be material (the causing of the evil will be partial and accidental) when one has a sufficient reason for acting "anyway", as we have said. But, perhaps cooperation will also be material when the causing of the evil can be considered *praeter intentionem* according to Long's broader sense. In other words, if providing a partial cause of evil is the only way under the circumstances to defend oneself, can it not be considered *per se* ordered to that end, such that the cooperation will be deliberately chosen but not (in the narrow sense) intended? According to this argument, the bank teller who hands over the money to robbers to save his life is doing much the same thing as a merchant who throws the client's goods into the sea to save his life.[55] This approach shows how important it is to be able to define precisely what is or is not *per se* ordering. It is an argument that seems to suit some classic cases of cooperation such as the bartender filling up drinks for an intoxicated and potentially belligerent customer. Choosing to make him drunk could be *praeter intentionem*, if it is *per se* ordered to pacifying him, in the same way that choosing to drink to excess before an operation is not counted as the sin of drunkenness. The argument, we recall, is that one would not be ordering an evil means to a good end if the means chosen naturally tends to the end, or the end naturally requires it. Then, if the means is proportionate to the end, the action would be simple and good. One way of checking this result is to ask if handing over money to bank robbers and keeping troublesome customers quiet with extra drinks is part of the description of what good bank clerks and bartenders, respectively, do. So it seems to be.

This line of argument cannot, however, justify the servant in Proposition 51. In the first place, the harm suffered by the girl is not proportionate to goods sought by the servant, even the preservation of his life. In this regard, the discussions regarding what help a captured soldier could offer his captors seems quite accurate. Help that would lead to the loss of property is one thing, but help that would lead to maiming or killing of innocent people is another. Similarly, we have observed that throwing someone's goods overboard in a storm is one thing; throwing him overboard (as was done to Jonas) is another. Sins against chastity are not something that can be weighed against greater goods, so intimately is human dignity involved. Even in the case of a servant facilitating not a rape but a tryst, direct participation should be considered wrong. Moreover, it may be that this lack of proportion corresponds to a lack of *per se* ordering and thus to the existence of a self-standing action (facilitation of the crime) which is accidentally ordered to a good end (self-defense). It is not entirely clear in Steven Long's presentation whether *per se* ordering and proportionality between object and end are independent variables.[56]

What is clear, however, is that applying these notions to concrete cases will never be unproblematic. By way of illustration, consider the abuse of the conjugal act as it relates to cooperation. In this regard Pope Pius XI wrote that:

> Holy Church knows well that not infrequently one of the parties is sinned against rather than sinning, when for a grave cause he or she reluctantly allows the perversion of the right order. In such a case, there is no sin, provided that, mindful of the law of

> charity, he or she does not neglect to seek to
> dissuade and to deter the partner from sin.[57]

Thus, "reluctantly allow[ing] the perversion of the right order" means consenting to relations despite the expectation that the other will somehow abuse the act. Nonetheless, the scope of the ability to cooperate materially is not as great as one might at first imagine. The Holy See originally made this declaration in regards to *coitus interruptus*,[58] but then ruled that it does not apply to condomistic intercourse[59] nor to relations with a diaphragm.[60] In regards to the latter situation, the warning that such behavior should not be condoned even when "a husband cooperates materially" should be interpreted narrowly; in other words, it may indicate only that the husband does not share the same goal as the wife, not that his choice constitutes "material cooperation" or in this case "immediate material cooperation" (see pp. 275–276). It would seem then that, in order to claim that one is being "sinned against rather than sinning," more is needed than a non-involvement in the abuse of the act itself. If steps have been taken to render the act perverse, then consenting to the act is wrong. Only in the case of *coitus interruptus* is the act essentially good until deformed. In other terms, the fact that the woman has employed such a device is a condition affecting the object; having relations of this sort is not something a good husband would do "anyway", foreseeing a subsequent abuse. In this case, the abuse is already underway, and his contribution cannot be considered *per se* ordered to any good end.

Notes

1   We refer to the "early" Häring, as he expresses himself in *The Law of Christ*, tr. E. G. Kaiser (Westminster, MD: Newman Press, 1961).

2   Interestingly, in his discussion of whether one can employ a usurer without sin, St Thomas speaks of the cooperator "using the evil of the other" rather than of the principal agent abusing the good deed of the cooperator: "pro aliquo incommodo vitando potest homo licite uti malitia alterius." *De Malo* q. 13, a. 4, ad 18 and 19.

3   McIntyre, "Doing Away," p. 243.

4   Liguori, *Theologia moralis*, lib. II, tr. 3, cap. 2, dub. 5, art. 3, n. 65.

5   Cf. *ST* I-II, q. 6, a. 3 "Utrum voluntarium possit esse absque omni actu."

6   This defect is found, for instance, in Bishop Fisher's mention of a "manufacturer of morphine" needing to justify "unintentional participation in the evil of drug addiction." Fisher, "Cooperation in Evil," p. 18.

7   In his article on restitution (*ST* II-II q. 62, a. 7), St Thomas lists the traditional nine ways of cooperating and asserts that four do not require restitution because they are not always "efficacious" causes of the theft ("non semper est efficax causa [rapinae]"). Both "participans" and "non obstans" are included with the five that do require restitution, although Thomas admits, in his reply to the third objection, that one is only obliged to intervene (*obstare*) when it is one's office and the danger is not too great. There is no such qualification for one taking part.

8   B. Ashley and K. O'Rourke, *Health Care Ethics: a theological analysis*, 4th ed. (Washington DC: Georgetown University Press, 1997), p. 194. Häring's view is apparently being drawn from his *Law of Christ*: "In formal cooperation, one's action of itself is to be characterized as an influence, as partial cause of an evil effect which must be avoided. Wherefore it is evil, although the agent himself may deplore the evil effect" (I, p. 293). Again, "one who intends the cause intends and wills also the effect which is intrinsically bound up with the cause" (I, p. 292).

9   J. Rojas, "St Thomas on the Direct/Indirect Distinction," *Ephemerides Theologicae Lovanienses* 64 (1988), pp. 371–392, at p. 387.

10   *Ibid.*, p. 383.

[11]   Rojas notes, in connection with a helmsman running his boat aground through negligence, that "the effect of a voluntary omission (indirectly voluntary) could in fact also be willed in itself (*voluntarium secundum se*)." *Ibid.*, p. 382.

[12]   Cf. Kramer, *Indirect Voluntary*, pp. 22–24. "But later, when treating the voluntariness of omissions and their effects [Billuart] adds an explanation that may offer a key to the solution of the whole question of the indirect voluntary" (pp. 22–23).

[13]   Perhaps J. O. Urmson's observations regarding cause and explanation are relevant: "It would indeed be absurd in ordinary circumstances to give the fact that a piece of glass has the (ordinary) brittleness of glass as the cause of it breaking; but in ordinary circumstances it would be very proper to mention the (unusual) brittleness of an aircraft wing as the cause of the wing falling off, and quite ridiculous to mention the fact that wind was pressing against the wing in quite a normal way, if investigating the cause of an accident." J. O. Urmson, "Motives and Causes," in *The Philosophy of Action*, ed. A. R. White, pp. 153–165 (London: Oxford University Press, 1968), at pp. 163–164.

[14]   Kramer, *Indirect Voluntary*, p. 28.

[15]   Anscombe, "Modern moral philosophy," p. 12.

[16]   Reichberg, "Aquinas on Defensive Killing," p. 345 (italics mine).

[17]   Flannery, *Acts amid precepts*, pp. 192–193, for instance. In this light, it is particularly interesting that Melina quotes John Paul II as saying that illicit cooperation debases the noble profession of pharmacists. Melina, "La cooperazione," p. 488, citing John Paul II, "Discorso alla Federazione Internazionale dei farmacisti Cattolici," in *L'Osservatore Romano*, November 3, 1990.

[18]   Note well: we are not simply repeating the first condition of the classical formulation of the PDE. Rather, we have criticized the requirement that "the cause be good or indifferent" as implying the separation of the behavior from its effects. In this perspective behavior can become atomized, separated from act-specifying circumstances and deprived of its built-in proximate intention, which is genuine physicalism.

[19]   Fisher, "Understanding the issues," p. 51.

[20]   Fisher does not give specific examples of these misunderstandings. It seems that the examples of the former are much more plentiful than the latter.

[21]   Ugorji, *Principle of Double Effect*, 137. See also p. 32.

22   The following passage of *Veritatis Splendor* seems opposed to such a position: "It is never acceptable to confuse a 'subjective' error about moral good with the 'objective' truth rationally proposed to man in virtue of his end... It is possible that the evil done as the result of invincible ignorance or a non-culpable error of judgment may not be imputable to the agent, but even in this case it does not cease to be an evil, a disorder in relation to the truth about the good." John Paul II, *Veritatis Splendor*, 63.

23   Brock, *Action and Conduct*, p. 223, fn. 63, citing K. L. Flannery, "Natural Law *mens rea* versus the Benthamite Tradition," *American Journal of Jurisprudence* 40 (1995), pp. 377–400, at p. 399.

24   Porter, "The Moral Act in *Veritatis Splendor*," p. 223.

25   Klueg, "Sin, cooperation in," p. 246.

26   "Qu.: 1. Potestne medicus rogatus a duellantibus duello assistere cum intentione citius finem pugnae imponendi, vel simpliciter vulnera ligandi ac curandi, quin incurrat excommunicatioem Summo Pontifici simpliciter reservatam? 2. Potestne saltem, quin duello sit praesens, in domo vicina vel in loco propinquo sistere, proximus ac paratus ad praebendum suum ministerium, si duellantibus opus fuerit? 3. Quid de confessario in iisdem condicionibus? Resp.: Ad 1. Non posse, et excommunicationem incurri. Ad 2. et 3. Quatenus ex condicto fiat, item non posse et excommunicationem incurri." "Response of the Holy Office to the Bishop of Poitiers," May 31, 1884, DS 3162.

27   This characterization of the policeman's action will surely be controversial. It may help to imagine an analogous case of policemen arresting abolitionist protestors interfering with a slave auction. We can imagine what Henry David Thoreau would think about the idea that one could with honor intact *help put* just men into prison from his glorious remark: "Under a government which imprisons unjustly, the true place for a just man is also in prison...the only house in a slave state in which a free man can abide with honour." H. D. Thoreau, "On the Duty of Civil Disobedience," in *Walden and On the Duty of Civil Disobedience* (New York: Collier, 1962), p. 245. Thoreau refers to those who work for the state in such circumstances as not men but machines (p. 238). This contrasts instructively with the suggestion made occasionally that one test of material cooperation is whether one could imagine a machine performing the action in question.

28   Often the situation of a mailman is presented, in which it is supposed that the mailman realizes that a certain item he delivers

with some regularity is pornographic material, but not such as to be prohibited by the mail system. Does he do wrong to deliver it? It may be argued that his job is to deliver packages without assessing their content, just as a policeman's job is to take away trespassers without assessing their motives for trespassing. However, there must be a point, difficult as it may be to define abstractly, at which people may not claim to be "just doing their job," a point at which their actions no longer correspond to their job, which is noble in itself (facilitating communications for a mailman or keeping the peace for a policeman). One avenue that may help distinguish the two cases: the mailman's cooperation seems to be legitimately classifiable as an *omission*: he omits removing the offensive piece from his bag, or from the recipient's pile of mail. It is perhaps inaccurate to characterize his cooperation positively as "delivering pornographic material." The policeman's action, on the other hand, "arresting trespassers", is not readily described as an omission.

²⁹ Kaveny, "Appropriation of Evil," p. 302.

³⁰ In footnote 11, Cavanaugh labels this tendency "Cartesian" (cf. *Double-Effect Reasoning*, p. 67). In support of this assertion, we cite what Ilham Dilman says in another context: "The philosopher who is troubled by 'our knowledge of the mind'... is strongly inclined to hold that our knowledge of our own mind is *direct* and *immediate*, whereas our knowledge of other people's minds is *indirect* and *inferential*. This is one of the central doctrines of the Cartesian view of the mind." I. Dilman, *Matter and Mind: two essays in epistemology* (London: MacMillan, 1975), p. 213. As we have indicated earlier, while there is certainly no way of knowing what another person intends to do before he does it, or what further intentions might motivate his doing it, there is not such a great difference between our awareness that we are intentionally making tea and our judgment that another person is. If there is an inference made, it is analogous to that involved in saying that "I see Daires' son," when "one cannot know a person's identity or familial relationships from sensation alone." Pilsner, *Specification*, p. 93.

³¹ Pilsner, *Specification*, p. 88.

³² Crawford, "Conjugal Life," p. 506. Noting that *Veritatis Splendor* uses the phrase "kinds of behavior" seven times, Crawford continues, "actions can be described objectively—without violating the perspective of the acting person—according to their intelligible

structure and meaning in relation to the vocation of human nature."

[33] K. L. Flannery, "Placing Oneself 'In the Perspective of the Acting Person': *Veritatis Splendor* and the Nature of the Moral Act," in *Live the Truth: the Moral Legacy of John Paul II in Catholic Health Care*, ed. E. J. Furton, pp. 47–67 (Philadelphia: National Catholic Bioethics Center, 2005) at p. 52.

[34] Brock, *Action and Conduct*, p. 240.

[35] G. E. M. Anscombe, "The Two Kinds of Error in Action," in *Ethics, Religion and Politics: Collected Philosophical Papers, Volume III*, 3–9 (Minneapolis: University of Minnesota Press, 1981), at pp. 5–6.

[36] For a thorough summary from a proportialist perspective, see B. Hoose, *Proportionalism: The American Debate and its European Roots* (Washington, DC: Georgetown University Press, 1987), Chapter 3.

[37] See, for instance, Cavanaugh, *Double-Effect Reasoning*, pp. 125–135. The law is frequently quite at odds with the moral viewpoint, as, for instance, when two drunk drivers *do* the same thing from a moral point of view ("from the perspective of the acting person") but the one who *happens* to hit a person instead of a fire hydrant is punished a great deal more.

[38] "Etenim, morali spectata re, non licet expresse cum malo operam sociare. Adesse consociatam operam constat cum perfectum opus, vel suapte natura vel ob speciem quam in certo quodam contextu ipsum praebet, se patefacit directo veluti actum contra vitam hominis innocentis patratum aut veluti immorale propositum cum agenti principe communicantem." John Paul II, *Evangelium Vitae*, 74, p. 487. The definition speaks of sins "against life" because of the context in which it appears, but it is obviously applicable to cooperation with evil of any sort.

[39] "Immediate material cooperation is wrong, except in some cases of duress. The matter of duress distinguishes immediate material cooperation from implicit formal cooperation. But immediate material cooperation—without duress—is equivalent to implicit formal cooperation and, therefore, is morally wrong." National Conference of Catholic Bishops, *Ethical and Religious Directives* (1995), p. 29.

[40] Catholic Health Association of the United States, "Report on a Theological Dialogue," p. 10. "*There was agreement that this text in EV does not represent new teaching on the principle of coopera-tion*, but, rather, is an expanded explanation of formal cooperation

in the context of discussing civil laws which permit euthanasia and abortion." *Ibid.*, p. 8.

[41] T. Kopfensteiner, "The Meaning and Role of Duress in the Cooperation in Wrongdoing," *Linacre Quarterly* 70 (2003), pp. 150–158, at p. 152.

[42] T. Kopfensteiner, "For Reflection: A Sample Case Study on Cooperation," in *Report on a Theological Dialogue on the Principle of Cooperation*, Catholic Health Association, 2007, p. 23. One is not surprised to learn that Fr Kopfensteiner was one of the authors, with Fr James Keenan, of the now retracted appendix to the ERD's (cf. Fisher, "Understanding the Issues," p. 35).

[43] Jorio, *Theologia moralis*, p. 205.

[44] Fabbro, *Cooperation in evil*, p. 19, citing Merkelbach, *Summa theologiae moralis*, I, p. 401 and Zalba, *Theologiae moralis compendium*, II, p. 125.

[45] The Congregation for the Doctrine of the Faith, "Some Observations on the November 1993 Draft of the Ethical and Religious Directives for Catholic Health Care Facilities of the U.S. Bishops' Committee on Doctrine," cited by Kopfensteiner, "Meaning and Role of Duress," p. 152. First use of italics added by me, second found in original document.

[46] "Difficultas applicandi principii de voluntario in causa in praxi est magna quia: a) interdum difficulter discernitur cooperatio materialis a formali implicita... Actio cooperatrix analyzanda est non in se ipsa et abstracte, sed cum circumstantiis et adiunctis concretis; non secundum meram materialitatem... sed secundum significationem et qualitatem moralem talis actionis." Zalba, *Theologiae Moralis Compendium*, II, p.125.

[47] Kopfensteiner, "Meaning and Role of Duress," p. 157.

[48] Merkelbach, *Summa theologiae moralis*, I, p. 401.

[49] Catholic Health Association of the United States, "Report on Theological Dialogue," p. 14.

[50] Ethicists, The, "Cooperating with Non-Catholic Partners," *Ethics and Medics* 23 (1998), pp. 1–5.

[51] *Ibid.*, p. 2.

[52] *Ibid.*, p. 2.

[53] *Ibid.*, p. 3. Both these ethicists and Ashley—O'Rourke (see next footnote), say that immediate material cooperation is to be excluded but deny that it is implicitly formal. This raises the question: what then is the reason for *always* prohibiting it? If the

intention is not necessarily bad (by virtue of the object), then it seems that it might sometimes be good (e.g. under duress). If the intention is necessarily bad, it is implicitly formal.

54 Benedict Ashley and Kevin O'Rourke seem to be developing on this point but in the wrong direction. Up to the third edition of their popular bioethics text, we read: "When such material cooperation is *immediate* (e.g. nurses who assist physicians to perform an abortion, which they personally disapprove), it amounts to the same as formal cooperation because it is a direct contribution to an evil act in which the cooperator shares the responsibility for the act." B. Ashley and K. O'Rourke, *Health Care Ethics: a theological analysis*, 3rd ed. (St Louis, MO: Catholic Health Association of United States, 1989), p. 188. This statement, written in 1989, perfectly anticipates the definition found in *Evangelium Vitae* six years later. However, in the fourth edition, which came out two years after that encyclical, a notable change is introduced in their treatment. Now the authors rule out immediate material cooperation if the assistance is necessary to the bringing about of harm and if the principal action is intrinsically evil. However, they explicitly refuse to equate it with formal cooperation. "If one's action contributes to the active performance of to [sic] the evil action so much so that the evil action could not be performed without the help of the cooperator, then this is known as immediate material cooperation. This method of cooperation involves the cooperator acting in conjunction with the person primarily responsible for the evil action. If the act in question is intrinsically evil, then immediate material cooperation is always prohibited." Ashley—O'Rourke, *Health Care Ethics*, 4th ed., p. 194.

55 Perhaps this also provides the underlying logic for Thomas's approval of taking a loan from a usurer or giving money to brigands in exchange for one's life. "Ita etiam in proposito dicendum est quod nullo modo licet inducere aliquem ad mutuandum sub usuris, licet tamen ab eo qui hoc paratus est facere et usuras exercet, mutuum accipere sub usuris, propter aliquod bonum, quod est subventio suae necessitatis vel alterius. Sicut etiam licet ei qui incidit in latrones manifestare bona quae habet, quae latrones diripiendo peccant, ad hoc quod non occidatur, exemplo decem virorum qui dixerunt ad Ismahel, noli occidere nos, quia habemus thesaurum in agro, ut dicitur Ierem. XLI" (ST II-II, q. 78, a. 4). Thomas notes that one is not giving scandal, but only foreseeing "passive" scandal. Furthermore, the physical harm

foreseen is done to oneself, not to a third party. In the case of loss or damage to possessions, however, this fact is not so significant. There is the doctrine of the universal destination of goods, the legitimate expectation of owner's permission, and the possibility of making up for the loss.

[56] They seem to be more clearly distinct in *Teleological Grammar*, but almost interchangeable in the earlier "Brief Disquisition". There we read: "The Abelardian position denies the natural moral teleology of each act... In St Thomas's view, by contrast, a relation and proportion to the end is included in the object of the external act..." S. A. Long, "*A Brief Disquisition regarding the Nature of the Object of the Moral Act*," *Thomist* 67 (2003), pp. 45–71, at p. 59. This would have the effect of linking act-specifying "circumstances", proportionality, and *per se* ordering, as Long sometimes appears to do: "Homicide is permitted in justified defense only insofar as it is either the only or the best means to justified defense. When this is true there is no doubt that it is naturally ordered to its end, and hence that what is intended is not killing but defense, although killing is chosen as a means to defense." *Ibid.*, p. 63. If "circumstances" were such that there were many non-lethal ways of stopping an attack, lethal means would no longer be proportionate; would they then cease to be *per se* ordered to defense? He writes: "Whereas [in contrast to fornication], to slay an assailant is always or for the most part to stop the assault, and so such slaying is *per se* ordered to defense when it is chosen precisely under that *ratio* (for one might deliberately provoke an attack in the hope of being able to slay someone, which clearly is not a defensive act but rather the pretext for wrongful homicide)." Long, *Teleological Grammar*, p. 49.

[57] "Optime etiam novit Sancta Ecclesia, non raro alterum ex coniugibus pati potius quam patrare peccatum, cum ob gravem omnino causam perversionem recti ordinis permittit, quam ipse non vult, eumque ideo sine culpa esse, modo etiam tunc caritatis legem meminerit et alterum a peccando arcere et removere ne negligat." Pius XI, *Casti Connubii*, 59, p. 561.

[58] "Response of the Sacred Penitentiary," April 23, 1822, DS 2715.

[59] "Response of the Sacred Penitentiary," April 19, 1853, DS 2795. "Qu.: 2) An uxor in congressu condomistico possit passive se praebere? Ad 2) Negative; daret enim operam rei intrinsece illicitae."

[60] "Decree of the Holy Office," April 2, 1955, DS 3917a. "The Sacred

Congregation particularly raises its voice utterly to condemn and reject as intrinsically evil the application of pessaries (sterilet, diaphragm) by married couples in the exercise of their marital rights. Furthermore, Ordinaries shall not permit the faithful to be told or taught that no serious objection may be made according to the principles of Christian law, if a husband co-operates materially only with his wife who uses such a device. Confessors and spiritual directors who hold the contrary and thus guide the consciences of the faithful are straying far from the paths of truth and moral righteousness" (Original in English).

CHAPTER 12

CONSEQUENCES OF THIS NOTION OF FORMAL COOPERATION

1. Proximate/remote distinction

ACCORDING TO OUR understanding of formal cooperation as defined by John Paul II, formal cooperation will be implicit if the cooperator directly participates in the commission of the evil act, even though he may not share the principal agent's evil intention or goal, in the sense of *finis operantis*. We argued that what is usually referred to as "immediate cooperation", participating in the commission of the act itself, is certainly direct. This does not mean, however, that the quality of being "direct" is a function of proximity. Certainly, the more proximate one's cooperation, the more likely it is to be necessary to the accomplishment of the evil deed. Yet, as we observed, the key to being direct participation is only that there is no explanation for positing the act other than the furtherance of the evil. It is not something good in itself that the agent would have done "anyway", that is, in situations unrelated to evil deeds. There was a confusion in days gone by between the *degree* of involvement (or proximity) and the issue of *directness* which should admit of no gradations. We noted, as early as Chapter 2, that some authors were speaking incongruously of cooperation that is more or less *per se*.

If the formal/material division (relating to the direction, or intrinsic meaning of the action) is genuinely distinguished from the proximate/remote division (relating to the degree of contribution to the evil), there appears to be no reason why the latter distinction should not be applied to formal cooperation as well. Implicitly formal cooperation is making some contribution to the commission of evil that has no legitimate reason for being posited. But this contribution could be exceedingly remote, even practically imperceptible. It is striking that in the long history of development of the cooperation doctrine very little attention has been given to this possibility. It was assumed that the very smallness of a contribution indicated material cooperation. This would seem to be a result of defining formal cooperation as either the explicit approval of the evil or, for some authors, virtually doing it oneself (immediate cooperation). It was presumed that one who contributed to the "physical" act while disapproving of the evil was committing but material cooperation, because the *type* of contribution was not sufficiently considered. Is the contribution essential (direct) or accidental (indirect)? Once the possibility of a direct contribution by a disapproving cooperator is seriously entertained, it is clear that this contribution can also vary along the whole gamut from remote to proximate.

Another reason for the lack of interest in this possibility is that very proximate cooperation, such as that of the servant, was considered justifiable by the majority. If the servant could hold the ladder to save his life, then *a fortiori* one could fetch it or perform increasingly remote acts under duress. There appeared to be no need to ask whether a very small contribution to an evil was worth resisting at great cost.

Again, formal cooperation seems to make the cooperator guilty of the very same crime as the principal agent. In Joseph Boyle's words: "When one cooperates formally one does not so much contribute to wrongdoing as do it, or do part of it, oneself ... a formal cooperator in abortion is guilty of abortion, not primarily of cooperation with it."[1] This perspective restricts the range of formal cooperation dramatically: it is hard to see how the servant could be guilty of the very same crime as the master, when he never even entered the house. Yet, it could be maintained that a cooperator could perform an act of the same species, which would be intrinsically evil, yet only venially so. Intrinsic evil is not a subset of mortal sin.

The problem of remote formal cooperation

Whatever the reason may be, the fact is that the concept of "remote formal cooperation", while not contrary to the tradition, is not discussed by it. It seems certain that raising the issue would stir up an outcry from persons insisting that it must be wrongheaded because of the immediate consequence: many people would be put in extremely awkward positions. There lingers unspoken the sense that moral theologians are to be "benign", trying to get people out of awkward positions, instead of "consistent", pointing the way to holiness however steep and narrow the path. How could people be expected to function in society if, for instance, not only the owner of the pharmacy that decides to order illicit drugs, but the chief pharmacist, his assistant, the clerk, and perhaps even the cashier might all be guilty of varying degrees of formal cooperation?

Before considering the consequences of such a view on a vast scale, let us analyze the individual case. Suppose that an intern pharmacist is told that to keep his job he must provide value-neutral answers to questions regarding contraceptive drugs. Although he hates contraception, he is concerned that explaining to people about proper dosage and so forth or even where to find them in the store is illicit (implicitly formal) cooperation. Many would consider such an understanding of the situation, which would demand he quit rather than do so, to be intolerably rigorist. Yet, what about the common situation of an employee who is told to misrepresent the truth to clients? Should one lose a job that might be very necessary rather than tell a small lie? Are not salespeople often asked to push overstocked items, telling customers that they are excellent products? The tradition has been as uncompromising on lying as it is on formal cooperation. In the perplexing moral problems that can arise with lying, we have a parallel to what would ensue from admitting a greater frequency of formal cooperation. In both cases, there is the apparent choice between committing a small sin (remote formal cooperation, small lie) or permitting a possibly very great harm (dismissal from work). The tradition has maintained that one cannot commit even a venial sin, regardless of the motive. This position has been stated with characteristic force and eloquence by Blessed John Henry Newman:

> The Catholic Church holds it better for the sun and moon to drop from heaven, for the earth to fail, and for all the many millions on it to die of starvation in extremest agony, as far as temporal affliction goes, than that one soul, I will not say should be lost, but should commit one single venial sin, should tell one willful untruth, or should steal one poor farthing without excuse.[2]

Dare we add to his list: "or directly participate in evil, even remotely"? The instinctive resistance to such a prospect seems to have led to a curious fact. During nearly four centuries of discussion of this question, mortal sin is mentioned quite often, but venial sin not at all. Proposition 51 condemned the idea that a servant could hold a ladder for the reasons enumerated without *mortal* sin, but no one seems to have considered that his holding it could be but a venial sin. Always the effort was to justify the cooperation, to show that he committed no sin in holding the ladder. It seems to have been taken for granted that his acquiescence, if formal, would be mortal sin, since he would be joining in an intrinsically evil act of the master who undoubtedly sinned mortally.[3] Certainly, the duress factor could diminish his responsibility, rendering his sin venial, but the possibility that the cooperation *itself*, due to its causal distance from the evil, would be venial sin is nowhere contemplated. Typical is an analysis such as that of a local ecclesial authority reported by Waffelaert: a believing architect who cooperates in the construction of a schismatic temple would sin mortally, but Christian construction workers could cooperate without sin.[4] Should one not expect a level of involvement that would be, of its nature, venial?

Lying and venial sin

Remote formal cooperation, we suggest, should be seen as essentially analogous to the classic problem of a confrontation with the Gestapo, seeking victims hiding in one's house. Formal cooperation is a breach of a *negative* commandment, as is lying, never to be allowed. Yet, drastic harms including the loss of life can be avoided by an apparently small infraction of these norms—hence, the dreadful problem. We believe that an incisive article by Lawrence Dewan on the problem of lying not only sheds great light on the Gestapo question but on our theme as well.[5]

Dewan begins by reminding the reader about the tradition's understanding of venial sin. It must be radically different from mortal sin, or else, were they just gradations of sin, we would have to admit that there is some point of transition which is only incrementally worse yet deserving, all of a sudden, of eternal punishment. This obviously is not the case. Hence, as Dewan observes, marshalling texts from Aquinas, there is an infinite difference between mortal and venial sin.[6] The word "sin" is only predicated of them analogically, because venial sin is not so much "contra legem" as "praeter legem". [7] Venial sin is, consequently, to be called "bad" in a qualified sense (*secundum quid*).[8] Moreover, the commission of a venial sin does not, of itself, diminish the agent's charity or friendship with God.[9] Dewan also reminds the reader that venial sins can be forgiven collectively, even without sacramental confession, and that the great majority of men contract them daily.[10] The reminder of the prevalence of venial sin should go a long way to reconciling us to the possibility that, assuming remote formal cooperation can be venially sinful, many people do in fact commit it. Still, Dewan's reminder about the nature of venial sin should not lead us to think that remote formal cooperation with evil can be ignored, still less approved. For one thing, he mentions that venial sin disposes one to commit mortal sin, an observation which seems to echo the intuition of many authors that cooperation, though considered material, can lead easily to cooperation that is formal.

Next, Fr Dewan shows, on the authority of St Thomas, that some lies are venial by nature. This does not particularly concern our theme, although his explanation of why even venial lies should not be employed to prevent great evils agrees with the natural meanings theory of action and Steven Long's take on self-defense.[11] Interestingly, Dewan points out that while it is never permissible to tell a lie to save someone from harm, doing so will be an even slighter venial sin than to tell a lie for comic purposes.[12] Finally, it is recalled that seeking to protect the innocent persons from harm remains a good end, even if the means used are bad. This point is made clear by Thomas's treatment of the Egyptian midwives, in which he follows Augustine.[13] They observe that, as the Book of Exodus reports, God rewarded the midwives; this is not interpreted as an approbation of the means they chose but of their good will towards the Israelite children.

A mind raised on casuistry will rebel at the notion that the midwives, or the man confronted by the Gestapo, should be put in a situation in which God wishes them to preserve the lives in danger and yet not tell a lie. It seems to violate the premises of the problem as defined by casuists; God would seem to be asking something impossible. The tradition, beginning at least with St Augustine, suggests that there are other options; some manner of misleading the persecutor without lying is permissible.[14] Yet, it is certainly *imaginable* that some circumstances— such as an interrogator who knows Catholic teaching on the matter—will make an attempt to escape the dilemma by mental reservation impossible. Nonetheless, the insistence of the great saints that a lie remains a moral evil and their refusal to condone it, even to save a life, does not mean that they are endorsing the turning over of the innocents.[15] Indeed, common intuition tells us that this would be a much worse sin. Does this mean that one can be in a situation where one must sin? Not exactly. Such a conclusion overlooks two important points. First, life is not a casuist's puzzle. Simply because life presents us with situations requiring tremendous prudence does not mean that it ever presents us with a lose-lose situation, unless we have contributed through our own fault.[16] Second, the prudence or courage required to resolve such difficult situations without any sin at all may be truly superhuman. We must maintain that God can provide a "third option" to those who have merited it by leading holy lives. Nonetheless, we frankly acknowledge, as does Dewan, that the majority of men, possessing but ordinary virtue, will choose to lie as their best option.[17] Once again, this is not the same thing as condoning this course of action. St Augustine sums up the situation marvelously:

> Those who merely tell lies such as [the Egyptian midwives, whose object is someone's safety or advantage] will deserve in time to be set free from all dissimulation, for in the perfect not even these are to be found... If this is at present beyond us, we must at least admit of lies only in strict necessity. We may then deserve to get rid even of white lies, if we do no worse, and receive strength from the Holy Ghost to make light of any suffering for truth's sake ...[18]

Duress and heroism

Certain martyrs have provided particularly eloquent examples of resistance to remote formal cooperation. We can but marvel at the courage of Blessed Michael Nakashima, a Jesuit brother who lived contemporaneously with the golden age of post-Tridentine probabilism, taking place in the West. The authorities persecuting the missionaries in Japan regularly passed through Nagasaki asking for small donations of firewood with which to burn arrested priests. On September 3, 1628, Brother Michael received such a visit. He replied that he would not contribute to the perpetration of such an injustice. The consequences of his refusal are detailed in the Appendix.

More recently, the case of Blessed Franz Jägerstätter has gained renown. Drafted by the Nazi army after the Anschluss of Austria, Franz immediately felt the pangs of conscience. To wear the uniform of an army bent on evil seemed to him an offense against God. He would have consented to serve as a medic, but not as an infantryman.

The vast majority of his fellow countrymen complied with the demand against their will; Franz's pastor and bishop assured him that he could do so without sin. He disagreed and suffered execution on August 9, 1943.

Many people will think that these and other saints are honored by the Church for having gone above and beyond the demands of basic Christian living. However, any distinction between "good" and "better", any claim to the existence of a class of supererogatory works, must remain in the realm of positive norms. If all are called to help the poor, surely not all are called to live exactly as St Francis did. However, this logic cannot apply to the infraction of negative commandments, even slightly. Although a special call leads people to exercise heroism in the fulfillment of positive commands, it is by an apparently random process, or one whose providential design remains hidden from us, that people find themselves in situations requiring heroism to avoid breaking negative commandments. The distinction between act and omission is of vital importance here.

Moreover, the claim that there are two tracks of Christianity, one for ordinary Christians and another for saints, while never explicitly endorsed, is in our day decidedly to be rejected.[19] The Second Vatican Council's renewal of the universal call to holiness has coincided with the affirmation of at least a remote call to evangelical radicality and mystical prayer for all Christians. One of the pre-conciliar defects of moral theology was surely the tendency to identify a minimum Christian obligation beyond which one could aspire if one wished or if one received a special call. Such an error seems to be the import of the following observation dating from 1938: "In any case, the moral theologian, by declaring the obligation to be inexistent, abstains from any judgment on the question of perfection, which he leaves entirely to the ascetical theologian."[20] How different is the comment made by the representative of Pope Benedict XVI when he beatified Franz Jägerstätter:

> His path is a challenge and an encouragement for all Christians who can take an example from him, by which to live their faith with coherence and radical commitment, even up to the most extreme consequences, if necessary. The blesseds and saints have always given the example of what being Christian means and entails, even in particular concrete moments of history.[21]

There are, moreover, several arguments which counter the idea that an ordinary Christian would be committing no moral evil whatever if he were to contribute wood the missionary's pyre or enlist in an army engaged in an unjust war. Firstly, those who do capitulate and do these things, although telling themselves that they have no choice, are never proud of what they have done. They regret their compliance bitterly. Second, the injustice lies precisely in the fact that such people are being made to do something *wrong*. Suppose that they are told that their cooperation is material, that, in other words, their action is fundamentally good and only abused by the persecutors. Not only does this description not correspond to their regret for having to do it, but it also absolves the persecutors! If they are not forcing people to do something wrong, then in what lies the injustice of their request? Finally, if the cooperation of people under duress is not a moral evil, even a slight one, then it becomes very implausible to say that Brother Michael or Franz Jägerstätter did well to resist. The latter not only gave up his life but abandoned his wife and three children. How could this be virtuous, if there was a morally upright alternative?[22]

2. A social perspective

Thus far we have been considering the question of the obligation of the servant to refuse compliance from the perspective of the individual agent. This is the context in which the question arose and on which Catholic moral theology typically focused: what judgment is to be made in a case of conscience, when a single individual is faced with a difficult choice? While this certainly is the fundamental perspective for moral questions, as ultimately all moral evil comes down to personal choices, it has its limits. In the case of cooperation with evil, this perspective can actually be misleading. This is so because many difficult cooperation cases involve both a craft (or some similar activity in which one might legitimately engage) and duress. Frequently, the more people who maintain the integrity of the craft, the less forceful the duress becomes. We typically imagine a pharmacist faced with the choice of selling contraceptives or resigning his position as if he were the only conscientious pharmacist on earth. This is not the real situation, however, but a product of the casuist method, which, as in the case of lying, tends to eliminate precisely the other options which an agent may licitly choose. In the case of pharmacists, this could be banding together in associations to demand freedom of conscience. In the case of the servant, the master is less likely to dismiss or injure his servant seriously if he knows that the servant's successor would probably behave in much the same way.

Utilitarian models

Helpful ideas for viewing cooperation from a social perspective can be found in surprising places, such as utilitarian models of ethics. In his popular book, *Reasons and Persons*, Derek Parfit reminds us of the famous "Prisoner's Dilemma" schema.[23] It supposes that two prisoners, who are unable to communicate with each other, will both be given light sentences for keeping silent and moderate sentences for confessing. However, if one keeps silent and the other confesses, the former gets the stiffest penalty and the latter goes free. The best outcome for all can only be obtained by each agent's willingness to forego an even better outcome for himself individually.

		You	
		confess	keep silent
I	confess	Each gets 10 years	I go free, you get 12 years
	keep silent	I get 12 years, you go free	Each gets 2 years

At first glance, this schema does not appear very helpful for two pharmacists eager to avoid cooperation with a coercive law. This is so firstly because the penalty incurred is so great that risking it does not often even appear as a realistic option. Moreover, the refusal by both parties to comply does not lead to an amelioration of the outcome, but to the worst of all possible cases.

		Pharmacist #1	
		sells	doesn't sell
Pharmacist #2	sells	Each prospers at the cost of moral compromise	#2 prospers with moral cost, #1 is ruined
	doesn't sell	#1 prospers with moral cost, #2 is ruined	Both are ruined

However, while Two-Person Prisoners' Dilemmas may surface regularly in departmental lounge debates, Parfit points out that *Many-Person* Dilemmas abound in real life. After considering commuters, soldiers, fisherman, and population rates, Parfit observes: "There are countless other cases. It can be better for each if he adds to pollution, uses more energy, jumps queues, and breaks agreements; but, if all do these things, that can be worse for each than if none do."[24] In a "many-person" version of cooperation cases, the situation is dramatically altered. The efficacy of coercive powers, be they democratically elected legislative bodies or ruthless tyrants, depends upon the fact that the threat of punishment will make the majority comply. The resistance of a few provides an opportunity to show that the threat of punishment is credible, but the resistance of many threatens the coercive system itself. In our pharmacist example, if a significant number of pharmacists were involved, the box corresponding to joint refusal to sell could represent the *best* outcome for all: prosper, while maintaining principles, at the cost of some risk and effort.[25]

From this perspective, the evil involved in cooperating with another goes beyond the harm one helps facilitate on this particular occasion. Viewing oneself as an isolated moral agent instead of a member of a profession or social group means ignoring a duty of solidarity. Perhaps it often happens that the greater harm caused by a cooperator is that of increasing the burden on others who are considering resistance. Surely, it is by the compliance of many individuals that situations of duress become institutionalized. It is highly significant that the Catechism of the Catholic Church mentions "structures of sin" immediately after the number on cooperation.[26] Structures of sin are the product of large-scale cooperation with evil. Likewise, the concept of a "culture of death" implies something created and sustained by a large section of society, not only by the more outspoken or influential promoters of evil practices. Surely, the silent majority of reluctant coopera-tors cannot be exculpated so easily for the existence of an evil so great as the culture of death. Intuitively, there is a moral duty to join in solidarity with other victims of pressure to do evil, but, in fact, it is difficult to demonstrate the existence of this duty, especially when hope of immi-nent success is lacking.

Problems for the social perspective

The policy of acting not for one's own best interest, but for the best possible outcome for all, including oneself, is dubbed by Parfit "sufficient altruism".[27] Why do agents not seem easily disposed to practice even sufficiently altruistic behavior? Indeed, why is it difficult for theorists even to show they are morally bound to do so? Parfit suggests the need for a principle that "revises the ordinary use of the words 'benefit' and 'harm'... [proposing that] I benefit someone even when my act is a remote part of the cause of the receiving of this benefit ... Similar claims apply to 'harm'."[28] He identifies what he calls "Five Mis-takes in Moral Mathematics", which obscure the account-ability of individual agents for their contributions to collective harms. For instance, the contribution of a single member of a collective action may be of uncertain effect, especially if the effect is "overdetermined". In traditional cooperation terms, this means that such cooperation would be "contingent" or "non-necessary"; the evil would happen without my help. Again, the contribution of a cooperator to collective action may seem insignificant because of the small chance of its making a difference or because of the negligible or imperceptible effect it will have. Parfit notes that the ancient paradox known as the

Sorites problem (or Paradox of the Heap) lies at the root of this factor.[29] So, in various ways the presence of many agents and the diffusion of harm obscure the connection between the choice of an individual and resulting evil.

In a remarkably clear and penetrating book, Christopher Kutz notes the same chief problems mentioned by Parfit: overdetermination and the causal insignificance of marginal contributions. Kutz agrees that in our "collective age" these factors can combine to make individual accountability disappear altogether. Yet, he does not accept Parfit's solution, which amounts to "simply asserting an ethical link between individual acts and collective harms."[30] For Kutz, any utilitarian approach is bound to fail, for it is based upon a causal relationship between an individual's action and the effects it produces. Such an approach underlies the commonsense notions that one is accountable only for the difference one makes to a harm's occurrence and that one is accountable only if one can control the occurrence of harm. These principles will not hold in collective contexts.[31]

Kutz also rejects a Kantian solution to the problem.[32] He shows that many collective harms (such as firebombing or selling weapons to thieves) seem more acceptable the greater one's assurance that others will do likewise; on the contrary, the classic example for Kantians—lying—tends to make communication harder the more it is universalized. Besides, even if a world of universalized firebombing would be unlivable, Kutz thinks that Kantians have not explained why marginal participation is wrong. He proposes "the logic of collective action" as a complement to the Kantian perspective: "I now want to pursue the insight that marginal participation is wrong primarily by virtue of the will of the participating agent, rather than the effects of that will."[33] Focus upon the will of the participator means locating accountability in the cooperator's intention, an idea fully compatible with the traditional Catholic perspective.[34]

Complicity principle

In Kutz's view, the key to explaining individual accountability for collective action is what he calls the "Complicity Principle": "I am accountable for what others do when I intentionally participate in the wrong they do or harm they cause... independently of the actual difference I make."[35] Kutz does not simply assert this principle but tries to justify it (see his Chapters 3-5). In order to make sense of collective action it must be redescribable as the actions of the individuals involved.[36] His approach is broad enough to cover types of collective action lacking a principal agent as well as the classic case of cooperation, which Kutz treats under the rubric "facilitation", a subset of "structured collective action".

Clearly, the Complicity Principle is also broad enough to include both formal and material cooperation, although these terms are not used. Kutz realizes the need to distinguish levels of accountability; in fact, he criticizes criminal law for failing to distinguish between principal agents and accomplices. Nonetheless, Kutz means to define "participatory intention" to include participants that do not share the harmful goal but are cooperating for some other reason.[37] He writes: "I will defend the claim that agents who intentionally perform their part of some joint act, but who lack a group-intention of realizing that joint act, nonetheless intentionally perform an act as a means to the joint end."[38] Here we see the use of group intention vs. participatory intention to approximate the formal/material distinction. His preferred binomial for this purpose seems to be exclusive intentionality (that held by those interested in the goal of the collective action) vs. inclusive intentionality (that held by those participating for some other reason).[39]

Those with an inclusive intention (even the shipping clerk at a land mine company) will still have some responsibility for the evil to which they contribute. He asserts that there is a normative difference between the two sorts of involvement, but he seems at a loss to demonstrate in what it consists. At one point he observes, rather vaguely, that accountable does not necessarily mean blameworthy.[40] He wishes to avoid "some deep metaphysics of causal responsibility"[41] or falling back on the individual difference principle. Nonetheless, in the final analysis, his explication of the responsibility of different employees in the land mine company seems to hinge upon proximate/remote distinctions (what he calls a "spatial metaphor",[42] as if originating the idea) and direct participation more or less as we have described it. The latter is dubbed by Kutz the "functional" orientation of one's actions; what makes them "functionally intelligible".[43] In sum, while Kutz's analysis does not seem to advance us terribly far in the precise question under consideration in this study, it does strongly support the claim that marginal contributors often bear a responsibility that differs from that of the principal agents only in degree. Moreover, Kutz's placing of the question in a broader context and his introduction of new terminology can serve as a valuable stimulus to discussions in Catholic circles.

The need for witnesses

Both Parfit[44] and Kutz[45] argue that the world has changed in ways that make ethical reflection about collective action essential. From the perspective of Catholic moral theology, we believe that this amounts to saying that the traditional thinking on cooperation needs to be updated. The immense harm caused by large scale cooperation of a small and seemingly negligible variety argues strongly in favor of viewing much remote cooperation as morally negative. Kutz comes very close to supporting our position that all participation, however slight, is wrong if it is essentially directed to fostering the harm. He seems less able or interested in identifying and exonerating a category of cooperators that the Catholic tradition rightly calls material.

On the other hand, Kutz is less strict than Catholic theology with those making a slight but functionally relevant contribution. Not surprisingly, when the collaboration of other conscientious persons is foreseen to be lacking and the value of altruistic action is thus apparently reduced to that of a symbol, Kutz refuses to demand coherence. "It is doubtful whether any plausible construction of morality could require outcome-independent self-sacrifice."[46] In short, Kutz correctly identifies the source of the problem—multiple individual choices leading to collective harms and evil social structures—but he hesitates to demand the only solution.

Aleksander Solzhenitsyn is well-known for his view on the same reality—forced participation of a great number of marginal contributors. He credits this participation with sustaining one of the most evil social structures in history, and he boldly demanded that the solution be implemented.

> When violence breaks out amid peaceful human life—its face burns with self-assurance. It carries it thus on a banner and cries: 'I am violence! Get away, flee—I will crush you!' But violence quickly grows old. A few years pass, and it is no longer so sure of itself, and, so as to hold up, so as to appear respectable, without fail it summons to itself as support—the Lie. Indeed: violence is covered by nothing, except by Lie, and Lie can only hold up by violence. Not every day, nor on every shoulder does

> violence lay its heavy paw: it demands from us only submission to Lie, daily participation in Lie—and in that consists all loyalty. Though scorned by us, here lies the most simple, most attainable key to our liberation: *personal non-participation in Lie*! Let Lie cover all, let Lie control all, but in even the smallest degree we will be firm: let it dominate but *not through me!*[47]

Not all people will choose the path of heroism, following in the footsteps of Solzhenitsyn, Martin Luther King, and the martyrs we have mentioned. However, we do a disservice to those who would follow them by releasing them of all obligation. Courageously declaring such cooperation to be *venially sinful* provides true light for the conscience. For many, it will be the necessary encouragement to resist, and the most blessed consolation in their trials. Talk of a "coercion-induced change of obligations"[48] will leave people like Franz Jägerstätter without moral support and those who comply without an explanation for their limited but real remorse. Moreover, we must recall that failing to disclose the full moral truth and to encourage generous coherence will perpetuate the cause of woe.[49] Perhaps not so very many persons considering cooperation will need to resist for the burden of duress on all to be made light. In that same essay Solzhenitsyn reminds us that it does not take so many heroes and martyrs to destroy evil: "[we would] be amazed how quickly and helplessly the Lie falls away."

Parfit seems to think that a greater familiarity with Prisoner's Dilemmas would bring more people to act for the greater good.[50] Kutz admires but cannot "endorse martyrdom or the absolutism of Solzhenitsyn."[51] We admit that one feels guilty of a shameful temerity to suggest that such demands be made, to claim—from the safety of one's study—that the call to heroism should not be considered optional for those in difficult situations. It must, however, be recognized that there is no other way to prevent the coming to be of pernicious structures, evil empires, and corrupt cultures, nor is there any other means to destroy them. The need for witnesses to absolute moral truth is unavoidably necessary. There are many degrees of heroism and self-sacrifice, and many if not most Christians are called to some degree of it. As Pope John Paul II reminded us in *Veritatis Splendor*: "Although ... relatively few people are called [to martyrdom], there is nonetheless a consistent witness which all Christians must daily be ready to make, even at the cost of suffering and grave sacrifice."[52] As we said at the outset, Christians are not Christians unless they refuse to do evil; this is the minimum level of Christian witness, which may, at the same time, require a very high degree of virtue.

We must always remember that while moral theology describes actions to be taken in this life, the goods for which we act are not of this world. This brings hope to otherwise desperate circumstances. Let Franz Jägerstätter, inspired as he was by the spirit of God, remind us of this truth in his own simple way:

> Today one often hears it said that there is nothing to be done: if anyone says something he would end up in jail or be killed. It is true, we cannot do much to change the events of the world: one would have had to begin more than a hundred years ago. But I believe that it is never too late to save oneself, and also to win some souls for Christ as long as we have life.[53]

Notes

1   Boyle, "Collaboration and Integrity," p. 192.

2   J. H. Newman, *Apologia pro vita sua* (New York: Appleton, 1865), p. 272.

3   Consider, for example, the statement of Joannes Maria Sbogar: "Ratio est, quia qui influit scienter ad lethale, peccat lethaliter, sed famulus adjuvando herum ad luxuriam, influit scienter ad lethale, ut supponitur, ergo peccat lethaliter..." Sbogar, *Theologia radicalis*, Tract. 79, cap 1, n. 6.

4   Waffelaert, *Coopération*, p. 44.

5   L. Dewan, "St Thomas, Lying, and Venial Sin," *Thomist* 61 (1997), pp. 279–299.

6   *Ibid.*, p. 284, citing *ST* I-II, q. 87, a. 5 ad 1; q. 88, a. 4.

7   *Ibid.*, p. 284, citing *ST* I-II, q. 88, a. 1, ad 1.

8   *Ibid.*, p. 285, citing *ST* I-II, q. 78, a. 2, ad 1.

9   *Ibid.*, p. 282, fn. 13, citing *ST* II-II, q. 24, a. 10, ad 2; I-II q. 88, a. 1, ad 2 and 3. Gonzalez de Santalla will cite Bellarmine in a similar vein, saying of venial sin: "Non excludit Dei gratiam, non tollit principium vitae, sed tantum impedit aliquo modo fervorem charitatis, & ideo proprie non efficit maculam seu deformitatem." Gonzalez de Santalla, *Selectarum*, III, disp. VIII §1, n. 11, p. 108.

10   Dewan, "Lying," p. 285.

11   *Ibid.*, pp. 287, 298–299.

12   *Ibid.*, p. 290, citing *ST* II-II, q. 110, a. 4.

13   *Ibid.*, pp. 290–293.

14   Cf. *Ibid.*, p. 287.

15   Here, again, what looks like an omission "not protecting them" may be more of a commission "turning them over." However, there must be a moral option available, even if it is only to be found by those assisted by the gifts of the Holy Spirit. This is another manner by which to render palatable Billuart's conclusion that the bank clerk who hands over the keys is guilty of theft. He failed to find a moral way out of his predicament, but chose the least bad by far.

16   See St Thomas on whether an erroneous conscience binds, for instance, *De Ver.* q. 17, a. 4, ad 8.

17   "However, given the human condition, most good people, most saints (we might even say), will tell the lie, that is, will commit the venial sin." Dewan, "Lying," p. 292. I would have omitted the part

about saints, since that which makes one holy is the operation of the gifts of the Holy Spirit, and it is this which would enable one to triumph in situations that are too much for ordinary virtue.

[18] Augustine, *On the Psalms*, vol. 1, Ancient Christian Writers, trans. S. Hebgin and F. Corrigan, no. 29, pp. 53–54, (New York: Newman Press, 1960), cited by Dewan, "Lying," p. 290, fn 36.

[19] Joel Feinberg, in the introduction to a volume of essays that he edited, speaks of the two track theory as if it is the classic Catholic view as opposed to the view of Luther. He provides one example from an editorial in a Catholic newspaper that certainly exemplifies how such an impression could have been given: "... a clear distinction must be maintained between the minimum requirements of morality, beyond which there is sin, and the ideal of the evangelical counsels given by Christ. To avoid sin one does not have to be heroic. One may turn the other cheek; one is not always obliged to do so. One may go the second mile; one does not sin if he does not. One can give away one's cloak; one may keep it without culpability...." *The Providence* [Rhode Island] *Visitor*, October 19, 1961, cited by J. Feinberg, "Introduction," in *Moral Concepts*, ed. J. Feinberg, (London: Oxford University Press, 1969), p. 10.

[20] "En toute hypothèse, le théologien moraliste, en déclarant l'obligation inexistante, s'abstient de tout jugement sur la question de perfection, qu'il laisse tout entière à la ascétique." E. Dublanchy, "Cas de conscience," in *Dictionnaire de théologie catholique*, II, 2, col. 1817.

[21] "Il suo cammino è una sfida ed un incoraggiamento per tutti i cristiani che possono prendere esempio da lui, per vivere con coerenza ed impegno radicale la loro fede, anche fino alle estreme conseguenze se necessario. I beati e i santi hanno sempre dato l'esempio di cosa significhi e comporti l'essere cristiani, anche in particolari concreti momenti della storia." Homily of Cardinal José Saraiva Martins on the occasion of the beatification of the Servant of God, Franz Jägerstätter, at Linz, Austria on October 26, 2007 (http:// www.vatican.va/ roman_curia/ congregations/ csaints/ documents/ rc_con_ csaints_ doc_ 2007 1026_beatif jagerstatter_it.html, accessed on January 5, 2009).

[22] "In 1946 Bishop Fliesser wrote of his conversation with Franz Jägerstätter: 'I explained in vain to him the moral principles on the degree of responsibility that the private citizen has for the actions of the authorities, and reminded him of the much higher responsibility he had for those around him and particularly his family.'

After the war ended the bishop suppressed publication of the affair in his district." Cf. C³ - Center for Culture and Communication, http://www.c3.hu/~bocs/jager-a.htm, accessed January 12, 2009.

23 D. Parfit, *Reasons and Persons*, (Oxford: Clarendon Press, 1984), pp. 56–62.

24 *Ibid.*, p. 62.

25 Christopher Kutz provides detailed "collective action" grids demonstrating how outcomes vary depending upon the likelihood of other actors complying or not. See Kutz, *Complicity*, Chapter 6.

26 "n. 1868 Sin is a personal act. Moreover, we have a responsibility for the sins committed by others when we cooperate in them: by participating directly and voluntarily in them; by ordering, advising, praising, or approving them; by not disclosing or not hindering them when we have an obligation to do so; by protecting evildoers.n. 1869 Thus sin makes men accomplices of one another and causes concupiscence, violence, and injustice to reign among them. Sins give rise to social situations and institutions that are contrary to the divine goodness. 'Structures of sin' are the expression and effect of personal sins. They lead their victims to do evil in their turn. In an analogous sense, they constitute a 'social sin'."

27 Parfit, *Reasons and Persons*, p. 66.

28 *Ibid.*, p. 69.

29 *Ibid.*, p. 78. The problem concerns entities, like a heap of sand, which continue to exist when one grain is removed, but which will at some point cease to exist, if grains are continually removed. The paradox consists in the inability to identify any such point.

30 Cf. Kutz, *Complicity*, p. 137. Also pp. 130–131, 172.

31 *Ibid.*, pp. 116–118.

32 *Ibid.*, pp. 135–136.

33 *Ibid.*, p. 136.

34 Interestingly, while the emphasis in much of the Catholic tradition lay in *exculpating* an agent by denying the necessity of intending harm when causing harms (PDE), Kutz is concerned to *implicate* agents as intending harm even if their causing of harms is marginal, unnecessary or without effect.

35 *Ibid.*, p. 122.

36 *Ibid.*, p. 73.

37 He is searching for "what can warrant responses of accountability in the absence of causation and simple intention." *Ibid.*, p. 184.

38 *Ibid.*, p. 100.

[39] *Ibid.*, pp. 105–106. He equates this distinction with that of "direct action" vs. "complicit participation" (p. 146).

[40] *Ibid.*, p. 199.

[41] *Ibid.*, p. 139.

[42] *Ibid.*, p. 159.

[43] Cf. *Ibid.*, pp. 162–163.

[44] Parfit notes that people used to live in small communities in which a connection between individual agents' actions and repercussions on others were traceable. In the modern world, by contrast, "we can have real though small effects on thousands or millions of people ... [effects which] may be either trivial, or imperceptible. It now makes a great difference whether we continue to believe that we cannot have greatly harmed or benefited others unless there are people with obvious grounds for resentment or gratitude." Parfit, *Reasons and Persons*, p. 86.

[45] "The consolidation of social and economic life threatens the possibility of individual accountability... With respect to the collective harms that threaten our global age, all individual actions are essentially insignificant." Kutz, *Complicity*, p. 258.

[46] *Ibid.*, p. 191.

[47] From an essay, "Live not by Lies," dated February 12, 1974, the day before he was exiled to West Germany (http://www.solzhenitsyn.ru/ 01_proizvedeniya/ 10_publizistika/ 01_stat'i_i_rechi/ 01_v_sovetskom_soyuze/ 07_jzit'_ne_po_ljzi.pdf). Translation mine.

[48] Boyle, "Collaboration and Integrity," p. 194.

[49] Edmund Burke has been paraphrased as saying something to the effect that: "All that is necessary for evil to triumph is for good men to do nothing." While he would undoubtedly subscribe to this view, one of his verifiable statements is perhaps even more apropos: "When bad men combine, the good must associate; else they will fall one by one, an unpitied sacrifice in a contemptible struggle." E. Burke, *Thoughts on the Cause of the Present Discontents*, 3rd ed. (London: J. Dodsley, 1770), p. 106.

[50] "The moral solutions are, then, often best; and they are often the only attainable solutions. We therefore need the moral motives. How could these be introduced?... Our need is to make these motives stronger, and more widely spread. With this task, theory helps. Prisoner's Dilemmas need to be explained. So do their moral solutions. Both have been too little understood." Parfit, *Reasons*

   and Persons, p. 65.

51   Kutz, *Complicity*, p. 190.

52   John Paul II, *Veritatis Splendor*, 93.

53   "Oggi si sente spesso dire che non si può fare nulla: se qualcuno
     dicesse qualcosa finirebbe in carcere o verrebbe ucciso. È vero,
     non si possono cambiare di molto gli eventi del mondo: si sarebbe
     dovuto iniziare già cento e più anni fa. Ma credo non sia mai
     troppo tardi per salvare se stessi, e anche guadagnare qualche
     anima a Cristo finché abbiamo vita." P. Vanzan, "Franz Jägerstät-
     ter: il contadino che rifiutò Hitler in nome di Dio," *La Civiltà
     Cattolica* 157 (2006), II pp. 345–354, at p. 350, fn. 13.

CHAPTER 13

GENERAL CONCLUSIONS

T HE ITINERARY FOLLOWED in this study may seem to have raised more questions than it has settled. So many disagreements between brilliant and well-intentioned authors, secular and Catholic alike, have only been grazed. They will be clarified gradually, as the discussion called for by the Second Vatican Council and continued by *Veritatis Splendor* bears its fruit. We hope that the tentative positions taken in regard to the under-lying philosophical and theological questions have allowed us, nonetheless, to come to well-founded conclusions in regard to the specific theme of cooperation with evil. Indeed, if these conclusions are convincing, they may provide support for the positions assumed on the deeper issues.

We began by presenting the intellectual climate which produced the opinion on cooperation condemned by the Holy See as Proposition 51. In the context of the other condemned propositions, we concluded that the element deemed objectionable by Pope Innocent was more than the claim that *notable* duress sufficed to excuse the servant, when in fact only *extreme* duress could do so. Rather, the problem seemed to concern a deeper tendency of thinkers influenced by probabilism to attend not so much to the intrinsic moral value of the action as to the permissibility of performing it in difficult circumstances. The question of what acts *in principle* can never be justified had receded before the question of what actions *in practice* are to be excused. Those seeking to analyse a given act on a speculative level were easily branded as "rigorist", while those pointing to *incommoditas* and the opinions of reputable thinkers appeared "benign". The first attempts to interpret Innocent XI's condemnation by the anti-probabilist side were not entirely successful. We noted a persistent confusion of the order of intention (direct/indirect) with the order of causation (proximate/remote). Acts of cooperation were treated as being closer to formal, the more proximate they were.[1] Later, in the Manualist period, this confusion resulted in the dilemma concerning immediate material cooperation: as material, it should be justifiable in theory in some cases, but as immediate (indistinguishable from the evil act itself) it should be just as wrong as it is for the principal agent. We observed in Chapter 11 that this same problem continued to divide the members of the panel convened by the Catholic Health Association of the United States even in our own day.

The latter part of Chapter 3 presented the new direction set by St Alphonsus. We should emphasize that the very use of the distinction between formal and material cooperation in this study testifies to the enduring value of the holy doctor's efforts. Nonetheless, we argued that a legalist point of view inherited by Alphonsus, which essentially viewed a moral act as intention added to a physical event, meant that his solution would need to be adjusted. Chapters 5 and 6 followed the development of his approach into the modern era, with the introduction of the categories of implicitly formal cooperation and immediate material cooperation. Despite this development, we saw that both in St Alphonsus and during the Manualist period the error remained of viewing the servant's act as what he physically did (hold a ladder) combined with his reason for holding it. This inadequate

approach, which we argued was transformed by proportionalists into a much greater error, caused much formal
cooperation to be considered material. This unwarranted
expansion of the material cooperation category produced
several stress points. These weaknesses in the apparently
clear formal/material distinction correspond to more
general issues concerning intention and action. Thus, for
instance, we objected first of all to the practice of treating
an act of cooperation, which certainly appears to be a
positive contribution to a harm, as negative agency or
"failure to impede". This has much to do with the understanding of omissions and the interpretation given in the
manuals to Thomas's notion of "indirect voluntary". A
second issue regards the description of an act of cooperation prescinding from the aspect of cooperation itself,
which leads to the hasty, or rather circular, definition of
material cooperation as an action not wrong it itself.
Clarification of this matter requires further thought on
the nature of circumstances and context in regard to the
specification of the moral object. Thirdly, there is the
remarkably persistent practice of assuming that material
cooperation does not violate the third condition of the
principle of double effect. The few attempts to face the
issue head-on are guilty of circularity for the reason given
in the preceding point. A fourth weakness in the tradition
was the continuing confusion of cooperation and scandal.
It seems that the refusal to consider the harm done (e.g.
to the virgin) as a direct effect of the cooperator's action
led writers to think that cooperation would only be wrong
absolutely, if there were a direct effect on the principal
agent, inducing, confirming or somehow influencing his
bad will. Finally, the circumstance of duress was pressed
into service to cover up some of these trouble spots. Rather
than simply reduce culpability should it be objectively

established, duress was thought either to indicate the presence of material cooperation (since a forced cooperator does not *approve*) or to take away voluntariness completely, rendering the moral question moot.

During the Manualist period deeper reflection on what is now called "action theory" was mirrored by the work of British philosophers. In Chapter 4, we tried to draw from their work some insights for our problem. The key issue for "implicitly formal cooperation" concerns whether or not an evil effect is merely foreseen or somehow intended by the cooperator. Many secular thinkers, who criticize the Catholic tradition for its development of the principle of double effect, would dispute the idea that the servant could say to the girl, in essence, "I intend you no harm," while helping her attacker through the window. We concluded that they have a point. There appear to be consequences of our actions (in this case, the harm to the girl) which are not causally required for our goal (the preservation of the servant's life), yet which count as means chosen to attain our end. We agreed with the utility of a concept like "oblique intention" to describe the relation of the agent's will to consequences which are not "aimed at" by an agent, but which are caused directly by him. In this way, we rejected a separation between certain effects not aimed at and the means (in the strict sense). In other words, the claim that "the merchant doesn't intend the ruination of his goods, only getting them off the ship" is both true and not true. We argued that one must admit that the merchant destroyed the goods as a *means* to saving his ship.

In the hope that both the insufficiencies of the Manualists and the excesses of the consequentialists could be avoided, we turned to contemporary Catholic moral theologians. Responding to the crisis that broke after the appearance of *Humanae Vitae*, attempts were made to recuperate and interpret Thomistic action theory both with its insight into the centrality of intention for constituting moral action and with its realism, opposed to any form of subjectivism. Even if *Veritatis Splendor* does not work out a detailed theory of action, it clearly points to the indispensability of these two pillars. So treacherous is this terrain that even prominent, faithful theologians disagree about the interpretation of a key passage in the encyclical. In Chapters 8 and 9 we argued that Germain Grisez and Martin Rhonheimer make essentially the same error of "putting the cart before the horse" as was made by St Alphonsus in applying his formal/material distinction. Just as the saint reasoned (in modern terms) that the lack of intention of the servant to harm the girl implied that his choice was simply to hold the ladder, so Grisez and Rhonheimer emphasize the role of intention in constituting the object of the act without paying sufficient attention to whether the matter can receive such a form. They admit, of course, that there is a limit to what intention may inform a given concrete behavior, but they reject the interpretation of St Thomas which we have given, namely, that only *one* proximate intention can inform a behavior *if adequately described.*[2] In other words, we argued that the proximate intention, or moral object, is distinguished from further intentions by the fact that it is *not* up to the choice of the agent. In choosing to act, or to perform a given behavior in certain (act-specifying) circumstances, the agent *adopts*, or makes his own, a determinate proximate intention, be it good or evil.[3]

Finally, in the next chapter, we considered Steven Long's presentation of Thomistic action theory. His explanation of mixed voluntary (self-defense and the jettisoning of goods by the merchant) appeared as a promising avenue to incorporate the notion of "oblique intention" insisted upon by the secular thinkers into Catholic thought. He describes the death of an assailant as a "chosen means", which is only *praeter intentionem* because *per se* ordered to the intended end. If the agent *accidentally* orders a means to an end, both will be intended. As applied to cooperation: if the action that *de facto* facilitates the doing of evil is being posited for some other reason, to which it is *per se* ordered, then the facilitation can be considered *praeter intentionem* (and material cooperation). If it is posited because of duress, affording the facilitation sought by the principal agent will be a means chosen to the end of personal security. The harm aimed at by the principal agent will be a direct result of the cooperation offered. Even though the harm itself is not aimed at or needed by the cooperator, it will be ("obliquely") intended as a means. This, in Long's terms, is because the facilitation is not *per se* ordered to the cooperator's security.

Our position has dramatic consequences for the notion of formal cooperation with evil, the chief ones being the following:

1. While the formal/material distinction, as proposed by St Alphonsus, remains valid, a category of implicitly formal cooperation must be understood to be included therein. This implicitly formal category really constitutes the main arena of interest and debate.

2. Implicitly formal cooperation is cooperation in which the *finis operis* of the cooperator will be wrong due to direct participation in the evil activity of the principal agents. The "directness" of the contribution and the correspondingly disordered proximate intention of the cooperator will be determined neither by an exaggerated first-person stance (focusing on the cooperator's

goals or proposal) nor by an exaggerated third-person stance (focusing on the causal effects of his action) but by a consideration of the natural teleology or intrinsic meaning of the behavior itself. An informed agent performing a given behavior in certain act-specifying circumstances will necessarily act with a definite proximate intention. In other words, he will choose a definite moral object, "which determines the act of willing on the part of the acting person."[4] Actions which are so closely related to those of the principal agent as to be labeled, traditionally, "immediate" will be examples of implicitly (if not explicitly) formal cooperation. (See p. 367).

3. Duress does not turn implicitly formal cooperation into immediately material cooperation. Either the duress completely removes the cooperator's action from the realm of human acts or it does not. When it *does*, it may only be called "material" cooperation in a different sense, as in "material adultery" (see p. 346). When the duress *does not* wholly deprive the agent of responsibility (as is normally the case), the cooperator's action will remain formal cooperation.[5] The culpability may be reduced or practically eliminated, of course, but that is another question. Material cooperation, on the other hand, refers to a kind of cooperation that is not wrong in species or *ex obiecto*.

4. The proximate-remote gradations do not enter into the question of the directness of participation. Consequently, cooperative actions that are essentially ordered to bringing about the evil (formal) and those that do so accidentally (material) will both admit of being more or less significant contributors to the harm. In the case of material cooperation, the more remote the cooperation, the more likely that it will be a

prudent choice, according to traditional teaching. In the case of formal cooperation, the more remote the cooperation, the more probable that it will be but venially sinful to choose.

It may appear that these positions radically alter the landscape of cooperation. Perhaps they do. Still, we believe that our conclusions are the authentic expression of recent Magisterial statements. In this light, our conclusions can also be viewed as simply clarifying the sounder intuitions of traditional teaching. For instance, a cashier who has to handle pornographic magazines would usually be told that this is remote material cooperation, but that he has an obligation to look for another kind of work. In light of our proposals, such a person should be considered in a situation of venial sin until he did make such a change. As we pointed out before, but underline again, a proper understanding of venial sin reminds us that most people commit venial sins every day. Is it surprising that in our sinful world, many people should find themselves in jobs where they are asked to do so? There is no more reason to suppose that the pressure under which a venial sin is committed would alter the objectively sinful character of the act than would similar pressure in a case involving grave matter.

Reminding the faithful of the true character of such cooperation will be a valuable stimulus to reviving a sense of sin and an awareness that ordinary Christian life is a dramatic challenge, requiring grace and courage to meet. Moreover, the Church as a whole will begin to recognize this sad truth: the very grave cultural diseases among which we live could not exist but for the marginal yet widespread cooperation of so many of Christ's faithful. As this awareness grows among the faithful, we can expect the emergence of many heroes and heroines, leading a unified refusal to participate in vile acts. This at last will sound the death knell for the "culture of death" itself.

> *Rememoramini autem pristinos dies,in quibus illuminati*
> *magnum certamen sustinuistis passionum ...*
> *nam et vinctis compassi estis*
> *et rapinam bonorum vestrorum cum gaudio susceptistis,*
> *cognoscentes vos habere meliorem substantiam et manentem.*
> *Nolite itaque abicere confidentiam vestram,*
> *quae magnam habet remunerationem ...*

Hebrews 10:32-35[6]

Notes

[1]   This error is ascribed by St Alphonsus to Cardenas and Milante. In reaction to it he proposes his own solution. Cf. Liguori, *Theologia Moralis*, lib. II, tract. III, cap. ii, dub. v, art. iii, n. 63. However, the tendency did not thereby disappear.

[2]   *ST* I–II, q. 1, a. 3, ad 3.

[3]   A statement of Lottin confirms this view. "La définition du chancelier Philippe conserve toute sa valeur: S. Thomas s'y appuie lui-même et il la reprend au cours de son exposé en définissant le *bonum ex genere* ou *ex obiecto* par les termes: *bonitas quae est ex debita materia*. Per *materia*, en effet, on entend la *materia circa quam* qui n'est autre que l'objet ou, si l'on veut, la fin, pourvu qu'on vise le fin prochaine de l'acte, non une fin ultérieure ajoutée par l'agent moral, qui est une circonstance de l'acte." O. Lottin, "Le problème de la moralité intrinsèque d'Abélard à Saint Thomas d'Aquin," *Revue Thomiste* 39 (1934), pp. 477–515, at p. 511.

[4]   John Paul II, *Veritatis Splendor*, 78.

[5]   Accordingly, we must consider Livio Melina's conclusion to be in need of revision: "Va quindi rilevato che la cooperazione immediata si identifica con quella formale ed è pertanto sempre illecita; tuttavia può darsi una cooperazione immediata non formale

quando si è di fronte ad una costrizione. Per la verità, qui si dovrebbe dire che non si tratta più di un atto umano in senso proprio, ma in fondo è solo questione di linguaggio." Melina, "La cooperazione," p. 478.

[6]   "But recall the former days when, after you were enlightened, you endured a hard struggle with sufferings ... for you had compassion on the prisoners, and you joyfully accepted the plundering of your property, since you knew that you yourselves had a better possession and an abiding one. Therefore do not throw away your confidence, which has a great reward."

APPENDIX

WITNESSES TO
NON-COOPERATION

1. Blessed Michael Nakashima (1582–1628)[1]

MICHAEL NAKASHIMA WAS born in Machiai, in today's prefecture of Kumamoto, Japan, of non-Christian parents. He was baptized at the age of eleven by Fr John Baptist de Baeza, and as a young man, he took a private vow of chastity and to live a life of piety and penance. As Christianity was outlawed in Japan and the missionaries had to go underground, Michael invited Fr Baeza to live with him in his Nagasaki home where the latter lived in hiding for twelve years until his death in 1626. Thereafter, Michael invited another priest to live his house, although he was aware that he was taking great risk, but he considered it worthwhile, as he had the joy of frequently attending Mass. While the priests were with him, he brought Christians home for Mass and to receive the Sacraments, taking circuitous routes to confuse the spies so that they would not suspect him of helping missionaries. He continued his activity although the risk was growing greater.

Michael was received into the Society of Jesus as a Brother in 1627. In August that year he was brought before the district governor, and though nothing was proven against him, he was placed under house arrest for a year which he accepted with serenity and continued to live a penitential life.

In Nagasaki, it was customary for the people of the city to supply the wood for the fiery death punishment of missionaries. On September 3, 1628, a wood collector called at Brother Nakashima's house, but he refused to contribute, saying that he wanted no part in the unjust killing of a minister of God. When his remark was reported to the governor, Brother Nakashima was arrested, his house confiscated, and he was beaten with clubs and imprisoned. He was later stripped and beaten with clubs to get him to deny his faith, but he remained steadfast in upholding his faith and would not deny his Lord, saying: "tear me to pieces and rip my soul from my body, but you will never force that detestable word of denial from my mouth." His torturers resorted to water torture where they would pour gallons of water into his body using funnels placed in his nostrils. The torturers would then repeatedly jump on his abdomen to force the water out. Brother Nakashima remained undaunted and refused to apostatize. He wrote about this experience to a friend saying: "When the pain became too intense, I invoked our Lady, the Blessed Virgin, and my pain instantly ceased."

Brother Nakashima's repeated refusal to renounce his faith greatly enraged his persecutors and they decided to subject him to the scalding sulphurous waters at Unzen which the Japanese dubbed "the mouths of hell." On December 24, 1628, after another round of water torture to no avail, they dragged him into a shallow pool of bubbling waters and made him stand there for a while before putting him into a deeper pool by which time portions of his flesh fell from his feet. He was then put into a second pool where the bubbling waters covered his neck. When they pulled him out, Brother Nakashima was unable to walk; his body was an open wound, and in places his bones were exposed. They left him to spend the cold December night in the open, lying on hay.

Early the next morning at sunrise, the torturers were at work again, but, as Brother Nakashima was unable to stand and go to the boiling water, they devised a way of pouring the scalding fluid over his head and body. For two hours, Brother Nakashima endured the cruel treatment, and the only words that he uttered were the names of Jesus and Mary. While the Christian world was thinking of Christ's birth on earth, Brother Nakashima was thinking of his own birth in heaven, and that morning he made his way to God.

Brother Michael Nakashima was beatified by Pope Pius IX in 1867, together with 204 other martyrs.

2. Blessed Franz Jägerstätter (1907–1943)[2]

Franz Jägerstätter was born on May 20, 1907 in St Radegund, Upper Austria, to his unmarried mother, Rosalia Huber, and to Franz Bachmeier, who was killed during World War I. After the death of his natural father, Rosalia married Heinrich Jägerstätter, who adopted Franz and gave the boy his surname of Jägerstätter in 1917.

Franz received a basic education in his village's one-room schoolhouse. His step-grandfather helped with his education and the boy became an avid reader. It seems Franz was unruly in his younger years; he was, in fact, the first in his village to own a motorcycle. However, he is better known as an ordinary and humble Catholic who did not draw attention to himself.

After his marriage to Franziska in 1936 and their honeymoon in Rome, Franz grew in his faith but was not extreme in his piety. Besides his farm work Franz became the local sexton in 1936 and began receiving the Eucharist daily. He was known to refuse the customary offering for his services at funerals, preferring the spiritual and corporal works of mercy over any remuneration.

In the mid to late 1930s, while much of Austria was beginning to follow the tide of Nazism, Franz became ever more rooted in his Catholic faith and placed his complete trust in God. While carrying out his duties as husband and bread-winner for his wife and three daughters, this ordinary man began thinking deeply about obedience to legitimate authority and obedience to God, about mortal life and eternal life and about Jesus's suffering and Passion.

Franz was neither a revolutionary nor part of any resistance movement, but in 1938 he was the only local citizen to vote against the "Anschluss" (annexation of Austria by Germany), because his conscience prevailed over the path of least resistance.

Franz Jägerstätter was called up for military service and sworn in on June 17, 1940. Shortly thereafter, thanks to the intervention of his mayor, he was allowed to return to the farm. Later, he was in active service from October 1940 to April 1941, until the mayor's further intervention permitted his return home. He became convinced that participation in the war was a serious sin and decided that any future call-up had to be met with his refusal to fight.

Jägerstätter was at peace with himself despite the alarm he could have experienced witnessing the masses' capitulation to Hitler. Mesmerized by the National Socialist propaganda machine, many people knelt when Hitler made his entrance into Vienna. Catholic Churches were forced to fly the swastika flag and subjected to other abusive laws.

In February 1943, Franz was called up again for military service. He presented himself at the induction centre on March 1, 1943 and announced his refusal to fight, offering to carry out non-violent services: this was denied him.

He was held in custody at Linz in March and April, transferred to Berlin-Tegel in May and subjected to trial on July 6, 1943, when he was condemned to death for sedition. The prison chaplain was struck by the man's tranquil character. On being offered the New Testament, he replied: "I am completely bound in inner union with the Lord, and any reading would only interrupt my communication with my God."

On August 9, before being executed, Franz wrote: "If I must write ... with my hands in chains, I find that much better than if my will were in chains. Neither prison nor chains nor sentence of death can rob a man of the Faith and his free will. God gives so much strength that it is possible to bear any suffering ... People worry about the obligations of conscience as they concern my wife and children. But I cannot believe that, just because one has a wife and children, a man is free to offend God."

Franz Jägerstätter, who would not bow his head to Hitler, bowed his head to God, and the guillotine took care of the rest. He was obviously called up to serve a higher order.

Notes

[1] This short biography is taken verbatim from the website of the Jesuits of Singapore. http: // www.jesuit.org.sg/ html/ companions/ saints.martys/ december/ michael.nakashima. html, accessed January 4, 2009.

[2] This biography is taken from the Vatican website. http://www.vatican.va/ news_services/ liturgy/saints/ ns_lit_doc_20071026_jagerstatter_en.html, accessed March 23, 2009.

Bibliography

1. Magisterial documents

Denzinger, H. and A. Schönmetzer. *Enchiridion symbolorum: definitionum et declarationum de rebus fidei et morum.* Barcelona: Herder, 1973.

Congregation for the Doctrine of the Faith. "Declaration on Euthanasia, *Iura et Bona.*" *Acta Apostolicae Sedis* 72 (1980), pp. 542–552.

John Paul II. *Catechism of the Catholic Church* (October 11, 1992).

_____. *Reconciliatio et Paenitenia* (December 2, 1984). *Acta Apostolicae Sedis* 77 (1985): I, 185–275.

_____. *Veritatis Splendor* (August 6, 1993). *Acta Apostolicae Sedis* 85 (1993), pp. II, 1134–1228.

_____. *Evangelium Vitae* (March 25, 1995). *Acta Apostolicae Sedis* 87 (1995), pp. I, 401–522.

_____. "Letter to German Bishops" (January 11, 1998). *Acta Apostolicae Sedis* 90 (1998), pp. 601–607.

_____."Allocution to the Officials of the Roman Rota" (January 28, 2002). *Acta Apostolicae Sedis* 93 (2002) I, 340–346.

National Conference of Catholic Bishops. *Ethical and Religious Directives for Catholic Health Care Services.* Washington DC: United States Catholic Conference, 1995.

Pius XI. *Casti Connubii* (December 31, 1930). *Acta Apostolicae Sedis* 22 (1930), pp. 539–592.

Pius XII. "Allocution to the meeting of Italian Catholic Obstetricians" (October 29, 1951). *Acta Apostolicae Sedis* 43 (1951), pp. 835–854.

_____. "Allocution to the participants in the XXIV congress of the Italian Association of Urologists" (October 8, 1953). *Acta Apostolicae Sedis* 45 (1953), pp. 673–679.

_____. "Allocution to the directors and members of the Italian Association of Cornea Donors" (May 14, 1956). *Acta Apostolicae Sedis* 48 (1956), pp. 459–466.

_____. "Allocution to the Second World Congress on Fertility and Sterility" (May 19, 1956). In *The Human Body*, ed. The Monks of Solesmes. Boston: St Paul Editions, 1960.

2. Before 1900

Anonymous. "Letter to Diognetus." In *The Apostolic Fathers*. The Fathers of the Church, ed. Ludwig Schopp, vol. 1. New York: Christian Heritage, 1947.

Antoninus Florentinus. *Summa theologica: ad vetustiores libros exacta et correcta, adnotationibus subjectis, praelectionibus illustrata, vita auctoris aucta.* Verona: apud Carattonium, 1740.

Aquinas, T. *De Malo (Quaestiones disputatae)*; *In libros Physicorum (Commentaria in Aristotelem)*; *Quaestiones de quolibet*; *Scriptum super Sententiis*; *Summa Theologiae*. See Corpus Thomistcum Project of the University of Navarre at www.corpusthomistcum.org

Aristotle. *Nichomachean Ethics*. tr. H. Rackham. Cambridge, MA: Harvard University Press, 1982.

Augustine. *On the Psalms, vol. 1*. Ancient Christian Writers, trans. Scholastica Hebgin and Felicitas Corrigan, no. 29. New York: Newman Press, 1960.

Billuart, C. R. *Summa Sancti Thomae.* 9th ed. Paris: apud Victorem Palmé, 1847.

Bossuet, J-B. *Oeuvres complètes de Bossuet*, ed. F. Lachat. Paris: Louis Vives, 1885.

Burke, E. *Thoughts on the Cause of the Present Discontents.* 3rd ed. London: J. Dodsley, 1770.

Cajetan, T. de Vio. *Summula peccatorum.* Leiden: G. a Portonarijs, 1565.

Cardenas, J. de. *Crisis theologica.* Venice: Pezzana, 1700.

Castro Palao, F. *Operis moralis: de virtutibus et vitiis contrariis.* Venice: Pezzana, 1690.

Concina, D. *Theologia christiana dogmatico-moralis.* Rome: apud Simonem Occhi, 1749–1751.

Duarte, D. *Brevis expositio propositionum.* Rome: ex typis haered. Corbelletti, 1712.

Elbel, B. *Theologia moralis decalogis.* Augsburg: sumptibus Mathias Wolff, 1733–1741.

Foot, P. "Hume on Moral Judgement." In *Virtues and Vices and Other Essays in Moral Philosophy,* pp. 74–80. Oxford: Clarendon Press, 2002.

Genet, F. *Theologia moralis, juxta sacrae scripturae, canonum, & SS. Patrum mentem.* 2d ed. Lat. Venice: apud Paulum Balleonium, 1705.

Gonzalez de Santalla, T. *Selectarum disputationum ex universa theologia scholastica.* Salamanca: apud Lucam Perez, 1680–1686.

_____. *Fundamentum theologiae moralis: id est, Tractatus theologicus de recto usu opinionum probabilium.* Rome: J. J. Komarek, 1694.

Gregory of Valencia, *Commentariorum theologicorum tomi 4.* Ingolstadt: Sartorius, 1603.

Kugler, J. *Brevissima atque acuratissima explicatio LXV Propositionum ab Innoc. XI damnatarum.* Pavia: apud Petrum Antonium Magrium, 1714.

Lacroix, C. *Theologia moralis antehac exprobatis auctoribus.* Koln: apud Servatium Noethen, 1710–1720.

Laymann, P. *Theologia moralis quinque libros complectens.* Lyon: Aubin, 1681.

Liguori, A. M. de. *Instruzione e practica pei Confessori.* Milan: Volpato, 1855.

_____. *Theologia moralis.* 9th ed. (Gaudé). Rome: Vatican, 1905.

_____. *Practica del confessore per ben esercitare il suo ministero.* Modena: Tip. Immacolata Concezione, 1948.

Lobkowitz, J. C. *Theologia moralis fundamentalis.* Lyons: Laurentii Anisson, 1657.

Lumbier, R. *Observationes theologicae morales.* Barcelona: typ. Mathevat, 1682.

Mandonnet, P. F. "Le Décret d'Innocent XI contre le Probabilisme." *Revue Thomiste* 9 (1901), pp. 460–481.

Masius, L. *Incommoda probabilismi,* 2nd ed. Valencia: apud Josephum Thomam Lucas, 1767.

Mazzotta, N. *Theologia moralis in quinque tomos distributa.* Venice: typ. Remondiniana, 1760.

Medina, B. *Expositio in primam secundae...d. Thomae Aquinatis.* Venice: apud Bernardum Basam, 1590.

Mercorus, J. *Basis totius moralis teologiae, hoc est praxis opinionum limitata: Adversus nimis emollientes, aut plus aequo exasperantes iugum Christi.* Mantua: apud Osanas, 1658.

Milante, P. T. *Exercitationes dogmatico–morales in propositiones proscriptas.* Naples: ex typographia Januarii, 1738–1740.

Moya, M. *Adversus quorundam expostulationes contra nonnullas Iesuitarum opiniones morales.* Bamburg: Nicolaum Bua, 1657.

Newman, J. H. *Apologia pro vita sua.* New York: Appleton, 1865.

Pascal, B. *Pensées et les Provinciales.* Paris: Booking International, 1995.

Roncaglia, C. *Universa moralis theologia.* Venice: typ. Francisci Pitteri, 1740.

Salmaticenses. *Cursus theologiae moralis.* Madrid: apud haeredes D. Michaelis Francisci Rodriguez, 1751.

Sanchez, T. *Operis moralis in praecepta Decalogi tomus.* Lyons: Laurentii Anisson, 1661.

Sbogar, J. M. *Theologia radicalis,* 3rd ed. Prague: Typ. Caroli Jannis Hraba, 1725.

Sporer, P. *Theologiae moralis super decalogum.* Venice: apud Nicolaum Pezzana, 1726.

Tamburini, T. *Explicatio decalogi duabus distincta partibus.* Lyons: Ioan. Ant. Huguatan, 1659.

Thoreau, H. D. *Walden and On the Duty of Civil Disobedience.* New York: Collier, 1962.

Tournely, H. de—P. Collet. *Universa moralis theologia, sive Praelectionum theologicum.* Venice: Pezzana, 1736–1758.

Trotta, B. *Brevis et clara expositio et impugnatio omnium et singularum propositionum,* Neapoli, 1707.

Vitoria, F. de. *Relecciones teologicas.* In *Obras,* vol. 198. Madrid: La Editorial Catolica, 1960.

Viva, D. *Damnatae theses ab Alexandro VII, Innocentio XI, & Alexandro VIII,* 9th ed. Padua: apud Joannem Manfre, 1720.

Waffelaert, G. J. *Ètude de théologie morale sur la coopération et sur l'Espèce morale du Scandale.* Bruges: Vandenberghe-Denaux, 1883.

3. After 1900

Abbá, G. *Felicità, vita buona e virtù.* Rome: Libreria Ateneo Salesiana, 1989.

Aertnys, J. and C. Damen. *Theologia moralis secundum doctrinam S. Alfonsi de Ligorio Doctoris Ecclesiae,* 17th ed. Rome: Marietti, 1956.

Alonso, V. M. *El principio del doble efecto en los commentadores de Santo Tomas desde Cayetano hasta los Salmanticenses.* Rome: Pontifical Gregorian University, 1937.

Amman, E. "Laxisme." In *Dictionnaire de théologie catholique,* ed. A.Vacant and E. Mangenot, IX i, col. 82. Paris: Librairie Letouzey et Ané, 1938.

Annas, J. "How basic are basic actions?" *Proceedings of the Aristotelian Society* 78 (1977–78), pp. 195–213.

Anscombe, G. E. M. "Modern Moral Philosophy." *Philosophy* 33 (1958), pp. 1–19.

_____. "On Brute Facts." *Analysis* 18 (1958), pp. 69–72.

_____. *Intention.* Oxford: Blackwell, 1963.

_____. "Under a Description." *Nous* 13 (1979), pp. 219–233.

_____. "The Two Kinds of Error in Action." In *Ethics, Religion and Politics: Collected Philosophical Papers,* Volume III, 3–9. Minneapolis: University of Minnesota Press, 1981.

_____. "Medalist's Address: Action, Intention, and 'Double Effect'." In *The Doctrine of Double Effect: Philosophers Debate a Controversial Moral Principle,* ed. P. A. Woodward, 50–66. Notre Dame, IN: University of Notre Dame Press, 2001.

_____. "War and Murder." In *The Doctrine of Double Effect: Philosophers Debate a Controversial Moral Principle,* ed. P. A. Woodward, 247–260. Notre Dame, IN: University of Notre Dame Press, 2001.

Ashley, B. and K. O'Rourke. *Health Care Ethics: a theological analysis,* 3rd ed. St Louis, MO: Catholic Health Association of United States, 1989.

_____. *Health Care Ethics: a theological analysis.* 4th ed. Washington DC: Georgetown University Press, 1997.

Aulisio, M. P. "In Defense of the Intention/Foresight Distinction." American Philosophical Quarterly 32 (1995), pp. 341–353.

_____. "On the Importance of the Intention/Foresight Distinction." *American Catholic Philosophical Quarterly* 72 (1996), pp. 189–205.

Austin, J. L. "A Plea for Excuses." In *The Philosophy of Action*, ed. Alan R. White, pp. 19–42. London: Oxford University Press, 1968.

Baier, A. C. "Act and Intent." *Journal of Philosophy* 67 (1970), pp. 648–658.

Ballerini, A. Vindiciae alphonsianae seu Doctoris Ecclesiae s. Alphonsi M. de Ligorio doctrina moralis vindicata a plurimis oppugnationibus, cura et studio quorumdam theologorum e Congregatione SS. Redemptoris. Rome: Propaganda Fide, 1873.

Beabout, G. "Morphine Use for Terminal Cancer Patients: An Application of the Principle of Double Effect." In *The Doctrine of Double Effect: Philosophers Debate a Controversial Moral Principle*, ed. P. A. Woodward, 298–311. Notre Dame, IN: University of Notre Dame Press, 2001.

Belmans, T. *Le sens objectif de l'agir humain: Pour relire la morale conjugale de Saint Thomas*, Studi Tomistici, vol. 8. Vatican City: Vatican Press, 1980.

_____. "Saint Thomas et la notion de 'moindre mal'." *Revue Thomiste* 83 (1983), pp. 40–57.

Bennett, J. F. *Events and their Names*. New York: Oxford University Press, 1988.

Beylard, H. "Le péché philosophique." *Nouvelle revue théologique* 62 (1935), pp. 591–616.

Boelaars, H. "Riflessioni sull'atto umano effettivo." *Studia Moralia* 13 (1975), pp. 109–142.

Bouquillon, T. J. "Moral Theology at the End of the Nineteenth Century." In *The Historical Development of Fundamental Moral Theology in the United States*, ed. Charles Curran and Richard McCormick, 91–114. Readings in Moral Theology, vol. 11. New York: Paulist Press, 1999.

Bourke, V. J. *History of Ethics.* Garden City, NY: Doubleday, 1968.

Boyle, J. M. "*Praeter Intentionem* in Aquinas." *Thomist* 42 (1978), pp. 649–665.

_____. "Human Action, Natural Rhythms, and Contraception: a response to Noonan." *The American Journal of Jurisprudence* 25 (1980), pp. 32–46.

_____. "Collaboration and Integrity: how to think clearly about moral problems of cooperation." In *Issues for a Catholic Bioethics*, ed. Luke Gormally, pp. 187–199. London: Linacre Centre, 1999.

_____. "Toward Understanding the Principle of Double Effect." In *The Doctrine of Double Effect: Philosophers Debate a Controversial Moral Principle*, ed. P. A. Woodward, pp. 7–20. Notre Dame, IN: University of Notre Dame Press, 2001.

Brock, S. L. *Action and Conduct: Thomas Aquinas and the Theory of Action*, Edinburgh: T&T Clark, 1998.

_____. "*Veritatis Splendor* §78, St Thomas, and (Not Merely) Physical Objects of Moral Action." *Nova et Vetera*, English Edition, 6 (2008), pp. 1–62.

Bucceroni, J. *Institutiones theologiae moralis secundum doctrinam S. Thomae et S. Alfonsi*, Rome: Pontifical Institute of Pius IX, 1914.

Cataldo, P. J. "Compliance with contraceptive insurance mandates: licit or illicit cooperation in evil?" National Catholic Bioethics Quarterly 4, no. 1 (Spr 2004), pp. 103–130.

Catholic Health Association of the United States. "Report on a Theological Dialogue on the Principle of Cooperation." *Health Progress* 88 (2007), pp. 68–69 [Summary with link to full text at www. chausa.org/coopdialogue].

Cavanaugh, T. A. "The Ethical Relevance of the Intended/Foreseen Distinction." Philosophical Papers 25 (1996), pp. 171–188.

_____. "Aquinas's Account of Double Effect." Thomist (1997), pp. 107–121.

_____. *Double-Effect Reasoning: Doing Good and Avoiding Evil*, New York: Oxford University Press, 2006.

Cessario, R. *Introduction to Moral Theology*, Washington, DC: Catholic University of America Press, 2001.

Chisholm, R. M. "The Structure of Intention." *Journal of Philosophy* 67 (1970), pp. 633–647.

Clark, P. A. "Morphine vs. ABT–594: A Reexamination by the Principle of Double Effect." Linacre Quarterly 70 (May 2003), pp. 109–120.

Cole, B. "Is the Moral Species of Craniotomy a Direct Killing or a Saving of Life?" *Nova et Vetera*, English edition , vol. 3, No.4 (2005), pp. 689–702.

Connery, J. R. "Grisez on Abortion." *Theological Studies* 31(1970), pp. 170–176.

_____. *Abortion: the Development of the Roman Catholic Perspective.* Chicago: Loyola University Press, 1977.

Coughlin, J. J. "Lawyers and cooperation with evil in divorce cases." In The Catholic Citizen: debating the issues of justice: proceedings from the 26th annual conference of the Fellowship of Catholic Scholars, September 26–28, 2003, Arlington, Virginia, ed. K. D. Whitehead, pp. 151–164. South Bend, IN: St Augustine's Press, 2004.

Crawford, D. S. "Conjugal Love, Condoms, and HIV/AIDS." *Communio* (Fall 2006), pp. 502–512.

Curran, C. E. "Cooperation: Toward a Revision of the Concept and Its Application." *Linacre Quarterly*, 41 (Aug 1974), pp. 152–167.

D'Arcy, E. *Human Acts: An essay in their Moral Evaluation.* Oxford: Clarendon Press, 1963.

Danto, A. C. "Basic Actions." *American Philosophical Quarterly* 2 (1965), pp. 141–148.

Davidson, D. "Agency." In *Essays on Actions and Events*, by Donald Davidson, pp. 43–62. Oxford: Oxford University Press, 1980.

Davis, H. *Moral and Pastoral Theology*. London: Sheed and Ward, 1958.

Davis, N. "The Doctrine of Double Effect: Problems of Interpretation." In *The Doctrine of Double Effect: Philosophers Debate a Controversial Moral Principle*, ed. P. A. Woodward, pp. 119–142. Notre Dame, IN: University of Notre Dame Press, 2001.

Dedek, J. F. *"Intrinsically evil acts: an historical study of the mind of St Thomas." Thomist* 43 (1979), pp. 385–413.

Deman, Th. "Probabilisme." In *Dictionnaire de théologie catholique, ed.* A.Vacant and E. Mangenot, XIII–i, 417–619. Paris: Librairie Letouzey et Ané, 1938.

Dewan, L. "St Thomas, Lying, and Venial Sin." *Thomist* 61 (1997), pp. 279–299.

DiIanni, A. "The Direct/Indirect Distinction in Morals." In *Moral Norms and Catholic Tradition*, ed. Charles Curran and Richard McCormick, 215–243. Readings in Moral Theology, No. 1. New York: Ramsey, 1979.

Dilman, I. *Matter and Mind: two essays in epistemology.* London: MacMillan, 1975.

Donagan, A. *The Theory of Morality*, Chicago: Chicago University Press, 1977.

Dublanchy, E. "Coopération." In *Dictionnaire de théologie catholique, ed.* A.Vacant and E. Mangenot, III, 1762–1770. Paris: Librairie Letouzey et Ané, 1938.

Duff, R. A. "Absolute Principles and Double Effect." *Analysis* 36 (1976), pp. 68–80.

_____. *Intention, Agency and Criminal Liability*. Oxford: Blackwell, 1990.

Ethicists, The. "Cooperating with Non-Catholic Partners." *Ethics and Medics* 23 (1998), pp. 1–5.

Fabbro, R. *Cooperation in evil: a Consideration of the Traditional Doctrine from the Point of View of the Contemporary Discussion About the Moral Act.* Rome: Pontifical Gregorian University, 1989.

Fahey, M. "Janssens, Louis 1908–2001." Theological Studies, 63 (2002), pp. 1–2.

Fanfani, L. J. *Manuale theoretico-practicum theologiae moralis ad mentem D. Thomae.* Rome: Ferrari, 1950.

Feinberg, J. "Introduction." In *Moral Concepts*, ed. Joel Feinberg. London: Oxford University Press, 1969.

Ferreres, J. *Casus conscientiae.* Barcelona: Eugenii Subirana, 1908.

Finance, J. de. *Essai sur l'agir humain.* Rome: Culture et Vérité, 1997.

Finnis, J. M. "Intention and side-effects." In *Liability and Responsibility: essays in law and morals*, ed. R. G. Frey and C. W. Morris, pp. 32–64. Cambridge: Cambridge University Press, 1991.

_____. "Object and Intention in Moral Judgment according to Aquinas." Thomist 55 (1991), pp. 1–27.

_____. *Aquinas: Moral, Political, and Legal Theory.* Oxford: Oxford University Press, 1998.

_____ and G. Grisez. "The Basic Principles of Natural Law: A Reply to Richard McCormick." *American Journal of Jurisprudence* 26 (1981), pp. 21–32.

_____, G. Grisez, and J. M. Boyle. "*Direct* and *Indirect*: A Reply to Critics of our Action Theory." *Thomist* 65 (2001), pp. 1–44.

_____, J. M. Boyle, and G. Grisez. *Nuclear Deterrence, Morality, and Realism.* Oxford: Clarendon, 1987.

Fisher, A. "Cooperation in Evil." *Catholic Medical Quarterly 44 (Feb.* 1994), pp. 15–22.

_____. "Cooperation in Evil: Understanding the Issues." In *Cooperation, Complicity and Conscience: Problems in Law and Public Policy,* ed. Helen Watt, pp. 27–64. London: Linacre Centre, 2005.

Flannery, K. L. "What is included in a Means to an End?" *Gregorianum* 74 (1993), pp. 499–513.

_____. *Acts amid Precepts: the Aristotelian Logical Structure of Thomas Aquinas's Moral Theory.* Washington, DC: Catholic University of America, 2001.

_____. "The Multifarious Moral Object of Thomas Aquinas." *Thomist* 67 (2003), pp. 95–118.

_____. "Placing Oneself 'In the Perspective of the Acting Person': *Veritatis Splendor* and the Nature of the Moral Act." In *Live the Truth: the Moral Legacy of John Paul II in Catholic Health Care,* ed. E. J. Furton, pp. 47–67. Philadelphia: National Catholic Bioethics Center, 2005.

_____. "The Field of Moral Action according to Thomas Aquinas." *Thomist* 69 (2005), pp. 1–30.

_____. "*The Teleological Grammar of the Moral Act* by Steven Long." *Thomist* 72 (2008), pp. 321–325.

Foot, P. "Morality, Action, and Outcome." In *The Doctrine of Double Effect: Philosophers Debate a Controversial Moral Principle,* ed. P. A. Woodward, pp. 67–82. Notre Dame, IN: University of Notre Dame Press, 2001.

_____. "The Problem of Abortion and the Doctrine of the Double Effect." In *The Doctrine of Double Effect: Philosophers Debate a Controversial Moral Principle,* ed. P. A. Woodward, pp. 143–155. Notre Dame, IN: University of Notre Dame Press, 2001.

Garrigou-Lagrange, R. *De virtutibus theologicis.* Turin: Berruti, 1949.

Genicot, E. *Theologiae moralis institutiones,* 3ʳᵈ ed. Louvain: Polleunis et Ceuterick, 1900.

Gerardi, R. *Storia della morale: Interpretazioni teologiche dell'esperienza cristiana.* Bologna: Edizioni Dehoniane, 2003.

Ghoos, J. "L'acte à double effet, étude de théologie positive." Ephemerides theologicae Lovanienses 27 (1951), pp. 30–52.

Gilby, T. "Ends and objectives." In *Summa Theologiae,* vol. 18, app., pp. 176–79. London: Blackfriars, 1970.

Gonzalez, A. M. *Moral, razón y naturaleza: una investigación sobre Tomás de Aquino.* Pamplona: Eunsa, 1998.

Gormally, L. "Marriage and the Prophylactic Use of Condoms." *National Catholic Bioethics Quarterly* 5, no. 4 (Win 2005), pp. 735–49.

_____. "Personal and social responsibility in the context of the defence of human life: the question of cooperation in evil." In *Christian Conscience in Support of the Right to Life: Proceedings of the Thirteenth Assembly of the Pontifical Academy for Life, Vatican City, 23–25 February 2007,* eds. Elio Sgreccia and J. Laffitte, pp. 92–111. Vatican City State: Libreria editrice Vaticana, 2008.

Grisez, G. *Contraception and the Natural Law.* Milwaukee: Bruce, 1964.

_____. "A New Formulation of a Natural-Law Argument against Contraception." *Thomist,* 30 (1966), pp. 343–361.

_____. *Abortion: The Myths, the Realities, and the Arguments.* New York: Corpus Books, 1970.

_____. "Public Funding of Abortion: a reply to Richard A. McCormick." *Homiletic and Pastoral Review,* 85 (June 1985), pp. 32–51.

_____, J. Boyle, J. Finnis and W. E. May, "Every Marital Act Ought to be Open to New Life: Towards a Clearer Understanding." *Thomist* 52 (1988), pp. 365–426.

_____. *The Way of the Lord Jesus. Vol. 1, Christian Moral Principles*. Chicago: Franciscan Herald Press, 1983.

_____. *The Way of the Lord Jesus. Vol. 2, Living a Christian Life*. Quincy, IL: Franciscan Press, 1993.

_____. *The Way of the Lord Jesus. Vol. 3, Difficult Moral Questions*. Quincy, IL: Franciscan Press, 1997.

Guevin, B. "The Conjoined Twins of Malta: direct or indirect killing?" National Catholic Bioethics Quarterly 1, no. 3 (Aut 2001), pp. 397–405.

_____. "A Debate on Condoms and AIDS." National Catholic Bioethics Quarterly 5, no. 3 (Spr 2005), pp. 37–39.

Gury, J.–P. *Compendium theologiae moralis*. Rome: Polyglotta, 1878.

Haldane, J. (ed.). *Mind, Metaphysics and Value in the Thomistic and Analytic Traditions*. Notre Dame, IN: University of Notre Dame Press, 2002.

Häring, B. *The Law of Christ*, tr. Edwin G. Kaiser. Westminister, MD: Newman Press, 1961.

Hart, H. L. A. "Problems of Philosophy of Law." In *Encyclopedia of Philosophy*, ed. P. Edwards, VI, 267–8. New York: Macmillan, 1967.

_____. *Punishment and Responsibility: two essays in the philosophy of law*. Oxford: Oxford University Press, 1968.

Hendriks, N. *Le moyen mauvais pour obtenir une fin bonne. Essai sur la troisième condition du principe de l'acte à double effet*. Studia Universitatis S. Thomae in Urbe, v. 12. Rome: Herder, 1981.

_____. "La contraception artificielle: conflit de devoirs ou acte à double effet." *Nouvelle revue théologique* 104 (1982), pp. 396–413.

Hittinger, R. "The Pope and the Theorists." *Crisis* 11 (1993), pp. 31–36.

Hoffmann, T. "Moral Action as Human Action: End and object in Aquinas in comparison with Abelard, Lombard, Albert, and Duns Scotus." *Thomist* 67 (2003), pp. 73–94.

Hoose, B. *Proportionalism: The American Debate and its European Roots.* Washington, DC: Georgetown University Press, 1987.

_____. "Circumstances, Intentions and Intrinsically Evil Acts." In *The Splendor of Accuracy: an examination of the assertions made by Veritatis Splendor,* ed. J. Selling and J. Jans, pp. 136–152. Kampen, Netherlands: Kok Pharos Publishing House, 1994.

Janssens, L. "Ontic Evil and Moral Evil." In *Moral Norms and Catholic Tradition,* ed. Charles Curran and Richard McCormick, pp. 40–93. Readings in Moral Theology, No. 1. New York: Ramsey, 1979.

Jensen, S. J. "A Long Discussion regarding Steven A. Long's Interpretation of the Moral Species," *Thomist* 67 (2003), pp. 623–643.

Jonsen, A. R.—Stephen Toumlin. *The Abuse of Casuistry.* Berkeley: University of California Press, 1988.

Jordan, J. "The Doctrine of Double Effect and Affirmative Action." In *The Doctrine of Double Effect: Philosophers Debate a Controversial Moral Principle,* ed. P. A. Woodward, pp. 234–238. Notre Dame, IN: University of Notre Dame Press, 2001.

Jorio, T. A. *Theologia moralis,* 4th ed. Naples: M. D'Auria Editore Pontificia, 1953.

Kaczor, C. R. "Double Effect Reasoning from Jean Pierre Gury to Peter Knauer." *Theological Studies* 59 (1998), pp. 297–316.

Kaveny, M. C. "Appropriation of Evil: Cooperation's Mirror Image." *Theological Studies* 61 (2000), pp. 280–313.

_____ and J. F. Keenan. "Ethical Issues in Health Care Restructuring." *Theological Studies* 56 (1995), pp. 136–150.

Kenny, A. "Happiness." In *Moral Concepts*, ed. J. Feinberg, pp. 43–52. London: Oxford University Press, 1969.

_____. "History of Intention in Ethics." In *The Anatomy of the Soul: Historical Essays in the Philosophy of Mind*, by Anthony Kenny. Oxford: Blackwell, 1973.

Klueg, F. E. "Sin, cooperation in." In *New Catholic Encyclopedia*, 13, pp. 245–246. New York: McGraw Hill, 1967.

Knauer, P. "La détermination du bien et du mal moral par le principe du double effet." *Nouvelle revue théologique* 87 (1965), pp. 356–376.

Kopfensteiner, T. "The Meaning and Role of Duress in the Cooperation in Wrongdoing." *Linacre Quarterly* 70 (2003), pp. 150–158.

_____. "For Reflection: A Sample Case Study on Cooperation." In *Report on a Theological Dialogue on the Principle of Cooperation*, Catholic Health Association, 2007, published online at www. chausa.org/coopdialogue.

Kramer, H. G. *The Indirect Voluntary or Voluntarium in Causa*. Washington DC: Catholic University of America, 1935.

Kravesac, E. "The Good that We Intend, and the Evil that We Do: a new look at *Praeter Intentionem* in Aquinas." *Angelicum* 79 (2002), pp. 833–854.

_____. "Can Effects that are Inevitable and Instrumental be *Praeter Intentionem*?: Another Look at Aquinas's understanding of 'Sit Proportionatus Fini'." *Angelicum* 82 (2005), pp. 77–88.

Kutz, C. *Complicity: Ethics and Law for a Collective Age*. Cambridge: Cambridge University Press, 2000.

Lee, P. *Abortion and Unborn Human Life*. Washington, DC: Catholic University of America, 1996.

Lehmkuhl, A. *Theologia moralis*. Freiburg: Herder, 1887.

Long, S. A. "St Thomas Aquinas through the Analytic Looking Glass." *Thomist* 65 (2001), pp. 259–300.

_____. "A Brief Disquisition regarding the Nature of the Object of the Moral Act." *Thomist* 67 (2003), pp. 45–71.

_____. *The Teleological Grammar of the Moral Act.* Naples, FL: Ave Maria University, 2007.

_____. "The False Theory Undergirding Condomitic Exceptionalism: A Response to William F. Murphy Jr. and Rev. Martin Rhonheimer." *National Catholic Bioethics Quarterly 8, no. 4* (Win 2008), pp. 709–731.

_____. "*Veritatis Splendor* §78 and the Teleological Grammar of the Moral Act." *Nova et Vetera* 6 (Win 2008), pp. 139–156.

Lottin, O. "Le problème de la moralité intrinsèque d'Abélard à Saint Thomas d'Aquin." *Revue Thomiste* 39 (1934), pp. 477–515.

Luscombe, D. E. *Peter Abelard's Ethics.* Oxford: Clarendon Press, 1971.

Mangan, J. T. "A Historical Analysis of the Principle of Double Effect." *Theological Studies* 10 (1949), pp. 41–61.

Mausbach, J. and G. Ermecke. *Teología moral católica*, 2d ed. Pamplona: Ediciones Universidad de Navarra, 1971; orig. *Katholische Moraltheologie*, 9th ed. Münster: Aschendorff-shche Verlagsbuchchandlung, 1959.

May, W. E. "*Aquinas and Janssens on the Moral Meaning of Human Acts.*" *Thomist* 48 (1984), pp. 566–606.

_____. "Using Condoms to Prevent HIV." *National Catholic Bioethics Quarterly* 4, no. 4 (Win 2004), pp. 667–668.

_____. Catholic Bioethics and the Gift of Human Life, 2nd ed. Huntington, IN: Our Sunday Visitor, 2008.

McCormick, R. A. "Ambiguity in Moral Choice." In *Doing Evil to Achieve Good*, eds. Richard A. McCormick and Paul Ramsey, pp. 7–53. Chicago: Loyola University Press, 1973.

_____. "Medicaid and Abortion." *Theological Studies* 45 (1984), pp. 715–721.

_____. "Document Begets Many Legitimate Moral Questions." *National Catholic Reporter* 29: 17 (Oct 15 1993): p. 17.

_____. "Moral Theology 1940–1989: an Overview" In *The Historical Development of Fundamental Moral Theology in the United States*, ed. Charles Curran and Richard A. McCormick, 46–72. Readings in Moral Theology, vol. 11. New York: Paulist Press, 1999.

McEvoy, J. "The Teleological Perspective upon Nature." In *Finalité et intentionnalité: doctrine thomiste et perspectives modernes, ed.* Jacques Follon and James McEvoy, pp. 1–8. Louvain-la-Neuve: Editions de l'Institut Supérieur de Philosophie, 1992.

McHugh, J. and C. Callan. *Moral Theology: a complete course.* London: Herder, 1929.

McIntyre, A. "Doing Away with the Double Effect." *Ethics* 111 (2001), pp. 219–255.

Meiland, J. W. *The Nature of Intention.* London: Methuen, 1970.

Melina, L. "*La cooperazione con azione moralmente cattive contro la vita umana.*" In *Commento interdisciplinare alla 'Evangelium Vitae'*, ed. E. Sgreccia and R. Lucas Lucas, pp. 467–490. Vatican City: Libreria Editrice Vaticana, 1997.

Merkelbach, B. H. *Summa theologiae moralis ad mentem D. Thomae*, 10th ed. Bruges: Desclée Brouwer, 1956.

Morlino, R. C. *The Principle of the Lesser of Evils in Today's Conflict Situations: new challenges to moral theology from a pluralistic society.* Rome: Pontifical Gregorian University, 1990.

Murphy, W. F. "*Veritatis Splendor* and 'Traditionally Naturalistic' Thomism: the object as proximate end of the acting person as a test case." *Studia Moralia* 45 (2007), pp. 185–216.

Murtagh, J. *Intrinsic evil: an examination of this concept and its place in current discussions on absolute moral norms.* Rome: Pontifical Gregorian University,1973.

Noldin H. and A. Schmitt. *Summa theologiae moralis iuxta codicem iuris canonici.* Regensburg: Oeniponte/Lipsiae, 1941.

Noonan, J. T. "Natural Law, the Teaching of the Church and Contraception." *The American Journal of Jurisprudence* 25 (1980), pp. 16–37.

Oleson, C. "Nature, 'Naturalism', and the Immorality of Contraception: A Critique of Fr Rhonheimer on Condom Use and Contraceptive Intent." *National Catholic Bioethics Quarterly* 6, no. 4 (Win 2006), pp. 719–729.

Palazzini, P. "Cooperazione." In *Encyclopedia cattolica*, 496–500. Vatican City: Ente per l'Enc. Cat. e per il libro Cattolico, 1950.

_____. *Dictionarium morale et canonicum.* Rome: Officium libri catholici, 1966.

_____ and A. Jorio, *Casus conscientiae propositi ac resoluti a pluribus theologicis ac canonistis urbis.* Rome: Marietti, 1958.

Parfit, D. *Reasons and Persons.* Oxford: Clarendon Press, 1984.

Peschke, K. H. *Christian Ethics: Moral Theology in the Light of Vatican II, vol. 1, General Ethics, revised ed.* Alcester: Neale, 1986.

Pilsner, J. *The Specification of Human Actions in St Thomas Aquinas.* Oxford: Oxford Theological Monographs, 2006.

Pinckaers, S. "La structure de l'acte humain suivant Saint Thomas." *Revue thomiste*, 55 (1955), pp. 393–412.

_____. "Le rôle de la fin dans l'action morale selon Saint Thomas Aquin." *Revue des sciences philosophiques et théologiques* 45 (1961), pp. 393–421.

_____. "La question des actes intrinsèquement mauvais et le 'proportionalisme'." *Revue Thomiste* 82 (1982), pp. 181–212; 84 (1984), pp. 618–24.

_____. "Le probléme de l'intrinsece malum." *Frieb. Zeitschrift für Phil. und Theol.* 29 (1982), pp. 373–388.

_____. *The Sources of Christian Ethics.* Edinburgh: T&T Clark, 1995; orig. *Les sources de la morale chrétienne.* Fribourg: University Press Fribourg, 1985.

_____. *Ce qu'on ne peut jamais faire: la question des actes intrinsèquement mauvais—histoire et discussion.* Paris: Cerf, 1986.

Pitcher, G. "'In Intending' and Side Effects." *Journal of Philosophy* (1970), pp. 659–668.

Porter, J. "The Moral Act in *Veritatis Splendor* and Aquinas's *Summa Theologiae*: A Comparative Analysis." In *The Historical Development of Fundamental Moral Theology in the United States,* ed. C. Curran and R. McCormick, 219–241. Readings in Moral Theology, vol. 11. New York: Paulist Press, 1999.

Privitera, S. "Principi morali tradizionali." In *Nuovo dizionario morale,* eds. F. Compagnoni, G. Piana and S. Privitera, pp. 993–994. Milan: Edizioni San Paolo, 1990.

Prümmer, D. M. *Manuale theologiae moralis secundum principia S. Thomae Aquinatis,* 6th ed. Fribourg: Herder, 1931.

Reichberg, G. M. "Aquinas on Defensive Killing: A Case of Double Effect?" *Thomist* 69 (2005), pp. 341–370.

Rey-Mermet, T. *Moral choices: the Moral Theology of Saint Alfonsus Liguori.* Liguori, MO: Liguori Press, 1998.

Rhonheimer, M. *Natural Law and Practical Reason: a Thomistic View of Moral Autonomy,* trans. G. Malsbary. New York: Fordham University Press, 2000; orig. *Natur als Grundlage der Moral: Die personale Struktur des Naturgesetzes bei Thomas von Aquin: eine Auseinandersetzung mit autonomer und teleologischer Ethik.* Innsbruck: Tyrolia-Verlag, 1987.

_____. "Contraception, Sexual Behavior, and Natural Law." *Linacre Quarterly* (1989), pp. 20–57.

_____. "Intrinsically Evil Acts and the Moral Viewpoint: clarifying a central teaching of *Veritatis Splendor.*" *Thomist* 58 (1994), pp. 1–39.

_____. *La prospettiva della morale: fondamenti dell'etica filos-ofica*. Rome: Armando, 1994.

_____. "Intentional Actions and the Meaning of Object: a reply to Richard McCormick." *Thomist* 59 (1995), pp. 279–311.

_____. "The Moral Significance of Pre-rational nature in Aquinas: a reply to Jean Porter (and Stanley Hauerwas)." *American Journal of Jurisprudence* 48 (2003), pp. 253–280.

_____. "The Perspective of the Acting Person and the Nature of Practical Reason: the Object of the Human Act in Thomistic Anthropology of Action." *Nova et Vetera* 2 (2004), pp. 461–516.

_____. "A Debate on Condoms and AIDS." *National Catholic Bioethics Quarterly* 5, no. 3 (Spr 2005), pp. 40–48.

_____. "On the Use of Condoms to Prevent Acquired Immune Deficiency Syndrome." *National Catholic Bioethics Quarterly* 5, no. 1 (Spr 2005), pp. 40–48.

_____. "The Contraceptive Choice, Condom Use, and Moral Arguments Based on Nature: a reply to Christopher Oleson." *National Catholic Bioethics Quarterly* 7, no. 2 (Sum 2007), pp. 273–291.

Ripperger, C. "*The Species and Unity of the Moral Act.*" *Thomist* 59 (1995), pp. 69–90.

Roberti, F. and P. Palazzini. (ed.), *Dizionario di teologia morale.* Rome: Studium, 1968.

Rojas, J. "St Thomas on the Direct/Indirect Distinction." Ephemerides Theologicae Lovanienses 64 (1988), pp. 371–392.

Rossi, L. "Diretto e indiretto in teologia morale." *Rivista di teologia morale*, 3 (1971), pp. 37–65.

Roy, R. "*La coopération selon Saint Alphonse de Liguori.*" *Studia Moralia* 6 (1968), pp. 377–435.

_____. *Notion de la coopération selon Saint Alphonse et ses sources*. Rome: Pontifical University of St Thomas Aquinas in the City, 1969.

Sabetti, A. and T. Barrett. *Compendium theologiae moralis*, 24ᵗʰ ed. Regensburg: Frederick Pustet, 1916.

Saraiva Martins, J. "Homily on the occasion of the beatification of the Servant of God, Franz Jägerstätter," given at Linz, Austria on October 26, 2007. http:// www.vatican.va/ roman_curia/ congregations/ csaints/ documents/ rc_con_ csaints_ doc_ 2007 1026_beatif-jagerstatter_it.html. Accessed on January 5, 2009.

Schüller, B. "Direct Killing / Indirect Killiing." In *Moral Norms and Catholic Tradition*, ed. Charles Curran and Richard McCormick, pp. 138–157. Readings in Moral Theology, No. 1. New York: Ramsey, 1979.

_____. "The Double Effect in Catholic Thought: a reevaluation." In *Doing Evil to Achieve Good*, ed. Richard A. McCormick and Paul Ramsey, pp. 185–191. New York: University Press of America, 1985.

Searle, J. *Intentionality: an essay in the philosophy of mind*. Cambridge: Cambridge University Press, 1983.

Sgreccia, E. *Manuale di bioetica*, 3ʳᵈ ed. Milan: Vita e Pensiero, 1999.

Shaw, R. "The Making of a Moral Theologian." *The Catholic World Report* 6 (March 1996), pp. 46–53.

Smith, J. E. *Humanae Vitae: a Generation Later*. Washington, DC: Catholic University of America, 1991.

_____. "*Veritatis Splendor*, Proportionalism, and Contraception." *Irish Theological Quarterly* 63 (1998), pp. 307–326.

_____. "The Error of Proportionalism." In *Ethical Principles in Catholic Health Care*, ed. E. J. Furton, pp. 67–71. Boston: National Catholic Bioethics Center, 1999.

_____. "The Morality of Condom Use by HIV-Infected Spouses." *Thomist* 70 (2006), pp. 27–69.

Smith, R. E. "Duress and Cooperation." *Ethics and Medics* 21 (1996), pp. 1–2.

Solzhenitsyn, A. "Live not by Lies." (February 12, 1974), http://www.solzhenitsyn.ru/ 01_proizvedeniya/ 10_publizistika/ 01_stat'i_i_rechi/ 01_v_sovetskom_soyuze/ 07_jzit'_ne_po_ ljzi.pdf.

Sterba, J. "Reconciling Pacifists and Just War Theorists." *Social Theory and Practice* 18 (1992), pp. 21–37.

Sullivan, D. F. "The Doctrine of Double Effect and the Domains of Moral Responsibility." Thomist (2000), pp. 423–448.

Theron, S. "Two Criticisms of Double Effect." New Scholasticism 58 (1984), pp. 67–83.

Therrien, M. "Did the Principle of Double Effect Justify the Separation?" National Catholic Bioethics Quarterly 1, no. 3 (Aut 2001), pp. 417–427.

Ugorji, L. I. *The Principle of Double Effect. A Critical Appraisal of its Traditional Understanding and its Modern Reinterpretation.* Frankfurt: Peter Lang, 1985.

Urmson, J. O. "Motives and Causes." In *The Philosophy of Action*, ed. A. R. White, pp. 153–165. London: Oxford University Press, 1968.

Vacek, E.V., "Proportionalism: One View of the Debate." *Theological Studies* 46 (1985), pp. 287–314.

Van der Mark, W. "Vruchtbaarheidsregeling: poging tot antwoord op een nog open vraag (Régulation de la fécondité: tentative de réponse à une question encore ouverte)." *Tijdschrift voor Theologie* (*Revue de théologie*) 3 (1963), pp. 378–413.

Van der Poel, C. J. "The Principle of Double Effect." In *Absolutes in Moral Theology*, ed. Charles Curran, pp. 186–210. Washington: Corpus Books, 1968.

Vanzan, P. "Franz Jägerstätter: il contadino che rifiutò Hitler in nome di dio." *La Civiltà Cattolica* 157 (2006) II, pp. 345–354.

Vereecke, L. *Da Guglielmo d'Ockham a sant'Alfonso de Liguori: saggi di storia della teologia morale moderna 1300–1787.* Milan: Edizione Paoline, 1990.

Vermeersch, A. "Encyclical *Casti connubii* annotationes." *Periodica de re morali, canonica, liturgica* 20 (1931), pp. 42–68.

_____. "De Causalite per se et per accidens, seu directa et indirecta." *Periodica de re morali, canonica, liturgica* 21 (1932), pp. 101*–116*.

_____. "Avortement direct ou indirect: réponse au T. R. P. Gemelli, O.F.M." *Nouvelle revue théologique* 60 (1933), pp. 599–620.

_____. *Theologiae moralis.* Rome: Pontifical Gregorian University, 1947.

Woodward, P. A. "Nancy Davis and the Means-End Relation: toward a defense of the doctrine of double effect." *American Catholic Philosophical Quarterly* 77 (2003), pp. 437–457.

Zalba, M. *Theologiae moralis compendium.* Madrid: Biblioteca autores cristianos, 1958.

_____. "Cooperatio materialis ad malum morale." *Periodica de Re Morali Canonica Liturgica* 71 (1982), pp. 411–441.

Index of Names

Index of Subjects

Lightning Source UK Ltd.
Milton Keynes UK
UKHW011131220222
399070UK00001B/248